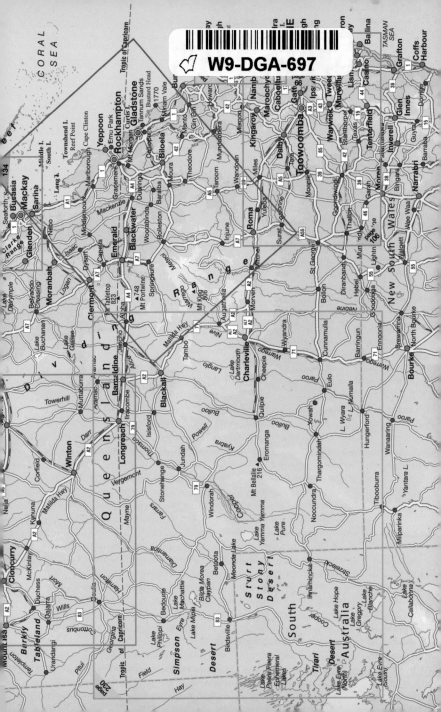

Map Legend

═══	Freeway
═ ═ ═	Freeway (under construction)
═══	Dual Carriageway
═══	Main Road
═══	Secondary Road
═══	Minor road
───	Track
━ ━	Regional Boundary
─ ─ ─	Province Boundary
▒▒▒	World Heritage Area
─ • ─	National Park/Reserve
─ ─ ─	Ferry Route
✈✈	Airport
✝ ⛪	Church (ruins)
✝	Monastery
∴	Archaeological Site
∩	Cave
★	Place of Interest
⌂	Mansion/Stately Home
✳	Viewpoint
⚑	Beach
═══	Freeway
═══	Highway
═══ }	Main Roads
═══ }	Minor Roads
═══	Footpath
▢	Pedestrian Area
▮	Important Building
▮	Park
❶	Numbered Sight
🚌	Bus Station
❶	Tourist Information
✉	Post Office
✚	Cathedral/Church
☾	Mosque
✡	Synagogue
⚲	Statue/Monument
▯	Tower
⌘	Lighthouse

INSIGHT GUIDES

QUEENSLAND
& THE GREAT BARRIER REEF

Discovery
CHANNEL

APA PUBLICATIONS

Part of the Langenscheidt Publishing Group

INSIGHT GUIDE
Queensland
& The Great Barrier Reef

Editor
Jerry Dennis
Managing Editor
Cathy Muscat
Art Director
Klaus Geisler
Picture Editor
Hilary Genin
Production
Kenneth Chan
Cartography Editor
Zoë Goodwin
Editorial Director
Brian Bell

Distribution

Australia
Universal Publishers
1 Waterloo Road
Macquarie Park, NSW 2113
Fax: (61) 2 9888 9074

New Zealand
Hema Maps New Zealand Ltd (HNZ)
Unit D, 24 Ra ORA Drive
East Tamaki, Auckland
Fax: (64) 9 273 6479

UK & Ireland
GeoCenter International Ltd
Meridian House, Churchill Way West
Basingstoke, Hampshire RG21 6YR
Fax: (44) 1256-817988

United States
Langenscheidt Publishers, Inc.
36–36 33rd Street, 4th Floor
Long Island City, NY 11106
Fax: (1) 718 784 0640

Worldwide
**Apa Publications GmbH & Co.
Verlag KG (Singapore branch)**
38 Joo Koon Road, Singapore 628990
Tel: (65) 6865 1600. Fax: (65) 6861 6438

Printing

Insight Print Services (Pte) Ltd
38 Joo Koon Road, Singapore 628990
Tel: (65) 6865-1600. Fax: (65) 6861-6438

©2006 Apa Publications GmbH & Co.
Verlag KG (Singapore branch)
All Rights Reserved

First Edition 2006

ABOUT THIS BOOK

The first Insight Guide pioneered the use of creative full-colour photography in guidebooks in 1970. Since then, we have expanded our range to cater for our readers' need not only for reliable information about their chosen destination but also for a real understanding of that destination. Now, when the internet can supply inexhaustible (but not always reliable) facts, our books marry text and pictures to provide that much more elusive quality: knowledge. To achieve this, they rely heavily on the authority of locally based writers and photographers.

How to use this book

The book is structured to convey an understanding of Queensland:

◆ To understand the state today, you need to know something of its past. The first section covers its people, history and culture in livel_ essays written by specialists.

◆ The Places section provides a ful run-down of all the attractions wortl seeing. The main places of interes are coordinated by number with ful colour maps. Margin notes provide background information and tips or how to save time and money.

◆ Photographic features illustrate unique aspects of Queensland, like reef life and the rainforest.

◆ Photographs are chosen not only to illustrate geography and buildings but also to convey the moods of the city and the life of its people.

◆ The Travel Tips listings section pro vides a point of reference for infor mation on travel, hotels, shops and activities. Information may be located quickly by using the index printed on the back cover flap – and the flaps are designed to serve as bookmarks.

the *Brisbane Courier Mail*. He won Australian journalism's highest accolade, the Gold Walkley; only one such award is made each year and he received it for his exposé of the Helen Demidenko literary hoax. In a previous life he wrote *In a Broken Dream*, a hit for Python Lee Jackson – a group fronted by a young Rod Stewart. David recently released his fourth album, *Last Man Standing* with himself on vocals. Today, David can be found at his boutique hotel, Leopard Lodge, in Brisbane's Kangaroo Point.

Another passionate (and sixth generation) Queenslander is **Anna King Murdoch**, who contributed the features on the Great Barrier Reef and Queensland's people. Anna was on the staff of *The Age* and *Sydney Morning Herald* for many years and is now a freelance travel writer.

For the Surf Culture piece we needed to look no further than **Tim Baker**, who writes for *Surfing World* and *Tracks* (the "surfer's bible") magazines. He recently edited *Waves: Great Stories from the Surf.*

The Travel Tips have been painstakingly researched by **Christine Long**, a journalist of several years' experience, with *The Age*, *Sydney Morning Herald* and *Travel + Leisure Australia* on her CV.

The project was managed by **Cathy Muscat**, with the assistance of **Siân Lezard** and **Jeffery Pike**. **Neil Titman** proofread the text, and **Helen Peters** compiled the index.

The contributors

This new *Insight Regional Guide: Queensland* has been put together by commissioning editor, **Jerry Dennis**, who also took the bulk of the photographs. Dennis has worked on countless Insight Guides, primarily as a photographer, and his work has been appearing in travel publications and other media for many years.

To create this guidebook, he enlisted the skills of several writers and researchers with special knowledge of the state. Prime amongst them was **David Bentley**, who wrote the Places section as well as the history feature, the essays on Aboriginal Land and on culture, and many of the restaurant reviews.

David's extensive knowledge of the state derives from many years as a news reporter, travel writer and restaurant critic, much of the time for

CONTACTING THE EDITORS

We would appreciate it if readers would alert us to errors or outdated information by writing to:

Insight Guides, P.O. Box 7910, London SE1 1WE, England. Fax: (44) 20 7403-0290. insight@apaguide.co.uk

NO part of this book may be reproduced, stored in a retrieval system or transmitted in any form or means electronic, mechanical, photocopying, recording or otherwise, without prior written permission of *Apa Publications*. Brief text quotations with use of photographs are exempted for book review purposes only. Information has been obtained from sources believed to be reliable, but its accuracy and completeness and the opinions based thereon, are not guaranteed.

www.insightguides.com
In North America:
www.insighttravelguides.com

Contents

LEFT: Great Keppel Island.

Maps

Map Legend **facing title page**

Travel Tips

THE BEST OF QUEENSLAND

Nature parks, island resorts, family outings, historic towns ... Here, at a glance, are our top recommendations

ISLANDS

- **Magnetic**
Just over the water from Townsville but a world away. Hire a Mini Moke and explore. *See page 163.*
- **Thursday**
Up at the top of Cape York, this former base for pearl divers is now a quiet outpost with a largely Aboriginal population. *See page 205.*
- **The Whitsundays**
Pick any one of them. Whether you want a bustling resort or a quiet retreat and some pampering, they are all outstanding. *See pages 152–7.*
- **Stradbroke**
Or rather Stradbrokes: North for relaxed DIY holidays, perhaps taking a tent, and South for the eco-

friendly luxury of Couran Cove Resort. *See page 101.*
- **Lizard**
The furthest north of a handful of islands which are home to a single exclusive up-market resort. Save up. *See page 200.*
- **Great Keppel**
Mostly National Park and unspoiled; there's a holiday village to stay in and white beaches to lounge on. *See page 141.*
- **Fraser**
Endless beaches on this giant sand bar, which has some densely forested interior. Popular with 4WD drivers but testing too. *See page 125.*

BEST SURFING

- **Surfers Paradise**. Not always the best waves but a good place for lessons. *See page 94.*

- **Burleigh Heads**
Seriously good waves; a popular spot for

serious surfers. *See page 97.*
- **Noosa** It was a surf centre before its gentrification and the waves are still there. *See pages 121–2.*
- **Coolangatta** Great spot at the base of the Gold Coast. *See pages 98–99.*
- **Moreton Island**
Close to Brisbane but not too many crowds. *See pages 82–3.*

ABOVE: bank on a good holiday in the Whitsundays. **LEFT:** surf action. **BELOW:** help is never far away.

LOCAL SPECIALITIES

- **Rum in Bundaberg**
Sip a "Bundy" in the distillery where it's made after being guided through the production process. *See page 135.*

- **Beef in Rockhampton**
The giant steaks served in the restaurants of "Rocky" are legendary. This is the beef capital of Oz, after all. *See page 139.*
- **Moreton Bay bugs**
One of Australia's many delicious crustaceans takes

its name from the bay just off Brisbane. *See page 82.*
- **XXXX beer**
There may be a bar not selling XXXX but you'll have a hard job finding it. *See pages 242–3.*
- **Pineapples in Nambour**
It's the home of the "Big Pineapple" and centre of the pineapple industry so where else would you buy them? *See page 128.*

FOR KIDS

- **Movie World**
Stunt shows, hair-raising rides, movie characters parading along Main Street all make for a rewarding day out. *See page 93.*
- **Australia Zoo**
A chance to see the Crocodile Hunter in his natural habitat. *See page 117.*
- **Lark Quarry**
See the tracks left by real dinosaurs and preserved in mud for thousands of years. *See page 225.*
- **The Strand, Townsville**
A fine example of how to revitalise a

seafront with water parks, playgrounds, cafés and the emphasis on family fun. *See page 161.*
- **Streets Beach, South Bank, Brisbane**
Building an artificial beach in a city just kilometres away from some of the world's best real beaches seems misguided but somehow it works. *See page 75.*
- **Cairns Lagoon**
Lifeguards patrol this tranquil swimming spot which has become the focus of the waterfront in Cairns. *See page 178.*

WILDLIFE SPOTTING

- **Whale watching in Hervey Bay**
It's an awe-inspiring moment when you see your first whale breaching just metres away from your boat. The season runs from July to November. *See page 125.*
- **Platypus at Eungella NP or Atherton Tablelands**
Settle by a riverbank just after dawn or before dusk to catch a glimpse of these elusive creatures. *Pages 151 & 184.*
  - **Lone Pine Koala Sanctuary**
More than 130 koalas frolic in gay abandon close to Brisbane. OK, they sleep a lot, but there are other, more active

animals too. *See page 82.*
- **Australian Butterfly Sanctuary**
Hundreds of butterflies flutter in an aviary, often settling on visitors, in the hills above Cairns at Kuranda. *See page 181.*
- **Billabong Sanctuary**
Lots of hands-on introductions to wildlife at this pretty site near Townsville. *See page 163.*
- **Rainforest Habitat**
Animals and birds in the wild outside Port Douglas. *See page 191.*

TOP: gleaming cab at Movie World **ABOVE:** pineapples from the tropical north. **RIGHT:** turtle time at the Billabong Sanctuary. **FAR RIGHT:** a rainbow lorikeet.

NATIONAL PARKS

- **Boodjamulla**
Miles from anywhere but unmissable gorge. *See pages 215–16.*
- **Glass House Mountains**
Extraordinary stark rock formations not far from the Sunshine Coast. *See page 115.*
- **Carnarvon Gorge**
Stunningly beautiful area. Deserves as much time as you can spare. *See page 143.*
- **Hinchinbrook Island**
Unspoilt wilderness, sheer granite mountains and empty beaches make this irresistible to walkers. *See page 169.*
- **Daintree**
If the environmental miracle of the rainforest weren't enough, there's dramatic Cape Tribulation to top it off. *See page 190.*
- **Undara Volcanic**
Unique lava tube formations make this one very unusual destination. *See page 209.*

COLONIAL STREETSCAPES

- **Rockhampton**
Quay Street down by the river and East Street just behind it have magnificently preserved Victorian frontages. *See pages 139–41.*
- **Bundaberg**
Elegant town centre and some lovely Queenslander houses on the outskirts. *See pages 133–6.*
- **Cooktown**
Terrific atmospheric pubs and commercial buildings create a distinctive personality. *See pages 197–200.*
- **Charters Towers**
Testament to what can happen when gold wealth and good colonial architects combine. *See pages 165–6.*
- **Brisbane**
Well-preserved city with pockets of Victoriana that would have succumbed to development elsewhere. *See pages 69–85.*
- **Ipswich**
Quietly stylish old town in the hinterland west of Brisbane. *See pages 105–6.*

MUSEUMS

- **QANTAS Founders Outback Museum, Longreach**
Hangars filled with exhibits in the airline's home town. *See page 230.*
- **Australian Workers' Heritage Centre, Barcaldine**
Fascinating museum, less earnest than the title suggests. *See page 232.*
- **Cosmos Centre, Charleville**
Try for one of the night sky sessions at this heavenly space. *See page 235.*
- **Australian Stockman's Hall of Fame, Longreach**
Great building devoted to all things rural. A must see. *See page 230.*
- **Ripley's Believe It Or Not! Museum, Surfers Paradise**
Intriguingly weird. *See page 96.*
- **Queensland Maritime Museum, Brisbane**
Boats and barnacles by Brisbane bridge. *See page 75.*
- **Cobb & Co. Museum, Toowoomba**
Stagecoach company's hall of fame. *See page 112.*

LEFT kayaking in Lawn Hill Gorge. **RIGHT** cattleman at the Stockman's Hall of Fame. **BELOW:** old warehouse in Rockhampton's East Street.

BOAT TRIPS

- **Great Barrier Reef**
There are a variety of ways of getting out to the Barrier Reef by boat, from vast cruisers that head for their own viewing platform permanently moored to the reef, to small specialist dive vessels which will tweak their itinerary to suit that day's customers. *See pages 53–7.*

- **Sailing the Whitsundays**
If you haven't chartered your own boat look at joining an organised trip. It's worth checking noticeboards in Airlie Beach where last minute requests for crew are posted. *See page 152.*
- **Take the Citycat in Brisbane**
It's public transport and it's a delightful way to get a feel for the layout of the city as you meander from bank to bank along the Brisbane River. *See pages 246–7.*
- **Rafting in Tully Gorge**
The place to come for that aquatic adrenaline fix. There are several operators catering for every level of experience. *See page 170.*
- **Fishing in the Gulf of Carpentaria**
Charter a boat or rent a "tinnie" in Karumba and spend a few hours fishing on the Norman River. The place can get packed with anglers who know a productive waterway when they see one. *See page 214–5.*

ABOVE: rafters tackle the rapids in Tully Gorge.
LEFT: most trips to the Barrier Reef allow some time for snorkelling.

MONEY-SAVING TIPS

Free bus: There is a free council-run bus service which operates in a loop around the central business district (CBD) in Brisbane. It takes in many of the city's main landmarks, including Central Station, Queen Street Mall, the City Botanic Gardens and the Riverside Centre. It runs every ten minutes or so from 7am to 6pm Monday to Friday and is an excellent way for visitors to orientate themselves. Look for the distinctive red bus stops.

BYO: There are restaurants and cafés across Queensland which do not have licenses to sell alcohol but are happy for you to bring your own (advertised as BYO), for which they add a small corkage charge to the bill. This not only allows wine buffs to drink exactly what they want with their meal but also seriously reduces the cost of dining out. Even some establishments that *do* have licenses will allow BYO wine, but the corkage tends to be set a bit higher and you need to look at the marginal benefits.

Theme park passes: If you or your loved ones are adrenaline junkies holidaying within range of the Gold Coast, consider purchasing a Theme Park Superpass. This allows 14 days unlimited entry to Warner Brothers Movie World, Wet 'n' Wild Water World and Sea World. Savings start to kick in if you make more than four visits. If you're not sure at the outset, you can buy a ticket to one of the attractions and then upgrade it to a super pass at the end of the day.

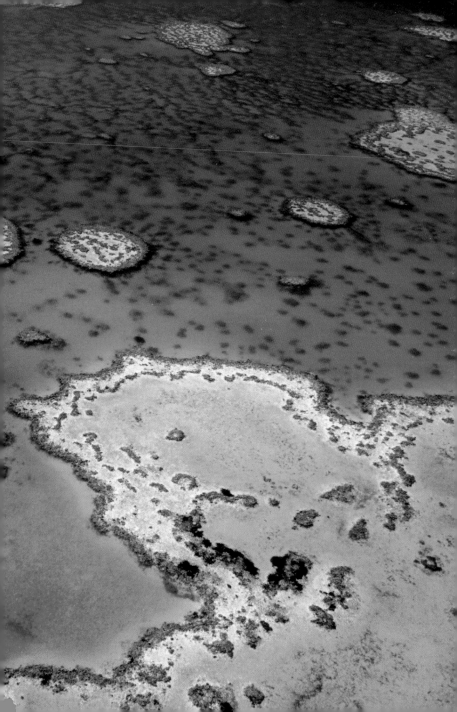

THE BIG COUNTRY

A huge area of contrasting and remarkable
features, Queensland somehow coheres as a
distinctive state with a character all of its own

Size isn't everything, but it is a factor when considering Queensland. This may be only the second largest state in Australia (after Western Australia) but its 1.73 million square km (667,000 square miles) would comfortably swallow a good selection of European countries or a couple of other Australian states. However, within this vast area there are only 4 million people – equivalent to the population of Sydney.

For the visitor it can still seem busy since so many are drawn to the high-rise high-gratification zone of the Gold Coast, where crowds are part of the atmosphere. Anywhere else, though, and this is one relaxed and friendly place; even in Brisbane, where the café culture usually associated with the southern cities of Sydney and Melbourne has burgeoned in recent years.

The coast – thousands of kilometres of it – gives everyone their own little piece of paradise. And from most of it there's access to the wonder that is the Great Barrier Reef. The reef stretches all the way to the tropical north, and towns like Cairns and Port Douglas have boomed on the back of it. Many Australian visitors have been so taken with the natural beauty and easy way of life that they've made the "sea change" and opted to settle in Queensland, in the process turning it into the fastest growing state in the country.

This has created pockets of frenetic coastal development, not all of it harmonious. The antidote is to head inland. This is where it gets really empty and, for some, where the real Australia begins – in the Outback. You don't have to go as far as Birdsville and its iconic pub in the far west or up to the rough, often impassable dirt tracks of Cape York. Just move in from the coast and within an hour or so the country will change, whether to the green hills of the Dividing Range in the south, the empty dry plains in the centre or the dense rainforest in the north. ❑

PRECEDING PAGES: aerial view of Hardy Reef; Eungella National Park.
LEFT: the parched red earth of southwest Queensland.

THE MAKING OF QUEENSLAND

Aborigines lived here for 50,000 years before the arrival of Captain Cook and the colonists who followed in his wake. They paved the way for an energetic population – the intrepid explorers, emancipated convicts and free settlers who carved out a life in Queensland's fertile hinterland

About 15 million years ago, the Australian continent broke away from an ancient land mass known as Gondwanaland and gradually drifted northwards to its present location. Due to periodic ice ages, sea levels were lower than today – so low that anyone reaching New Guinea from eastern Asia could continue the journey to north Queensland on foot. These first eastern Asian migrants, ancestors of Australia's Aborigines, dispersed along the Gulf of Carpentaria, spreading south and west until, with the warming of the planet, the sea rose to isolate them from the rest of the world. Thus, human history in Queensland began at least 50,000 years before the arrival of colonising Europeans.

The original inhabitants evolved a nomadic way of life based on hunter-gatherer techniques and seasonal migration. Tribes traded with one another and also with Torres Strait Islanders. Their life in the harsh landscape of Australia consisted of the men hunting and the women fishing and gathering. A good hunter knew intimately the habits of the creatures he stalked, was an expert tracker and understood the seasons and the winds. He took only what he needed to feed himself and his people and hence was able to keep in balance with his supply. Conservation was the Aborigine's way of avoiding starvation; in a country that would kill many white pioneers, the Aborigine was perfectly at home.

The first Europeans

Some historians argue that Portuguese mariners charted the northern coastline of Queensland as early as the 16th century, but that they kept their maps secret lest they fell into the hands of the Spanish. Nonetheless, Dutchman Willem Janssen, who sailed the *Duyfken* into the Gulf of Carpentaria in 1605, is generally cited as the first European to "discover" Australia.

Another Dutchman, Abel Tasman, visited the Australian coastline twice – in 1642, when he charted parts of Tasmania, and in 1644, when he traced the northern coast from Cape York to Port Hedland. English buccaneer William Dampier sailed to the west Australian

LEFT: an early European impression of an Aboriginal camp. **RIGHT:** a Dutch crew in the *Duyfken* (Dove) discover the Gulf of Carpentaria.

coast in 1697 and in 1699. However, credit for charting the eastern coastline goes mainly to Captain James Cook, whose 1770 voyage opened the way to colonisation *(see box below)*.

The penal years

Thus the east coast of Australia became a dumping-ground for Britain's criminal element. In 1788 and 1790 fleets of convict ships arrived at Port Jackson, Sydney's great harbour-to-be, and the colony stumbled into life. Poor soil and harsh conditions overrode thoughts of further exploration until 1799, when Governor Hunter dispatched Lieutenant Matthew Flinders in the *Norfolk* to look more closely at the north.

Flinders charted much of Moreton Bay, in southern Queensland, but failed to notice the mouth of the Brisbane River that emptied into it. The honour of "discovering" the Brisbane River fell to three convicts – John Finnegan, Thomas Pamphlet and Richard Parsons – whose boat washed up on Moreton Island in 1823 after being swept northwards in a gale. With no idea where they were, these marooned ticket-of-leave men paddled to the mainland in a makeshift canoe, and followed the Brisbane River as far as Oxley Creek before retracing their steps to Moreton Bay.

They were a motley crew. Parsons made several attempts on Finnegan's life, then wan-

CAPTAIN JAMES COOK

Captain Cook (1728–79), who may have been informed by a Portuguese map, followed the shore from Cape Everard on the Victorian coast to Botany Bay, then northwards to Cooktown and the Torres Strait. The place names he left behind give a clue to his travails – Point Danger and Mount Warning at the southern extreme of Queensland and Cape Tribulation and Weary Bay to the north. Specifically, the names express Cook's dismay at having hit a coral reef, a misfortune that obliged him to beach the *Endeavour* for repairs in the river that now bears its name.

He remained at present-day Cooktown for nearly seven weeks. Having restored the *Endeavour* to sea-worthiness, he continued to Possession Island at the tip of Cape York where, on 22 August 1770, he claimed the east coast for King George III.

His report was positive, but incited no rush to establish a colony. As far as the British government was concerned, the new continent was mainly useful as a repository for felons, whose numbers exceeded the ability of British jails to accommodate them. Of around 1,300 people who left Britain aboard the First Fleet, more than half were convicts. The new arrivals set up camp at Port Jackson on 26 January 1788 – an occasion of dubious celebration to the original inhabitants.

dered off on his own. The other two ended up on Bribie Island, where they were spotted by surveyor-general John Oxley. He had been sent to locate the site for a northern outpost where fractious convicts might be exiled. Having investigated Port Curtis and found it unsuitable, he called into Moreton Bay on his return journey to Sydney. When Finnegan showed him the Brisbane River, Oxley was impressed. So, too, was Governor Brisbane, who, in the following year, dispatched Oxley to establish a new penal settlement in Moreton Bay.

Oxley's party comprised Lieutenant Henry Miller, botanist Allan Cunningham, various

Investigators supposed that Aborigines had ambushed Logan. But the captain had made a great number of enemies, and many believed that he had been ambushed and beaten to death by escaped convicts exacting revenge. Either way, Logan's demise was like an epitaph to an era of hardship, merciless discipline and relentless toil, when convicts were whipped to death and prisoners cast lots to slit one another's throats to escape torment.

Logan's reputation for cruelty eclipsed his work as an explorer. Posterity rarely remembers him for locating the river that bears his name, nor for his significant contribution to the exploration of the Tweed.

Penal station at St Helena. Moreton Bay. Queensland

assistants and family members, plus 14 soldiers and 29 convicts, including Finnegan.

For five years, until his death in 1825, Moreton Bay commandant Captain Patrick Logan ruled the fledgling colony with a severity bordering on the sadistic, while devoting his leisure hours to the gentlemanly pursuit of exploration. In October 1830, while mapping the headwaters of the Brisbane River, Logan disappeared. After a four-day search, his body was found face-down in a shallow grave.

LEFT: Captain Cook taking possession of the Australian continent on behalf of the British Crown.
ABOVE: penal station at St Helena, Moreton Bay.

The land rush
As the penal years receded into history, free settlers would reap the benefit from the sweat and misery of the lash-scarred wretches who cleared the bush, established farms and erected public buildings. Nonetheless, Brisbane's progress was slow compared with the rural areas around it.

Surveyor-general Allan Cunningham's discovery of a pass to the Darling Downs in 1828 encouraged pastoralists to push north, a land rush spearheaded by brothers Patrick and George Leslie, who drove 5,000 sheep from New England. By the late 1840s, more than 45 stations had been established on the Downs, with only slightly fewer on the eastern side of the Great Dividing Range. The first sheep farmers were "squatters", illegally occupying Crown grazing land. But by the late 1840s, the authorities recognised their economic worth for the colony, and issued them leases for their sheep runs. Soon squatters outnumbered Brisbane's meagre population of 540 people, and many became wealthy landowners.

Leichardt's great expeditions

As gentlemen graziers carved out dynasties on the Downs, they wondered whether greener pastures lay beyond. In 1844, a Prussian adventurer, Ludwig Leichardt, set out from named after a woman who helped outfit his expedition; Charley's Creek, near Chinchilla, immortalised his tracker; and Kent's lagoon celebrated the quartermaster who supplied him with chocolate.

The expedition was fraught with setbacks. Hostile Aborigines killed one of his party and badly injured two others, while packhorses drowned, forcing him to jettison scientific experiments. Yet he won through – 14 months after their departure and long after being given up for dead, Leichardt and his party staggered into Port Essington. Returning by sea to Sydney, these "men from the grave" were fêted as national heroes.

Moreton Bay to find out. Unlike many early explorers, Leichardt was not a career soldier. He viewed exploration as a spiritual quest, and his journeys were financed not by the government, but by land-hungry squatters.

Once he had found sufficient backers, he gathered an expedition team of 10 companions, Aboriginal guides and a bullock herd, and set off on a 5,000-km (3,000-mile) expedition from Brisbane to Port Essington in the Northern Territory. Where military explorers named rivers and mountains after government luminaries who might forward their careers, Leichardt honoured benefactors who had given practical help. The Burdekin River was

Generous government grants and public subscriptions encouraged Leichardt to explore further. In 1847, his next expedition, which he said would take him "through the interior of Australia to the Swan River on the west coast", foundered after seven months. His bid to cross central Australia to the west in the following year fared worse. The party of six whites and two Aborigines left Mount Abundance in April 1848, never to be seen again.

By that time, Aboriginal attitudes to white intruders had hardened. Even outlying tribes knew that white men herding livestock (as Leichardt's party did) intended to seize rivers and hunting lands for themselves. A form of guerrilla warfare prevailed. Squatters drove off Aborigines by fair means or foul, and, when Aborigines retaliated, native policemen from other tribal areas exacted retribution, massacring entire communities.

It may be that Aborigines mistook Leichardt, his men and livestock for settlers come to steal their land. It may also be that Leichardt inadvertently stumbled onto sacred ground – and paid the ultimate price. Ironically, his lost expedition succeeded in opening up vast tracts of Queensland. Rescuers searching vainly for Leichardt returned with glowing reports of the terrain that had swallowed him up.

So dramatic were Leichardt's journeys that the expedition of his rival Sir Thomas Mitchell to find a route from Sydney to the Gulf of Carpentaria paled almost to insignificance, and as Leichardt pressed on into Port Essington at the triumphant conclusion of his journey, Mitchell turned back. He gave up too soon. He had located pastoral land in interior and southern Queensland, but stopped tantalisingly short of valuable grazing country Leichardt's route had bypassed.

Kennedy's expedition

Edmund Kennedy, who had been Mitchell's deputy on the Queensland expedition, attempted to consolidate the work of Leichardt and Mitchell by sailing to Rockingham Bay on Cape York's eastern seaboard, then overlanding to meet supply ships at Princess Charlotte Bay and Port Albany. Tragically for Kennedy, the marine surveyors who recommended Rockingham Bay had made their assessment from the deck of a ship. What they took to be gently wooded hills were, in fact, impenetrable tropical jungles.

Landing in May 1848, Kennedy found steep mountains blocking the way north and mangroves blocking the way west. He had to lead 12 men, 27 horses, 11 sheep, a ton of flour and three carts through trackless rainforest. Six months later, having survived skirmishes with Aborigines and trudged through the rough terrain, the exhausted explorers reached Weymouth Bay, where eight of the men, too sick to

travel, stayed behind with a supply of provisions. The expedition was further depleted near Shelbourne Bay, when one man could go no further, and the party's blacksmith accidentally shot himself in the chest. Kennedy left a third man to care for them until help arrived and pressed on with his Aborigine guide, Jacky Jacky, for Port Albany.

After hacking through scrub for a month, they sighted their destination just 30 km (19 miles) away. It was here, in a swamp by the Escape River, that Aborigines who had been tracking them moved in for the kill. Kennedy was killed but Jacky escaped with a head wound. He struggled through the jungle to the

Cape and informed the waiting schooner of the whereabouts of the other survivors who were stranded on the coast. Of the eight men at Weymouth Bay, two survived. The three at Shelbourne Bay were never seen again. Jacky Jacky enjoyed a brief glow of celebrity but died six years later after falling into a camp fire. Kennedy's remains were never found.

Burke and Wills

In August 1860, Robert O'Hara Burke embarked on a hugely ambitious expedition – his intention was to lead the first party to cross the continent from coast to coast, south to north. The explorers were given a ceremonious

LEFT: the starting of the Leichardt search expedition.
RIGHT: explorer Edmund Kennedy is killed by Aborigines.

send-off by gold-rich Melbourne burghers who felt it their patriotic duty to lift the mantle of mystery shrouding the Australian interior. As it set out, the expedition resembled a travelling circus. Burke, a former officer in the Austrian cavalry, cut a dash in red shirt, blue coat and tall black hat at the head of a cavalcade of 18 men, 23 horses, 27 camels and wagons with 21 tons of stores. However, the pomp of departure soon turned to dust. Morale plummeted in the eight weeks that it took to reach Menindie. When deputy leader William Landells dropped out, Burke appointed 26-year-old surveyor William Wills as his second-in-command.

through mud until they reached the Gulf of Carpentaria.

On the return journey, Gray died of exhaustion. In April, the three emaciated survivors, Burke, Wills and King, staggered into the base camp on the Cooper, where they found the warm ashes of a fire and the words "Dig.3ft.N.W.April.21, 1861". Wills and King unearthed meat, rice, flour, sugar and a letter from depot leader William Brahe, who said that, since no one had arrived with supplies, he was turning back. Brahe had waited four months – a month longer than his orders. He had left just seven hours before Burke, Wills and King returned. Burke and Wills died of

They headed for Cooper Creek, planning to travel overland to the known rivers of the Gulf of Carpentaria and, under pressure to beat rival explorer John Stuart to the Gulf, Burke left some of his party at Menindie while he forged ahead. In theory, the Menindie group would bring the stores to the Cooper, but after five weeks nothing had arrived, and Burke lost patience. Leaving William Brahe and three others at the Cooper, he set out for the Gulf with Wills, John King and Charlie Gray. The monsoons hit in January. Burke's camels slithered in the quagmire, until, on 17 February, Burke and Wills left King and Gray at their last camp and sloshed

starvation. Only King, cared for by Aborigines, survived to tell the story.

An independent Queensland

The first half of the 19th century saw a change in European settlement in Australia. The transportation of convicts was phased out, and by 1860 the continent had been divided into seven colonies, one of which was Queensland. At that time the European population numbered only 23,520, and no industry had yet been established, although gold had been discovered in 1858.

Labour shortages continued, despite the conscientious efforts of Henry Jordan, the colony's immigration agent in London, who by 1865 had enticed 50,000 British workers to try their luck in Queensland. At about the same time, cotton grower Captain Robert Towns embarked on a scheme to recruit indentured Kanakas from the Pacific Islands to do the work that white men could or would not do.

Kanakas provided muscle for sugar plantations along the tropical seaboard, particularly in Maryborough, Mackay, Bundaberg and Innisfail, where they died in alarming numbers. The system trod a fine line between indenture and slavery. When crew members of the recruiting ship, the *Hopeful,* were found guilty of murdering their "cargo", the 1866 bank crash that caused funds for railway projects and public buildings to dry up. Workers went unpaid, and riots erupted in the streets. Only a miracle could save Queensland. It came in the form of a gold strike near Gympie, where, in 1867, prospector James Nash made a major find, sparking a rush that would last for five decades. Finds were reported at Cape River, inland from Bowen; at Ravenswood, 130 km (81 miles) southwest of Townsville; and, in 1871, at the Charters Towers goldfield, which at one point attracted a population of 27,000.

More gold was found the following year in the Palmer River, southwest of Cooktown, sparking another major gold rush that attracted

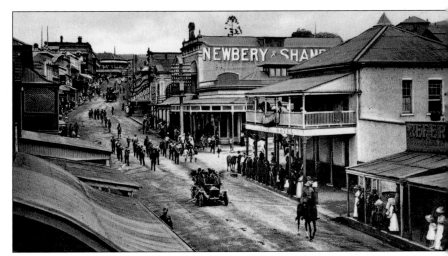

government attempted, with mixed results, to stop the human traffic. In the event, the Kanaka system thrived for another decade, until 1904, when the new Federal Government prohibited the entry of Kanakas to Australia, and initiated a programme of repatriation.

The Queensland gold rushes

Queensland's progress to this point had been characterised by reckless optimism, alarming setbacks and lucky breaks, exemplified by the

LEFT: the exploring party of Burke and Wills comes upon an Aboriginal encampment. ABOVE: crowds attending a parade in Upper Mary Street, Gympie.

large numbers of Chinese immigrants. By 1876, Chinese miners outnumbered European ones, who expressed their displeasure by burning down Chinese dwellings. The government eventually legislated against the Chinese, banning them from new goldfields for the first three years.

Station hands sinking postholes at Croydon, in the Gulf of Carpentaria, made discoveries that sparked the last of the big Queensland gold rushes. Despite its isolation, Croydon at its zenith had 36 hotels catering to a population of 7,000. The get-rich-quick gold-mining era was dwindling by the 1890s, but mineral wealth remained important to the economy.

As gold deposits depleted, miners turned their attention instead to copper, tin, silver and coal. Nonetheless, gold, more than anything else, provided the catalyst for the establishment of many of the state's cities and ports.

Towards the end of the century the increase in population, the advance of social legislation in Europe and the depression of the 1890s encouraged the growth of trade unionism and led to the emergence of a Labor Party with well-defined policies. In 1891 the Shearers' Union organised a seven-month strike in Queensland after the ranch-owners began employing non-union labour at lower wages. The strike was finally broken, but subsequent legislation provided shorter working hours and improved working conditions. In December 1899, Queensland had for six days the first Labour government in the world (though a minority one).

Federation and war in Europe

In September 1900, Queen Victoria regally proclaimed that, on 1 January 1901, a new nation would be born – the Commonwealth of Australia, which included the state of Queensland. The 1901 census recorded 498,129 inhabitants in the state, excluding Aborigines. Brisbane was proclaimed a city in 1902.

The queen remained head of state, retaining power over all foreign affairs; her direct representative in Australia was the governor-general. Mother Britain did not let the new nation escape the interests of imperialism. She expected, and got, continuing support in her military involvements, and ample returns on her substantial investments in Australia.

When Britain declared war on Germany in August 1914, Australia, as a member of the British Empire, was automatically at war, too. Of the 330,000 troops dispatched to Europe to fight, 226,000 were casualties, a greater percentage by far than had been suffered by any other country among the Allies.

In 1915 Queensland got its first majority Labor government – which would remain in power until 1929, then again from 1932 until 1957. The first half of the 20th century saw the state's economy grow quickly, boosted by improved farming methods, irrigation, insecticides, communications and new markets at home and in Japan.

In 1922, at the instigation of the ruling Labor government, the Legislative Council (the upper house of the state parliament) was abolished, leaving Queensland as the only Australian state with a single-chamber parliament, the Legislative Assembly. Three years later, Greater Brisbane was established as the largest municipal council in Australia. From the first, the Brisbane council was elected by a complete adult electorate (women had had the vote in Queensland since 1904).

In 1923 vast silver-lead-zinc deposits were found at Mount Isa, but the Depression of the late 1920s and early 1930s was hard on Queensland. In 1929, amid rising unemployment,

THE BRISBANE LINE

On 19 February 1942, after Japanese planes bombed Darwin, the Allies expected a full-blown land invasion, starting in north Queensland. The Japanese dropped bombs in the Torres Strait, Townsville and Mossman, and the area north of Rockhampton was designated a war zone. American troops arrived to defend the "Brisbane Line" against the anticipated Japanese invasion. As it turned out, the only conflict was between the American and Australian servicemen, due to friction over supplies and amenities. The "Battle of Brisbane" was fought on 26 November 1942. It escalated into an ugly riot, in which one Australian was shot, and 14 others wounded.

falling incomes and social distress, the Labor government was ousted by the Country Party.

During its five-year tenure, the Country Party abolished state trading and established the Bureau of Economics. But it was unable to stem the tide of the Depression, and was replaced in 1934 by the Labor Party, which attempted to stimulate the economy through large capital improvement projects, including the Story Bridge, the Stanley River Bridge and the construction of the University of Queensland at St Lucia. By now, the worst of the Depression was over, and many social services, suspended during the bad economic times, were reinstituted.

duced in 1946, and the government began large-scale irrigation projects, which included the Burdekin and Tully hydroelectric scheme.

The 1950s also saw the rapid development of the coastal strip south of Brisbane. Originally a secluded holiday destination for the Brisbane middle classes, its property values soared in the post-war period, leading one journalist to dub the area the "Gold Coast". There was a rush to build large beachfront holiday apartments and hotels, to support the rapidly growing tourist market. In 1958 the South Coast Town Council was renamed "Gold Coast Town Council": it now administers Australia's seventh-largest (and fastest-growing) city. By the 1960s the

War and peace

When Britain went to war against Germany in September 1939, Australia once more automatically entered the conflict. Of the one million Australian servicemen and women who had enlisted, almost 10,000 died in Europe and more than 17,000 in the Pacific. Of those taken prisoner by the Japanese, 8,000 did not survive the terrible privations and humiliations to which they were subjected. Meanwhile, in Queensland, free hospital service was intro-

LEFT: Australian plane destroyed during the Japanese raid of Brisbane. **ABOVE:** Surfers Paradise in the 1960s, a boom time for Queensland.

DIRE STRAITS

The Torres Strait Islands had become part of Queensland in 1879, following legislation by the Queensland and British parliaments. In 1936, the islanders took strike action against the state administrators, in an effort to take control of their own affairs and gain fairer treatment. This resulted in the Torres Strait Islanders Act of 1939, which established an elected local government council giving the people of these communities a greater role in how the islands were run. But the first islander permitted on the mainland to cut cane did not arrive until 1947, and only in the 1960s were the islanders free to work and settle elsewhere.

beachfront had been all but completely developed, and the urbanisation of the surrounding farms and wetlands began.

Modern politics

The long tradition of Labor politics in Queensland fell apart in the mid-1950s, with fiercely conflicting views on the influence of communism in the Labor Party and the trade unions. After 25 years in power, the party split into competing factions, and promptly lost the next election, ushering in 32 years of rule by the National Party.

For two decades, politics and social life in Queensland were dominated by one man, Sir

leader Wayne Goss in the 1989 state election ended 32 years of continuous National Party rule in Queensland.

Goss, a solicitor, enacted many of the reforms recommended by the Fitzgerald Inquiry, which had been set up to investigate corrupt practices under Bjelke-Petersen. He won a second term but lost Green Party support in 1995 over a government plan to subsume koala habitat for road widening. A recount in the Townsville seat of Mundingburra in the narrowly contested election led to a hung parliament. When the Gladstone-based Independent Liz Cunningham gave her support to the Rob Borbidge-led National-

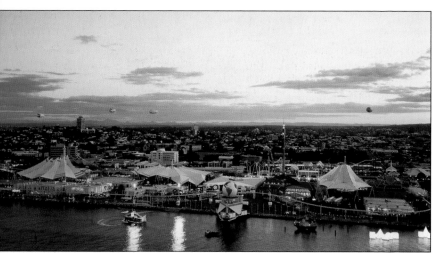

Joh Bjelke-Petersen *(see page 27).* Sir Joh's era was characterised by confrontation with unions and civil-rights advocates. He finally lost the National Party leadership in 1987, having made firm friends and bitter enemies, and eventually outstaying his welcome.

Queensland politics entered a period of turmoil when Bjelke-Petersen's long era of dominance came to an end. His successor, Mike Ahern, adopted a moderate approach that displeased Nationals accustomed to Sir Joh's bulldozer tactics. In September 1989, Ahern was toppled as leader by hardliner Russell Cooper, a cattle breeder who remained premier for just six weeks. His defeat at the hands of Labor

Liberal Coalition, Goss resigned as premier.

The lacklustre Borbidge government lost office in 1998, and Labor's Peter Beattie began his reign as premier. Like others in the rough and tumble of Queensland politics, Beattie has had to weather scandal – most memorably in 2000, when a number of prominent Labor Party figures were implicated in electoral fraud. Beattie was perceived as having handled the crisis fearlessly and with honesty – emerging victorious in the 2001 and 2004 elections. ❑

ABOVE: dusk view of the World Expo '88 held in Brisbane with the theme "Leisure in the Age of Technology".

Joh Bjelke-Petersen

It is impossible to chart Queensland's history without invoking the memory of the idiosyncratic right-wing premier who ruled for 19 years from 1968, and was known far and wide simply as "Joh".

Sir Johannes Bjelke-Petersen died in 2005, aged 94. Even in death, he remains a controversial figure, with opponents first contesting his right to a state funeral, then, more recently, moves to name an important bridge in his honour.

The eccentric, despotic and sometimes naive reign of this fundamentalist farmer has left an indelible imprint on the state – as much for his ruthless silencing of dissent as for his unsentimental approach to development.

Yet Joh accomplished much. The 1982 Commonwealth Games and the building of the Cultural Complex at South Bank were achieved under his government. World Expo '88 – arguably the event that elevated Brisbane from big country town to cosmopolitan city – was another of his initiatives. But although he built up Queensland into an economic power and Brisbane into a thriving capital, he also demonstrated arrant chauvinism, hostility to social and environmental concerns, and disregard for alleged police corruption and brutality.

To opponents, the human cost of Joh-style progress was unacceptable. When protesters marched in support of civil liberties, Joh mobilised the police to quell them, a response that frequently led to violence and mass arrests. Progress was his mantra. Anything that stood in its way was bulldozed into oblivion. Thus Brisbane lost some of its most iconic buildings – the gracious and historic Bellevue Hotel in George Street and the hilltop Cloudland Ballroom were both demolished under cover of darkness.

Poverty and struggle in his rural childhood left him with no sympathy for those who thought themselves above hard work. The years of hardship may well have filled the reservoir of energy which, combined with an innate craftiness, enabled him to crush opponents, big and small, during his tumultuous and sometimes precarious career. He came to be seen as invincible, a strongman who brooked no challenge to his authority. He took on powerful unions – and won. When the Queensland Liberals defected from the coalition, he went to the polls without them – and still won.

In 1975 he deliberately appointed a federal senator hostile to Prime Minister Gough Whitlam and helped to precipitate

Whitlam's dismissal from office. In the end, Joh decided he would run for prime minister himself. Like the mythical Icarus, he flew too close to the sun and fell from grace. His era ended badly, amid accusations of bribery and corruption. The Fitzgerald Inquiry uncovered corruption on a significant scale. Even when he was deposed by his own National Party, he at first refused to vacate the premiership. He finally yielded to reality, relinquishing both the premiership and the parliamentary seat he had held for 41 years. His 1991 trial for perjury ended with a hung jury. ❏

RIGHT: Petersen and Thatcher in 1984.

1885 Legislation is passed to discontinue the "recruiting" of Pacific Islanders for Queensland's tropical agriculture.

1887 Brisbane is connected by rail to Sydney. Difficulties (which still exist) arise because of Queensland's choice of narrow gauge, which does not match that of southern states.

1890s Economic depression leads to industrial unrest and a series of violent confrontations. A shearers' strike at Barcaldine is a catalyst in the organisation of labour and the establishment of a union movement.

1891 The Cairns to Kuranda railway line opens.

1896 The first sugar cane is crushed at the Mulgrave Central Mill at Gordonvale.

1901 The six independent colonies are federated into the Commonwealth of Australia under a common constitution.

1914 The first Australian troops leave home to join the Allies in World War I.

1920 Passenger ships offer one-day stopovers on a Whitsunday "tropical island", heralding the area's success as a tourist destination. QANTAS is founded at Longreach.

1928 The Royal Flying Doctor Service (RFDS) is established in Cloncurry by John Flynn, a bush clergyman.

1933 The Surfers' Paradise township is named after James Cavill's hotel of the same name.

1939 Outbreak of World War II. Australian forces again leave to fight in Europe and the Middle East. Later in the war, Australia's military forces fight the Japanese in the Pacific.

1941 First convoy of American servicemen arrives in Brisbane, which becomes the base for hundreds of thousands of them.

1942 Japanese planes attack Darwin. Naval bases are established at Cairns and Thursday Island. The Battle of the Coral Sea is fought from 4–8 May. Catalina flying boats operating from Cairns attack Japanese positions in the Pacific islands.

1947 Airline owner Reg Ansett introduces big business into the Whitsundays with his acquisition of Hayman Island.

1951 Bush Pilots Airways, established to open up communications and transport on Cape York, makes its first scheduled flight.

1968 Joh Bjelke-Petersen begins a 19-year reign as state premier, and a ruthless, ultimately corrupt, period of government ensues.

1976 The Great Barrier Reef Marine Park Authority is established, with responsibility for protecting the extensive coral reefs.

1982 The 12th Commonwealth Games (previously the British Empire Games) are held in Brisbane.

1984 Cairns International Airport is opened. A track negotiable only by off-road vehicles is opened up between Cape Tribulation and the Bloomfield River despite considerable protest.

1988 Amid Australia's bicentenary celebrations, Brisbane hosts World Expo '88 with the

Queensland-friendly theme: "Leisure in the Age of Technology". World Heritage status is accorded to 900,000 hectares (2.25 million acres) of North Queensland's tropical rainforests.

1992 The Australian High Court rejects the *Terra Nullus* (empty land) concept which had existed since the time of European discovery, and instead rules that the native title has survived the annexation of the country.

1990s Brisbane's population reaches the 1.5 million mark.

2001 Centenary of Australian Federation.

2006 Cyclone Larry devastates the state's northeast coast around Innisfail, causing millions of dollars worth of damage. ❑

LEFT: Burke, Wills and companions set out on their ill-fated expedition to the interior in 1860.

RIGHT: Townsville in the early '70s.

QUEENSLAND PEOPLE

The early settlers had a tough start amid harsh conditions, but Queenslanders have developed into a relaxed, friendly bunch of people with a strong sense of community. Their region is becoming a magnet for outsiders, keen to share its natural beauties and laid-back lifestyle

A Melbourne journalist once observed that Queensland was so different from the rest of Australia that it was always a surprise that you didn't need a visa to go there. The houses on stilts, the tropical vegetation and flowering trees with musical names – frangipani, jacaranda, poiciana, bauhinia – the heat, the vivid light, the vast distances and the people themselves – so much more laid-back, friendly and direct than southerners, made it seem like another country.

In a typical Queensland childhood, a baby will be placed in a hole at the water's edge on the Sunshine Coast or the Gold Coast and sit with the waves pounding beside it. Several childhood holidays a year may be spent playing on these long, wide, white beaches. Surfing the waves, with your body or your board, becomes as natural as breathing. To the Queenslander, the Pacific Ocean is a necessity of life.

Space is also something that Queenslanders take for granted. In 1901 there were just half a million people in an area of 1,734,189 sq. km (670,000 sq. miles), two-and-a-half times the size of Texas. More than a century later, there are four million, but that still means there is one square kilometre of space for every 2.3 people – possibly the most space per person anywhere on earth. It is further from Brisbane to Cooktown in the far north than Brisbane to Tasmania. And with 1.8 million people living in the Brisbane area, that leaves just 2.2 million spread around the rural towns, cities and properties.

Queensland had a rough start. When it was separated from New South Wales in 1859 and became an independent colony, this vast state had a population of only 23,520. Brisbane was originally the Moreton Bay penal colony for the toughest of convicts who had reoffended while serving out their sentences in New South Wales.

Nature could be harsh and threatening. The Queensland Club in Brisbane, an elegant colonial sandstone building with verandas and wrought-iron railings, is a bastion of the old established WASP families, yet in the entrance lies a stuffed crocodile – a reminder of the country's primordial nature, a symbol of how different this state is from the milder south.

LEFT: a stockman in the Outback. **RIGHT:** surfing: as natural as breathing to ocean-loving Queenslanders.

The Catholic–Protestant divide used to be significant, with Irish Catholics dominating the law and medicine, the pubs and racing. These days Catholics from all countries make up about a quarter of the population, and, though the migrant population has increased, they still comprise just a sixth of the national total. The atmosphere is still overwhelmingly white Anglo-Celtic.

The pioneers, threatened by a harsh, immense bush and often hostile Aboriginal people, had to be resourceful, with a sense of adventure and an independent spirit. This developed into a kind of patriotism. Even as recently as the 1980s, during the State of Origin rugby league matches

good training to send talented youth up north for a bit of toughening experience in the tropics.

But although southerners could be patronising, there was a sense that with its mineral wealth, size, diversity and its sheer beauty, Queensland was a place of immense potential. In the last 20 years, it has been living up to that sense of promise in unforeseen ways.

A fast-growing state

Queensland currently has the fastest-growing population of any state in Australia (more than 200 people are moving in every day) and arguably the most solid economy. Part of this increase is from overseas migration, but it is the

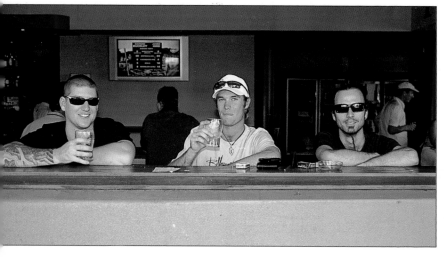

against New South Wales, whenever they were under the cosh, one of the Queensland team would yell out: "Queenslander! Queenslander!" and immediately they would be galvanised. They won over and over.

Although outstanding Queenslanders have often left the state in search of greater opportunities, they can never forget it. As local writer Hugh Lunn says: "There's no such thing as an ex-Queenslander, only a lapsed Queenslander."

In the south, Queenslanders have often had a reputation for being uncultured, with "redneck" attitudes to the Aboriginal people and other migrants. There was a time when those in industry and big business down south considered it

interstate migrants – here for the greater opportunities, the climate and the relaxed atmosphere – who are changing Queensland most dramatically. They include a lot of young people, entrepreneurs eager to take advantage of the biotechnology boom, and prosperous southern baby-boomers and retirees bringing their wealth north to buy property all along the coast.

Brisbane has become a place that is full of people from somewhere else. Euan Murdoch, from Victoria, created a hugely successful pharmaceutical company in Brisbane, sold it, and now heads a research-and-development company. Brisbane people, he says, are "more open and flexible in their attitude in the workplace".

Professor Allan Paull, of the School of Mechanical Engineering at the University of Queensland, is researching technology that will help make international travel faster and provide an inexpensive method for launching satellites. He says that while failure means death to projects in some parts of the world, in Queensland "it is part of the course of learning – the first failure doesn't mean doom".

The capital

Even in the 1980s, Brisbane was hardly more than a large country town from which every young person with nous or ambition wanted to escape. But then came the 1982 Commonwealth

ney or Melbourne. In summer, it is normal to see people watering their gardens at sunrise or taking a quiet walk around the streets. Brisbane children are still more carefree than in the southern cities, and are often seen barefoot in the streets and parks.

Nature has a powerful presence even in the middle of the city, where there are thriving mangroves on the river banks, and seagulls, hawks, cormorants and pelicans on the river. In bush suburbs only 20 minutes' drive from the city centre, there are poisonous brown snakes. Backyard hens' eggs can be taken by carpet snakes, while the redback spider can live in gardens and under houses in the inner city.

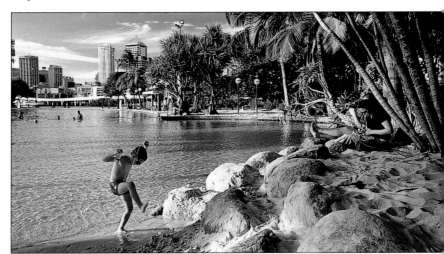

Games and the '88 Expo – a celebration of the bicentenary of the First Fleet, attracting tourism and interest from all over the world. The Fitzgerald Inquiry exposed the corruption of the long-term Jo Bjelke-Petersen government; and a new period of Labor rule began. Brisbane started to be seen as a place that was moving ahead and yet getting the balance right: it was neither hidebound by tradition like Melbourne nor tough like Sydney.

Despite its rapid growth, Brisbane still offers a slower and less complicated lifestyle than Syd-

And there is another natural danger. Living in some of the most intense sunlight on earth, Queenslanders have the world's highest rate of skin cancer. But the fair-skinned are learning. In the south of the state, at least, you no longer see the same number of baked-brown faces.

Brisbane people are still comparatively conservative. You won't see many solar heating panels on top of the houses or water tanks, despite generous rebates. Family values are very strong. And although the city has many more fashion designers, including the international duo Easton Pearson, the general community still tends to dress down. Thongs (flip-flops) and shorts remain a common sight.

LEFT: sinking a cool one.
ABOVE: Brisbane children lead a charmed life.

Betty Churcher, the first woman to run Australia's National Gallery in Canberra, says that the quality of her Brisbane childhood was essential to her success. "The subtropical climate gives you a sense of openness and freedom."

The regions

Queensland is Australia's most decentralised state. Large communities live on the Gold Coast (the state's second-largest city was formed in 1959 to unite several small centres along the strip), on the Sunshine Coast, and in Rockhampton, Townsville, Mackay, Cairns, Gladstone, Toowoomba and Mount Isa. With huge distances between them and with populations

Speech gets slower and each comment invariably ends in "eh". Cape York Peninsula has some of the country's biggest cattle stations, some up to 400,000 hectares (1 million acres) or more. One of the most important social occasions – the annual race meeting – might involve hours of driving along hundreds of kilometres of road, much of it dirt.

The west – roughly a three-hour drive in every direction from Longreach, home of Qantas – has a special spirit. Flat and dry, with huge skies, the landscape can be interpreted as harsh, but the space generally brings a profound sense of freedom and peace. The stars out there seem brighter than anywhere else on earth.

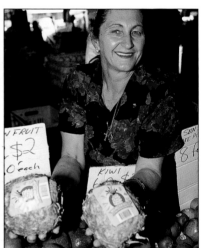

of varying ethnic mixes, these areas have developed their own distinct identities.

The primary industries – wheat, tropical and temperate fruit, cattle, cotton, sugar cane, viniculture, wool, bauxite, coal, copper, silver, lead and zinc – have largely depended on the hard work of immigrants from more than 200 nations. Some have congregated to great effect: the Germans on the Darling Downs, Australia's largest population of South Sea Islanders in Mackay, the Italians of Innisfail, the Finns and Yugoslavs of Mount Isa, and the Hmong from Laos in northern Queensland.

The further north you go, the hotter and more humid it gets and the more extreme the accent.

Families have run properties in the west for generations and continue to do so, despite the economic pressures, whereas in other areas of the country the population turnover is much greater. Western Queenslanders are known for their hospitality. Humour, trustworthiness and mutual help have always been necessary for survival in Queensland's remote communities.

Queensland's indigenous people

According to the 2001 census, about 126,000 Aborigines and Torres Strait Islanders live in the state. There is no escaping the fact that the Aboriginal people of Queensland have had a tragic existence since white settlement: killed in huge numbers by imported diseases, living at the mercy of discriminatory laws and damaged by alcohol and drugs. For a brief period, many lived in peace in family communities on the stations of their employers and were respected for their skills as stockmen and trackers. Then came the reservations, handouts and access to alcohol. There have been decades of government largesse and many dedicated people working to improve conditions – prominent among them poet and activist Kath Walker (whose traditional name is Oodgeroo Noonuccal, *see page 40*), but many policies have been misguided, and Aboriginal people still have a life expectancy decades less than that of the white community.

much of the state's great natural beauty and lifestyle. In 2005 the state government revealed its vision for managing growth in southeast Queensland up to 2026. Brisbane resident Dr Aila Keto, an environmentalist with a global reputation, has devoted her life to preserving Queensland's natural heritage. It is thanks to her and her husband Keith Scott that the Wet Tropics of Queensland, Fraser Island and the central-eastern rainforest of Australia are World Heritage-listed. But she says that her joy at seeing so much preserved has been "tinged with a sense of tragedy" at the amount of destruction in the southeast of the state. Meanwhile, the developers gleefully rub their hands.   ❑

Despite the grim reality, there are Queensland successes, like William Barton, the Brisbane-based Aboriginal didgeridoo player, the artist Judy Watson, and high-profile achievers such as Olympic gold medallist Cathy Freeman and television personality Ernie Dingo who are positive role models for the younger generation.

The future

There are fears that overdevelopment and too rapid a rate of population increase could destroy

LEFT: flying the flag; pineapple grower. **ABOVE LEFT:** Kath Walker, poet and activist, who died in 1993. **ABOVE RIGHT:** William Barton and his didgeridoo.

NOTABLE QUEENSLANDERS

Out of this state have come the Nobel Prize-winning scientist Peter Doherty, poets Kath Walker, Judith Wright and Peter Porter, writer David Malouf, painters Margaret Olley and William Robinson, the actor Geoffrey Rush, the didgeridoo player William Barton, the band Powderfinger, and many great sports people: cricketers Matthew Hayden and Andrew Symonds, tennis players Rod Laver (the Rockhampton Rocket), Roy Emerson and Pat Rafter, golfer Greg Norman (the Great White Shark), rugby union player Michael Lynagh and captain John Eales, Olympic gold medal runner Cathy Freeman and rugby league player Wally Lewis (King Wally).

ABORIGINAL LAND

Despite two centuries of cultural attrition, the Aboriginal people have retained a strong sense of identity and a fierce pride in their heritage. The land is a crucial part of their being, and the fight for "land rights" goes on

When James Cook took possession of the eastern coast of Australia in the name of King George III on 22 August 1770, he created a minefield of perplexing landownership issues. According to 18th-century law, the ways to gain legal sovereignty over new lands were by conquest, by the indigenous populace ceding sovereignty or by declaring the land *terra nullius*. The first two options carried an obligation to negotiate just reparations for the alienated occupants of the lands. The third option was based on the notion that the territory lacked human habitation and could therefore be obtained for free.

The British government went for the last option. The first settlers to arrive on Australia's remote shores could not understand the Aboriginal people's nomadic lifestyle or their profound connection to their tribal lands. It seemed that they came and went without reason across the sparse landscape. Ignoring the presence of an estimated 300,000 indigenous people who had been pursuing their culture for 50,000 years, the British government conveniently declared Terra Australis to be a *terra nullius* – an uninhabited void that could be occupied without further thought. The results were devastating for Aboriginal culture.

The colonial curse

When the First Fleet arrived, no war was declared. White settlers simply occupied land and Aboriginal resistance was met with sav-

age reprisals. Those living in the vicinity of Port Jackson were the first to lose their territory. As white settlement expanded, so began the cycle of attack and reprisal. Previously unknown European diseases brought death and misery, while survivors were reduced to living in abject squalor around the periphery of white settlements. An ugly war of attrition prevailed, and massacres were exacted upon people who often had taken no part in any transgressions.

As the spread of settlement advanced, Aboriginal people ejected from their tribal lands were forced into territory belonging to their neighbours – adding internal conflict to an

---

LEFT: Torres Strait Islander in traditional dress. **RIGHT:** an early European impression of an Aboriginal camp.

already difficult predicament. Either way, spears stood no chance against bullets, and, sadly, some of the worst atrocities were carried out by native police trained by the settlers in the use of carbines.

Last of the tribes to succumb were the Kalkadoons, whose territory once encompassed the land on which the mining city of Mount Isa now stands. The Kalkadoons engaged native police and squatters in wily guerrilla warfare for more than a decade, striking unexpectedly then melting into the hills. Lured into open conflict at Battle Mount, north of Cloncurry, in 1884, they were finally mown down by native police.

late and "protect" the surviving Aboriginal people from white society – a strategy designed to keep the Aboriginal "problem" hidden.

Nonetheless, in the late 1890s, it became apparent that ruthless whites were taking advantage of indigenous people – preying on their women, exploiting their children, paying subsistence wages to their men. The government reacted by passing the Aboriginal Protection and Restriction of the Sale of Opium Act 1897, which made the majority of Aboriginal people wards of the state. People were relocated from their traditional lands to government reserves and church missions, and families dispersed to different reserves. Few

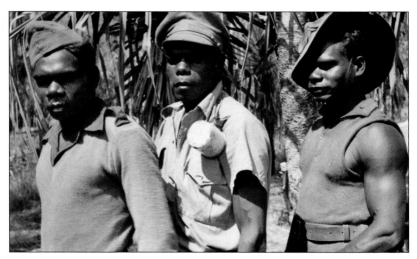

Australia's apartheid

Survivors of this colonial holocaust lived as refugees – marginalised in wretched shanties on the outskirts of white settlements or occupying squalid humpies (temporary shelters) on pastoral properties. Some graziers treated Aboriginal stockmen and servants with kindness and consideration, but, for the most part, graziers paid Aboriginal people subsistence wages and denied them basic human rights.

By 1888, Australia's Aboriginal population had declined to around 80,000 – but, to the disappointment of white supremacists, it showed no sign of dying out completely. The Queensland government embarked on a policy to iso-

freedoms applied. Permits were required in order to work outside the reserves; income was managed by the state; and Aboriginal people wishing to marry required permission from the chief protector.

Dissent

There is a perception that Aboriginal dissent did not surface until the 1960s and 1970s. In fact, an Aboriginal rights association existed in Sydney as early as 1924. Indeed, the Melbourne-based Australian Aborigines Advancement League petitioned King George V for special indigenous electorates in 1932. If white Australians believed (as many did) that Aboriginal people owed them a debt of gratitude for having brought civilisation to *terra nullius*, they were disabused by the Aboriginal Progressive Association manifesto of 1938. Issued on the 150th anniversary of the landing of the First Fleet in Botany Bay, this document declared 26 January a "day of mourning" – a theme that would be repeated over ensuing decades. "You took our land away from us by force," the manifesto said. "You have almost exterminated our people, but there are enough of us remaining to expose the humbug of your claim as white Australians to be a civilised, progressive, kindly and humane nation. By your cruelty and callousness towards the

act confirming that those who could vote in their states could vote for the Commonwealth. Interestingly, Aboriginal people in all states except Queensland and Western Australia had been entitled to vote in state elections from the 1850s. They didn't vote because noone told them their rights. (Queensland accorded state voting rights to Aboriginal people in 1965 – the last Australian state to do so.)

The Stolen Generation

If Aboriginal people were hazy about their rights, so too were the police and welfare officers who forcibly removed up to 100,000 children from their parents between 1910 and

Aborigines you stand condemned in the eyes of the civilised world."

World War II brought white Australians and Aboriginal people into closer communion, particularly within the armed forces. At the same time, better communications made it harder to get away with abuses in remote areas. By the 1940s, various lobby groups were championing Aboriginal political rights, and in 1949 the Chifley government passed an

1970. The idea was to "assimilate" mixed-blood Aboriginal children into European society over one or two generations. They were fostered into white homes and forbidden to speak their own language. Most were given menial jobs, many suffered abuse, and nearly all experienced psychological damage. They became known as the Stolen Generation.

Aboriginal activists

The referendum of 1967, in which 90 percent of Australians voted to allow the Commonwealth to make laws for Aboriginal people, marked the turning point in attitudes to Aboriginal rights. The year before, Aboriginal

LEFT: Aboriginal servicemen, 1943.
ABOVE: Still from the 2002 movie *Rabbit-Proof Fence*, a moving testimony to the suffering of the Stolen Generation.

stockmen at Wave Hill Station, 600 km (375 miles) southwest of Katharine, had staged their historic "walk-off", sparking the land-rights movement. Previous Aboriginal protests had been easily crushed, but the Gurindji people stood firm for nine years, expanding their cause from a plea for fair treatment to a demand for the return of traditional lands.

Having walked off, the tribe set up camp at Wattie Creek, naming the new settlement Daguragu while pursuing a campaign that would lead to the Commonwealth Land Rights Act (Northern Territory), 1976. The build-up to all of this was characterised by 1960s radicalism. Inspired by the US civil-

country speaking in favour of land rights. In 1971, the Yirrakala people on the Gove Penin-sula in the Northern Territory mounted a land claim to win back control of traditional land where mining company Nabalco had estab-lished a bauxite project. In support of their claim, activists set up a "tent embassy" out-side Parliament House, demanding legal title to and control of mining rights on existing reserve lands, preservation of sacred sites and A$6 billion compensation. Justice Blackburn ruled against the Yirrkala people in the subse-quent court action. Nonetheless, their gutsy stand signalled new confidence among Abo-riginal activists.

rights movement, Aboriginal activist Charles Perkins led a series of "freedom rides" through Outback Queensland and northwest New South Wales, bringing his message to the most remote communities. At a time when feelings were running high over apartheid in South Africa and racial discrimination in the American Deep South, Perkins visited Aus-tralian towns where Aboriginal people were banned from pubs, RSL (Returned and Ser-vices League) veterans' clubs and community pools. By highlighting Australian discrimina-tion, Perkins did much to eliminate it.

Later that year, Aboriginal poet Kath Walker (Oodgeroo Noonuccal) toured the

Towards self-determination

This new-found political consciousness forced the Federal Australian Government to come up with a new policy, "self-determination". This allowed Aboriginal people to make deci-sions affecting their own future, retain their cultural identity and values, and achieve greater economic and social equality.

The Department of Aboriginal Affairs was established in 1972, followed by the Aborigi-nal Development Commission (ADC) in 1980. The concept was to develop programmes that would bring economic independence to Abo-riginal people by fostering the development of business enterprises – but it didn't happen overnight. Since the 1970s, Aboriginal people have become involved in the development of government policies that affect them and in the delivery of services. More importantly, a wide range of organisations, from medical and legal services to Land Councils (which govern the affairs of different regions), have been established; there are now more than 1,200 Aboriginal community organisations.

In 1988, while the rest of Australia celebrated 200 years of white settlement at the Bicentennial, Aboriginal activists staged peaceful protest marches. The international media carried their message around the world, and white Australians were forced to admit that Aboriginals had very little to celebrate. The events of 1988 pushed Aboriginal issues to the forefront of the political agenda.

Land rights

For all Aboriginal groups, "land rights" have always been the top priority. The land is a crucial part of their being, and the responsibility for protecting significant sites is central to their spiritual life. It has been a source of profound distress that they have been pushed from their traditional homes, and seen sacred sites mined, built on, flooded or otherwise destroyed. The Northern Territory Land Rights Act, passed in 1975, allowed Aboriginal people to make claims to vast swaths of the Outback on the basis of traditional ownership. The act also gave them significant control over mining and other activities. Royalties from mining operations were distributed to Aboriginal groups throughout the territory.

Land-rights acts have been passed in various states, and in 1985 the Federal Government attempted to introduce national land-rights legislation. There was strong opposition – particularly in Queensland and Western Australia, where mining lobbies are powerful – and Canberra backed down, agreeing that a state-by-state approach was more appropriate.

Perhaps the most symbolic change occurred in 1992, when the High Court of Australia overturned the legal fiction of *terra nullius* – the assumption that people previously living in the region had been too primitive to qual-ify as human beings. The judges agreed that "native title" had always existed for land that had been continuously occupied by Aboriginal people. Where a traditional connection to land and waters had been maintained and where government acts had not removed it, the law recognised this as native title.

In 1993 the government set up a Native Title Tribunal to regulate claims. As time went on, however, it appeared that the tribunal would achieve little in practice: since 19th-century missionaries had moved indigenous peoples around, often splitting up clans and lumping them together again in remote areas, few Aboriginal groups could prove continu-

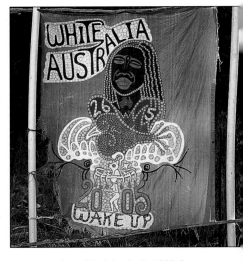

ous occupation of their lands. In 1998, however, the Western Yalanji people of north Queensland were formally recognised as the native titleholders of a pastoral property called Karma Waters, although their rights are limited because of the government's pastoral lease and other actions in the past.

Lack of progress has been frustrating for Aboriginal people, and the emotional land-rights debate remains one of the most contentious issues in Australia today. Aboriginal dissent continues to be a feature of Queensland's political life, but, while the situation is far from perfect, it has improved significantly since the mid-1990s. ❏

LEFT: "Freedom Ride" bus tour led by Charles Perkins.
RIGHT: a wake-up call for white Australia.

SURF CULTURE

Introduced to Australia in 1912 by Duke Kahanamoku of Honolulu, surfing has become a way of life for many of the continent's coastal dwellers. With ideal waves and weather, southeast Queensland is a surfer's paradise that has produced both champions and drop-outs

If you hit the southeast coast of Queensland when the surf's up you may wonder if anyone here goes to work or school. On a good day at Noosa Heads, Burleigh, Snapper Rocks or dozens of other Queensland surf beaches, thousands of surfers of all ages and on all kinds of equipment clog the line-ups. From Brisbane, drive for an hour north to the Sunshine Coast, or south to the Gold Coast, and you can't help but be struck by the all-pervasive surf obsession.

The lure of warm water, long point breaks, sand-bottomed tube rides and a balmy subtropical climate have drawn surfers here for generations. Australian surfing may have begun at Sydney's Freshwater Beach, when visiting Hawaiian champion Duke Kahanamoku put on his historic display in 1914, but the surfing lifestyle seems to have reached its zenith here in Queensland. The idea of a life spent lolling under pandanus trees on a grassy headland overlooking a glistening Pacific Ocean, in between idyllic surf sessions, is rooted deep in the Australian surfer's psyche.

The history of surfing

Early European settlers initially frowned upon surf bathing, as both physically and morally dangerous. Mixed genders in minimal clothing frolicking in the surf were regarded as an almost certain prelude to the breakdown of civilisation. Slowly but surely, though, the

surf's siren song proved irresistible. Surf life-saving clubs were formed in the early 1900s to protect public safety, and quickly grew as social hubs for the emerging beach culture.

There is some evidence of a surf culture among pre-European, indigenous Australians. They were adept at fishing, even enjoying the aid of dolphins to herd schools of fish shorewards, and they fashioned canoes out of bark that were seaworthy even in rough surf. Indigenous Australians were almost certainly competent and confident in the surf – the foundation meeting of the Greenmount Surf Club in 1908 paid tribute to a local Aboriginal man, called Churaki, for the many daring

LEFT: riding a tube.
RIGHT: Hawaiian champion Duke Kahanamoku.

rescues he carried out in the surf prior to the club's formation.

Early surfcraft were cumbersome, 5-metre (16-ft) "toothpicks", hollow plywood paddleboards, nicknamed for their narrow, pointed appearance. Surfboats were built for ocean rescues and manned by teams of earnest paddlers, but proved poorly designed for rough ocean conditions, and probably caused as many casualties as they prevented. More successful was the belt and reel, introduced to Queensland by a pair of Sydney visitors, the Bennett brothers, in 1915.

Surf clubs remained unchallenged as the seat of beach culture until the 1950s, when a rebellious new surf culture. Freshly inspired surfers rejected the stuffy, regimented conservatism of the surf clubs and ditched their voluntary beach patrols for the freewheeling lifestyle of the wave-chasing surfie.

Simmering tensions between the life-savers (or clubbies) and the surfers occasionally boiled over, with surfers claiming the life-savers erected their swimming flags where the waves were best, or steered their unwieldy surfboats through packs of surfers. Life-savers claimed surfers were endangering public safety and often confiscated their boards.

The late 1960s "shortboard revolution" further exacerbated tensions, as surfers began to

group of Americans visited Australia to coincide with the 1956 Melbourne Olympics. Their surfriding displays at Torquay in Victoria, and Manly and Avalon in Sydney, on revolutionary, short, light Malibu boards, reverberated around the country.

Surfers of the sixties

The introduction of a new, radical style of surfing on more manoeuvrable equipment coincided with the emergence of a new culture of independence and social revolution among Western youth. The same circumstances that gave rise to rock and roll inspired

SURFING LINGO

The following is a short glossary of surfing terms to help the uninitiated:

Belt and reel: a life-saver's tackle.

Clubbies: surf life-saving club members.

Hotdog surfing: agile style of surfing based on abrupt direction changes.

Kneeboarder: one who surfs on their knees.

Lineups: areas where waves are ridden at a surf break.

Long pointbreak: a wave that breaks for long distances along a point of land, or headland.

Shorebreak: where waves dump abruptly onto the beach.

chop a foot or more at a time off their old longboards, in the quest for ever lighter, more manoeuvrable equipment with which to enact the new "hotdog" style of surfing.

Queensland's Noosa Heads, with its long, perfectly peeling pointbreak, provided the perfect test track for surfing's new experimentalists. American kneeboarder and filmmaker George Greenough, surfboard shaper Bob MacTavish and 1966 world champion Nat Young formed the vanguard of this revolution, enjoying long, uncrowded sessions at Noosa to push the limits of wave-riding. A new generation of freedom-seeking surfers grew their hair, defied the austere post-war work ethic of their parents and were ready, in the words of acid guru Timothy Leary, to "turn on, tune in and drop out". Queensland's beaches provided the perfect environment to do just that.

In the late 1960s and early 1970s, surfing's public image reached an all-time low, associated as it was with laziness, drug use and antisocial behaviour. Vagrancy laws were enacted to lock up surfers who weren't carrying a specific amount of money. Drug raids on surfer households were commonplace, carried out by a Queensland police force renowned for their heavy-handedness.

But the waves kept on rolling in, and this period is still revered today as a golden era of uncrowded surf, with consistent, ruler-edged cyclone swells pouring into the pointbreaks. In Queensland, under an ever-shining sun, it was all too easy to surf all day and not worry about tomorrow.

Going professional

Beneath the hippy trappings, however, a new revolution began bubbling away in the quiet Queensland town of Coolangatta. The dream of professional surfing, to be paid to ride waves as a legitimate sporting career, took hold of a small group of top practitioners. Intense rivalry between Coolangatta's top three 1970s surfers, Michael Peterson, Peter Townend and Wayne "Rabbit" Bartholomew, provided the spark for this hyper-competitive push. Coolangatta's neighbouring pointbreaks of Snapper Rocks, Greenmount Point and

Kirra were the scene of groundbreaking performances in the new hotdog surfing and the advent of deep tube-riding. While the three vied for the title of the best surfer in town they were pushing each other to heights that would see them acclaimed as the best in the world.

A loose collection of surf contests scattered around the globe were first cobbled together into a unified world tour in 1976, to anoint Peter Townend, the Coolangatta Kid, as pro surfing's first world champion. But the real birth of pro surfing was at Burleigh Heads in 1977, when former Queensland and Australian champion Peter Drouyn masterminded the first Stubbies Classic. Under his innovative man-on-man format (still used today),

judging was made fairer, and a major mainstream sponsor put up serious cash for the winners. Thousands of spectators crammed Burleigh Heads to see all the giant surfing talents of the day do battle in Burleigh's perfect barrels. Peterson emerged victorious, with a then staggering A$5,000 prize, and swiftly vanished into a drug-and-paranoia-fuelled oblivion. It was left largely to Townend, Rabbit and a handful of their contemporaries to steer professional surfing towards mainstream acceptance and respectability.

Rabbit went on to claim the world title in 1978, and hold down a top-five world ranking up until 1984, as a new era of big money and

LEFT: Peter Townend, the original Coolangatta kid.
RIGHT: Mick Fanning, one of today's Coolangatta kids.

media coverage dawned. But, strangely, few of Rabbit's Queensland peers seemed ready to follow in his wake. The most common theory is that the Queensland surfing lifestyle is so pleasant, the living so easy, the lure of generous unemployment benefits, frenetic nightlife, a seductive climate and sheer overindulgence rendering the typical Queensland surfer of the day unsuited to, or simply uninterested in, the demands of world travel and elite competition. Queensland's surfing history is littered with monumental talents who burned out on a "too-much-too-young" trajectory. It seems you can have too much of a good thing. Queensland's status as the skin-cancer capital of the world

wide boom of the surf industry means that professional surfers have the opportunity to set themselves up financially for life. Young surfers barely out of their teens drive luxury 4WD vehicles and buy million-dollar mansions. Home-grown surf label Billabong, started on the kitchen table of a rented Gold Coast apartment some 30 years ago, is now a publicly listed, Top 100 company on the Australian Stock Exchange. And its founder, Gordon Merchant, a nomadic surfboard shaper, and a handful of his senior management, are wealthy beyond their wildest dreams.

Surfing today is as mainstream as tennis, golf, cricket or football, regularly splashed all

seems to stand as a kind of metaphor for flying too close to the sun in this alluring lifestyle.

Surfing today

Yet a new generation of talented Queensland surfers seems to have learned the cautionary lessons of their elders well. Today, a new trio of gifted Coolangatta Kids – Mick Fanning, Dean Morrison and Joel Parkinson – is mimicking the rivalry of their predecessors, pushing themselves towards surfing greatness. Lucrative careers with million-dollar salaries and worldwide superstardom beckon. Legions of success-hungry grommets (junior surfers) vie for supremacy in their wake. The world-

over the front and back pages of the local newspapers. Rabbit Bartholomew is president of the Association of Surfing Professionals, presiding over a multimillion-dollar world tour from his Coolangatta head office overlooking the waves he grew up riding. Government departments undertake weighty studies of the economic and social value of surfing. The Quiksilver Pro at Snapper Rocks is estimated to inject A$5 million into the local economy each year.

The old surfer/clubbie rift has long since healed. Queensland's twin surf cultures now coexist and overlap, and local kids grow up riding every kind of surfcraft imaginable. If you come across a Saturday morning "nippers" (junior surf life-saving session), with kids who look as if they're barely out of nappies charging in and out of the waves, you would swear they're breeding a new, genetically modified amphibious race here. Webbed hands and feet and gills are surely only a few generations away.

Those old surf clubs with their prime beachfront positions are still the social hubs of the Queensland coast, where you can enjoy a cheap meal, a cold beer, or succumb to the dreaded "pokies" (fruit machines), all with unmatched ocean views. The old, framed black-and-white photos of past surf champions peer down curiously, echoing earlier, simpler times. Surf clubs act as village square, public house, gymnasium and ceremonial site for rituals into adulthood.

Or you can walk around those mighty headlands at Noosa, Burleigh, Kirra, Greenmount or Snapper and watch new generations of surf-crazed kids or ageless grown-ups happily feeding an unstoppable addiction. On a full moon, you'll even find a few hardy souls surfing it up in the silvery light, just to escape the incessant crowds and threat of melanoma.

For the quintessential Queensland surf experience, have a surf lesson, sit under a pandanus tree with a pie and a chocolate milk, go for another surf, then retreat to the surf club for a steak and a beer as the sun sets over the mountain hinterland. Just see if you don't feel strangely good about the world. Then go to bed, wake up and do it again. Ad infinitum.

Wave etiquette

More than 1,000 Australians move to southeast Queensland every week, and, along with a couple of million tourists a year, it seems as if they all want to surf. If you plan on entering the fray, think about a surf lesson first, and learn some of the basic rules. Unwritten codes of conduct govern the safe functioning of a busy surf spot, and you are advised to respect them. The surfer on the wave has right of way. The surfer closest to the curl (the breaking part of the wave) has first priority. Learn to handle your board, to paddle and duck-dive away from

more experienced surfers and challenging waves. Find a little beachbreak to yourself to flounder around in while you learn the basics, rather than being one of the hundreds of visiting surfers who paddle out at Snapper Rocks, or Burleigh, or Kirra, just so they can tell the folks back home they did it. Give space to more experienced and local surfers. Don't drop in on someone else's wave. Never throw your board in the face of an oncoming wave if it's going to endanger others. And one last thing. You would hardly credit that it needs saying (but it clearly does): make sure you can swim proficiently before you try to surf. Stay safe and have fun. ❑

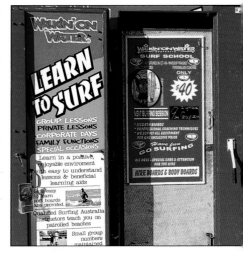

LEFT: Quicksilver Pro 2006.

RIGHT: there are surf schools at all major surf beaches.

CULTURAL QUEENSLAND

Queensland was once regarded as a cultural desert, but the last few decades have seen exciting advances made in all the art forms, some sponsored by the government, others by private initiatives

Queensland was somewhat unfairly perceived as a cultural desert from the 1950s to the 1970s, but its cultural scene has blossomed visibly over recent decades, although most of it is concentrated in Brisbane. Concerts, festivals and celebrations now punctuate the events calendar. The Queensland Performing Arts Complex at South Bank in Brisbane regularly hosts performers of international renown and blockbuster exhibitions are the norm rather than the exception at the Queensland Art Gallery. The city is home to a fine symphony orchestra, an accomplished ballet, professional opera and theatre companies, as well as an active art and literary scene.

To complement – and to some extent challenge – mainstream cultural events, the city has nurtured alternative venues devoted to cutting-edge performances and exhibitions, notably the Brisbane Powerhouse and the Judith Wright Centre of Contemporary Arts. Brisbane also demonstrates a knack for producing internationally successful actors and rock bands. Diane Cilento, Billie Brown, Geoffrey Rush and Mount Isa-born Deborah Mailman have all achieved prominence. Home-grown pop bands include Savage Garden, Powderfinger, george, The Go Betweens and The Saints.

The desert blooms

It would be an exaggeration to portray mainstream Queenslanders as voracious culture vultures. Thanks to a sunny outdoor lifestyle and the hero worship accorded sporting stars, the arts play second fiddle to sport. Nonetheless,

Brisbane has a lot to offer, a change largely brought about by Expo '88 coupled with clever programming on the part of former Queensland Performing Arts Complex director Tony Gould and long-serving Queensland Art Gallery supremo Doug Hall.

Gould successfully enticed people out of their homes and into QPAC's performing spaces for sell-out seasons of musicals, plays, ballets, operas and concerts. Hall, for his part, lent entrepreneurial zest to the QAG, attracting massive crowds to blockbuster exhibitions. In a sense, the gallery's 1982 opening symbolised a watershed for the arts. Until then, the state gallery had been without a permanent base since its beginnings in 1895. Today QAG not only has its own impressive headquarters but a sister gallery, the Queensland Gallery of Modern Art, exhibiting 20th- and 21st-century art. There are also many significant regional galleries around the state, notably Artspace Mackay, the Bundaberg Arts Centre, the regional galleries of Cairns, Caloundra, Gladstone and Rockhampton, and the Perc Tucker Regional Gallery and the Umbrella Studio of Contemporary Arts in Townsville.

Queensland painters

Of course, Queensland was never completely culturally arid. In the 1950s and 1960s Bris-

ings in the style of Gauguin. His works are in major collections, including the National Gallery of Australia and the Vatican Collection in Rome. Fellow Archibald Prize-winner (1986) Davida Allen, known for her images of female sexuality, lives and paints in Ipswich; while Aboriginal artist Rosella Namok, whose work has been curated into more than 30 national and international exhibitions, maintains her close association with the Lockhart River Gang, which generates some of the most exciting Aboriginal paintings in Australia.

Funding the arts

The arts are not starved for cash. In 2005–6 the government devoted A$300 million to expan-

bane nurtured an important school of painters, including such acclaimed artists as Lawrence Daws, Margaret Olley, Charles Blackman, Andrew Sibley and Jon Molvig. A number of these pioneers have died or moved on, but the brilliant Daws, one of the state's most revered and recognisable artists, continues to work in his Glasshouse Mountains studio. Cairns-based Ray Crooke, winner in 1969 of the Archibald Prize, Australia's oldest and most prestigious visual arts award, produces sought-after paint-

LEFT: concert at the Queensland Performing Arts Complex, Brisbane. **ABOVE:** The Go Betweens.

sion of the State Library and construction of the new Gallery of Modern Art. Another A$3 million went on the 280 events of the biennial Queensland Music Festival, held in more than 20 locations over a fortnight.

Opera Queensland's annual A$6 million spend is funded partly by government subsidy (to the tune of around 40 percent of the total), partly from box-office receipts.

Interestingly, the Queensland Ballet was not established with government patronage but by expatriate Frenchman Charles Lisner, who danced with Edouard Borovansky's ballet company and the Royal Ballet in London before arriving in Brisbane in 1953 to found the Queensland Ballet, remaining at its helm until 1974. The company's major performances are staged at QPAC's Playhouse, but the thrice-annual Vis-à-Vis performances at the company's heritage-listed headquarters (424 Montague Road, West End; tel: 3013 6666) are a must if you are keen on dance.

Regional arts

Inevitably, the primary cultural focus falls on Brisbane, but with more than 35 percent of the state's 3.5 million population living in regional, rural and remote centres, touring has become an essential aspect of taxpayer-funded

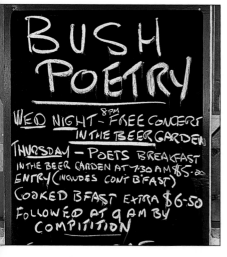

arts organisations. Part of the Queensland Ballet's annual allocation of around A$1.8 million is spent touring the company's 22 dancers around Queensland – Cairns, Townsville, Mackay and Maryborough. Every other year, the company tours smaller Outback centres – Chinchilla, Roma, Stanthorpe, Milmerran, Emerald and further afield.

As well as delivering four to six major productions and concerts in Brisbane annually, Opera Queensland takes productions to regional centres around the state in alternate years. In addition it pursues a state-wide programme of about 60 community concert tours extending deep into far north Queensland and

spilling south into northern New South Wales. Similarly, the Queensland Theatre Company's play-reading tours cover vast tracts of southeast Queensland, with performance artists travelling as far afield as Weipa and Cairns to mentor local productions.

At the same time, regional centres have established their own events. Townsville's annual Australian Festival of Chamber Music, for example, presents 10 days of concerts by distinguished soloists and chamber musicians from around the world.

Alternative venues

In Brisbane, it is entertaining to compare the delightfully old-fashioned Brisbane Arts Theatre (210 Petrie Terrace) with the stylishly grungy Brisbane Powerhouse (119 Lamington Street, New Farm) and the lively Judith Wright Centre of Contemporary Arts (420 Brunswick Street, Fortitude Valley). BAT, as the Arts Theatre is popularly known, has been churning out amateur drawing-room comedies, Agatha Christie-style mysteries, musical comedies and pantomimes in a crowd-pleasing manner since 1936. It's light years away from the Powerhouse, which operates within a formerly derelict building where graffiti and industrial machinery lend an edge to performance spaces mainly dedicated to the avant-garde. The Brisbane Pride Festival is orchestrated here each June, and a range of events from alternative drama to children's workshops take place throughout the year.

Literature

As for literature, the Brisbane Writers Festival (tel: 3255 0254), held annually in mid-September, features prominent writers in four days of panel sessions, performances, book launches, discussions and interviews. The festival brings renowned international authors to a city with a long literary pedigree of its own.

Within Toowong Cemetery, in Brisbane's inner west, a visitor may like to track down the red-granite headstone that marks the final resting place of Arthur Hoey Davis, aka Steele Rudd, creator of the immortal rural characters Dad and Dave (look for his grave in portion 29a, off Fourth Avenue). Davis died on 11 October 1935. His best-known book, *On Our Selection*, sold more than 250,000 copies, and all 21 of his titles were reprinted a total of 239 times. In his time he matched the popularity of Henry Lawson (1867–1922), who wrote about life in the Australian bush, and Andrew Barton (Banjo) Paterson (1864–1941), known as "the man from Snowy River", after his poem of the same name. Paterson also wrote the song that is regarded as Australia's unofficial national anthem: *Waltzing Matilda*.

If anything, the absence of cultural celebration in early Brisbane appears to have inspired its writers to fresh heights. Certainly it stimulated David Malouf's famous quotation about the city where he was born in 1934 in his acclaimed novel *Johnno*: "Brisbane is so sleepy, so slatternly, so sprawlingly unlovely! I have taken to wandering about after school looking for one simple object in it that might be romantic, or appalling even, but there is nothing. It is simply the most ordinary place in the world." Such is the confidence of modern Brisbane that these words have been enshrined on a pavement plaque in the inner city, as if to demonstrate how much things have changed since the 1940s.

To pursue Brisbane's literary legacy further, it is worth obtaining a copy of a new book, *Words to Walk By: Exploring Literary Brisbane* by Todd Barr and Rodney Sullivan. It includes a literary map of the landmarks that provided backdrops for stories by local authors such as Hugh Lunn, Matt Condon, John Birmingham, Nancy Cato, Nick Earls, Bruce Dawe and Andrew McGahan. Lunn, a long-time correspondent on *The Australian* newspaper is Brisbane's best-known author, most famous for his tales of growing up in Queensland.

Outside the principal conurbations literature can take on quite a different hue. An evening of bush poetry in an Outback pub may not satisfy literary purists but it can tell you as much about life as it's lived in Queensland as any of the garlanded writers competing for space in the bookshops.

Eclectic musical offerings

Musically, Brisbane is something of a smorgasbord. The Queensland Orchestra delivers a programme of more than 70 concerts annually,

from classics, new commissions and baroque recitals through to cinema favourites. It also accompanies artists as diverse as violinist Nigel Kennedy, Harry Connick Jr, k. d.lang and Dionne Warwick.

Public radio station 4MBS conducts a Festival of Classics annually in May, when hundreds of local classical musicians perform around Brisbane. Contemporary music also has its place, with at least three ensembles pursuing paths less followed. Brisbane quintet Topology performs in theatres, art galleries, clubs and occasionally with pop groups.

Elision, another respected new-music ensemble, explores contemporary opera, site-

specific installations, improvisation and electronic music, while the emerging Brisbane string quartet, Zhivago, fuses gypsy and jazz elements with world music.

Brisbane also has a thriving jazz scene, partly centred around the Brisbane Jazz Club at Kangaroo Point, partly in Fortitude Valley bars such as Ric's, The Press Club and The Bowery *(see page 81)*.

To find out about all kinds of cultural and entertainment events when you visit the city, check the useful Brisbane listings website: www.brisbane247.com. For more information on galleries, theatres, performance venues and events in Queensland, *see pages 263–5.* ❏

LEFT: culture in the Outback. **RIGHT:** Cairns art gallery has an emphasis on indigenous art.

THE GREAT BARRIER REEF

The Great Barrier Reef, a protected World Heritage Area,
is one of the most beautiful and diverse natural sites
in the world, but many aspects of contemporary
life are threatening its existence

The Great Barrier Reef, one of the Seven Natural Wonders of the World, is an aquatic wilderness bigger than the UK, Holland and Switzerland put together. The reef extends over 250,000 sq. km (96,500 sq. miles) and comprises some 3,000 individual coral reefs and 940 islands running along the Queensland coast from north of Cape York Peninsula to just north of Fraser Island.

Declared a World Heritage Area in 1981, it is an extraordinarily complex ecosystem, a dazzlingly beautiful universe of low-wooded islands, mangrove estuaries, seagrass beds, algae and sponge gardens, sandy and coral cays, mud floors and deep ocean troughs.

The largest structure built by living organisms on earth, the reef contains one-third of the known species of soft corals and more than 360 hard corals. It is also the home of 1,500 species of brilliantly coloured and patterned fish (of which the most prized are the long-lived coral trout, red emperor and red-throat emperor), dugongs, marine turtles, dolphins, whales, seasnakes, seals, crocodiles, seahorses, seadragons, pipefish, birds, sharks, rays and skates (see pages 56–7).

Thirty years ago, the Great Barrier Reef Marine Park Authority was set up to protect this unique wonderland of colour and lifeforms. And in July 2004 the Australian government increased the area protected from fishing from 4.6 percent to 33.3 percent of the 344,000-sq. km (133,000-sq. mile) park, mak-

ing it the largest protected marine area in the world. Arguably, the reef has generated more superlatives than anything else in the world, as well.

Crucially, the Great Barrier Reef brings A$5.1 billion into the Australian economy from more than two million tourists who visit each year, and more than 60,000 people earn a living from it.

Threats to the reef

Of the many threats to the reef, the worst is coral bleaching. Some marine scientists are now warning that the Great Barrier Reef could be nothing more than a vast skeleton by 2030

LEFT: aerial view of waves breaking on the reef.
RIGHT: school of yellowfin goatfish.

if global warming caused by greenhouse gases (most significantly carbon dioxide, produced by deforestation and through burning fossil fuels) continues.

If the clear, tropical waters remain too warm for too long, corals expel their photo-synthesising zooxanthellae and become colourless. Bleached corals are not necessarily dead and can regain their original algae if not too stressed, but if the water does not cool within about a month the coral will die.

Maximum summer sea temperatures only 2–3 degrees centigrade above normal can kill corals. The summer of 1997–8 was the hottest recorded on the reef since records began in the

late 19th century. Then, in the summer of 2002, the worst bleaching ever recorded occurred, with 60–95 percent of the marine park affected.

Up to 5 percent of the Great Barrier Reef has been severely damaged during each of the last two major bleaching events, and this process has revealed that many of the corals are now living at the top of their temperature tolerance. Increased temperatures from global warming are also thought to cause more violent tropical storms, but fortunately the reefs are resilient and do recover from storm damage. Cyclones – there have been 130 in Queensland waters over the past 30 years – are

one of the most powerful natural impacts on the reef, albeit indirectly. Flooding onshore results in millions of litres of earth-laden fresh water flowing into the sea, and this has a detrimental effect on the balance of the reef.

Corals are damaged by anchors, the dredging of harbours and channels for boats and marinas, sewage from resorts, divers and snorkellers, commercial reef lines, recreational and charter-boat fishing and aquarium fish collecting (the coral trout is the most sought after by fishermen and collectors). Line fishing, which puts the most pressure on reef fish, is at least being controlled by licensing, gear restrictions, size and bag limits and seasonal closures.

The dugong and all six of the reef's marine turtle species are threatened, with the loggerhead most in danger because of the loss and degradation of their habitat, and commercial and traditional fishing nets, shark nets and illegal nets as well as foxes taking their eggs on land. The loggerhead turtle population has dropped by up to 90 percent since the 1960s. Turtles are long-living and slow-growing, and it can take decades to perceive changes in their population. The correlative is that it can take decades to recover from any downturn.

One creature that is thriving is the Crown of Thorns starfish, a natural predator of coral and thought to be indestructible. However, even this creature's cycles are being affected by the decline in water quality caused by excess nutrients from farm run-off.

The reef's human history

The course of Australian history might have been very different had Captain James Cook been less fortunate when his ship *The Endeavour* ran aground on the reef in June 1770. By jettisoning a load of heavy cargo his crew managed to repair the ship and return to sea. Not all seafarers were so lucky; 30 shipwrecks lie in the reef's waters.

Many ruins and lighthouses on the cays and islands, as well as relics from World War II, tell of the European presence. But the shell middens, rock paintings, artefacts and story sites suggest that it has been of great importance to Aboriginal tribes all along the coast.

When the Europeans settled, they cleared forests, mined, engaged in agriculture and established towns. It is unfortunate that, unlike most other reefs, the Great Barrier Reef runs along a string of major centres – Cairns, Townsville, Mackay, Rockhampton and Gladstone. Coastal wetland forest is still being cut down to make room for the beef cattle, sugar cane, cotton industries and banana plantations close to the coast, which result in large quantities of fertilisers running into the sea.

Sediment levels are now four times what they were before European settlement. Hundreds of reefs are at risk from the sediment and chemical run-off from farming, and from the loss of the coastal wetlands that have acted as a natural filter in the past.

gas emissions by 85 million tons, although, given that it has not signed up to the Kyoto Protocol, there are some who question how serious it is about this commitment.

What is more, the Great Barrier Reef Marine Park Authority has established a A$2-million programme to boost the resilience of the reef while also sustaining the industries and communities that depend on it. Using a combination of satellite imagery and aerial and underwater surveys, the country's best marine scientists can quickly determine the extent of coral bleaching and analyse the effects on the reef. It is to be hoped that these measures are not too little, too late. ❏

About a fifth of Queensland's population lives along the coast adjacent to the reef, and with the current interstate and overseas migration to the state (about 215 people per day), communities continue to grow. How to manage water quality, tourism and commercial and recreational fishing is a major concern.

Limiting the damage

In response to the enormous threat of climate change, the Australian government has said it is committed to reducing annual greenhouse

LEFT: Crown of Thorns starfish, predator of coral.
ABOVE: diver watching a graceful bullray.

HOW TO SEE IT

There are numerous ways to investigate the reef. Cairns and Port Douglas are the main starting points, and you will be spoilt for choice; it really depends how active you want to be. The biggest operator is Quicksilver, which has a fleet of custom-built catamarans that transport vast numbers to the outer reef for snorkelling. Numerous dive operators cater for everyone from the novice upwards, while the moneyed can take a scenic flight and get some grasp of the sheer scale of the thing. In Townsville and other centres further south, reef exploring is less commercialised and sophisticated, and none the worse for that (for more information, see page 270).

Reef Life

The largest, most accessible reef on earth is one of the natural wonders of the world

When the reef was put forward for World Heritage listing, the nomination said: "Biologically, the Great Barrier Reef supports the most diverse ecosystem known to man. Its enormous diversity is thought to reflect the maturity of an ecosystem which has evolved over millions of years..."

At the heart of that ecosystem is the humble polyp, a tiny animal consisting of not much more than a mouth and surrounding tentacles to feed it – plus, of course, a limestone skeleton into which it withdraws during the day. It is the remains of these skeletons that form the basis of the reef. Individual polyps are linked by body tissue (to share the colony's food), but the main source of a photosynthetic coral's food is algae cells within its tissue called zooxanthellae, which convert the sun's energy into nutrients for the coral. This massive accumulation of plant and animal life can truly be said to be the largest living thing in the world.

Other Inhabitants

The reef is home to a fantastic variety of marine life, including more than 1,500 species of fish, from the relatively plain to the ornately bizarre. They include sharks (such as the white-tipped reef shark), the huge but strictly vegetarian manta ray, and some of the largest black marlin in the world. There are thousands of different crustacea (crabs, lobsters and shrimps), starfish with feathery arms or brittle, spiny fingers, sea urchins and sea slugs, and a seemingly infinite variety of shellfish. Dugongs feed here, and it is a breeding area for the humpback whale and green and loggerhead turtles.

Above: grey reef shark. **Below Left:** clown fish live symbiotically with sea anemones. The anemone is not a plant but an animal, closely related to coral. **Below Right:** a soft coral (Dendronephyta), but it is the hard coral, of which Acropora or staghorn corals are the most common, that form the foundations of the reef. They appear in many forms and colours, including a beautiful lilac version *(pictured above left)*.

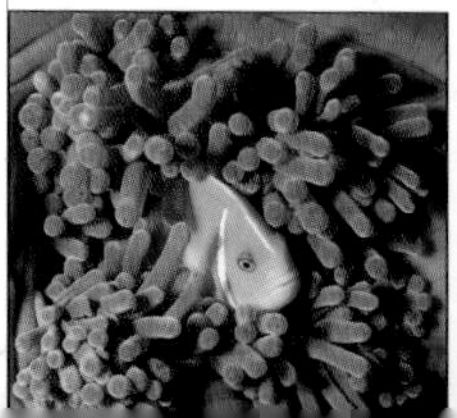

THE ISLANDS

The 20 or so resort islands inside the Great Barrier Reef Marine Park offer many attractions: lodging varies from five-star resorts to backpacker hostels and campgrounds; some are dry, barren and windy; others are lush and covered with rainforest. The islands can be reached by fast catamaran, sea-plane, light plane or helicopter. The best time of year to visit the reef is May–October. The major islands for visitors from north to south are:

The Southern End: Lady Elliot Island *(see page 136; pictured above)*; Lady Musgrave Island *(see page 136)*; Heron Island *(see page 139)*; Great Keppel Island *(see page 141)*; Brampton Island *(see page 153)*; the Whitsunday group *(see pages 152–7)*

The Centre to the North: Magnetic Island *(see page 163)*; Orpheus Island *(see page 167)*; Hinchinbrook Island *(see page 169)*; Dunk Island *(see page 171)*; Green Island *(see page 187)*; Lizard Island *(see page 200)*

ABOVE: the Great Barrier Reef is not just the largest mass of living organisms on earth, but is also an incredibly complex and diverse ecosystem, home to 1,500 species of brilliantly coloured and patterned fish.

BELOW: The sea fan belongs to a group known as Gorgonians (other members include sea whips and sea feathers). They all have a flexible spine of horn-like material.

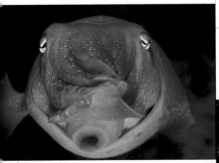

ABOVE: face to face with a broadclub cuttlefish (Sepia latimanus), one of many cephalopod species found on the reef.

PLACES

Queensland is a state on the move. As more and more visitors discover its appeal, it is revealing new facets which refute its old image as a destination for unsophisticated hedonism

So much has changed in Brisbane since the 1950s, when author David Malouf could describe his city as "so sleepy, so slatternly, so sprawlingly unlovely". Today the Queensland capital exudes a sparkle that other cities would envy. A mini-Manhattan sprouts from its centre, well-tended parklands border its river banks, and its million-strong population has embraced café society.

Then there's the sea. Few destinations boast such diversity of surf beaches, coral cays and islands. Surfers Paradise, south of Brisbane, is as famous for its glitter as for its surf beaches. Noosa, to the north, offers gastronomy and fashion. Of course, a good proportion of the A$8 billion generated by tourism each year stems from the Great Barrier Reef. Many resorts cling to the peripheries of this living miracle, and three of them – Green Island off Cairns, Heron Island off Gladstone and Lady Elliot Island off Bundaberg – stand on the reef itself.

There's glorious rainforest to be found in the Far North, and, if you keep on going, the isolated communities at the top of Cape York and on the Torres Strait Islands will provide succour after the often tortuous journey there. The Outback rewards travellers willing to get off the beaten track, and sights that would attract thousands anywhere else, like the Aboriginal cave paintings in Laura, the breathtaking Lawn Hill Gorge, the site of the dinosaur stampede at Lark Hill Quarry – all of these can be enjoyed in peace, often with a bare handful of other explorers.

There are other worlds, too. Mount Isa and Cloncurry are burly mining towns, but enter one of the numerous bars and you'll soon be assimilated. Or drunk. Probably both. Sing in the bar at the North Gregory Hotel where Banjo Paterson first banged out *Waltzing Matilda* on the pub piano in 1895. Take in the Stockman's Hall of Fame in Longreach. Seek out the Dig Tree in the desert on the border with South Australia and contemplate the story of Burke and Wills and the opening up of this unforgiving country.

Choose a corner or two, make the most of them, and start planning the next trip. ❏

PRECEDING PAGES: Brisbane's Central Business District lines the banks of the Brisbane River; pristine surfing conditions at Snapper Rock, Gold Coast. **LEFT:** Queensland's beaches are a child's dream.

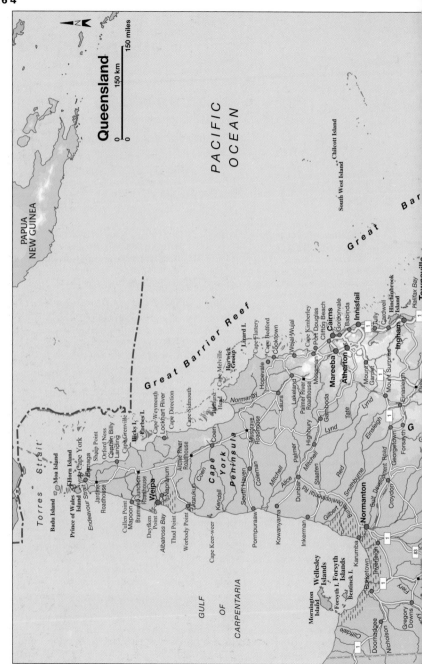

Queensland

150 km

150 miles

PAPUA NEW GUINEA

PACIFIC OCEAN

Torres Strait

Badu Island

Moa Island

Prince of Wales Island

Horn Island

Cape York

Endeavour Strait

Bamaga

Sharp Point

Orford Ness

Caathin Billy Landing

Jardine Roadhouse

Cullen Point

Mapoon

Bramwell Junction Roadhouse

Duyfken Point

Albatross Bay

Weipa

Napranum

Thud Point

Wordboy Point

Aurukun

Cape Keer-weer

Pormpuraaw

Kowanyama

Inkerman

GULF OF CARPENTARIA

Wellesley Islands

Mornington Island

Forsyth I. Forsyth Islands

Bentinck I.

Cliffdale

Doomadgee

Nicholson

Gregory Downs

Hicks I.

Forbes I.

Cape Grenville

Cape Weymouth

Lockhart River

Cape Direction

Cape Sidmouth

Archer River Roadhouse

Coen

Cape York Peninsula

Kendall

South Haven

Coleman

Mitchell

Alice

Palmer

Dunbar

Staaten

Mitchell

Red

Gilbert

Smithburne

Karumba

Normanton

Burketown

Inverleigh

Croydon

Burke Development Road

Georgetown

Forsayth

Gulf Development Road

Great Barrier Reef

Lizard I.

Cape Flattery

Hurlwick Group

Cape Melville

Hopevale

Cooktown

Cape Bedford

Cape Kimberley

Port Douglas

Clifton Beach

Cairns

Mossman

Gordonvale

Babinda

Innisfail

Mareeba

Atherton

Mount Garnet

Mount Surprise

Einasleigh

Ingham

Cardwell

Tully

Hinchinbrook Island

Halifax Bay

Townsville

Wujal Wujal

Mulfurst

Normanby

Laura

Lakeland

Palmer River Roadhouse

Gamboda

Lynd

Tate

Lynd

Highbury

Musgrave Roadhouse

G

South West Island

Chilcott Island

Great Bar

83

1

1

1

1

1

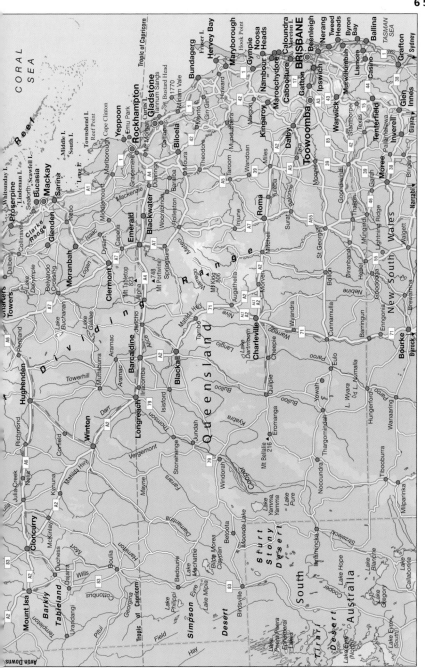

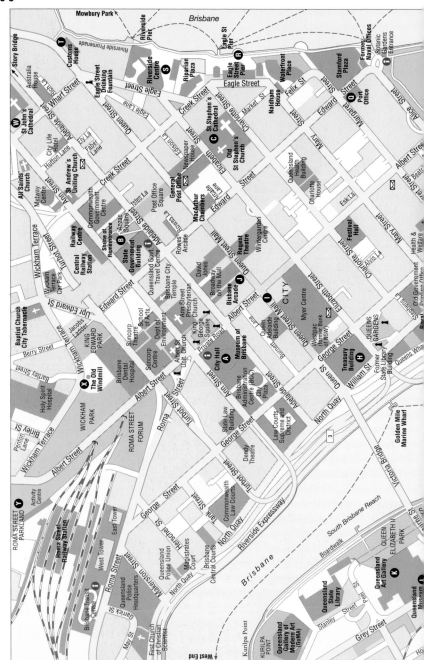

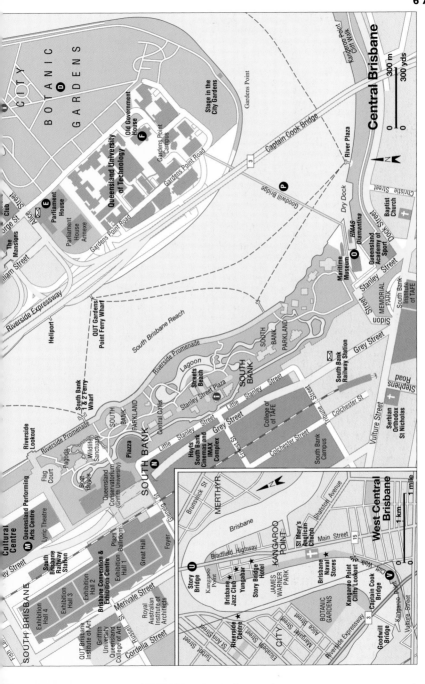

Central Brisbane

N

300 m
300 yds

BOTANIC GARDENS
CITY
D
Botanic Gardens
Old Government House F
Parliament House E
Queensland University of Technology
Gardens Point Campus
Stage in the City Gardens
Gardens Point
Parliament House Annexe
Alice Street
George St
The Mansions
Club
William Street
Gardens Point Road
Riverside Expressway
Heliport
QUT Gardens Point Ferry Wharf
South Brisbane Reach
Captain Cook Bridge
Gardens Point Road
3
Goodwill Bridge
P
River Plaza
Dry Dock
HMAS Diamantina
Queensland Academy of Sport
Maritime Museum
O
Kangaroo Point Cliff Walk
Christie Street
Dock Street
Stanley Street
Baptist Church
MEMORIAL PARK
Sidon
Stanley Street
South Bank Institute of TAFE
South Bank 1 & 2 Ferry Wharf
Riverside Promenade
SOUTH BANK PARKLAND
Riverside Lookout
Lagoon
Streets Beach
Stanley Street Plaza
Central Cafés
Pagoda
Wildlife Sanctuary
Boat House
SOUTH BANK PARKLAND
SOUTH BANK
SOUTH BANK
Little Stanley Street
Grey Street
Stephens Road
South Bank Railway Station
College of TAFE
Vulture Street
Serbian Orthodox St Nicholas
Grey Street
Colchester St
Piazza
N
Hoyts South Bank Cinemas and IMAX Complex
Little Stanley Street
Ernest St
Grey Street
Tribune Street
Colchester Street
South Bank Campus

West Central Brisbane

N

1 km
1 mile

Story Bridge U
Kangaroo Point
Brisbane Jazz Club
Yungaba
Story Bridge Hotel
Bruntswick St
MERTHYR
Brisbane
Main Street
St Mary's Anglican Church
Shafston Avenue
Bradfield Highway
KANGAROO POINT
JAMES WARNER PARK
Brisbane Naval Stores
Kangaroo Point Cliffs Lookout V
Captain Cook Bridge
Goodwill Bridge
BOTANIC GARDENS
CITY
Riverside Centre
Elizabeth Street
Margaret Street
Alice Street
Ann Street
Riverside Expressway
Cliff Walk
Kangaroo Point
Vulture Street
15
3
Turbot Street

Cultural Centre
M Queensland Performing Arts Centre
Lyric Theatre
South Brisbane Railway Station
Exhibition Hall 2
Brisbane Convention & Exhibition Centre
Exhibition Hall 3
Exhibition Hall 4
Great Hall
Plaza Ballroom
Foyer
Exhibition Ballroom
QUT Brisbane Institute of Art
Griffith University Queensland College of Art
Royal Australian Institute of Architects
SOUTH BRISBANE
Fish St
ey Street
Merivale Street
Russell St
Grey Street
Cordelia Street
Queensland Conservatorium (Griffith University)
SOUTH BANK

BRISBANE

Brisbane has shaken off its image as a sleepy backwater and emerged as a cosmopolitan city, with a thriving arts scene, vibrant nightlife and world-class cuisine. But Australia's third-largest city still retains something of a country heart

Brisbane

Map on pages 66–7

The southern approach to Brisbane presents a striking picture: rounding a bend on the Pacific Motorway you see weatherboard stilt houses on leafy hills, with the thrusting towers of the Central Business District (CBD) beyond. Crossing Captain Cook Bridge, you catch glimpses of the serpentine Brisbane River, bordered by skyscrapers on one side and lush parkland on the other. It's hard to believe that, only a few decades ago, this impressive waterway was polluted and neglected. Today's sparkling river is at the hub of city life and is the pride of its inhabitants. It serves as an aquatic highway for ferries connecting riverside suburbs and is the focal point for festivals and celebrations. The motorway follows the river's edge, swooping above the bank and through luxuriant mangroves – an unexpected sight deep in the heart of Australia's third-largest city.

Nearly half of Queensland's population of four million lives within Brisbane's statistical boundaries – a sprawling 4,673 sq. km (1,800 sq. miles) – one of the reasons why the city's reputation as the "world's biggest country town" lingered for so long. The catalysts for change were the 1982 Commonwealth Games and the Expo '88 which put Brisbane on the cultural map. Inevitably, some-thing of the city's laid-back character has been lost in transition from sleepy backwater to cosmopolitan hub. The new Queenslander may wear board shorts but, in business, he or she is as hard-nosed as anyone from Sydney or Melbourne. More than likely, the new Queenslander *is* from Sydney or Melbourne. Yet there remains some truth to the old saying: "In Melbourne they ask what school you went to, in Sydney, they ask how much you earn, in Brisbane they ask if you'd like a beer."

LEFT: McWhirter's old department store (1912), a historic landmark. **BELOW:** the riverside skyscrapers of Brisbane's CBD.

Inside City Hall is a museum "for and about the people of Brisbane". Free concerts are also held here throughout the year.

BELOW: soldiers preparing for an Anzac Day ceremony in Anzac Square.

Rough edges remain, but there's a new sophistication, as evidenced by a healthy restaurant culture and the number of people able to spout knowledgeably about wine. Add Brisbane's hip young generation to the mix and you have a sassy, confident city. Young people no longer feel the imperative to leave. This, plus a surge of interstate migration, has caused Brisbane's population growth to outpace that of every other Australian capital. The climate – subtropical summers and mild, sunny winters – has undoubtedly played a part but the reasons for Brisbane's rise are many and complex.

Brisbane's recognition of the value of its architectural heritage came too late to save many iconic buildings destroyed during the development frenzy of the 1980s. Still, enough historic architecture remains to show what used to be. Many of the city's distinguished colonial-style residences were wrenched from their stumps in leafy Ascot or Hamilton and relocated, iron-lace and all, to exclusive outer suburbs like Brookfield and Pullenvale.

Brisbane City Hall

A suitable place to begin exploring the city is **Brisbane City Hall** Ⓐ (Mon–Fri 8am–5pm, Sat–Sun 10am–5pm; guided tours Mon–Fri; tel: 3403 8888) on King George Square. Designed on grand neo-classical lines, with massive sandstone columns, City Hall held the record as Brisbane's tallest building until the early 1960s – and even now provides excellent views from the soaring 92-metre (300-ft) clock tower. Installed in 1929, it features a cast-iron tower bell weighing 4.32 tons and four smaller bells of more than 3 tons apiece. Initially, these massive bells chimed 24 hours a day and were audible in faraway Wynnum, leaving the citizenry bleary-eyed. Nowadays the bells peal in daylight hours only.

The **Museum of Brisbane** (daily 10am–5pm) on the ground floor is dedicated to the city's social and cultural history, as well as contemporary visual art, crafts and design.

City Hall flanks **King George Square**, a public space notable for its eclectic collection of statuary. Works include a 1938 statue of King George V on horseback and a 1988 tableau depicting members of early Brisbane pioneers, the Petrie family.

Anzac Square

From King George Square, proceed along Ann Street (away from North Quay) to **Anzac Square** Ⓑ and the **Shrine of Remembrance** – taking time to marvel at one of Australia's more intriguing examples of far-sighted urban design. Position yourself at the shrine's upper level, looking across Anzac Square and neighbouring Post Office Square to the clock tower of the **General Post Office** (261 Queen Street) two blocks away, erected between 1871 and 1879. Now take a 180-degree turn and you'll see the **Central Railway Station** clock tower, opened in 1901. Both towers stand in perfect alignment with the sacred flame and war memorial in the square directly below.

Descend the curved steps beside the shrine, past commemorative bottle trees and symbolic date palms to **Post Office Square**. Legend has it that a secret tunnel once connected the post office with the former AMP (Australian Mutual Provident Society) building at the corner of Edward Street and Queen Street, now known as MacArthur Chambers (and converted into an upmarket apartment hotel). US Army General Douglas MacArthur commanded the Allied forces in the southwest Pacific from this building during World War II *(see page 25)*. The **MacArthur Museum Brisbane** (Tues–Thur and Sun 10am–3pm ; entry by gold coin donation), containing MacArthur memorabilia, has been established on the eighth floor of his former HQ.

Having given the GPO's colonnades and Corinthian columns the once-over, follow the narrow lane flanking the building to Elizabeth Street and **St Stephen's Cathedral** ⓒ (tours Mon–Fri 10.30am, Sun after mass; tel: 3336 9111). Within this precinct you will find the gracefully weathered Pugin's Chapel, also known as old **St Stephen's Church**, completed in 1850 to a design by celebrated neo-Gothic architect Auguste Welby Pugin. Beside it, the more imposing cathedral replaced the church as Brisbane's seat of Catholicism in 1874.

City Botanic Gardens

Wander through the church precinct, passing by the large bell into Charlotte Street. Turn right into Charlotte Street, then left at the next junction, following Edward Street to the **City Botanic Gardens** ⓓ (entrance in Alice Street). Covering 20 hectares (50 acres) laced with footpaths and trails, these remarkable gardens offer a peaceful oasis amid inner city bustle. Established in 1828 to provide vegetables for the penal settlement, the gardens boast a 150-year-old row of weeping willows planted by the first gardens director, Walter Hill. There are open spaces, fragrant

Map on pages 66–7

TIP

The Brisbane Council Translink Loop operates a free bus service that circles Brisbane's CBD every 10 minutes (weekdays approx 7am–6pm). Stops include Central Station, Queen Street Mall, City Botanic Gardens, Riverside Centre, QUT and King George Square. Visit www.translink. com.au (tel:13 12 30).

BELOW: St Stephen's Cathedral.

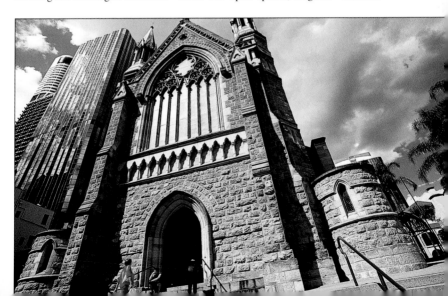

corners, an ornamental lake bordered by palms and bamboo and a **mangrove boardwalk** skirting the river.

Parliament House precinct

Overlooking the gardens is one of Queensland's best-loved landmarks, **Parliament House**  (corner of George and Alice Streets; guided tours on request; Mon–Fri 9am–4pm, Sat–Sun 10am–2pm; www.parliament.qld.gov.au). The grand French Renaissance-style building, designed by Charles Tiffin, eloquently expresses Queensland's satisfaction at having achieved separation from New South Wales in 1859. Near by, **Old Government House** , another grand Tiffin design, was built in 1862 when Queensland's population stood at a mere 6,000. The porphyry and sandstone structure remained the governor's official residence until 1910, when it became the first University of Queensland. The building is now administered by the Queensland University of Technology.

Opened in 1884, the **Queensland Club** (intersection of Alice and George Streets) exudes an air of superiority. The Italianate three-storey building, with its spacious verandas and cast-iron balustrading, was designed by Francis Stanley as a bastion of gentility – and so it remains today.

Further along George Street **The Mansions** is an ornate row of terrace houses built in 1889 as residences for the gentry. Here you'll find Augustine's restaurant *(see page 84)*, a favourite haunt among high-ranking politicians.

Near the river, another historic landmark is the **Commissariat Store**  (William Street; Tues–Fri 10am–4pm, Sun irregular hours, phone ahead; tel: 3221 4198). It was built in 1829, one year before Moreton Bay's tyrannical commandant Captain Patrick Logan was struck down and killed on a mapping expedition in Brisbane River headwaters *(see page 19)*. Built as a government store, the Commissariat also houses a museum documenting the early history of Brisbane.

The authentic array of convict memorabilia includes shackles, lashes and a macabre glass tube

Visitors will need to find a member to vouch for them if they are to get beyond the front door of the illustrious Queensland Club.

BELOW: the Mansions.

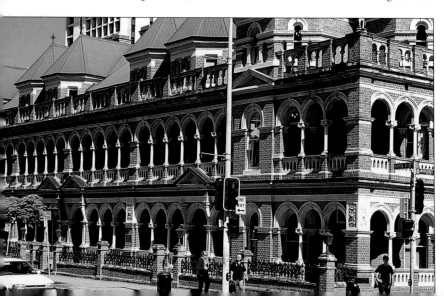

containing convicts' fingertips, sliced off by their owners to avoid work.

The casino

On the corner of Elizabeth Street and William Street stands the former **Treasury Building** , converted to a casino in 1995. The main entrance is in Queen Street Mall, but no one will mind if you slip in by the rear door to try your luck at the 80 gaming tables and 1,300 slot machines that occupy this formerly dignified space. The casino is open 24 hours a day with a selection of bars, restaurants and even hotel rooms for those who can't tear themselves away. There's a nearby pawnshop where high rollers hock cars and watches for another round with Lady Luck. Despite sincere attempts to preserve the building's heritage values, strident casino culture overwhelms the building's sombre architecture. For the record, work on the Treasury began in 1886 and was completed in 1928, when it was deemed one of the state's most notable buildings.

Queen Street Mall

The retail heart of Brisbane is the **Queen Street Mall** , a pedestrian area with more than 600 shops, 45 cafés and restaurants, two cinema complexes and 11 shopping zones. At first glance the bustling mall appears completely modern from street level – but look above the awnings and you'll see old-fashioned shop façades which have been faithfully preserved. Embedded in walls decorated with neo-classical columns, archways and keystones, you can still make out the names of hotels and stores that once thrived here. The precinct throbs with off-beat vitality. Professional acts perform in the rotunda, but the spirit of the mall is best expressed by its buskers and street performers: a soupy sax wobbling through *Waltz-ing Matilda*, trained poodles playing dead for loose change, or maybe a clown coaxing animal shapes from balloons for the amusement of small children. Pause for a coffee or lunch in one of the sidewalk cafés, and take it all in.

Pop in at the **Regent Theatre** (167 Queen Street) to admire the grand marble staircase, ornate ceilings and gilded walls in the lobby – virtually unchanged since 1929. The intermission organist, who magically appeared at the console of a Wurlitzer, disappeared for ever during the 1970s refurbishment that carved the large cinema up into small four ones.

Another slice of history remains in the refined Edwardian-style **Brisbane Arcade** , built in 1924, and now the city's oldest surviving shopping arcade. This charming row of shops, on two levels, connects Queen Street Mall with Adelaide Street. Upmarket boutiques occupy the lower level. The mezzanine floor has been colonised by milliners and fashion designers.

Similarly intact is the classical revival architecture of the former

Map on pages 66–7

TIP

While on the mall, why not indulge in a free facial at Mecca Cosmetica, Queens Plaza (tel: 1800 007 844) or browse through vintage apparel at the General Pants Co. (116–118 Queen Street Mall, tel: 3210 6638; www.generalpants.com.au).

BELOW: Brisbane Arcade.

Bank of NSW (now Westpac) at the corner of Queen and George Streets.

Queensland Cultural Centre

Having browsed the mall, cross **Victoria Bridge** to **South Bank**, where the **Queensland Cultural Centre** rises impressively. On one side of the street is the Queensland Performing Arts Complex, on the other the Queensland Art Gallery and the Queensland Museum South Bank (joined by a walkway). The opening of the Cultural Centre coincided with the opening of Expo '88 – an event that stimulated a burst of community confidence.

The **Queensland Art Gallery** (Mon–Fri 10am–5pm, Sat–Sun 9am–5pm; tel: 3840 7303; www.qag.qld.gov.au) is one of the most prestigious art galleries in the country. In addition to its extensive permanent collection of Australian, Aboriginal, European and Asian works, the gallery has a reputation for putting on outstanding international exhibitions. A second major gallery, the **Queensland Gallery of Modern Art** at nearby Kurilpa Point, is near completion. When it opens at the end of 2006, GoMA, as it is known, will be the biggest gallery of modern art in Australia.

The **Queensland Museum South Bank** (daily 9.30am–5pm; tel: 3840 7555; www.southbank.qm.qld.gov.au) tells the region's history through a fascinating display of exhibits from a Muttaburrasaurus, the most complete dinosaur skeleton found in Australia, to the tiny aeroplane Bert Hinkler flew from England to Australia in 1928. Kids love the **Sciencentre**'s hands-on interactive displays and the life-size models of humpback whales in the Whale Mall. Under the same roof, the **Dandiiri Maiwar** centre provides an insight into the Aboriginal and Torres Strait Islander cultures.

Also part of the complex, the **John Oxley Library** (Sun–Fri 10am–5pm; tel: 3840 7880) holds important archives relating to the history of Queensland.

The **Queensland Performing Arts Centre** (www.qpac.com.au) across the elevated walkway is a superb facility; it hosts a wide range

The present Victoria Bridge, unveiled in 1969, is the third bridge to be built on this site. As a consequence of floods and problematic foundations, early attempts at bridging the Brisbane River were short-lived. A leftover pylon from bridge number two, built in 1897, carries a poignant memorial to a Greek boy killed during the World War I victory celebrations.

BELOW: sculpture in front of Queensland Art Gallery.

Birth of South Bank

South Bank's present incarnation dates from the late 1980s when, except for a handful of historic buildings, the site was flattened for Expo. The Plough Inn and the nearby Caledonian Building, both built in 1885, survive from an era when Brisbane was ruled by rival councils, one for each side of the river. South Brisbane stood poised to overtake the north bank as the city's commercial hub until 1893, when the south side was totally inundated. After that, no one wanted to live there, and the area fell into dereliction until revived for Expo '88. Several former Expo pavilions have been converted into riverfront restaurants.

of world-class theatrical productions in four theatres, and includes restaurants, bars and a gift shop.

South Bank Parklands

The parklands take over where the Cultural Centre ends. Sprawling across the revamped Expo '88 site, **South Bank** has become an inner-city playground of parks, tropical gardens, lagoons, restaurants and boutiques. It's full of character and atmosphere, and you could easily spend a whole day or more here without finding yourself in the same place twice.

In recent years there has been a concerted push to lend this populist precinct a more sophisticated edge. Grey Street has been transformed into a leafy boulevard of smart apartments and exclusive shops.

The precinct's most popular attraction is **Streets Beach**, a large swimming lagoon where the essential elements of beach culture have been replicated: white sand, lapping water, lifeguards, tanned and toned bikini wearers and small children with buckets and spades.

Queensland Maritime Museum

Meandering south along the promenade that skirts the river you come to the **Maritime Museum** (daily 9.30am–4.30pm; admission charge; tel: 3844 5361; www.maritimemuseum.com.au) in Sidon Street. The museum focuses on Queensland's close links with the seaways and its dependence on them, then and now. Ever since Dutch explorer Willem Janssen and the crew of the *Duyfken* landed on Cape York Peninsula in 1606, the sea has shaped Queenslanders' lives and commerce. The museum features a wealth of artefacts reflecting the state's maritime history. These include a Royal Australian Navy frigate snug within a 19th-century dry dock, a Torres Strait pearling lugger and the 1925 steam tug, *Forceful*, which takes visitors for occasional day trips to Moreton Bay.

Near the Queensland Maritime Museum is the **Goodwill Pedestrian Bridge** , connecting South Bank with the CBD. Controversy surrounded the bridge's construc-

Map on pages 66–7

TIP

South Bank is the place to head on a sunny day for an outdoor meal. Brisbane, once a culinary desert, now enjoys a reputation for chefs who take advantage of their state's natural resources: giant mud crabs, ripe avocados, macadamia nuts, mangoes, barramundi, coral trout, oysters, as well as exotic tropical delights.

BELOW: the artificial Streets Beach in South Bank Parklands.

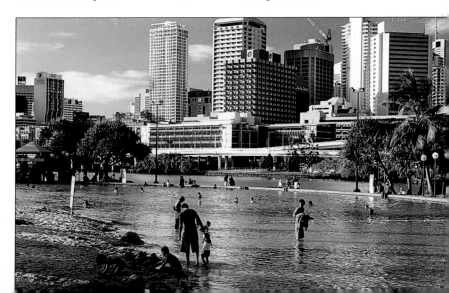

Queensland Maritime Museum has a fascinating collection of vessels to investigate, including a Torres Strait pearling lugger and the Royal Australian Navy frigate, Dia-mantina. *The 1925 steam tug,* Forceful, *makes regular trips down the Brisbane River to Moreton Bay (tel: 3844 5361).*

tion, but, to judge from the continuous stream of cyclists, roller bladers and commuters hurtling or hurrying by, fears that this bridge might become a white elephant have been without basis. Having arrived on the CBD side, retrace your steps past Parliament House and into Alice Street, where huge figs grow beside, and in some places engulf, the iron fence of the City Botanic Gardens.

Old maritime precinct

Within the CBD area roughly bounded by Edward, Eagle, Felix and Charlotte Streets, the historic architecture of Brisbane's dockland stands remarkably intact. The **Former Naval Offices** and the next-door **Port Office** ⓠ have been immaculately restored and subtly incorporated into the Stamford Plaza Hotel. The former headquarters of the Australian United Steam Navigation Company, **Naldham House** (Mary Street), now provides premises for the Polo Club. Flood markers on the side of the building are reminders of Brisbane's vulnerability to inundation during its early history.

In the 19th century the maritime precinct was a rumbustious blend of warehouses, engineering works, mercantile agencies, brothels, boarding houses and residences amid busy wharves, rough hotels, a ferry terminal and the Botanic Gardens. The raffish cosmopolitanism of those days finds a distant resonance in the array of fine dining restaurants lining **Eagle Street Pier** ⓡ, where Brisbane's expense-account set congregates to sluice and trough.

Riverside

From Eagle Street Pier, follow the boardwalk to Harry Seidler's remarkable **Riverside Centre** ⓢ. This bold tower stands head and shoulders above its neighbours in Brisbane's mini-Manhattan – albeit eclipsed by its twin, the **Riparian Plaza**. People love it, and it is widely admired within the architectural fraternity. Seidler once described his own design as "before its time and above all, an Australian building with a capital A". The Royal Australian Institute of Architects, which has honoured Seidler's vision with three of its most prestigious awards, obviously agrees.

Across Eagle Street, at its junction with Queen Street, stands the **Eagle Street Drinking Fountain** completed in 1880 as part of a beautification project. At some point in time, the public arrived at the mistaken conclusion that the fountain commemorated James Mooney, a volunteer fireman killed in active duty in 1877. The myth became so embedded in the public consciousness that in 1988 the Brisbane City Council made folklore into reality, adding a tablet honouring Mooney and other firemen.

Near by, the copper-domed **Customs House** ⓣ at 399 Queen Street lends a splash of colonial pomp to both the street and the riverfront. Once a source of maritime tax rev-

A Culinary Revolution

A couple of decades ago Brisbane was something of a gastronomic desert. The city's culinary development began in the early 1980s, with a food movement led by a group of young chefs who, having toiled in the fine hotels of Europe, returned home to fire up Brisbane's food revolution. They called themselves The Five Chefs and became Brisbane's culinary superstars. Three of the five – Philip Johnson, David Pugh and Russell Armstrong – continue to run successful restaurants. Younger chefs have followed in their footsteps. The subsequent appearance in Brisbane of accomplished European chefs like Romaine Bapst (Il Centro) and Romeo Rigo (Romeo's) has confirmed the city's culinary coming of age. It can now be said that the best restaurants of Brisbane have hit international standard.

Along with the numerous formal restaurants, you'll find an array of very good ethnic places (Thai, Indian and Vietnamese being the most usual). And Brisbane-ites still love steak and fish and chips – two of the city's most successful restaurants (Brett's Wharf and Pier Nine) have turned these most basic of dishes into art forms *(see pages 84–5 for full restaurant listings).*

enue, the building is now owned and operated by the University of Queensland as a heritage facility offering boardrooms, a ballroom, an art gallery and a waterside brasserie. Nor has its influence ceased, at least in the architectural sense, with copy-cat domes crowning several neighbouring towers.

Story Bridge

Of the many bridges across the Brisbane River, none holds a more lasting place in Queenslanders' affection than the iconic **Story Bridge** . Tram tracks were removed in 1959 but otherwise this elegant structure joining Kangaroo Point with the CBD stands unchanged since its opening on 6 July 1940.

At the time, it symbolised progress in an era of political and economic uncertainty. Hundreds of tradesmen and engineers worked on the project during the six years from design to completion – a task made perilous because the sandy bottom necessitated unusually deep foundations. Tragically, four men died during construction.

Today the Story Bridge carries 43 million vehicles annually. Lit by night, it is Queensland's most photographed landmark, appearing in countless books, brochures and postcards. For a remarkable 360-degree view of the city, sign up with Story Bridge Adventure Climb (170 Main Street, Kangaroo Point; tel: 3514 6900; www.storybridgeadventures.com.au). Supervised ascent of the arches takes around two-and-a-half hours.

Kangaroo Point precinct

The **Kangaroo Point Cliff Walk** offers great views of the city as it winds from South Bank to Dockside and beyond. Formed by convicts quarrying porphyry for building materials, this serene sliver of riverside parkland hums with wildlife: scurrying possums, long-legged seabirds, posturing lizards, jumping fish and, in the dead of night, soaring fruit bats. By day, it belongs to joggers, rollerbladers, rock climbers and cyclists. As shadows lengthen, picnickers, lovers and, occasionally, fire twirlers take over.

Map on pages 66–7

TIP

Eagle Street Pier is the departure point for paddlewheeler cruises on board the *Kookaburra River Queens I* and *II*. Lunch cruises depart daily at noon; dinner cruises Mon–Sat 7pm, Sun 6.30pm (tel: 3221 1300; www.kookaburrariverqueens.com).

BELOW: the Story Bridge at night from the Riverside Centre.

Examples of public artwork decorate the parkland around Brisbane Naval Stores.

BELOW: Brisbane Naval Stores.

The 130-year-old **St Mary's Anglican Church** (455 Main Street, Kangaroo Point) clings to the cliff edge. Near by, a ramshackle set of stairs tumbles down the cliff to the **Brisbane Naval Stores**, built in 1887 to accommodate the Queensland Navy. The old stores recently became HQ of the Riverlife Adventure Centre (tel: 3891 5766; www.riverlife.com. au), where, among other pursuits, you can have a go at kayaking, abseiling, rock climbing and rollerblading. To get there, catch the ferry to the Thornton Street Ferry Terminal then follow the signs along the river.

Whimsical examples of public art are dotted along this stretch of the parkland – among them Christopher Trotter's scrap-metal fish, Mona Ryder's sculpture of rowers at Thornton Street Ferry, and a solar sunflower that doesn't work. Elsewhere, the park serves as a repository for a series of one-dimensional sculptures, huge buoys, ancient anchors, rusty chains and unidentified nautical gewgaws. Gazebos, follies and jetties jut from the boardwalk.

As for Kangaroo Point itself, few traces remain of the gracious houses that lined River Terrace and the waterfront. **Yungabar**, built to accommodate immigrants in 1885–7, still stands, as does the old weatherboard lock-up at the corner of Main and Thornton Streets. The **Story Bridge Hotel**, at least 120 years old, is another enduring relic.

A short walk away, in a creaking boathouse on priceless riverfront real estate, stands the **Brisbane Jazz Club** (1 Annie Street, Kangaroo Point; tel: 3391 2006) – last bastion of mainstream jazz, traditional dixieland and big-band swing. This brave little club with its alarming sloping floor has battled for survival for 35 years – and shows no sign of stopping.

St John's Cathedral and Wickham Terrace precinct

Head back to the CBD and **St John's Cathedral** Ⓦ in Ann Street, where stonemasons toil on Australia's last uncompleted Gothic-style cathedral. Work started in 1901, new bays were completed in 1968 and,

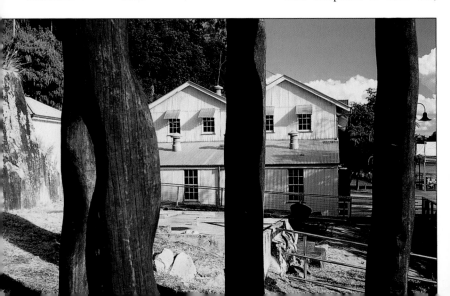

although the façade is well advanced, there are years of work ahead. Even as a work in progress, St John's is impressive. A scale model inside the cathedral shows how it will eventually look.

Within the grounds stands the **Deanery**, a two-storey porphyry building that served as the governor's residence from 1859 to 1862. Near by, in Ann Street stands **All Saints' Church** – the oldest Anglican church in Brisbane, opened in 1862 to minister to the spiritual needs of residents in what was then Windmill Hill. Cross into **Wickham Terrace** and discover a shady boulevard that has attracted specialist medical practitioners since the 1920s.

Many historic buildings line its length, but none so historic as **The Old Windmill** ❽ – built in 1829 and one of only two convict buildings surviving from the first wave of construction. Small and unprepossessing, the windmill has been many things since the convict era: a signal station, a fire lookout and, in 1935, the scene of Brisbane's first television broadcast. Its original purpose

was to grind the grain cultivated on the surrounding land. It was powered, partly by sails, partly by convicts slaving on a treadmill for up to 14 hours a day. Its designer, a convict miller named John Oseland, absconded within a couple of days of the sails turning and was never seen again.

An offbeat modern building in this precinct is the **Wickham Terrace Car Park**. Car parks are rarely seen as iconic, but this one, designed by James Birrell for Brisbane City Council in 1958, continues to excite comment.

Roma Street Parkland

Wickham Terrace provides an entry point to **Roma Street Parkland** ❿, the world's biggest subtropical inner-city garden. Formerly a railway shunting yard, the 16-hectare (40-acre) site has been planted with more than 100,000 varieties of shrub and 1,200 mature trees. The floral displays are breathtaking, with themed gardens that include a topiary maze, a lillypilly garden and a "wall" of epiphytes. Seasonal plants

Map on pages 66–7

Architect James Birrell won an award for the heritage-listed Wickham Terrace Car Park. Contemporary architects are still full of praise for his ingenious use of concrete.

BELOW: Roma Street Parkland.

scramble over Wendy Mills's stain-
less-steel sculpture, and the massed
displays of azalea, camelia and tropical rhododendron are spectacular.
Anyone with even a passing interest
in horticulture could spend a whole
day enjoying the orchids, ferns and
lilies of the forest and Fern Gully
walk. The bridge across Fern Gully
is just one of several vantage points
for superb views over the parklands
to the city centre.

Botanic Gardens, Mount Coot-tha

Quite different in character to the
Roma Street Parkland, but no less
visually arresting, are the **Botanic
Gardens ❶** in Mount Coot-tha
Road. Just 10 minutes from the city
centre, these gardens contain Australia's largest subtropical display of
flora, spread over 57 hectares (140
acres) of lakes, ponds and streams.
Attractions include a climate-con-
trolled dome filled with rare tropi-

cal plants, a planetarium and formal
Japanese garden. Further up Mount
Coot-tha Road, a popular lookout
provides a panoramic view of the
city and glimpses of Moreton Bay.

Fortitude Valley and Brunswick Street Mall

For urban recreation, head for **Fortitude Valley ❷** – once Brisbane's
premier commercial and retail hub,
now reborn as a cosmopolitan precinct of trendy bars, clubs and residential apartments. The area is
especially lively at weekends, with
most of the action concentrated
around the sidewalk cafés and bars in
and around **Brunswick Street Mall**.
One of the area's busiest clubs, the
GPO (corner of Ann and Ballow
Streets), occupies the former Fortitude Valley Post Office, an ornate
Victorian structure built in 1887 to
reflect the area's burgeoning importance (*for more nightlife venues, see
box, below right*).

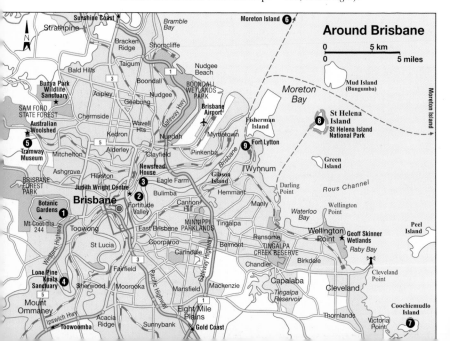

Other noteworthy buildings include **The Empire Hotel** (1880s), **McWhirter's Department Store** (1912), both in Brunswick Street, and the **Valley Police Station** (1936), corner of Wickham and Brooke Streets. The Empire is now given over to trendy bars and thumping music. McWhirter's has become residential apartments. Only the police station is used for its original purpose.

Adding to the Fortitude Valley mix is the **Judith Wright Centre** at 420 Brunswick Street. Named after the late Queensland poet and environmental activist, the contemporary arts centre incorporates a 200-seat performance space, art gallery, artist studios, screening room, administration and storage facilities, workshops and theatre, music, dance and circus rehearsal spaces.

Also integral to the Fortitude Valley precinct is **Chinatown Mall** in Duncan Street, where dining choices cover a wide range of Asian cuisines including Thai, Malaysian, Korean and Japanese... but not so much Chinese. Excellent Chinese

restaurants do operate within Chinatown but, in general, Chinese restaurateurs and shopkeepers have gravitated to **Sunnybank**, a well-to-do fringe suburb with a large expatriate Chinese community.

Newstead House

For more early Brisbane history, head to **Newstead House** ❸ (Newstead Park, Breakfast Creek Road, Newstead; Mon–Fri 10am–4pm, Sun 2am–5pm; admission charge; tel: 3216 1846; www.newstead house.com.au). Brisbane's oldest surviving residence has been quietly dominating Breakfast Creek since 1846, when pioneering Darling Downs pastoralist Patrick Leslie built the then two-storey house for his father William. Neither Leslie appears to have spent much time there. In the year after its completion the government resident Captain John Wickham moved in, establishing the building as the unofficial Government House. Across Breakfast Creek is the **Breakfast Creek Hotel**, famous for beer "off the wood", and good steaks.

The Police Station in Fortitude Valley, built in 1935, is a distinctive landmark in the area.

BELOW: mixing it at the Wickham Hotel.

Fortitude Valley Nightlife

I t's colourful, it's loud and, even if you don't feel like partying, the spectacle is reason enough to visit Fortitude Valley – the city's hot spot for music, food and good times.

At **Family** (8 McLachlan Street; Fri–Sun), the crowd raves to a pounding 33,000-watt sound system. Sunday is gay night, but not exclusively so. **The Press Club** (339 Brunswick St) is less noisy and more upwardly mobile than many of the bars and clubs in the valley. Another friendly and laissez-faire Fortitude Valley haunt is **The Beat Mega Club** (677 Ann Street), which offers themed bars on several levels. The **Wickham Hotel** (308 Wickham Street) is the centre of the gay scene, with a throbbing dance floor where female impersonators mime to tracks by gay icons. As the night wears on, stayers of all sexual persuasions gravitate to **Belushi's** (Brunswick Street Mall), where merrymakers are encouraged to dance on stage and generally shed inhibitions. Live-music venues include **Ric's Café**, opposite Belushi's, and **The Zoo** (711 Ann Street), where many a famous Brisbane band made their start. Adjoining Ric's is a 24-hour café where the Valley crowd gathers for breakfast of bacon and eggs to round off an evening of unrestrained partying.

TIP

On an upstream loop of the Brisbane River, Lone Pine can be reached by taxi or bus. Better still, at least in one direction, take a leisurely and scenic 19-km (12-mile) cruise up the Brisbane River on *Mirimar*, a stately, 60-year-old timber vessel that departs daily at 10am from North Quay at the top of Queen Street Mall (tel: 3221 0300; www.mirimar.com).

BELOW: a number of sanctuaries in Queensland, including Lone Pine, keep wombats.

Lone Pine Sanctuary

In such a sprawling city, it's impossible to see everything in one visit. Still, visitors who stay in Brisbane more than a day or two usually wind up nursing a koala at **Lone Pine Koala Sanctuary** ❹ (Jesmond Road, Fig Tree Pocket; daily 8.30am–5pm; admission fee; tel: 3378 1366; www.koala.net). Open since 1927 and noted in the *Guinness Book of Records* as the world's first and biggest koala sanctuary, Lone Pine also keeps kangaroos, wombats, birds, bats, reptiles, echidnas, a Tasmanian devil and dingoes.

Tramway Museum

At Ferny Grove, just northwest of Brisbane, you'll find the **Tramway Museum** ❺ (Tramway Street; Sun 12.30–4pm; admission charge; tel: 3351 1776; www.brisbanetramwaymuseum.org), where tram aficionados lovingly maintain a fleet rendered obsolete by the City Council's 1968 decision to end a tradition of transport that began with horse-drawn trams in 1885. Many of the exhibits here are true collectors'

items – from the 1901 Californian-built Car 47 that ran between Edward Street and the City Botanical Gardens, to Car 554, the last car to run officially on the tram system.

Moreton Bay

In many respects, **Moreton Bay** is Brisbane's best natural asset – stretching 160 km (100 miles) from Caloundra in the north to Southport, and encompassing some 360 islands. On **Moreton Island** ❻, Tangalooma Resort (tel: 3268 6333; www.tangalooma.com), built on the site of a whaling station where more than 6,000 humpback whales met their deaths between 1952 and 1962, now promotes whale-watching and dolphin studies. Just 75 minutes by catamaran from the CBD, it's close enough to call by for lunch. Departures are from Tangalooma Launch Terminal at Holt Street Wharf, Pinkenba, on the lower Brisbane River. A transfer coach (for which the resort charges A$5) operates daily from most CBD hotels and the Roma Street Transit Centre (tel: 1300 652 250). The transfer coach connects

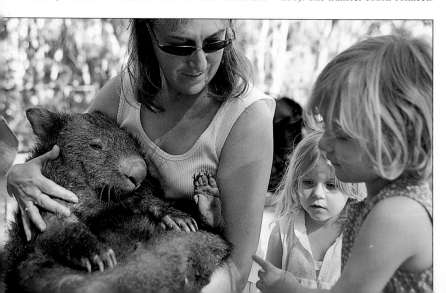

Map
on page
80

with the 10am service to the resort and the 4pm service from the resort only. The extended day tour (dolphin feeding inclusive) is A$90.

Captain Cook named the bay as he sailed past in 1770, but Matthew Flinders was the first European to enter its waters in 1779 – an event re-enacted annually by the residents of **Coochiemudlo Island** ❼. Flinders was followed by John Oxley who, with the assistance of three castaway convicts, explored the Brisbane River in 1823 *(see page 19)*. Located 40 km (25 miles) southeast of Brisbane, Coochiemudlo is accessed by ferry. From Brisbane take Cleveland Road towards Victoria Point; follow the sign at the main traffic lights in Victoria Point. (Contact Redlands Tourism, Shore Street West, Cleveland; tel: 3821 0057 for details.)

Stradbroke Island *(see page 101)*, meanwhile, has been identified by Brisbane's prosperous middle classes as a good place to build weekenders. Historically, the bay's most interesting island is **St Helena** ❽, 6 km (4 miles) southeast of the river mouth, where crumbling walls form the outline of a self sufficient prison farm that, at its zenith, held 300 prisoners – among them Captain Starlight (the sobriquet given to legendary hustler Henry Readford, who entered folklore in 1870 when he and two others stole around 1000 head of cattle from Longreach). The oldest ruins date from 1866. The prison was finally abandoned in 1933. (To get there, contact St Helena Ferries, tel: 3393 3726, or Brisbane Cruises, tel: 3630 2666.)

Fort Lytton

Visitors interested in military history should plan a visit to **Fort Lytton** ❾ (South Street, Lytton; Sun and public hols 10am–4pm; admission charge; tel: 3906 9111), near the mouth of the Brisbane River. Built to repel a feared Russian invasion in the late 19th century, the fort is shielded by earthworks and surrounded by a moat, with underground passages connecting its chambers. Invading navies would be met by a combination of heavy guns and controlled river mines. ❏

If you're not at Tangalooma in the whale-watching season, try your hand at sand tobogganing.

BELOW: whale-watching at Moreton Bay.

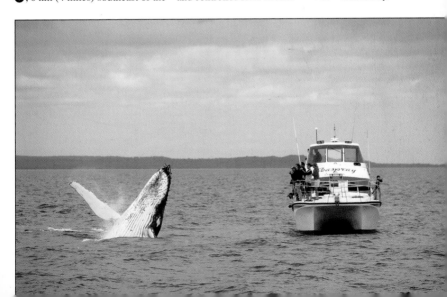

RESTAURANTS, CAFÉS & BARS

Most Brisbane precincts have at least one formal dining space and a selection of ethnic restaurants, the most common being Thai, Indian and Vietnamese. The cafés and bistros of Park Road, Milton; Brunswick Street, Fortitude Valley; Merthyr Road, New Farm; and Little Stanley Street, South Bank, offer reasonable fare in often sophisticated settings. Asian restaurants are mainly concentrated in Fortitude Valley, West End and Sunnybank.

Restaurants

Augustine's on George
40 George Street
Tel: 3221 9365
Open: L Mon–Fri, D Mon–Sat. **$$**
Hong Kong expatriate Augustine Tso has been a flag on Brisbane's fine-dining map for more than 25 years. The quality at this snug restaurant in historic George Street has never wavered: thoughtful, flavoursome dishes that sit lightly on the palate. Entrées such as grilled haloumi on onion jam with tomato terrine, tempura zucchini flower and basil oil set the scene for mains such as red braised duck with lentils, banana chili, Asian greens and kaffir lime broth.

Bespoke
317 Sandgate Road, Albion
Tel: 3262 5822
Open: L Tues–Fri, D Tues–Sat. **$$$**
A cool, sassy space with suede-and-silk banquettes and polished bamboo tables. Chef Robert Davis's open kitchen produces artful modern Australian dishes, with the menu changing to reflect seasonal produce.

Brett's Wharf
449 Kingsford Smith Drive, Hamilton.
Tel: 3868 1717
Open: L & D daily. **$$$**
Located beside the Brisbane River, with pelicans perched on the pylons outside. this is one for seafood-fanciers. The menu reflects what's biting, and on a good day, the fare is absolutely stunning. Restaurateurs Francis and Marilyn Domenech also own **Baguette**, in nearby Racecourse Road – another Brisbane institution.

Il Centro Restaurant
Eagle Street Pier
Tel: 3221 6090
www.il-centro.com.au
Open: L Sun–Fri, D daily. **$$$**
One of a trio of upmarket restaurants overlooking the Brisbane River at Eagle Street Pier. Alsace-born chef Romaine Bapst is a master of texture and flavour, delivering an Italian-inspired menu with great skill.

Cha Cha Char
5 Waterfront Place
Tel: 3211 9944
www.chachachar.com.au
Open: L Mon–Fri, D daily. **$$$**
Owner John Kilroy takes steak very seriously. His menu discusses the history of the beef you're about to eat, its age, provenance and the pasture on which it was raised. Regulars discuss steak as they do wine.

Circa
483 Adelaide Street
Tel: 3832 4722
Open: L Mon–Fri, D Mon–Sat. **$$$**
Modern Australian cuisine served in a cool, airy room overlooking the Brisbane River. Dishes run the gamut from Moroccan spiced milk-fed lamb with couscous, okra and fig jus to seared flounder fillets, tomato tart, snow peas and warm tartare sauce. Popular with well-heeled thirtysomethings.

E'cco
100 Boundary Street (corner Adelaide Street East)
Tel: 3831 8344
www.eccobistro.com
Open: L Tues–Fri, D Tues–Sat. **$$$**
One of Brisbane's most awarded bistros. Philip Johnson's mantra is simplicity, simplicity, simplicity. Essentially, his food relies on fresh ingredients and unfussy preparation. Settle in for field mushrooms, olive toast, rocket and parmesan, or try sautéed squid, cannellini beans, tomato, smoked chilli and salami. And that's just for starters.

Gianni Vintage Cellar Bar
12 Edward Street
Tel: 3221 7655
www.giannisrestaurant.com
Open: L Mon–Fri, D Mon–Sat. **$$$**
Award-winning restaurant offering innovative but accessible food to a dedicated inner-city following. Excellent wine cellar.

The Green Papaya
898 Stanley Street, East Brisbane
Tel: 3217 3599
Open: L Fri, D Tues–Sat. **$$**
Owner-chef Lien Yeomans offers a beguiling blend of classic and contemporary Vietnamese cuisine. Try the Saigon rocket – crabmeat filling with prawn in crispy fried rice paper, or the bouillabaisse spiced with lemongrass, galangal and coriander. BYO.

Isis Brasserie
446 Brunswick Street, Fortitude Valley
Tel: 3852 1155
www.isisbrasserie.com.au
Open: L Tues–Fri, D Tues–Sun. **$$$**
Isis has a casual yet elegant atmosphere. A thoughtful menu is supported by a top wine list and swift, unobtrusive service. Isis was awarded the Queensland Restaurant and Catering Award for 2005.

Michael's Riverside Restaurant
123 Eagle Street,
Riverside Centre.
Tel: 3832 5522
Open: L Sun–Fri, D daily. **$$$**
Beautifully positioned, overlooking two reaches of the Brisbane River, Michael's is a haunt of business types and politicians, offering impeccable food and flawless service. The menu has a lingering resonance of old-style fine dining but includes many modern dishes. Noted for its comprehensive wine cellar. A serious splurge.

Montrachet
224 Given Terrace,
Paddington
Tel: 3367 0030
www.montrachet.com.au
Open: L & D Mon–Fri. **$$$**
Lyon-born chef Thierry Galichet has been a significant presence on the Brisbane scene for years, operating a series of memorable restaurants across the city. Montrachet is his best yet. Main courses include baked rack of lamb with Roquefort soufflé and a fresh pea casserole.

Pier Nine
Eagle Street Pier
Tel: 3226 2100
www.piernine.com.au
Open: L Sun–Fri, D daily. **$$$**
In this self-styled "12-star fish-and-chip shop", the seafood is always fresh, served with zesty sauces and interesting accompaniments. The wine list is sublime

(owner Matthew Hill-Smith belongs to one of Australia's best-known wine families). Lots of expense-account diners.

Restaurant Two
2 Edward Street
Tel: 3210 1311
Open: L Mon–Fri,
D Mon–Sat. **$$**
Classic, restrained dining in a lovely high-ceilinged room with a stylish bar. Co-owner-chef David Pugh, one of Brisbane's "Five Chefs", emphasises freshness and natural flavour in his elegant dishes.

Romeo's Restaurant
216 Petrie Terrace
Tel: 3367 0955
www.romeos.com.au
Open: L Tues–Fri, D
Tues–Sat. **$$**
Italian chef Romeo Rigo arrived in Australia as the personal chef of the late Prime Minister Harold Holt, and became quite a celebrity in Melbourne during the 1960s. Exquisite antipasto dishes, creamy risottos and Romeo's signature tagliarini with Moreton Bay bugs.

Seasalt at Armstrongs
Incholm Hotel
73 Wickham Terrace
Tel: 3226 8888
Open: L Mon–Fri, D
Mon–Sat. **$$**
Russell Armstrong has been a stalwart of the Brisbane food scene for more than two decades – feisty, uncompromising, and arguably the best chef in Australia. Spe-

cialises in seafood.

Timmy's Restaurant
4b Galleria Complex,
Grey and Tribune Streets
Tel: 3846 0322
Open: L Tues–Sun, D
Tues–Sat. **$$**
Thai-born chef Timmy Kemp is Brisbane's fusion-food legend. His bill of fare includes a bit of everything – from beef brisket red curry, kaffir lime, grilled bread, crushed peanuts and Asian herbs to tortellini with ricotta, sweet potato and pine nut with sautéed chicken breast, asparagus and lemon oil. BYO.

Cafés and Bars

Cru Wine Bar (22 James Street, Fortitude Valley; tel: 3252 2400; www.crubar. com; open: L & D daily; **$$**) serves great wine and tapas and is a pleasant place to while away an

hour. Part bottle shop, part bar and part café, Cru is run by one of Brisbane's most successful food-and-drink teams. There are plenty of quiet corners for people-watching while enjoying a snack washed down with wine. For something altogether different, try **Belgian Beer Café Brussels** (Mary and Edward Streets; tel: 3221 0199; open: L & D daily; **$$**), where you can wash down authentic Flemish dishes with a selection of Belgian beers on tap.

PRICE CATEGORIES

Prices are for a three-course meal per person with house wine:
$ = A$60 and under
$$ = A$60–90
$$$ = A$90–120
$$$$ = A$120 and over

RIGHT: Michael's Riverside Restaurant.

SPORTS

It's difficult to tune into the local psyche without some grasp of sport. In Queensland there's plenty to choose from

No country's population is more passionate about sport than Australia's, whether as participants or spectators. And no region is more passionate than Queensland. Certainly some sports are favoured, but give Queenslanders something to cheer about and there's no stopping them, even if it's not a "local" game. The Brisbane Lions story *(see opposite)* is testimony to this.

But if there is a number one sport for Queenslanders it's rugby league. The Brisbane Broncos and the Queensland Cowboys are the state's NRL (National Rugby League) teams, and both attract passionate support. Historically the Broncos have had more attention, but it was the Townsville-based Cowboys who made it to the final in 2005. It's the State of Origin games, though, between the Maroons (Queensland) and the Blues (NSW) which really stir the blood in the depths of winter. In summer cricket is popular, with tests and state games at the Gabba in Brisbane, while soccer is growing as a participation sport, its profile raised by the national league set up in 2005; Queensland Roar, based on the Gold Coast, is the team. Basketball is popular, country rodeos have their own appeal and, if drinking is your thing, head to the infamous Birdsville Races in September.

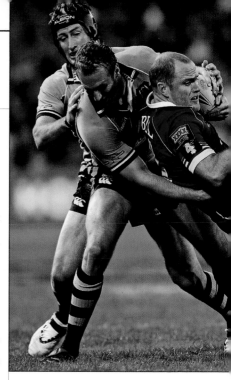

ABOVE: the State of Origin series between Queensland and New South Wales is the highlight of the rugby league calendar. The matches are played as a best of three every June and inspire passionate support from inhabitants of both states.

ABOVE: Broadbeach on the Gold Coast hosts the annual Australian National Lifesaving Titles. The summer contest attracts thousands of competitors from clubs in every state, and a vast number of spectators.

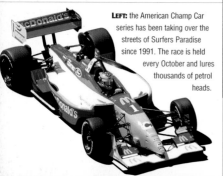

LEFT: the American Champ Car series has been taking over the streets of Surfers Paradise since 1991. The race is held every October and lures thousands of petrol heads.

AUSSIE RULES

For years Australian Rules Football was the preserve of Victoria, until it was decided that if the sport was to survive, it would need to build up its fan base. As part of this process the Fitzroy Lions from north Melbourne merged with Brisbane Bears in 1996 and the Brisbane Lions were born. Similar moves saw teams established in the other mainland states, but for some time the dominant clubs still came from Victoria. This began to change when the West Coast Eagles from Perth won championships in 1992 and 1994, but the real shift in attitudes came with the astonishing success of the Brisbane Lions, when the team won three consecutive Grand Finals from 2001 to 2003 under coach Leigh Matthews. With success came loyalty from local fans, and nowadays the team can attract 30,000 to the Gabba in Brisbane. The season runs from March to September, and there's always a willing local to explain the arcane rules to an overseas visitor.

ABOVE: Matthew Hayden, from Kingaroy, is one of the greats of world cricket. He's the one who's been trading records for highest scores with the West Indies' Brian Lara for the last few years, having made 380 in a test match in 2003. The left-hander plays for Queensland and debuted for Australia in 1993. He was the first man to make over 1,000 test runs in five seasons.

RIGHT: Ian Thorpe may be the poster boy of Australian swimming, but it's Queenslander Grant Hackett who's quietly breaking records and securing championships at a rate which suggests he may one day eclipse his great rival and Olympic teammate. As winner of the 1,500 metres freestyle at both the 2000 and 2004 Olympics, Hackett has established himself as one of the greats of distance swimming. He was made team captain of Australia as well.

GOLD COAST

Welcome to the subtropical pleasure zone, home of the bronzed, the toned and proudly hedonistic. Away from the flash and hoop-la, you can still find tranquil waterfalls, verdant rainforests and rolling cane farms

Brisbane

Map on page 90

outh of Brisbane, the 32-km (20-mile) stretch of coast from Coolangatta to Surfers Paradise – bushland just two generations ago – is the fastest-growing tourist and residential area in Australia. The Gold Coast is superficial and showy in parts, beautiful in others, but never dull. The beaches, particularly Burleigh Heads, set in national parkland, are strikingly gorgeous, while the high-rise skyline of Surfers Paradise, holiday headquarters for Australia's rich and hedonistic, must now rank with Ipanema, Miami and Cannes for architectural overkill: famously, the skyscrapers at Surfers cast shadows over the beach every afternoon. But that no longer matters by night, when the partygoers take over the streets, restaurants and nightclubs.

Soaring residential towers and conurbations line almost the entire length of this coastal stretch. Successive waves of development have all but obliterated the original shoreline. Only the sea remains untamed, as beachfront residents become painfully aware whenever turbulent seas threaten the dunes.

It's appropriate that this bright and brassy strip should be known as the Gold Coast – a headline dreamed up in the 1940s by journalists writing about the post-war real-estate boom (a boom, apparently, without end). The name stuck and became official in 1959. Ever since, the Gold Coast – Surfers Paradise in particular – has taken perverse pride in its embrace of glitz and pizzazz.

Gold Coasters live for the moment. They are fascinated by glamour. They love to flaunt. It's a happy hunting ground for wealthy retirees and divorcees. Tummy tucks and face-lifts are de rigueur. The young go surfing. The young-at-heart go partying. This is a proudly

LEFT strolling at Surfers **BELOW:** the extravagant 6-star Palazzo Versace.

hedonistic society that sees no contradiction in working extremely hard to maintain outward impressions of leisurely designer-clad affluence.

Main Beach

Just north of Surfers Paradise on the Gold Coast highway lies **Southport.** When Governor Sir Anthony Musgrave built a summer retreat here in the late 1880s, the town became all the rage. The cream of Brisbane society braved an arduous coach journey, ferry crossing and horseback ride to be close to the action. Nowadays, Southport is a relatively low-key residential area. The action long ago shifted across the Broadwater to **Main Beach ❶**, with its glittering hotels, resorts, theme parks, bars, boutiques and restaurants. The Spit is a 3-km (2-mile) sandbar running north of Main Beach separating the Broadwater from the Pacific Ocean. On one side of the main street running south to north stands **Shera-**

ton Mirage, the airy Honolulu-style resort. On the other is the decadent six-star *(sic)* **Palazzo Versace** where the floors are laid with fine Italian marble, the bellboys dress better than the clientele, and guests choose from six types of pillow.

Within the nearby **Marina Mirage Shopping Complex**, a twice-monthly farmers' market brings jolly cheese makers and weathered crayfish farmers into incongruous communion with boutique owners pandering to the Louis Vuitton set. Spice blenders, emu ranchers, bee keepers, sausage makers, organic fruit growers and what-have-you set up shop around the faux Renaissance fountain – making it one of the few places you can buy silk socks and smoked eel under one roof.

The precinct is also a fine-dining zone. Both Palazzo Versace and Sheraton Mirage maintain excellent restaurants. One of the Gold Coast's more elegant Italian eateries, **Ris-**

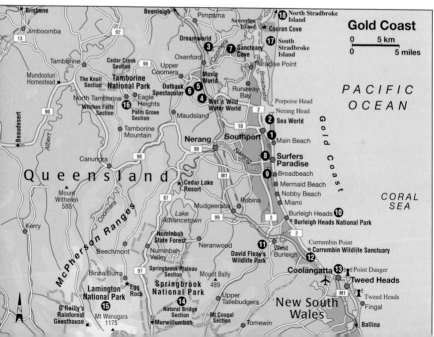

torante **Fellini**, occupies premises within Marina Mirage. For most visitors, however, it's enough to slip into one of the casual cafés lining the boardwalk, order something Mediterranean and watch the yachts scud gracefully across the Broadwater, with the towers of Southport beyond. At nearby Tedder Avenue in Main Beach, trendy bars, alfresco cafés and restaurants cater to a less pretentious crowd who nonetheless take pleasure in seeing and being seen.

Sea World

Beyond the upmarket shopping mall, crowds flock to the theme park **Sea World ❷** (Seaworld Drive, The Spit; daily 10am–5.30pm; admission charge; tel: 5588 2205; www.sea world.com.au). Attractions on offer include choreographed water-skiers, performing dolphins, polar bears in a replicated Arctic tundra, sharks swimming in a purpose-built lagoon system and dugongs grazing in a simulated Moreton Bay. For safe thrills, take a ride on **The Corkscrew**, a triple-loop roller-coaster, or snorkel amid benign reef sharks in a pool while beyond a glass partition, maneating tiger sharks cruise.

Dreamworld

The Gold Coast has no shortage of theme parks. Apart from Sea World, they are concentrated at the northwestern end of the coastal strip, off the Pacific Motorway.

Dreamworld ❸ (daily 10am–5pm; tel: 5588 1111; www.dream world.com.au) at Coomera combines gentle fun with adrenalin-pumping rides. The **Tower of Terror** hurls passengers 120 metres (395 ft) vertically into the firmament. If you can bear to open your eyes, there is, momentarily, a marvellous view of the surrounding countryside as the gondola teeters at the upper limit of its trajectory. **Wipeout** is another ride for thrill-seekers: a spin on this roller-coaster is likened to "windsurfing in a washing machine".

Among the gentler attractions are a carousel, bumper cars, the big red car ride at **Wiggles World**, the family roller coaster at **Nick Central** and interactive live entertainment shows for kids. There are wildlife

Map on page 90

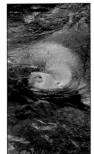

Polar bear at Sea World, a big theme park on the Southport Spit, where you'll find smoothly staged entertainment, all of it aquatic.

BELOW: the beach at Surfers Paradise.

Indy Racing

The Gold Coast Indy is Queens-land's noisiest and most glittering event – a high-octane cocktail of motor racing, big business and celebrity schmooz-ing. For four days in October, more than 300,000 spectators watch racing cars thun-der around a tortuous 4.47-km (2¾-mile) cir-cuit amid the hotels and residential towers of Surfers Paradise and Main Beach. Noth-ing if not panoramic, the circuit winds through the streets at the northern end of Surfers Paradise, veers north along Main Beach, twists into a couple of tight corners, then follows the Gold Coast Highway back to the starting grid.

For motor-sports fans, it's a rich feast of scorching rubber, engine fumes and motor-ing derring-do – with the limelight equally divided between open-wheeled Champ Cars and V8 Supercars. The Indy 300 Champ Car event is raced over more than 50 laps, with some cars capable of speeds upwards of 350 km per hour (220 mph), though few, if any, ever reach that velocity. The V8 Super-car racing is characterised by fierce rivalry between the manufacturers of Holden and Ford sedans. These race-modified V8s can

accelerate from 0 to 100 in 4 seconds, with a top speed just shy of 300 km per hour (185 mph).

It's non-stop action. F1-11s rumble over-head. There are stunt shows, burn-out dis-plays, precision driving expositions, even choreographed dance routines and beauty pageants to occupy empty moments.

A valuable money-spinner for the Gold Coast, the Indy has attracted more than three million spectators since John Andretti won the first Champ Car race through the streets in 1991. Criticism, trenchant at first, gradually turned to praise as politicians and tourist operators came to appreciate the pro-motional benefits of a glamorous motoring event telecast around the globe. For the Gold Coast business community, it repre-sents a welcome boost to the region's fis-cal health. When Indy is on, hotels are heavily booked, clubs do a roaring trade and gambling revenue goes through the roof.

These days, the Gold Coast Indy is recog-nised as a major motor-sport event in its own right – up there with the Monaco Grand Prix, California's Long Beach Grand Prix and the Australian Grand Prix in Melbourne.

For Australia's famous and nearly famous, the Indy presents an irresistible opportunity to see and be seen at a seem-ingly unending social round of concerts, nightclub parties and parades. The premier social occasion is the black-tie Indy Gala Ball – though hardcore race fans are more inter-ested in the Champ Car drivers' breakfast and V8 Supercar drivers' auction. The hoop-la of the Miss Indy contest and the thunder of live bands add to the fun, while organised trackside autograph sessions allow fans to meet their favourite drivers.

Tours of the Champ Car and the Supercar V8 pit areas are popular, with tickets avail-able from the Pit Walk booth on MacIntosh Island behind the pit area. Admission prices may change from year to year, but in 2006, tickets ranged from A$29 for a one-day pass on the first day to A$535 for a four-day "plat-inum club" grandstand pass – with many options between. Tickets through Ticketek (tel: 1300 303 103). ❑

LEFT: ring-side seats for the Gold Coast Indy race.

attractions, too – seven Bengal tigers, a Sumatran tiger and two cougars climb trees, adopt fight stances and generally do everything bar jumping through fiery hoops.

Wet 'n' Wild

For water-based spills and thrills, head to the nearby **Wet 'n' Wild Water World ④** at Oxenford (daily May–Aug 10am–4pm, Sept–Apr 10am–5pm, 27 Dec–25 Jan until 9pm; tel: 5573 2255; www.wetnwild. com.au). Spread over 10 hectares (25 acres) of subtropical gardens, this giant water-sports park makes a genuine attempt to please everyone. Activities run from the scary to the therapeutic. Eligibility for the more exciting rides is regulated by height, not age. Thus, you must be 110 cm (3 ft 7 inches) tall for the **Terror Canyon** or the **Twister**, but only 100 cm (3ft 3 inches) tall for the **Whirlpool** or **Mammoth River**.

Movie World

Not to be outdone, the nearby **Movie World ⑤** (daily 10am–5.30pm; tel: 5573 8485; www.movieworld.com. au) features the **Wild West Falls Adventure Ride**, an "action-packed, six-minute adventure propelled by more than a million litres of wicked water to a 20-metre (65-ft) heart-stopping final splashdown". One of Australia's biggest theme- park attractions, the ride is built in and around an artificial mountain, itself part of a Wild West movie set, complete with Indian reservations, ghost towns and wagon trains.

Movie World is interesting because it combines the functionality of a working film studio – not open to the public, by the way – with high-tech rides, staged stunts, animatronics and pyrotechnics. Clint Eastwood set the tone at the opening in 1991 when he pulled the first beer in the Dirty Harry Bar. While visitors are unlikely to spot any Hollywood stars, their chances of bumping into Daffy Duck or Yosemite Sam are quite good.

High-tech exhibits reflect Warner Bros. cinema hits. The **Scooby Doo Spooky Coaster**, for instance, is a A$13-million indoor ride inspired by the 2002 film shot at the Gold

Map on page 90

The Superman Escape ride at Movie World promises 0–100 km per hour in 2 seconds.

BELOW: Wet 'n' Wild's Super 8 Aqua Racer.

BELOW: some like it
hot, some like it wet.
More attractions at
Movie World.

Coast. **Lethal Weapon** delivers "drops, dives, rollovers, sidewinders, double spins, loops" and fast, upside-down thrills. The **Batman Adventure** simulates free flight as the Caped Crusader pursues The Joker and Cat Woman through Gotham City.

Movie World's newest rollercoaster, **Superman Escape**, accelerates from 0 to 100 kph (62 mph) in two seconds, traversing 760 metres (2,500 ft) of vertical climbs, weightless drops and giant G-force turns.

At **Looney Tunes Village** the little ones can have fun on the **Road Runner Rollercoaster**, get wet in the **Splash Zone** and hop on board for the Looney Tunes river ride.

Australian Outback Spectacular

Finally, for "a genuine Aussie Outback experience", there is Warner's new **Australian Outback Spectacular 6** (Tues–Sat 7.30pm; admission charge; tel: 5573 8289), located between Movie World and Wet 'n' Wild. Tuck in to a three-course barbecue while watching stockmen deal with wild horses and stampeding cattle. The A\$23-million extravaganza comes complete with audio and visual effects, an array of bush vehicles and a mustering helicopter.

It's a short drive from here to **Sanctuary Cove 7** (tel: 5577 6175), an enclave of mega-mansions and maxi-yachts belonging to the superwealthy Gold Coast elite. The late crooner Frank Sinatra launched this resort, which boasts two excellent golf courses, a country club, a "village" of bars, boutiques and restaurants, and the sumptuous Hyatt Regency Hotel.

To reach Sanctuary Cove, take exit 57 from the Pacific Motorway near Coomera, then drive down Casey's Road for 10 minutes or until you catch the whiff of money.

Surfers Paradise

Surfers Paradise 8 has meretricious charm, as befits the Gold Coast's iconic city. The surf rolls in. Tanned muscle-men and beautiful women strut their stuff on the beaches and in the bars. A sense of suntanned *joie de vivre* prevails.

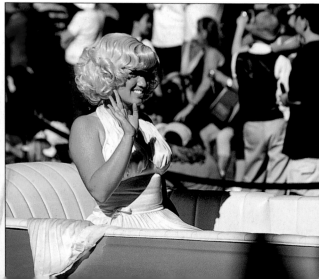

You see faces from Asia or the Middle East, hear the twang of American accents. Visionaries who dreamed that Surfers Paradise would one day become an international destination are having their day. It's cosmopolitan and saucy. **Orchid Avenue**, one of several busy thoroughfares within the main hub of the area, is a heady mix of luxury hotels, clubs, bars, strip joints, hot-dog stands, smart restaurants and boutiques selling Prada and Cartier.

Older locals speak wistfully of the 1950s and 1960s, when Surfers blossomed as a friendly resort filled with Runyon-esque characters with names like Cherokee Bill and the Mutton Bird Man. Pragmatists realise that Surfers Paradise has long since passed the point of no return. Its future lies as a party town, a place where people let their hair down. School-leavers descend en masse every November to carouse and celebrate the end of exams in "schoolies' week". Sometimes, in the nightclub strip, their antics tread a fine line between high jinks and sleaze.

Meanwhile, a surge of luxury development has created a new generation of upmarket restaurants, boutiques and spas – edging out the tacky arcades, gaudy signage and seedy shops that infested the CBD through the 1990s. Massive developments like the **Renaissance Towers** in Surfers Paradise Boulevard and the 80-storey **Q1** residential tower in Hamilton Avenue have set the tone for the future. The magnificent sand and surf of the foreshore play a curiously secondary role to the high-rise apartment blocks that overshadow them. Surfers continue to catch the waves, but thanks to successive skin-cancer awareness campaigns, Queenslanders spend less time on the beach than they used to.

Surfing and amusements

Ironically, it's for the entertainment more than the surfing that people flock to Surfers Paradise, even though it has several surf schools and is a good place for novices to get started.

Former world surfing champion Cheyne Horan (Cheyne Horan

Map on page 90

TIP

The Australian National Life Saving Titles attract thousands of competitors from clubs in every state, and a vast number of spectators. Competitions are held most frequently during the summer months, from around mid-September to the end of April. For information on contests, call the Queensland Surf Life Saving Association (tel: 3846 8000; www. lifesaving.com.au).

BELOW: this way to Paradise.

The Vomatron Sling Shot and the Fly Coaster. Apparently a Gold Coast traders' initiative to part punters from their lunches so they have to go and eat again.

School of Surf, corner Hanlan Street and The Esplanade, Surfers Paradise; tel: 1800 227 873; www.cheyne horan.com.au) promises to get his students riding in their first lesson. Beginner classes are daily 10am–noon, 2pm–4pm, and the school offers complimentary hotel pick-up. Another recommended surf school is Gold Coast Surf Coaching (154 Marine Parade, Rainbow Beach, Coolangatta; tel: 5599 5495), where former professional surfer Dave Davidson gives lessons for beginners daily 10am–noon (8am in summer); 2pm–4pm daily. *(See page 271 for more about surf schools.)*

For a blast of old-fashioned hoopla, check out **Ripley's Believe It Or Not! Museum** (Cavill Mall; daily 9am–11pm; tel: 5592 0040; www.ripleys.com.au). Within the museum's 12 themed galleries are displayed such bizarre items as "a rare shrunken head" and "a real Fiji mermaid". Visitors are invited to "stand next to the tallest and biggest men who ever lived".

Thrill-seekers are well catered for in Surfers Paradise. Heart-stopping

attractions include **The Flycoaster** (corner Gold Coast Highway and Cypress Ave; tel: 5539 0474; www.flycoaster.com) – a free-fall device that drops participants from a height of 12 storeys to 2 metres (6 ft) above the ground in 1.3 seconds – and **The Sling Shot** (6 Palm Avenue; daily; tel: 5570 2700; www.funtime.com.au) – a 52-metre (170-ft) high catapult that propels two passengers 80 metres (260 ft) into the air at speeds of more than 160 kph (100 mph) aboard an open-seat gondola attached by steel cables.

Back on terra firma, **The Infinity Funhouse** (Chevron Renaissance, corner Surfers Paradise Boulevard and Elkhorn Avenue; daily 10am–10pm; admission charge; tel: 5538 2988; www.infinitygc.com.au) is a disorientating but captivating series of futuristic mazes filled with special effects and illusions.

Broadbeach

A short drive from Surfers Paradise is **Broadbeach** ❾ – a rapidly developing precinct of residential towers, snazzy shopping zones and trendy eat streets. As the name suggests, Broadbeach has a top surf beach. Locals promenade along this sandy strip from 5.30am onwards. Broadbeach is also home to the **Kurrawa Surf Life Saving Club**, host of the annual Australian Surf Lifesaving Titles.

More family-orientated than Surfers Paradise, Broadbeach surged ahead during Surfers Paradise's period of stagnation and decline in the 1990s and now prospers as its more conservative twin. Broadbeach may seem less racy and frenetic than Surfers, but it still offers plenty of sun and fun, with crowd-pulling attractions of its own. More than 13,000 people daily pass beneath the rippling neon façade of **Jupiters Casino, Broadbeach Island** (tel: 5592 8100) to try their luck at the tables. The 24-hour casino has five

The Rise and Rise of the Gold Coast

In the 1840s cedar getters pushed into the Nerang Valley, setting up their loading stations on the Logan and Coomera Rivers. In their footsteps came graziers and cane farmers, whose agricultural methods irrevocably altered the wooded hills, river valleys, wetlands and low sand hills that the Aboriginal inhabitants, the Yugambeh people, had known. Nerang, the first town, was surveyed in 1865. Cobb & Co., the stagecoach operators, extended services to Southport in 1878, while steamers made regular voyages to and from Brisbane. The opening of the railway in 1889 accelerated progress. The completion of a coastal road in 1923 coincided with the arrival of dashing English swimming and surfing instructor James Cavill, who built a hotel at Elston which became known as The Surfers Paradise Hotel. The hotel proved so popular that in 1933 the entire township was renamed Surfers Paradise.

By the mid-1950s, thanks to the post-war economic boom and non-existent building regulations, the Gold Coast's destiny was already clear. The first high-rise – Kinkabool – went up at Surfers Paradise in 1959. The rest, as they say, is history.

restaurants, nine bars, a 600-room hotel and a 1,200-seat theatre. There's no need to leave until the money runs out.

A monorail connects the Jupiters with the Oasis complex across the Gold Coast Highway. Yet more alfresco dining places and wine bars line **Surf Parade**.

Burleigh Heads

Driving south from Surfers Paradise, the atmosphere becomes more laid-back as thrill-a-minute diversions give way to natural attractions in the form of nature reserves, wildlife parks and bird sanctuaries.

Burleigh Heads ⑩, 89 km (55 miles) south of Brisbane, is the Gold Coast's premier family destination and has been insulated from the excesses of development by preservation of the terrain around the Tallebudgera Creek Estuary. It is also a mecca for surfers, whose skills have become something of an attraction in themselves – sometimes observed by hundreds of spectators on **Burleigh Headlands** as they ride the southeasterly swell to the beach.

The small **Burleigh Heads National Park** embraces coastal rainforest and heathlands. A 3-km (1¼-mile) walking trail around the rocky headland departs from the Burleigh Heads Information Centre (1711 Gold Coast Highway, on northern side of Tallebudgera Creek). It leads past mangroves, eucalypts and pandanus which shelter reptiles, wallabies, bandicoots and koalas – all a world away from the concrete coastal jungle. The track emerges at Goodwin Terrace, at which point you can either follow the boardwalk along the foreshore or head back to the information centre via a steep rainforest walk.

Wildlife sanctuaries

West of Burleigh Heads, **David Fleay's Wildlife Park ⑪** (Kabool Road, West Burleigh; daily 9am–5pm; admission charge; tel: 5576 2411) is well worth a visit. The park functions both as a research centre and a sanctuary for endangered and injured wildlife. Now operated by the Queensland Parks and Wildlife Service, it continues the work of the

Map on page 90

TIP

Descendants of the Kombumerri people, who once inhabited the area around Burleigh Heads, operate guided tours that explain the significance of rock formations and middens (Paradise Dreaming; tel: 5578 3044).

BELOW: catching a wave at Burleigh Heads.

Feeding times for the squawking lorikeets which flock to the Currumbin Sanctuary are at 8am and 4pm. Wear easily washable clothing and a hat.

BELOW: Natural Bridge, Cave Creek.

late naturalist and platypus breeder Dr David Fleay, who established the park in the 1950s. It comprises five distinct habitats, from tropical rainforest, the habitat of tree kangaroos and cassowaries, to a nocturnal/arid zone, home to lesser-known species such as the great bilby and the yellow-bellied glider. It's a wonderful place to familiarise yourself with native Australian species.

Heading south to Coolangatta is **Currumbin Wildlife Sanctuary** ⓬ (28 Tomewin Street, Currumbin; tel: 5534 1266; www.currumbin-sanctuary.org.au), the Gold Coast's longest-running attraction, famous for its rainbow lorikeets. The story goes that founder Alex Griffiths began hand-feeding these chattering, brightly coloured parrots in the late 1940s to distract them from his favourite cultivated flowers, which they would attack in search of nectar. His feeding sessions attracted so many visitors that he formalised it into a business.

The sanctuary has evolved significantly since then. Run by the National Trust of Queensland since 1976, it now holds Australia's biggest collection of native animals, including 1,500 species of mammals, reptiles and birds. Nearly half a million visitors pass through the turnstiles annually to see birds of prey, cuddly koalas, crocodiles and wildlife shows featuring venomous snakes. It's a natural haven amidst the Gold Coast's surfeit of artificial splendours and excess.

Coolangatta

Coolangatta ⓭ is at the easy-going end of the Gold Coast, a border town that melds seamlessly with **Tweed Heads**, its twin on the southern side of the Queensland–New South Wales border. The Gold Coast's international airport is located at nearby Bilinga, but, thus far, Coolangatta has been spared the full brunt of high-rise development. Located 102 km (63 miles) south of Brisbane, the laid-back resort remains popular for family holidays and is a top surfing destination. It has great beaches, rolling surf and is well-positioned for day trips to the hinterland.

Local landmarks Point Danger and Mount Warning are among the few places Captain Cook felt inspired enough to name along this part of the coast. The town is named after the *Coolangatta*, an 88-ton brigantine that came to grief in 1843. Views from the Point Danger headland along the coast are lovely, plus it's a great spot to watch the surfing action. There's a memorial at the lighthouse to Captain Cook made of cast-iron ballast jettisoned from his ship, the *Endeavour*.

Springbrook National Park

Less than an hour's drive west of the Gold Coast, the **Springbrook National Park ⓮** (tel: 5533 5147; www.epa.qld.gov.au) offers a cool and tranquil refuge from the noisy, urbanised lowlands. The park occupies the northern rim of an ancient volcano, which was once centred on Mount Warning in New South Wales. It is made up of three reserves: the **Springbrook Plateau** section, the **Mount Cougal** section and the **Natural Bridge** section, remarkable for an intriguing rock-

arch formation over Cave Creek *(see Tip below)*. Listed as a World Heritage site, the park preserves subtropical rainforest, eucalypt forest and montane heath. It's a stunning landscape of ancient trees, gorges and waterfalls.

An extensive network of walking paths has been cut through all three sections of the park. The Springbrook Plateau section, in particular, has lookouts affording spectacular views, albeit shrouded in cloud on overcast days. There are information displays at all major track entrances, and a small information centre operates from the historic Springbrook schoolhouse, where you can pick up a booklet of the park's trail network.

Two bitumen roads lead to Springbrook Plateau, which is 29 km (18 miles) from Mudgeeraba and 34 km (21 miles) from Nerang.

Lamington National Park

The sheer beauty of **Lamington National Park ⓯**, another World Heritage site, defies description. The park lies in the McPherson Ranges directly behind the Gold Coast,

Map on page 90

Thanks to an hour's time lag between New South Wales and Queensland, New Year's Eve attracts big crowds, with revellers surging across the border in order to celebrate twice.

BELOW LEFT: koalas in their natural habitat.
BELOW RIGHT: Purlingbrook Falls, Springbrook National park.

TIP

A short circular walk affords marvellous views of the natural arch over Cave Creek *(pictured far left)*. Look out for noisy pittas, rainforest dragons and rainbow lorikeets in the forest. At night, you can see the large colony of glow-worms inside the cave under the rock arch. Natural Bridge is 30 km (18 miles) from Nerang *(see Springbrook National Park, above)*.

Bright green algae coats the swamps around the trees on South Stradbroke Island.

TIP

There are several places to stay in Lamington National Park. Two of the best are the sophisticated eco-resort, O'Reilly's Rainforest Guesthouse (tel: 5544 0644; www.oreillys.com.au), and the rustic retreat, Binna Burra Lodge (tel: 1800 074 260; www.binnaburra lodge.com.au). Or you can pitch a tent at one of the many bushcamp grounds under the aegis of Queensland Parks and Wildlife Service (tel: 5533 3584; www.epa.qld.gov.au).

RIGHT: the Couran Cove Resort.

about a 90-minute drive inland. This vast and dramatic park of subtropical rainforest, wild-flower heath, tall open forests and splashing waterfalls offers some of Australia's best bushwalking, with several appealing mountain lodges to stay in.

The park is also the natural habitat for a realm of rarely seen bird life – a place of pilgrimage for "twitchers" who come here in search of the rare, the exotic and the elusive. British television naturalist David Attenborough has filmed here, drawn by the usually elusive black-and-yellow regent bowerbirds that descend en masse to be hand fed. Satin bowerbirds, collectors of all things blue, also flutter amid the guests, vying with king parrots that perch on heads, hands and shoulders in noisy expectation of food. The resort's annual Bird Week draws twitchers on the lookout for such creatures as Albert's lyrebird, the rufous scrub bird and Baillon's crake.

Tamborine Mountain

Tamborine Mountain ⑯, 40 km (25 miles) from Southport, comprises three distinct settlements – Mount Tamborine, North Tamborine and Eagle Heights – dispersed around a compact mountain plateau (550 metres/1,800 ft) with stunning views. These so-called heritage communities have been taken over by craft shops, galleries and tearooms, set up to cater for the Gold Coast tour buses. The real attraction of the area is the natural beauty of the surrounding rainforests, streams and waterfalls within the 12 reserves that make up the Tamborine National Park.

Well-defined walking tracks mark the terrain at Joalah, Cedar Creek, The Knoll, MacDonald Park, Palm Grove and Witches Falls – among the most scenic spots. Contact Tamborine Mountain Visitor Information Centre (tel: 5545 3200) for detailed information or Queensland Parks and Wildlife Service (tel: 5576 0271; www.epa.qld.gov.au).

Thanks to rich volcanic soil and cooler temperatures, the region also supports avocado, kiwi fruit and rhubarb farms – and is an emerging wine district, with half a dozen

cellar-door outlets, including a distillery selling schnapps.

North and South Stradbroke Islands

These attractive bay islands were connected when Captain Cook sailed past in 1770 – and remained that way until 1896 when a storm caused a breakthrough at Jumpinpin.

South Stradbroke is the smaller and less populated island, with 22 km (14 miles) of ocean beach fringing national park containing remnant livistona rainforest and melaleuca wetlands. The main centre of civilisation is the multi-million-dollar **Couran Cove Island Resort** (tel: 5597 9000). Some of its 350 rooms are free-standing bush cabins; others perch on stilts over a lagoon. Four km (2½ miles) north of Couran Cove is the low-key **South Stradbroke Resort** (tel: 5577 3311), which began as a popular stopover for Moreton Bay yachties. Locals still refer to it by its original name, Tippler's. Access to South Stradbroke Island is by resort ferry (both resorts maintain separate services from Runaway Bay, 9 km (5 miles) north of Surfers Paradise or by water taxi.

Activity on **North Stradbroke Island** – "Straddie" to locals – focuses around the townships of Dunwich, Amity Point and Point Lookout. Barges and ferry offload visitors at **Dunwich**, a settlement dating to 1827 when convicts were deployed to load and unload ships unable to navigate the shallow waters of Moreton Bay.

The island's resorts are mainly clustered around **Point Lookout** and **Main Beach**. **Amity Point**, on the island's northern tip, retains the atmosphere of a fishing village and supports a community of fishermen.

North and South Gorge, high above the rocky headland at Point Lookout, afford sightings of migrating humpback whales from June to November. Turtles, manta rays and dolphins are seen all year round.

The stunning 445-hectare (1,100-acre) **Blue Lake National Park**, 10 km (6 miles) east of Dunwich, was subject to restricted access at the time of writing. For updates, contact QPWS (tel: 3821 9000). ❏

Map on page 90

Stradbroke Island-born Aboriginal poet and activist, the late Oodgeroo Noonuccal, formerly known as Kath Walker, led often bitter confrontations over mining damage to the environment. The Noonuccal Nughie Centre in Ballow Road conducts cultural tours and sells arts and crafts made by the island's Aboriginal community.

BELOW: shallow mid-off. The thrills of beach cricket.

RESTAURANTS, CAFÉS & BARS

Restaurants

The Gold Coast has an estimated 500 restaurants, but a high proportion of these are decidedly average – which makes the stand-out venues really stand out. Avoid the franchises. Rather, seek out the smaller, owner-operated dining venues that cater for locals as well as tourists. There are plenty of these along the coast outside the most concentrated shopping areas. Here are a few recommendations.

Absynthe
Q1 complex, 9 Hamilton Avenue, Surfers Paradise
Tel: 5504 6466
Open: L Mon–Fri, D Mon–Sat. **$$$**

Celebrated French chef Meyjitte Boughenout lends a dash of Gallic élan to the 80-storey Q1 building. Famous for juxtaposing the most unlikely of flavours to create taste sensations that are as beguiling as they are unexpected. His Golden Egg, for example, combines an egg-mousse bisque with soya jelly and edible gold leaf.

BlueFire Churrascaria
Shop 31 Marina Mirage, Seaworld Drive, Main Beach
Tel: 5557 8877
www.bluefiregrill.com.au
Open: L & D daily. **$$$**
Water views and flame-grilled meat dishes carved at the table make this a firm favourite with carni-

vores. The concept is Portuguese. It's cooking as entertainment. The bill of fare mainly comprises seafood, chicken, lamb, beef and pork grilled on skewers.

The Broadbeach Tavern
Old Burleigh Road, corner of Charles Avenue, Broadbeach
Tel: 5538 4111
www.broadbeachtavern.com.au
Open: L & D Mon–Sat. **$**
Good food from an extensive and surprisingly inexpensive menu. However, most people come here for the live entertainment, on seven nights a week. Check the website for details.

The Fireplace
The Hyatt Regency Sanctuary Cove
Tel: 5530 1234
www.bluefiregrill.com.au
Open: L & D daily. **$$$**
If you're not deterred by the expense, the Fireplace offers a wonderful gastronomic experience. Succulent grilled meats and seafood are the speciality of the house, and the ambience is reminiscent of a private dining room in a large manor house. Chefs are on show interacting with diners whilst meticulously preparing the freshest local produce.

Omeros Brothers Seafood Restaurant
Marina Mirage, 74 Seaworld Drive, Main Beach
Tel: 5591 7222
www.omerosbros.com

Open: L & D daily. **$$**
Ideal for decently cooked seafood with a minimum of fuss. The decor is lavish and the bill of fare is laced with retro favourites like Oysters Mornay, Mussels á la Parisienne, Steak Diane and Veal Funghi.

Oskars on Burleigh
43 Goodwin Terrace, Burleigh Heads
Tel: 5576 3722
www.oskars.com.au
Open: L & D daily. **$$$**
Oskars has been a Gold Coast institution for 25 years – and it's easy to see why. The menu changes daily, but the twice-baked sandcrab soufflé with tomato compote, rocket and walnut salad is a frequent entrée. The beach location, with sweeping ocean views north to Surfers Paradise, is a strong component of its appeal.

Ristorante Fellini
Marina Mirage, Seaworld Drive, Main Beach
Tel: 5531 0300
Open: L & D daily. **$$**
Brothers Carlo and Tony Percuoco dish up superb Italian cuisine within their elegant, award-winning restaurant. Try the *pasta linguette allo zafferano* – saffron-infused long flat pasta cooked with Moreton Bay bug meat in a light cream sauce. Like other entries on the menu, the dish makes a virtue of

simplicity, and is a perennial favourite with regulars. The restaurant looks across the Southport Broadwater, and behind it stands the brothers Percuoco's pasta shop, Pastificio Fellini, where the available lines include ravioli with fresh deep-sea ocean trout cooked in Sauvignon.

Shuck
20 Tedder Avenue,
Main Beach
Tel: 5528 4286
Open: L & D daily. **$$**
As the name implies, Shuck is noted for oysters. The kitchen also churns out excellent seafood chowder, crab lasagne and bouillabaisse dishes... as well as steaks. Seating is mainly alfresco, with courtyard tables overlooking a passing parade of poseurs. The Oz Mod cuisine, open-air setting, and general feeling of relaxation make it exactly right for this trendy Gold Coast precinct.

Volare
2729 Gold Coast Highway,
Broadbeach
Tel: 5592 2622
www.volarerestaurant.com.au
Open: L & D daily. **$$$**
Volare is a long-established Italian restaurant mainly specialising in seafood. House speciality is *zuppa di pesce*, an Italian version of bouillabaisse. Decor is big on embellishment and low

on understatement, with a wagon-wheel chandelier suspended above arches and statuary. Aimed towards tourists but good fun.

Cafés and Bars

Charlie's 24-Hour Café, Restaurant & Bar
Cavill Avenue,
Surfers Paradise
Tel: 5538 5285
Open: 24 hours a day. **$**
Everyone ends up at Charlie's sometime during their stay in Surfers Paradise. Well located and affordable, Charlie's hasn't closed its doors since 1976. Fare includes grilled fish, pizzas, pasta, steaks, salads and club sandwiches.

Chicane
6/20 Queensland Avenue,
Broadbeach
Tel: 5504 7611
Open: L & D daily. **$$**
Chicane serves up appealing dishes in stylish but relaxed surroundings. Try the blacklip mussels in ginger, tamarind and hot sour broth.

Dee and Paul's Rainbow Bay Café
13 Ward Street,
Rainbow Bay
Tel: 5536 4999
Open: daily 7am–6.30pm. **$**
One block from the beach, the Rainbow Café offers generous breakfasts and filling snacks. Scrambled eggs, bacon and toast

(A$7); mixed grill of steak, sausages, eggs, bacon, tomato, toast and chips (A$10). The café is decorated with surfing memorabilia, much of it contributed by the clientele. You could well find yourself rubbing shoulders with well-known surfing identities like Joel Parkinson, Mick Fanning and Dave Davidson.

Melba's
46 Cavill Avenue
Surfers Paradise
Tel: 5592 6922
www.melbas.net.au daily
Open: 7.30am–5am daily. **$$**
Wild nights have been known to begin and end in Melba's horseshoe-shaped bar and upstairs nightclub. Melba's restaurant offers steak, seafood and pizza. Breakfast is popular, but the place doesn't really start to pump until the

lunch crowd surges in. Locals who drop by for after-work drinks often stay until the wee small hours. Meals and drinks are affordable – but the longer you stay, the more you'll spend.

Sage
Shop 5, 20 Queensland Avenue, Broadbeach
Tel: 5538 9938
Open: L & D daily. **$$**
Sage enjoys a central location. It offers good food, efficient service – and makes a fine place to watch Gold Coasters promenade.

PRICE CATEGORIES

Prices are for a three-course meal per person with house wine:
$ = A$60 and under
$$ = A$60–90
$$$ = A$90–120
$$$$ = A$120 and over

Welcome to
**THE SURF CLUB
KURRAWA**

Voted
'Best Club Gold Coast'
'Best Supporters Club in
Queensland'

OPEN FOR
Breakfast from 8.00am
Lunch from 11.30am
Dinner from 5.30pm
7 DAYS A WEEK

...alfresco dining at its finest...
· Superb Food
· Magnificent Views
· Delightful Ambience

For Enquiries

LEFT: chefs at work.
RIGHT: good value food can be found in the clubs.

DARLING DOWNS

Inland from Brisbane, the countryside is almost entirely ignored by tourists. Here, the tablelands give way to the Darling Downs, a vast area of beautiful rolling plains and rich soil, and a centre for the dairy, beef, wool and horse-stud industries

Brisbane

Fat cattle, sheep farms, booming wineries and stately homes mark this fertile region, stretching north to Kingaroy in the South Burnett, west to Roma on the Warrego Highway and south to Goondiwindi and Stanthorpe, the only place in the world that celebrates Christmas twice. It's prime motoring territory, studded with bed and breakfasts and pretty towns – and, for bushwalkers, highland rainforest parks with surreal granite outcrops.

Ipswich

Thanks to a fast motorway, **Ipswich** ❶ lies within easy commuting distance of Brisbane (about a 40-minute drive). As Queensland's oldest provincial city, it has a rich history and is renowned for its architectural and cultural heritage.

Rivalry with Queensland's capital goes back to the 1860s, when Ipswich challenged Brisbane as the colony's pre-eminent city. The influential squatters' lobby favoured Ipswich as the starting point for a railway. The first section to Grandchester was opened in 1865, reaching Toowoomba and the Darling Downs a couple of years later.

For 130 years, the North Ipswich Railway Workshops remained a major economic and cultural force – employing more than 1,500 people at

any one time, and reaching a peak of 3,000 after World War Two. The complex has now been reborn as the **Workshops Rail Museum** (North Street, North Ipswich; daily 9.30am–5pm; admission charge; tel: 3432 5100; www. theworkshops.qm.qld. gov.au) and comprises a streetscape of robust brick industrial buildings in late Victorian style, the oldest of which date from 1878. Among the exhibits is Australia's oldest operating engine (from 1865) and a vice-regal car built in 1903 for the

Map on page 106

LEFT: the joey of an eastern grey kangaroo.
BELOW: trained sheep-dog in action.

exclusive use of the governor of Queensland and visiting royalty. There's a scale model railway of Queensland's rail network, and a working blacksmiths' shop.

Ipswich has 54 National Trust-listed buildings spread about the city, all described in the *Ipswich City Heritage Trails* pamphlet, available from the tourist information centre (corner of Brisbane Street and d'Arcy Doyle Place; tel: 3281 0555). Heading along Burnett, Limestone or Milford Streets, you'll see some of the fine old houses featured. **St Paul's Church** in Brisbane Street dates from 1859, making it the oldest Anglican church in Queensland, with the colony's first pipe organ.

After languishing for decades, the city has lately come to life. At the time of writing, plans are afoot to create a precinct linking the inner city with the railway workshops and the Bremer River. The population of 137,000 includes a strong multicul-tural component, which is reflected in the burgeoning art scene. Located in the Old Town Hall, the **Ipswich Art Gallery** (d'Arcy Doyle Place; daily 10am–5pm; tel: 3810 7222) offers a dynamic programme of visual arts, and has a popular children's gallery.

An alternative form of family entertainment is on show at **Willow-bank Raceway** (Champions Way, Willowbank; tel: 5461 5461; www.willowbank-raceway.com.au), which stages year-round drag-racing events.

Warwick

Warwick ❷, 162 km (100 miles) southwest of Brisbane, promotes itself as the 'Rose and Rodeo City' – after the signature rose that grows in its parks and because of its well-attended rodeo held every October. The arrival of the railway from Ipswich in 1871 sparked a boom that, by 1936, had established War-wick as the second-biggest city on

The stylish municipal incinerator, built in 1936 in Queen's Park, was converted to a theatre in 1969 and is now home to the Ipswich Little Theatre (tel: 3812 2389).

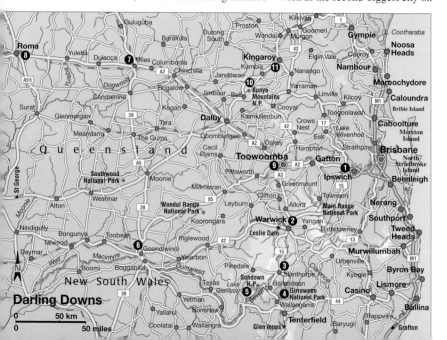

the Darling Downs. Essentially, it is an agricultural centre in a pleasant location with interesting architecture. Modern sprawl has obscured some of the town's early grandeur, but fine examples of colonial timber and sandstone architecture – churches, public buildings and grand residences – survive.

Something of the flavour of 19th-century Warwick can be gleaned from the former **St Mary's Church**, 163 Palmerin Street – dating from 1865, and the city's earliest sandstone church. However, the best way to begin an appraisal of Warwick's 30 heritage-listed sites is to visit **Pringle Cottage** (open Wed–Fri 10am–noon, 2–4pm, Sat and Sun 11am–4pm; tel: 4661 3234) in Dragon Street, within the grounds of the **Warwick and District Historical Museum** (tel: 4661 1527 for heritage trail booklets and tours by arrangement). This two-storey cottage, dating from the 1870s, is filled with an interesting collection of old contraptions, costumes, telephones and photos; it was the residence of John McCulloch, the mason responsible for most of the district's sandstone buildings – including the Court House (1885), St Mark's Anglican Church (1874), St Andrew's Presbyterian Church (1869), the Methodist Church (1875) and the Central School (1874).

Warwick Railway Station (mid-1880s) in Lyons Street is also worth looking at, as are Warwick's fine old hotels. O'Mahoney's (1890), formerly the National Hotel, in Grafton Street, and the Criterion Hotel (1917), in Palmerin Street, are still good for a beer.

The **Jackie Howe Memorial**, on the corner of Glengallan Road and the Cunningham Highway (notable for the large shears on top) honours Warwick's favourite son; legendary shearer Jackie Howe, born on Canning Downs Station in 1861, holds the record (established in 1892) of having shorn 321 sheep with a set of hand shears in under eight hours.

Excursions from Warwick

A popular local excursion is to **Leslie Dam** – 13 km (8 miles) west of Warwick along the Cunningham Highway on the road to Goondiwindi – where you can go fishing, swimming and boating; there are picnic areas for day visitors and camping areas for longer stays.

About 50 km (31 miles) northeast of Warwick on the Cunningham Highway, the **Main Range National Park** (tel: 4666 1133) forms the western part of a semi-circle of mountains known as the Scenic Rim. This impressive wilderness is mostly dense rainforest, but there are areas where picnic tables, wood barbecues and toilets are provided. Have a bush picnic beside West Gap Creek near Cunningham's Gap, at the Pioneer Picnic Area at Spicer's Gap, or at Queen Mary Falls. Around these areas are walking tracks – the rest of the park is suitable only for experienced, well-

Map on page 106

TIP

The Warwick Visitor Information Centre, at 49 Albion Street (Mon–Fri 8.30am–5pm, Sat–Sun 10am–2pm; tel: 4661 3122), has plenty of material on the "Rose and Rodeo City", and neighbouring South Downs towns.

BELOW: Warwick in bloom.

BELOW: filling up for a road trip.

equipped bushwalkers. For spectacular views, head for Governor's Chair, Sylvester's and Fassifern lookouts.

Stanthorpe

The pleasant highland town of **Stanthorpe ❸** is best known for its climate, which the inhabitants have turned into a tourist attraction. Sitting at 915 metres (3,000 feet), bracing winters have inspired a mid-year Christmas complete with crackling hearths and festive hoopla, known as the Brass Monkey Festival, part of a whole Brass Monkey season.

The four-season climate means that fruit and vegetables flourish in the Granite Belt region just south of town, around the village of **Ballandean**, especially wine grapes: there are around 40 wineries within 20 km (12 miles) of Stanthorpe. If you plan to tour the wineries, it's a good idea to sign up with a tour operator, such as the Grape Escape Tour Company (tel: 1300 361 150) or Granite Highlands Maxi Tours (tel: 4681 3969) – for a winery crawl with lunch.

The temperate climate also appeals to sun-baked Brisbane residents, who make the 220-km (137-mile) journey to attend the numerous seasonal festivals. The Apple and Grape Harvest Festival is held in the early spring in even-numbered years, with street parades, sheep shearing and grape crushing. The Spring Wine Festival takes place every October, while winemaker Angelo Puglisi organises "Opera in the Vineyard" concerts every May Day weekend.

Considering its size, Stanthorpe (population 11,000) is a remarkably cosmopolitan town. This is largely due to its substantial Italian community *(see margin note)*. Delicatessens stock Italian specialities, and local butchers routinely prepare cuts for osso bucco and other Italian dishes.

The town has a good number of heritage buildings. The Federation-style **Post Office** sports an illuminated clock installed in 1903; the **Railway Station** (1881) recalls Stanthorpe's moment of eminence as a railhead; and the **Central Hotel** is everything you would expect of an old-fashioned pub.

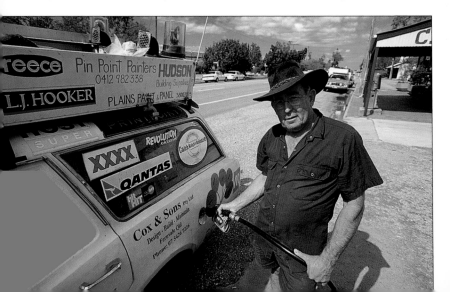

For a comprehensive rundown of where to go, and a copy of the district's *Cultural Heritage and Historic Building Trail* booklet, contact **Stanthorpe Visitor Information Centre** (28 Leslie Parade; daily 8.30am–5pm; tel: 4681 2057).

Girraween National Park

About 20 km (12 miles) south of Stanthorpe, on the border with New South Wales, a lovely place to enjoy the great outdoors is **Girraween National Park ◆**. Surreal granite outcrops, pristine forests and amazing wildlife are the highlights here, and there are plenty of walking trails to explore. Perhaps the best is the 10-km (6-mile) trek to the top of Mount Norman (1,265 metres/4,140 ft). Contact the visitors' centre (tel: 4684 5157) for information on camping and fees.

Sundown National Park

Another great place to explore is the **Sundown National Park ❺** (tel: 6737 5235), further west along the border with New South Wales (80 km/50 miles southwest of Stan-thorpe); it's a stunning wilderness area with spectacular steep-sided gorges, sharp ridges and towering granite rocks. Conventional vehicle access is at the southern end of the park. A four-wheel-drive route leads 16 km (10 miles) from Ballandean to the park's eastern boundary, followed by a rough 20-km (12½-mile) track to campsites at Burrows' Waterhole and Reedy Waterhole. Sundown has a history of grazing and mining – pastoral relics and old surface diggings remain.

Goondiwindi

West of Warwick, and still on the New South Wales border, **Goondiwindi ❻** is a rural community of about 5,000 people whose main distinguishing feature is a collective obsession with the racehorse Gunsynd, winner of races in the late 1960s and early 1970s. A **Monument to Gunsynd**, also known as the Goondiwindi Grey, stands beside the MacIntyre River in Apex Park. In the main street is the "Digger" statue, erected in 1922, and memorial gates (from 1949) in honour of

Map on page 106

Goondiwindi means "resting place for birds" and the area is true to its name, with over 200 species identified. Pick up a route guide from the tourist office to find the best bird-watching sites in and around town.

BELOW: paint that wagon. Then sit by it.

Goondiwindi's Victoria Hotel is one of the best-preserved colonial pubs in Queensland. Built in 1898, it has a display of memorabilia linked to a phenomenally successful racehorse: Gunsynd, the "Goondiwindi Grey".

BELOW: sheep farmers at auction.

the thousands of Australian soldiers who died in the two world wars.

Other eye-catchers are the **Victoria Hotel** and the **Customs House** – two well-preserved relics of Goondiwindi's 19th-century heyday. The pub closed its doors in 2005, but its ornate verandas and grandiose tower continue to dominate the street. The **Customs House Museum** (1 MacIntyre Street; Wed–Mon 10am–4pm; tel: 4671 3041) has a small collection of historical artefacts and a lovely flower-filled garden.

For more information, contact the tourist office at Goondiwindi-Waggamba Library (Bowen and McLean Streets; tel: 4671 2653; daily 9am–5pm).

Miles

In the small rural centre of **Miles ❼**, 220 km (137 miles) north of Goondiwindi, the highlight is the **Historical Village** in Murilla Street (daily 8am–5pm; admission charge; tel: 4627 1492). A 19th-century streetscape, including relocated heritage buildings, has been created by members of the local historical soci-

ety, and includes a general store, post office, bakery, barber shop, bootmaker, saddlery, café and bank.

The eccentric Prussian explorer Ludwig Leichardt *(see page 20)* established a crossroads here in 1844, and named it Dogwood Crossing after a locally occurring wild-flower. It was still known as Dogwood Crossing in 1878 when construction of the railway from Brisbane came to an unscheduled halt at Dogwood Creek. The delay dragged on so long that Dogwood Crossing became a temporary railhead for the west, complete with shops, stores and pubs. About this time, the town's name was changed to honour William Miles, the Queensland Colonial Secretary.

Today, **Dogwood Crossing** (Mon–Fri 8.30am–5pm; Sat–Sun 9am–4pm; tel: 4627 2455) is a community project illustrating how this small town was born, developed and prospered; it comprises a museum, library and multimedia resource centre, and gives a colourful insight into the growth of this little patch of the Downs.

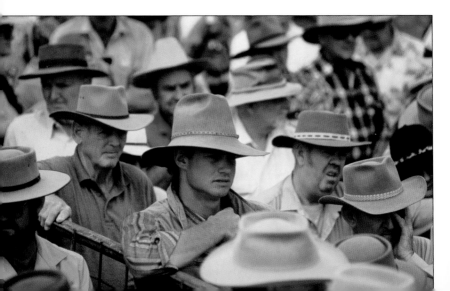

Roma

If you want to see how 10,000 head of cattle are sold in one morning, head for **Roma** ❽, 140 km (87 miles) west of Miles, which has Australia's largest cattle-selling centre – the **Roma Bungil Saleyard** (Quintin Street; Tues and Thur only; tel: 4622 1201).

Roma came to national attention in 1900 when a crew drilling for water hit gas by mistake. It was the first strike in Australia – and, to this day, sheep and cattle farms surrounding Roma are studded with oil and gas installations.

Roma's main tourist draw is **The Big Rig** (Riggers Road; daily 9am–5pm; admission charge; tel: 4622 4355) which traces the development of the industry through a series of interpretive panels and audio-visual presentations. Exhibits include a 1929 steam-powered oil-drilling rig that stands 45 metres (148 ft) high. The **Roma Visitor Information Centre** (tel: 1800 222 399) is in the same complex.

Another popular attraction is the **Romavilla Winery** (Injune Road; tel: 4622 1822). Established in 1863, it's Queensland's oldest winery.

Roma has its share of old pubs and *fin de siècle* houses, but its most arresting sight is the memorial avenue of bottle trees in **Wyndham Street**. Planted in 1920, each tree commemorates one of the 93 local men who fell during World War I.

The town comes alive over the Easter weekend, when it celebrates **Easter in the Country** with a rodeo, horseraces, parades and dancing.

Toowoomba

Hilly **Toowoomba** ❾ sits impressively on the rim of the Great Dividing Range, 700 metres (2,300 feet) above sea level, with the Darling Downs laid out before it. It's a pleasant place, with a passion for floral displays and in incredible 230 parks and gardens – hence its sobriquet, the "Garden City". It is colourful all year, but sensational in the springtime when flowers bloom.

At street level Toowoomba is very much a modern city, yet to raise your eyes above the awnings is to see façades little altered since the early decades of the 20th century. Toowoomba's beginnings date from around 1850, but it was the arrival of the railway in 1867 that brought prosperity, tree-lined streets and elegant Victorian buildings and the gardens it is so proud of. You can pick up a heritage trail brochure from the **Toowoomba Visitor Information Centre** (86 James Street; daily 9am–5pm; tel: 1800 331155 or 4639 3797).

Toowoomba **Railway Station**, opened in the 1870s, is a classic piece of Queensland architecture. The only thing which seems to have changed over time is the volume of passengers. In 1945, more than 230,000 people passed through; these days, the human flood has reduced to a mere trickle, with only one train per week connecting Toowoomba with Brisbane. The Railway Refreshment

Take a picnic to the **Ju Raku En Japanese Garden** (tel: 4631 2627), a few kilometres south of the centre of Toowoomba, in West Street. With walking trails around a lake, waterfalls and streams, it's a beautiful spot.

BELOW: an old petrol pump at Miles Historical Village.

Map on page 106

One council thoughtfully provides signs for those not blessed with a car full of impatient children.

BELOW: floral displays are lovingly maintained in Toowoomba, the "garden city".

Room next door functions as well as ever; it's elegant, old-fashioned and frequently booked out.

Other significant attractions include the **Cobb & Co. Museum** (27 Lindsay Street; daily 10am–4pm; admission charge; tel: 4639 1971), illustrating life in the horse-drawn age, and the **Royal Bulls Head Inn**, Drayton, where the original 1847 kitchen, hotel rooms and interior details have all been carefully restored. The **Empire Theatre** in Neil Street, built in 1911 and restored to art-deco splendour, is also worth a look. In Margaret Street, meanwhile, the post office and courthouse are two more majestic buildings dating from the 1870s.

Bunya Mountains National Park

Northwest of Toowoomba, the forested peaks of the **Bunya Mountains National Park 10**, 1000 metres (3,300 ft) above sea level, are home to a wide variety of wildlife, including wallabies, crimson rosellas and king parrots. The park is named after the bunya pines that thrive here.

Every few years these trees produce a crop of huge edible bunya nuts. But if you're walking in the forest during the nut season, between late January to April, beware of the falling fruits – they are heavy and the size of a pineapple. There's an extensive network of paths, ranging from a gentle discovery walk to a 10-km (6-mile) trek to the Big Falls Lookout. The three main camping and picnic areas are Dandabah, Burton's Well and Westcott. Dandabah has coin-operated barbecues and hot-water showers. Burton's Well has bush showers, Westcott does not. Cabins, guesthouses and rental houses are available near the park. Call the rangers, station (tel: 4668 3127) in Dandabah, near the southern entrance to the park, for more information.

Kingaroy

Kingaroy 11, 56 km (35 miles) northeast of the Bunya Mountains National Park, is the centre of Australia's most important peanut-growing area, and peanuts seem to dominate every facet of life in the town. Amongst Australians, the town is best known as the home of Queensland's notorious ex-premier, Sir Joh Bjelke-Petersen *(see page 27)*. Even in death, Sir Joh remains one the town's principal attractions, with twice-weekly tours of his property, **Bethany** (Peterson Drive, Kumbia; Wed, Sat 2pm; admission charge; tel: 4162 7046).

Kingaroy is the centre of a promising wine industry; the region produces award-winning wines and is rapidly challenging the Granite Belt's reputation as the state's premier wine area. The Kingaroy Information Art and Heritage precinct (1–8 Haley Street; tel: 4162 6272) has details of noted wineries and other South Burnett attractions – including the gastronomic pleasures of the district's olive groves, aquaculture farms and cheese factories. ❑

RESTAURANTS, CAFÉS & BARS

Ballandean

Barrel Room Café
354 Sundown Road
Tel: 4684 1226
Open: L daily. **$**
Pleasant Italian food
graciously served amid
130-year-old barrels
filled with port and
liqueur. Here you can
taste wines grown on
Stanthorpe's oldest
estate, established by
the Puglisi family in
1931 and still operated
by them.

The Vineyard Café
Vineyard Cottages, New
England Highway
Tel: 4684 1270
Open: L & D Sat–Sun. **$$**
In an old church and
surrounded by gardens
and vineyards, this
restaurant forms part of
a five-star resort.
Book ahead.

Bunya Mountains

Cider Gum Restaurant
20 Bunya Avenue
Tel: 4668 3131
Open: L daily, D Wed–Mon. **$$**
The menu incorporates
bush tucker-based
dishes such as quon-
dong aoli with bunya nut
and capsicum relish.

Goondiwindi

Gibbsy's Restaurant
Jolly Swagman Motor Inn,
1 Anderson Street
Tel: 4671 4560
Open: D Mon–Sat. **$$**
On the outskirts of
Goondiwindi, with an
extensive menu.

**The Townhouse
Restaurant**
110 Marshall Street
Tel: 4671 1855
Open: L Tues–Fri, D
Mon–Sat. **$$$**
In the main high street, a
popular place for special
occasions.

Ipswich

Cottons
Peppers Hidden Vale, 617
Mount Mort Road,
Grandchester
Tel: 5465 5900
Open: L & D daily. **$$$**
A 30-minute drive south-
west of Ipswich, this ele-
gant restaurant is part of
an upmarket resort.

Fentons Restaurant
17 Limestone Street
Tel: 3812 0424
Open: L Mon–Fri, D
Mon–Sat. **$$**
Delicious dishes show-
ing Western, Asian and
French influences.

Kingaroy

Bell Tower Restaurant
Corner of Schellbachs and
Haydens Road, Booie
Tel: 4162 7000
Open: L Tues–Sun,
D Fri–Sat. **$$$**
Located 6 km (4 miles)
from Kingaroy, this
stylish restaurant com-
mands fantastic views.

Burning Beats Café
194 Kingaroy Street
Tel: 4162 3932
Open: Wed–Fri 11am–late;
Sat 5pm–late. **$**
Award-winning formula of
live music and spicy

Asian food makes a
welcome change in
conservative Kingaroy.

Roma

**Golden Dragon
Restaurant**
60 McDowall Street
Tel: 4622 1717
Open: L Mon, Wed–Fri,
D daily. **$$**
Traditional Chinese cook-
ing adapted to Outback
tastes with happy results.

**The Overlander Home-
stead Motel**
44,767 Warrego Highway,
Tel: 4622 3555
Open: D daily. **$$$**
No-frills Outback restaur-
ant with good chargrilled
steak.

Stanthorpe

Anna's Restaurant
1 O'Mara Terrace,
Tel: 4681 1265
Open: D Mon–Sat. **$$**
Anna Pompetti's old-
fashioned eatery is a
Stanthorpe institution.

Toowoomba

Albert's Restaurant
Burke and Wills Hotel
554 Ruthven Street
Tel: 4632 2433
Open: D daily. **$$$**
This well-run restaurant
won the 2005 Darling
Downs Signature Dish
competition.

Fire+Ice
Ruthven Street
Tel: 1800 008 269
Open: L & D Mon–Sat. **$$**
A sleek restaurant which
has been garnering

awards from day one.

Gip's Restaurant
120 Russell Street
Tel: 4638 3588
Open: L daily, D Mon–Sat. **$$**
Asian and Western
fusion, including such
dishes as tempura barra-
mundi, and chili pork and
cuttlefish salad.

Picnic Point Restaurant
164 Tourist Road
Tel: 4631 5101
Open: L Tues–Sun, D
Tues–Sat. **$$**
Eclectic menu and won-
derful scenic location.

Warwick

Bramble Patch
8 Albion Street
Tel: 4661 9022
Open: L daily. **$**
Light meals feature
gourmet preserves and
ice creams from the
family berry farm.

**Spring Creek
Mountain Café**
1503 Spring Creek Road,
Killarny
Tel: 4664 7101
Open: L Wed–Sun, D by
appointment. **$$**
40 km (25 miles) south of
Warwick, this appealing
café offers great views
and food. BYO.

PRICE CATEGORIES

Prices are for a three-
course meal per person
with house wine:
$ = A$60 and under
$$ = A$60–100
$$$ = A$100 and over

SUNSHINE COAST

This area really lives up to the promise of its appealing name. There are golden beaches, volcanic peaks and verdant landscapes, together with towns that marry an affection for the past with an innovative approach to the future, whether they are concentrating on wildlife attractions or fusion food

Brisbane ●

The Sunshine Coast, about an hour's drive north of Brisbane, is one of the most gorgeous stretches of Queensland's coastline. The region extends from Caloundra at the tip of Bribie Island, beyond Noosa Heads to Rainbow Beach, its northernmost point. It is backed by the dramatic Glass House Mountains to the west, which rise sheer from the grassy plains. Less brash and commercial than the Gold Coast, its mix of high-rise development and relaxed beach accommodation is characterised by long expanses of golden beach. Laid-back resorts like Maroochydore and Coolum fill up with families during the school holidays, but it's the chic resort of Noosa that exemplifies the lifestyle of the Sunshine Coast. Inland, the national parks and mountain resorts – "the green behind the gold" – offer a refreshing alternative to the sea and sand.

Glass House Mountains National Park

Motoring north from Brisbane on the Bruce Highway, you'll catch your first glimpses of the **Glass House Mountains ❶** – a cluster of craggy volcanic peaks towering over a scenic patchwork of bushland, pine plantations and small farms. The steep-sided and heavily

eroded mountains were formed by volcanic activity millions of years ago. They are so named because of tricks of reflected light on the rain-damped peaks, first noted by Captain Cook from offshore, and the stuff of Aboriginal legend *(see box on page 117)*.

The well-drained slopes of rich volcanic soil are ideal for growing pineapples, which are sold at numerous roadside stalls, along with avocados and other locally grown fruit. The region is also the home of the

Map on page 116

LEFT: the Sunshine Coast lives up to its name. **BELOW:** climbing a dune in the Great Sandy National Park.

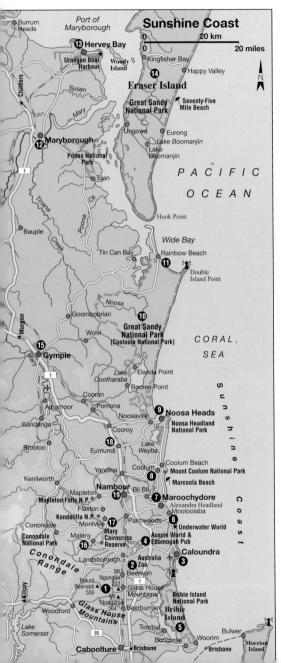

Sunshine Coast

Queensland nut, now better known worldwide as the macadamia nut.

Eight of the 16 peaks fall within the 920-hectare (2,270-acre) **Glass House Mountains National Park** (tel: 5494 3983), where remnants of eucalypt woodland and mountain heath provide refuge for rare and threatened plants.

For the best views of the region's geological showpiece, come off the Bruce Highway and join the slower scenic roads that snake their way among them. The Aboriginal owners, the Gubbi Gubbi people, regard the mountains as sacred, frowning on attempts to climb them, so trails have been created within the national park, presenting walkers with various levels of difficulty. The circuits on **Mount Beerwah** (556 m/1,824 ft) and **Mount Tibrogargen** (364 m/1,194 ft) are for experienced bush-walkers only. The track on **Mount Ngungun** (253 m/830 ft) is less taxing, though with challenging sections. Other tracks have been cut at **Mount Beerburrum**, **Wild Horse Mountain**, **Glass House Mountains Lookout** and the **Beerwah Forest**.

An excellent campground at Coochin Creek is accessed via a forestry track off Roys Road, east of Beerwah. For general information about national parks in Queensland, visit www.epa.qld.gov.au. For specific information about Glass House Mountains National Park contact the Queensland Parks and Wildlife officer at 61 Bunya Street, Maleny, tel: 5494 3983. For campground permits, call 13 13 04 or book online via the EPA website.

While in the vicinity, it's worth checking out the **Spirit of Cobb & Co.** complex (tel: 5496 9588) at the corner of Old Gympie Road and Mount Beerwah Road, in the township of Glass House Mountains. Built around an authentic 1860 Cobb & Co. changing station, the operation includes a working blacksmith's shop, where horse-drawn carriages are built from scratch. Visitors also learn how to make damper, Australian bush bread made from a simple water and flour dough, cooked in coals or a camp oven.

Steve Irwin's Australia Zoo

One of Queensland's top tourist attractions is crocodile-handler Steve Irwin's **Australia Zoo ❷** (daily 9am–4.30pm; admission charge; tel: 5436 2000; www.crocodilehunter. com), on the Glass House Mountains Tourist Drive at Beerwah. Irwin's television show, *The Crocodile Hunter*, earned him an international reputation – and he has translated that success into a multi-million dollar wildlife park. Australian wildlife is well represented in the park, though Irwin sees no problem in displaying tigers, cheetahs, Asian elephants, camels, Komodo dragons and even South American macaws alongside native species. It's all about spectacle. Irwin has built a 5,000-seat outdoor stadium – he calls it the Animal Planet Crocoseum – where, among other things, he hand-feeds croco-

diles, puts tigers through their paces and handles venomous snakes.

Caloundra

The first major town at the southern end of the Sunshine Coast is **Caloundra ❸**, a pleasant resort with a sparkling coastline and dramatic hinterland parks. Its magnificent beaches draw surfing and fishing fans, while a variety of man-made attractions, including Australia Zoo, Aussie World and the Ettamogah Pub, make it popular with families.

Caloundra has been transformed from a sleepy backwater into one of the fastest growing cities in Australia. In 1961, the population of the municipal area stood at less than 3,000. By 2005, it had reached 88,500, a good percentage of which is made up of commuters working in Brisbane. Given the town's proximity to Brisbane – about an hour's drive – it's surprising that the population explosion took so long to ignite.

Bulcock Street in Caloundra's Central Business District (CBD) has morphed, virtually overnight, into a busy food and retail precinct of

Map on page 116

Crocodile Hunter Steve Irwin's high profile (particularly in the USA) draws huge crowds to his Australia Zoo. The man himself is often on display.

BELOW: Mount Tibrogargen with Mount Coonowrin in the distance.

Mountain Spirits

Named by Captain Cook in 1770, the Glass House Mountains hold great significance for the Gubbi Gubbi Aboriginal people. According to legend, each peak represents one member of a family of mountain spirits, the offspring of Tibrogargen and his wife Beerwah. Fearful of flooding and the safety of his pregnant wife, Tibrogargen appealed to his eldest and strongest son, Coonowrin, to protect his mother, but the frightened boy abandoned her. Tibrogargen beat his son and cast him off, hence the wide valley between father and son. The many streams coursing through the mountains are the tears shed by the family over the disgraced Coonowrin.

TIP

If you like a thrill you can explore the Sunshine Coast on a Harley Davidson, in a souped-up trike or in a vintage Tiger Moth. **Freedom Wheels** (tel: 5448 4200; mob: 0403 680 507; www.free-domwheels. com.au) offers excursions lasting from an hour to a full day, as well as extended tours combining the thrill of both Harley Davidson and Tiger Moth.

BELOW: the Ettamogah Pub tilts in all directions.

boutiques, coffee bars, sidewalk cafés, pubs and restaurants. Residential towers have sprouted along the coastline, and property values in hinterland villages have skyrocketed.

While senior citizens continue to wet a line in Pumicestone Passage, the picturesque channel that separates Caloundra from nearby Bribie Island, Caloundra's recreational emphasis rests on the excellence of its surf beaches. Life Savers patrol Golden Beach, Bulcock Beach, Kings Beach, Dicky Beach, Currimundi, Wurtulla and Buddina. A coastal path from Golden Beach to Buddina has been designed to link with similar paths in Maroochydore and Noosa.

The **Old Lighthouse** on Canberra Terrace is the city's oldest building and one of the few historic structures still standing amid all the new development. First erected in 1896, this venerable structure used a kerosene lamp to guide shipping into Moreton Bay until 1942, then electricity until 1968 when it fell into disuse.

At the **Queensland Air Museum** (7 Pathfinder Drive, Caloundra Airport; daily 10am–4pm; admission charge; tel: 5492 5930; www.qam.com.au), aviation buffs will find 40 historic aircraft including a collection of post-World War II de Havillands and Australia's oldest DC3.

To find out more, contact the Caloundra Visitor Information Centre, 7 Caloundra Road, Caloundra, tel: 5420 6240; www.caloundratourism.com.au.

Aussie World and the Ettamogah Pub

For those who enjoy old-fashioned fun parks, a visit to **Aussie World** ❹ (daily 9am–5pm; admission charge; tel: 5494 5444; www.aussieworld.com.au) – off the Bruce Highway at Palmview, northwest of Caloundra – is just the ticket. This low-key park of about 30 rides and games is reminiscent of a 1960s fairground. Set in native gardens, it sells didgeridoos, dot paintings and other Aboriginal-themed merchandise.

Next door is the distinctive **Etta-mogah Pub**, a working tavern built to resemble the imaginary Outback hotel made famous by cartoonist Ken Maynard in *Australian Post* maga-

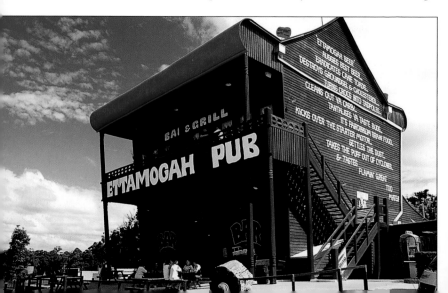

zine. Maynard's drawings pictured the building tilting crazily in all directions. The real-life Ettamogah Pub has been built exactly as Maynard drew it, only to larger-than-life scale.

Bribie Island

Across the Pumicestone Passage from Caloundra is the northern tip of **Bribie Island ❺**. Until the opening of a bridge in 1963, Bribie Island was mainly known as a destination for Brisbane-based excursion ferries bringing day trippers to a place of peaceful isolation. Today the island, which measures 34 km (21 miles) from end to end, functions as a dormitory suburb for commuters and a haven for retirees. Most of its 17,500 residents are gathered at the southern end, 70 km (43 miles) north of Brisbane, accessed via a turnoff from the Bruce Highway, near the Caboolture exit. The remaining 80 percent of its area is taken up by the bushland and beaches of **Bribie Island National Park** (Visitor Information Centre: 48 Bentbrow Street; tel: 3408 9026; www.caboolturetourism.com.au). This is a truly beautiful reserve. More

than 350 bird species have been identified within it, and sightings of turtles, dugongs and dolphins are frequent in the adjoining Moreton Bay Marine Park.

Mooloolaba and Maroochydore

North of Caloundra, the residential towers of **Mooloolaba ❻**, painted in Mediterranean hues, signal a brave new resort, quite literally on the way up. Just about every other prime site along Mooloolaba's esplanade has been redeveloped, with apartment towers offering the standard street level mix of sidewalk cafés, boutiqu-s and designer shops. Locals who have lived through Mooloolaba's pressure-cooker transition from fishing village to high-rise resort seem bemused by the changes, but they are outnumbered by new settlers smitten by the gloss.

Few café precincts in the world are better positioned to take advantage of crashing waves and spectacular sea views. The local council, for its part, has landscaped the seafront, installing fanciful bollards and surfboard-

Map on page 116

The first European to set foot on Bribie Island's sandy shores was Matthew Flinders in 1799. The township of Bongaree is named after Flinders's Aboriginal companion.

BELOW: Caloundra Head.

Life of a Recluse

Scottish-born Ian Fairweather (1891–1974), arguably Australia's greatest painter, lived the life of a recluse on Bribie Island. After serving in the British Army in India, he voyaged from Darwin to Indonesia on a homemade raft in 1952, settling on then remote Bribie Island in the following year. After Fairweather's death, vandals burned his Polynesian-style grass hut. A stone and plaque commemorates the site at the corner of First Avenue and Hunter Street, long since engulfed by suburbia.

shaped benches. Fine views are offered from any balcony or pavement café. The eye follows the tree-lined arc of the sandy Spit to Point Cartwright lighthouse. Trawlers chug down Mooloolaba Harbour, past canal developments and marinas. It's particularly picturesque when yachts taking part in the annual Sydney–Mooloolaba or the Auckland–Mooloolaba races weave among pleasure craft and charter boats coming and going.

Within the harbour, **Underwater World** (Parkyn Parade, Mooloolaba, daily 9am–6pm; admission charge; tel: 5444 8488; www.underwater world.com.au) is a marine park displaying sharks, rays, moray eels, turtles, octopi, reef fish, groupers and other sea critters. Visitors are invited to handle starfish and hermit crabs, swim with seals and scuba dive in the shark tank. There's also a 2.5-million-litre oceanarium containing thousands of reef fish.

The complex, spread over four levels, is itself part of a retail/restaurant precinct called **The Wharf**. While in the vicinity, do as the locals do and buy fresh prawns from the trawlermen's outlets near the Fisheries Board.

To Maroochydore

A few kilometres north of Mooloolaba is **Alexandra Headland** – a tower-strewn but relaxed coastal community known to locals as "Alex", where nothing much happens and that's the way they like it.

Alexandra Headland's beach segues into **Maroochydore Beach** and the estuary of the Maroochy River – which, in turn, flows through **Maroochydore ❼**, seat of local government and the commercial hub of the Sunshine Coast.

Located 98 km (61 miles) north of Brisbane, Maroochydore (pop: 13,000) is a pleasant place that keeps its feet firmly on the ground. As with most of the settled areas along the coast, the town has experienced a development boom – which, if nothing else, has brought good restaurants along with inflated real-estate values. The city's best asset is the **Maroochy River**, an easy-flowing waterway that imparts

Boats for hire, Maroochydore.

BELOW: the wharf at Mooloolaba.

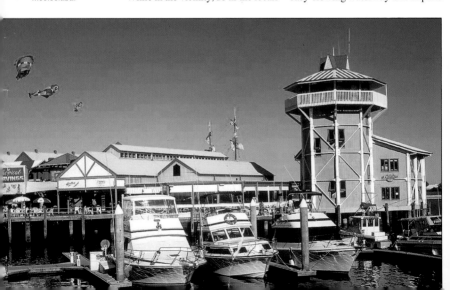

a sense of calm. **Cotton Tree Park**, on the south bank, is a sweet place to picnic. Conservation parks occupy the northern bank.

Coolum

Laid-back **Coolum** ❽ has two assets: the unspoiled **Marcoola Beach** and **Mount Coolum National Park**. The beach is overlooked by the swish 5-star Hyatt Regency hotel, complete with 18-hole championship golf course. The hotel grounds adjoin Mount Coolum National Park, which contains coastal wallum, paperbark wetlands and rainforest remnants that have virtually disappeared from the surrounding lowlands. Peregrine falcons nest along the cliff faces. After rain, waterfalls cascade down the sides. You can clamber up and down the craggy 208-metre (680-ft) peak. For more information contact Noosa National Park (tel: 5447 3243).

Noosa

Nestling beside the usually tranquil waters of Laguna Bay, **Noosa** ❾ has been called the Cannes of Australia, a heady blend of beauty, sophistication and high finance. Noosa Heads is the chic, high-density heart of the Noosa region. It comprises the iconic Hastings Street strip, nearby Noosa Hill and the adjacent national parks. Its real estate is highly sought after, with prices that reflect exclusivity and scarcity.

Only slightly less valuable is the real estate in Noosa proper – a region that begins at Peregian Beach, extending north through Marcus Beach, Sunrise Beach and Sunshine Beach to Noosa Heads, then along the southern bank of the Noosa River through Noosaville to Tewantin.

Noosa is the town that pioneered alfresco dining, fusion food and good ecological practice at a time when such ideas were considered dangerously radical. Locals now lament that Noosa's aestheticism has yielded to ostentation, its idealism to pragmatism – and that too much of its distinctive architecture has been bulldozed for pretentious mansions.

Hemmed in by sea and national parks, Noosa can't get bigger, only more elitist. As the population approaches saturation, this formerly

Map on page 116

TIP

Noosa Visitor Information Centre (Hasting Street, Noosa Heads; tel: 5447 4988) provides information about accommodation as well as events like the Noosa Long Weekend in June, the Celebration of Food and Wine in May and Noosa Jazz Festival in September.

BELOW: Noosa from the air.

bohemian enclave increasingly resembles an exclusive realm of Sydney and Melbourne plutocracies.

For battle-scarred veterans of the Noosa Parks Association, it's a cruel irony. Having shielded Noosa from rampant development, they discover themselves to be caretakers of a playground for the rich. Thanks to the association's quiet persistence, 35 percent of the shire's 875 sq km (340 sq miles) has been amalgamated into national park, state forest, fauna reserve and vacant government land.

All that said, Noosa remains an undeniably charming and atmospheric place. Hastings Street, its central hub, is a leafy, cosmopolitan thoroughfare of enticing restaurants and smart apartment buildings, thronged by the designer-clad well-to-do. The street leads down to a patch of sandy beach occupying reclaimed woodland on **Noosa Spit**, where children paddle and rainbow lorikeets screech in the she oaks.

Whatever else may happen, Noosa Heads will always enjoy the saving grace of the adjoining 477-hectare

(1,180-acre) **Noosa Headland National Park**, with its craggy cliffs, sheltered beaches, heathlands and rainforest.

Great Sandy National Park

About 30 km (19 miles) to the north of Noosa Heads is Lake Cootharaba, a wide expanse fed by the Noosa River – and an entry point to the 50,000 hectares (123,553 acres) of unspoiled tranquility that is the Cooloola section of the **Great Sandy National Park** ❿.

Here, at Boreen Point or Elanda Point, it is possible to rent a canoe and paddle along the glassy waters of Noosa River, cutting through rippling reflections of reeds, cabbage palms, cyprus, cotton trees, bloodwood and banksias.

Camping grounds lining the stream provide designated areas, some with basic amenities, others without. Motorised vessels are not permitted beyond a certain point. One of the sites, Harry's Hut, is accessible by road – but only by 4WD.

North from the Noosa River to Rainbow Beach, the Cooloola sec-

tion of the park is characterised by sand dunes, coloured sand cliffs, sweeping beaches, sandblows, freshwater lakes, tall forests, paperbark swamps and wild-flower heath. Plants and animals whose habitats have been compromised by coastal development – the Cooloola acid frog, for example – have found sanctuary here. The park is also home to one of Queensland's few remaining emu populations.

Providing you have a 4WD, it is possible to drive the 50 km (31 miles) from the north shore of Noosa Heads to Rainbow Beach and Inskip Point, which is a terminus point for barges to Fraser Island. Migrating humpback whales pass offshore between August and October. By way of relics, you'll see **Double Island Point Lighthouse**, built in 1884, and the now vestigial remains of the *Cherry Venture*, wrecked on **Teewah Beach** in 1973.

For more information about the Great Sandy National Park, contact the information centre at Tewantin (240 Moorindil Street; tel: 5449 7792) or visit www.epa.qld.gov.au.

Rainbow Beach

Rainbow Beach ⓫ is a cross between frontier town and fishing village – with a salty, come-what-may ambience that is most refreshing after prolonged immersion in the espresso-and-high-rise culture to the south. Originally established to serve the sand-mining industry, Rainbow Beach gradually turned into a fishing and retirement retreat, and now offers motel and caravan park accommodation to thousands of visitors annually.

Scuba diving and windsurfing are popular pursuits. A good spot to watch the sunset is from the **Carlo Point Marina**, which doubles as a restaurant and centre for charter boats and houseboat hire.

The Rainbow Beach office of the QPWS (tel: 5486 3160) is located on Rainbow Beach Road, as you enter town. The Rainbow Beach Tourist Information Centre is at 8 Rainbow Beach Road.

Maryborough

Maryborough ⓬ is a venerable Queensland city with much of its

Map on page 116

Rainbow Beach takes its name from the amazing multi-coloured sand cliffs near by, which offer a sweeping panorama from Fraser Island in the north to the lighthouse at Double Island Point in the south .

BELOW: sand dunes of Fraser Island, part of the Great Sandy National Park.

Maryborough's 19th-century Post Office, with its ornate tower.

BELOW: a grand old Victorian "Queenslander", Maryborough.

colonial architecture intact, and the placid Mary River flowing through. Located 264 km (164 miles) north of Brisbane, Maryborough creates a sense of unhurried permanence – due, perhaps, to its reliance, not on tourism, but on local industries based around timber, sugar and engineering.

First settled in 1847, Maryborough was already a busy immigration port when the Maryborough Sugar Company was established in 1865. The gold rush at nearby Gympie shortly afterwards assured its future. Grand public buildings erected during the late 19th and early 20th century express the optimism of the time. The 1866 **Post Office**, in particular, is an exercise in colonial gravitas, complete with arcaded verandas and clock tower. The original tower was equipped with a time ball that, at the stroke of 1pm, dropped noisily on the roof of the postmaster's residence. To the postmaster's relief, the time ball was jettisoned in 1869, and replaced by a clock in 1872.

Telling the time remained an issue until 1877 when Queensland premier John Douglas gave the city an 18th-century cannon, fired daily at 1pm for the benefit of ships' captains, and to alert Kanakas – South Pacific Islanders press-ganged into virtual slavery on the area's sugar plantations during the latter decades of the 19th century – that it was time for lunch. The actual gun, cast for the Dutch East India Company, is displayed in Maryborough's **Bond Store Museum** opening. A replica is fired at Heritage City Markets on Thursdays at 1pm.

Another Maryborough gem is **Brennan & Geraghty's Store**, 64 Lennox Street. Built in 1871 and restored in 1990, this remarkable museum, with its shuttered windows and Victorian façade, is a rare example of a late 19th-century retail outlet. The store traded continuously for 100 years until 1972, when its second-generation owner George Geraghty closed the doors on his treasure trove of merchandise, some of which had remained unsold since the store's opening.

To learn more about Maryborough's historic buildings, call into

Map on page 116

the Maryborough Visitor Information Centre (Bruce Highway; Mon–Fri 8.30am–5pm, Sat–Sun 10am–4pm; tel: 4121 4111) or Maryborough City Hall Visitor Information Centre (Kent St; Mon–Fri 9am–5pm; tel: 4190 5742).

Hervey Bay

The main portal to Fraser Island, **Hervey Bay** ⑬, 300 km (186 miles) north of Brisbane, is another sleepy seaside community experiencing the impact of development, albeit limited to six storeys.

Urangan Boat Harbour, the terminus for ferries to Fraser Island, has already been girdled by modern apartments – a trend reflected in the tourism-oriented villages of Torquay, Scarness and Pialba (less so at Point Vernon). Caravan parks, low-tariff motels and rental holiday homes continue to assert a presence but, assisted by direct flights from Sydney and Melbourne, Hervey Bay is redefining itself as a resort for retirees and families of more modest means.

Formerly associated with whaling (notice the harpoon mounted on the marina), Hervey Bay now provides a base for whale-watching excursions, as well as for game fishing and charter boats. The city (pop: 50,000) is also interesting for its memorial to Kanakas (the South Sea Islanders virtually kidnapped to work for low wages in the Queensland cane fields). Allow at least three-and-a-half hours for the drive from Brisbane to Hervey Bay.

QPWS camping and access permits for Fraser Island can be collected when purchasing barge tickets at the River Heads vehicular terminal. Note that permits have to be booked in advance. This can be done by contacting the Harvey Bay-Fraser Island Tourist and Visitors Centre, shop 2, 401 Charlton Esplanade, Torquay, Hervey Bay; tel: 4124 8741; www.herveybay-touristinfo. com.au or the Kingfisher Bay resort (tel: 1800 249 122). Permits can also be obtained online via Smart Service Queensland; www.qld.gov.au/ camping.

Fraser Island

Fraser Island ⑭ is justifiably known as one of the world's premier wilderness destinations. The burden of mass visitation has taken a toll, but conservationist John Sinclair's 1990 description of the island as "a magnificent mosaic of plant communities, lakes, swamps, sand blows, beaches and wetlands" holds true. If anything, Sinclair's rhetoric has proved too effective. Thanks to his environmental campaigns, the world's largest sand island has become an irresistible magnet to eco-tourists and 4WD aficionados.

Despite logging from 1863 until 1991, pockets of pristine rainforest survive on this 184,000-hectare (455,000-acre) island. Piccabeen palms hold back the sun; satinay and brush box trees flourish amid creepers, ferns, elkhorns and orchids.

Aside from its scenic wonders, Fraser Island is famous as the scene of a tragic encounter between Aborigines and a party of mariners whose ship came to grief on the Great Barrier Reef in 1836. Eliza Fraser, after whom the island is named, survived rough treatment at the hands of her captors until rescued by a search party. She eventually wrote a book about her experiences and became a celebrity.

BELOW: shark show, Hervey Bay.

Wild dingoes roam on Fraser Island. They're undeniably part of the native fauna but they do cause problems (there was a fatality in 2001). Fences circle picnic areas, and rogue dingoes are culled. Don't be tempted to feed them.

BELOW: driving on the beach is part of the Fraser Island experience. So is getting bogged.

Passenger ferries for Fraser Island depart from Urangan Boat Harbour in Hervey Bay, and vehicular barges from River Heads. Both dock at Kingfisher Bay and Wonggoolba Creek on the island (tel: 1800 249 122). At the upmarket end of the spectrum, Kingfisher Bay Resort attracts mainly "green" tourists who spend their days exploring walking paths or lazing on the beach.

Less visited than the more photogenic "blue" lakes, **Lake Boomanjin**, its water tannin-stained to the colour of strong coffee, is still one of the island's more beautiful lakes.

The island's roads, if you could call them roads, are impassable by anything other than 4WD vehicles – and, even then, motorists appear to spend most of their time extracting one another from bogs. If people always behaved as they do when mired in sand, the world would be a better place. Bogged motorists are unfailingly polite and grateful.

The ocean beach on Fraser Island is great fun in a 4WD. Salty breezes blow, terns wheel overhead and, at certain times, waders gather at the water's edge, building strength for their annual flight to Siberia.

A driving permit is required on Fraser Island, and fees apply for the use of camping facilities. Contact Queensland Parks and Wildlife Service (tel: 5486 3160), or Smart Service Queensland (tel: 13 13 04; www.qld.gov.au/camping).

Gympie

Gympie ⓯, 90 km (56 miles) south of Maryborough, falls outside the generally recognised boundaries of the Sunshine Coast, but, being roughly equidistant from Noosa Heads and Rainbow Beach, it warrants mention here.

A rip-roaring gold-mining town until the 1920s, Gympie now functions as a service town for the surrounding agricultural area. It has historic architecture but, as destinations go, the visual impact is less than riveting. That said, it should be remembered that Queensland might be a very different place if gold prospector James Nash had not struck it lucky in Gympie in 1867 – rescuing the then fledgling state

from bankruptcy. Almost 100 million grams of gold were obtained – a bonanza chronicled in informative attractions like the **Gympie Gold Mining and Historical Museum** (215 Brisbane Road; daily 9am–4.30pm; admission charge; tel: 5482 3995), and the **Woodworks Museum** on the history of forestry and timber (corner of Bruce Highway and Fraser Road; Mon–Fri 9am–4pm, Sun 1–4pm; admission charge; tel: 5483 7691).

The hinterland

Maleny ⓰, 100 km (62 miles) north of Brisbane, began as a timber-getting town in the 1870s, progressing to dairying and fruit crops as the land was cleared – finally adding tourism to its economic mix a few decades ago. At 450 metres (1,480 ft) above sea level, Maleny (pop: 5,000) offers a cool hill station for the coastal lowlands around Caloundra and Maroochydore: a verdant, scenic zone supporting a bewildering array of B&B operators as well as a large artistic community.

The agricultural ambience of the main thoroughfare, Maple Street, is leavened by the many galleries and craft outlets, supplemented by a handicrafts market at the community hall on Sunday (9am–2pm).

For a glimpse of what Maleny was like before timber-getters began chopping their way along the Blackall Range, look for the **Mary Cairncross Reserve**, 5 km (3 miles) east of Maleny in Mountain View Road. Named after the 19th-century conservationist, this 52-hectare (128-acre) patch of pristine rainforest contains a comprehensive array of native flora and fauna, including a huge strangler fig said to be 500 years old.

The Maleny Visitor Information Centre (tel: 5499 9033) has information about accommodation and can provide details of local attractions such as the Maleny Show in May and the Christmas Carnival.

Ten km (6 miles) to the north is the quaint township of **Montville** ⓱ – a community that strives to create the impression of having been transplanted from the Swiss Alps. You half expect the inhabitants to wear leather shorts and yodel. Judging by Montville's thriving galleries, speciality shops and tearooms, the Swiss Alps ploy is working a treat.

Two nearby settlements are so understated as sometimes to pass unnoticed. The hamlet of **Flaxton**, 4 km (2½ miles) along Flaxton Road from Montville, has a winery with clear-day views to Mount Coolum and Moreton Island. **Mapleton**, a few kilometres further on, comprises a general store, a French restaurant, a tavern and a petrol station. Contact Montville Tourist Information Centre (tel: 5442 9214) for information.

The Blackall Range

There are two parks within the Blackall Range area – **Kondalilla National Park** (3km/2 miles north of Montville) and **Mapleton Falls**

Map on page 116

TIP

When in Montville, make a detour to The Settlers Rise Vineyard and Winery (249 Western Avenue, Montville; daily 10am–5pm; tel: 5478 5558), to sample their award-winning wines.

BELOW: Gympie's Valley Rattler steam train runs Wednesdays and weekends.

TIP

If you are interested in plants and gardens, visit Fairhill Native Plants and Botanic Gardens (open Mon–Sat 8.30am–5pm; tel: 5446 7088) in Yandina. Pathways through this 3-hectare (7-acre) garden lead you round a mix of wild-flower and rain-forest flora, with more than 1,500 different species of native plants.

BELOW: pineapple farm, Nambour.

National Park (4km/2½ miles west of Mapleton) – both with spectacular waterfalls. Kondalilla National Park has tall open eucalypt and subtropical rainforest. The Kondalilla Falls drop 90 metres (300 ft) over Skene Creek into a rainforest valley. The Mapleton Falls are even more impressive, tumbling 120 metres (400 ft) down an escarpment from Pencil Creek. Both have lookouts with fabulous views over the rainforest.

Eumundi and Yandina

Eumundi ⓲, 20 km (12½ miles) west of Noosa, is a twice-a-week city, with up to 20,000 people rolling up for the Wednesday and Saturday markets – swelling the population 40-fold and lending this otherwise quiet hinterland city a carnival atmosphere.

The market's 500 stallholders, by themselves, double the population. It's noisy, colourful and unrelentingly jolly. All sorts of gewgaws are sold. People wear fancy dress, apparently for no better reason than that's what they like to do. Estab-lished in 1979 in an attempt to save this former timber and dairying community from fiscal extinction, the markets have revived the area's commercial life, with cafés and speciality shops now lining the street.

Ten km (6 miles) to the south is Yandina – another town that has embraced tourism. The Ginger Factory, 50 Pioneer Road (tel: 5446 7096), is the biggest producer of ginger in the world and now a tourist attraction – complete with cane train rides and a shop. There's also a pleasant garden in Fairhill Road (see Tip).

Nambour

Nambour ⓳, on the Brisbane Highway between Caloundra and Noosa, stands aloof from the tourism circus – happy to fulfil its traditional role as a service centre for the surrounding sugar-cane and pineapple farms. Settled in the 1860s by disappointed gold miners from Gympie, its 10,000 citizens embody the ideals of steady industry, with no interest in joining the frantic rush for tourist gold. Go there for a blast of ordinariness. You'll probably need it. ❑

RESTAURANTS, CAFÉS & BARS

Caloundra

Alfie's on the Boardwalk
Otranto and Esplanade
Tel: 5492 8155
Open: L & D daily. **$$**
Contemporary food with an Asian twist. The view over Pumicestone Passage is a bonus. BYO.

Coolum

Harvest
1806 David Low Way
Tel: 5446 4314
Open: D daily. **$$**
Chef Gary Skelton made a splash in Noosa with his cutting-edge restaurant Season – now he's doing it again here. This place was a magnet for foodies from day one.Great barbecued seafood antipasto.

Maroochydore

The Wine Bar and Restaurant
8 Duporth Avenue
Tel: 5479 0188
Open: L Mon–Fri, D Mon–Sat. **$$**
A cellar of 550 wines accompanies such dishes as lobster crêpes with carrot beurre blanc. One of a number of venues in this still-evolving precinct.

Mooloolaba

Earth Bistro
Esplanade and Venning Streets
Tel: 5477 7100
Open: L & D daily. **$$**
Casual is the buzzword

here. Cool, modern atmosphere with shutters opening to the sea. The tapas are perfect for a light lunch.

Noosa

Berardo's
52 Hastings Street
Tel: 5447 5666
www.berardos.com.au
Open: D daily. **$$$**
New Yorker James Berardo has given his adoptive home a very classy restaurant. Food is Mod Oz with a Mediterranean edge.

Berardo's on the Beach
On the beach, Noosa
Tel: 5448 0888
Open: L & D daily. **$$**
A delightful location for acclaimed chef Bruno Loubet's version of Noosa cuisine. The menu offers such delights as sugar-cured salmon with creamed lime mayonnaise, and chilli-salted baby octopus and Asian herbs.

Bistro C
On the beach, Hastings Street, Noosa Heads
Tel: 5447 2855
www.bistroc.com.au
Open: B, L & D daily. **$$**
Overlooking Laguna Bay, this casual restaurant is much favoured by locals. Some steak and seafood dishes cost up to A$30, but the menu includes plenty of affordable options.

Ma'Mensa
Hastings Street, Noosa Heads
Tel: 5449 2320
Open: L & D daily. **$$**
Thus buzzy, popular Italian trattoria offers such dishes as fettucine marinara and black mussels in tomato and basil sauce.

River House
301 Weyba Road, Noosaville
Tel: 5449 7441
Open: L Sun, D daily. **$$$**
The domain of British-born chef David Rayner, the River House has white walls with the occasional splash of colour. Dishes use the freshest ingredients. BYO.

Sails
Park Road and Hastings Street. Tel: 5447 4235
Open: L & D daily. **$$$**

A seafood-dominated Mod Oz menu and sweeping views across Laguna Bay. Sails is a fine place to watch the sunset.

Yandina

Spirit House
20 Ninderry Road
Tel: 5446 8977
www.spirithouse.com.au
Open: L daily, D Wed–Sat. **$$$**
Fragrant Thai food served beside a lily pond within a tropical jungle.

PRICE CATEGORIES

Prices are for a three-course meal per person with house wine:
$ = A$60 and under
$$ = A$60–100
$$$ = A$100 and over

RIGHT: crunchy crustacean.

BIG THINGS

It's one of those phenomena which seems amusing enough the first time you encounter one. But it's just possible that the march of the big things is getting out of hand

The first Big Thing in Australia wasn't even in Queensland. It was at Coffs Harbour on the New South Wales north coast that the Big Banana was erected in 1964 as a way of attracting custom to a plantation on the Pacific Highway. It was ludicrous, it was tacky and it immediately struck a chord with passers-by. It became a destination in itself, and once that happened every desperate or mediocre enterprise that had no other distinguishing feature considered adopting the idea. Queensland was fertile ground for big things and many a small company or local council has made the leap. At the last count there were close to 50 of the things around the state, some being quite distinguished feats of engineering and construction, some more simple but still alluring, and some, frankly, rubbish. Originality doesn't count for much either; there are two pineapples, two crabs and three crocodiles. Still, keep your eyes open and look out for that serendipitous moment when the Big Spanner looms over the horizon, or take a more planned approach and invest in the book *Big Things* by David Clark.

ABOVE: the Big Mango, in Bowen on the coast between Townsville and Mackay, was the archetypal community project aimed at raising the town's profile. When completed in 2002 it was substantially over budget and, according to some, upside down.
BELOW: Tully's Golden Gumboot would have been big enough to handle the town's record rainfall of 7.93 metres (26 ft) in 1950.

LEFT: the Big Peanut is on the Kennedy Highway between Tolga and Mareeba outside a produce shop otherwise entirely bereft of character. The peanut makes you stop for a photo. Then you buy vegetables. See, function fulfilled.

CANE TOAD

Sarina's Big Cane Toad is on the grass strip running down the middle of the main street, but isn't quite big or dramatic enough to cause the pile-ups of distracted drivers that would really put the town on the map. However, its rusty steel bulk is sturdy and nigh-on indestructible, which just happens to be a fine metaphor for the real-life cane toad. It was in 1935 that someone had the bright idea of introducing the chunky amphibian from Hawaii to deal with a plague of greyback beetles which was causing havoc on sugar plantations. The toads had little effect on the beetles (the adults lurked at the top of the canes and the larvae were underground), but did tuck into every other insect and, as a break from eating, bred energetically. They have no effective predators and are so toxic that any indigenous wildlife that tries to eat them just dies. Cane toads are spreading relentlessly across the country, and so far no one has come up with a way of stopping them.

ABOVE: angling is phenomenally popular across Australia, possibly because there are so many fish around that even the most pitiful incompetent can catch something. However, in serious fishing, size is what counts, and no true Aussie male likes to be outdone. The popular Big Barramundi Barbecue Garden in Daintree serves the big catch of the day.

BELOW: defying the logic of most big things, which tend to be about drawing attention to a town or attraction, the Big Deckchair in Winton can only be seen once you're inside the Royal Theatre.

CAPRICORN COAST AND ITS HINTERLAND

Queensland's central coast encompasses graceful coastal cities, rugged national parks and dreamy offshore islands. Here the attractions are many and varied. Go "fossicking" for sapphires, rum-tasting in Bundaberg, turtle-watching on Heron Island or trekking in the Carnarvon gorge

Brisbane ●

Straddling the Tropic of Capricorn, Queensland's central coast extends 750 km (470 miles) north from Bundaberg to just south of Mackay. Inland, it extends beyond Carnarvon Gorge to the tiny Outback town of Jericho, 550 km (340 miles) west of Rockhampton. In this region, the sugar barons of 19th-century Bundaberg vied with the mining magnates of Mount Morgan to build ever more grandiose civic buildings; and also here, in contrast, away from the modern resort developments (but within easy reach of them) you'll find some of the world's most spectacular national parks. The Great Barrier Reef begins offshore from Bundaberg at Lady Elliot Island, or you could head inland for the gemfields of central Queensland.

Bundaberg

Sitting alongside the Burnett River in the heart of sugar country is **Bundaberg ❶**, 371 km (230 miles) north of Brisbane. This little agricultural town is known for its most famous product – Bundaberg rum, distilled here since 1883. "Bundy" (as both the town and the tipple are affectionately known) is distinguished by elegant public buildings, venerable churches, a striking monument to Bundaberg-born aviator Bert

Hinkler and a remarkable turtle hatchery at Mon Repos Beach.

Commercial tourism has yet to take root in any crass way. Young travellers who come to pick fruit seem in no hurry to leave, blending with the locals, using the city as a base for excursions to the reef.

The heritage trail

Bundaberg's unhurried pace of life sits well with the colonial splendour of buildings such as the **School of Arts** (1888) in Bourbong Street and

Map on page 134

LEFT: a fringing reef, Lady Elliot Island.
BELOW: a tour of the Bundaberg Distillery.

Pioneering aviator Bert Hinkler (1892–1933) spent several years in England working as a test pilot. In 1983, his English house was shifted brick by brick from Southampton to its present location in his home town of Bundaberg where it is now a museum (see right).

the **Post Office** (1890) in Barolin Street. Its 30-m (98-ft) clock tower was built at the height of Bundaberg's prominence as a sugar town.

A number of impressive churches line the streets. The **Holy Rosary Church** (1875) in Woongarra Street is the oldest, with successive renovations resulting in a structure curiously reminiscent of a Roman temple.

Amid the cluster of heritage buildings in the city centre is the fascinating **East Water Tower** in Sussex Street (1902). Circled by actual and blind windows at each level, the eight-storey tower would not look out of place in a Tuscan hilltop town, and was considered a masterpiece of brickwork construction. Although the tower post-dates many of Bundaberg's impressive civic buildings by more than a decade, it symbolises the city's importance and prosperity during the 1880s when the sugar industry boomed.

Botanical Gardens

Located at the city's northern entrance, on the corner of Mount Perry Road and Young Street, are the **Bundaberg Botanical Gardens** (daily 6am–6pm; tel: 4153 2377), comprising 28 hectares (68 acres) of lush, well-tended parkland studded with landmarks of historical significance. The centrepiece is the **Hinkler House Memorial Museum** (daily 10am–4pm; admission charge; tel: 4152 0222; www.bundaberg onthe.net), which honours Bundaberg-born aviator Bert Hinkler. Contained within Hinkler's former residence *(see left)*, the museum overlooks the park where, in 1928, he completed his record-breaking England-to-Australia solo flight.

Another impressive attraction within the gardens is Fairymead House, a plantation homestead reborn as a **Sugar Museum** (Thornhill Street; daily 10am–4pm; tel: 4153 6786). Built in 1890, the house

testifies to the grand lifestyle enjoyed by Bundaberg sugar barons in the late 19th and early 20th century. Relocated from its original site in 1994, Fairymead House has been furnished in authentic style.

On Sundays and public holidays volunteers from the Bundaberg Steam Tramway Preservation Society (tel: 4152 6609) fire up their small fleet of steam locomotives for rides around the gardens. If you want more railway memorabilia, drop in at the **Bundaberg Railway Museum**, corner of Wilmot and Station Streets (Tues and Fri 9am–3pm; Sat 8am–4pm; tel: 4152 1267). Housed within the city's first railway station, displays include old rolling stock, photographs and uniforms.

Most visitors to the Botanical Gardens wind up having a snack at Ann's Kiosk (Mon 10am–3pm; Tues–Sun 10am–4pm; tel: 4153 1477), but the lily-fringed lagoons also make a delightful setting for picnics. More than 10,000 trees and shrubs have been planted since the gardens opened in the mid-1980s, creating a habitat for many waterbirds.

The distillery

No visit to Bundaberg is complete without paying homage to its famous export with a one-hour tour around the **Bundaberg Rum Distillery** (Whittred Street; tours every hour on the hour Mon–Fri 10am–3pm, Sat–Sun 10am–2pm; admission charge; tel: 4131 2999; www.bundabergrum. com.au). During the tour, you'll peer into deep pools of molasses, pose for photographs beside an outsized rum bottle, wander among tall storage vats and, finally, head to the bar for an invigorating slug of "Dad and Mum".

Close to the rum distillery is **Schmeider's Cooperage and Craft Centre** (5 Alexandra Street; Mon–Fri 9am–5pm, Sat 9am–3pm; free; tel: 4151 8233), where in-house artisans engage in barrel-making, woodturning, glass-blowing and pottery – as well as selling souvenirs.

Bundaberg's beaches

Southeast of Bundaberg, a 13-km (8-mile) drive through canefields leads to **Bargara**, set against a dramatic backdrop of black volcanic

Map on page 134

TIP

Once you've absorbed Bundaberg's history, take a stroll down by the Burnett River where trawlers and yachts line the banks and birdsong filters through the mangroves.

BELOW: turtles hatching at the Mon Repos rookery.

Some 28 km (17 miles) west of Bundaberg on the Gin Gin Highway lie the Mystery Craters (daily 8am–5pm; tel: 4157 7291), so named because they're so darned mysterious. Formed more than 25 million years ago, the 35 craters are still puzzling geologists. Some think they are meteorite fragments, others say they may be the result of volcanic disturbances or the action of an underground sea.

BELOW: Lady Elliot Island.

rock. This beach enclave has undergone swift and dramatic modernisation over recent years, with new apartments and boutiques. The dazzling bank of coral near the shore makes it very popular with divers and snorkellers.

About five minutes from Bargara is the beach at **Mon Repos**, the most accessible loggerhead turtle rookery in Australia, where, in season, you can watch these ancient creatures struggle up the beach to nest. Until a decade ago, it was "open slather", as the locals would have it (or unrestrained free-for-all), for turtle-watchers. Queensland Parks and Wildlife Service has since formalised Mother Nature's peep show with an information centre, video show, boardwalk and ticketing system. As a rule, turtles nest between mid-November and February. Hatchlings make their run from January to the end of March. Viewing takes place at night and is closely supervised (Bundaberg Region Tourism, 271 Bourbong Street; tel: 4153 8888; freecall: 1800 30 88 88; www.bundabergholidays.info).

Southern Reef islands

Bundaberg is also a gateway to the two southernmost islands of the Great Barrier Reef. Flights depart daily from Bundaberg Airport (Childers Road, Kensington; tel: 4155 1238; www.bundaberg.qld.gov.au) to **Lady Musgrave Island** ❷, in Capricornia Cays National Park, a beautiful, uninhabited coral cay, accessible by boat from Bundaberg to day trippers and campers. It offers excellent diving and snorkelling within a brilliant-blue lagoon; camping is only allowed with a National Parks permit (Bundaberg Region Tourism, tel: 4153 8888; or QPWS, tel: 4131 1600; www.epa.qld.gov.au). You can also fly to **Lady Elliot Island** to the south, another delightful coral cay, with a resort which provides easy access to snorkelling and diving (no camping).

Agnes Water and Town of 1770

About 120 km (75 miles) north of Bundaberg are the twin coastal resorts of Agnes Water and the Town of 1770, popular seaside destinations

surrounded by national parks, great beaches and the ocean. Although developing rapidly, they still retain a certain charm. **Agnes Water** is busier, with bustling shopping centres, coffee bars and restaurants; its main attraction is a magnificent surf beach (Queensland's most northerly), where the 1770 Longboard Classic, a major surfing competition, is held every March.

Just 5 km (3 miles) up the track is the **Town of 1770**. Until a few years ago, this sleepy seaside paradise was known only to a few; locals bought beer on credit and strangers got the stare treatment. Now the developers have moved in and many of the locals have moved out.

Bounded by national parks and the Great Barrier Reef, 1770 is a popular spot for fishing and boating, and is a departure point for neighbouring national parks and the southern cays of the Great Barrier Reef. Captain James Cook anchored the *Endeavour* off this coast on 23 May 1770 before venturing ashore with botanists Sir Joseph Banks and Dr Daniel Carl Solander to collect plants. While Banks and Solander were plunging through paperbark swamps in search of new species, Cook's men brought down a plains turkey, a bird that tasted so pleasing to the great navigator that he named the inlet **Bustard Bay**.

Amphibious buses known as LARCs, the military acronym for Lighter Amphibious Re-Supply Cargo vessels (tel: 4974 7555; www.1770holidays.com.au), depart from The Marina, Captain Cook Drive, Town of 1770, for **Bustard Head Lighthouse** (Mon, Wed, Sat only). The journey is an adventure in itself, involving four tidal creek crossings to reach the restored lighthouse, where a small but crowded cemetery underlines the hardship of a lighthouse keeper's life in the 19th century *(see box)*.

Coastal parks

To the northwest of Agnes Water is **Eurimbula National Park ❸**, a 12,500-hectare (30,900-acre) landscape of thick mangrove, freshwater paperbark swamps and eucalypt forest. An 11-km (7-mile) bush track

Map on page 134

The lighthouse at Bustard Head.

Lighthouse of Tragedy

From the moment it first lit up on 26 June, 1868, a heavy burden of tragedy descended on the gloomy lighthouse at Bustard Head. In all, the adjoining cemetery contains 11 graves, two unmarked, almost all of them underscored by tragedy. First to go was a carpenter accidentally hit on the head; next, in 1887, lighthouse keeper Nils Gibson's wife Kate slit her throat; two years later, Gibson's 20-year-old daughter Mary and two others died in a boating mishap. Six years after Mary's death, Gibson passed away; two months later, assistant lighthouse keeper Ernest Waye's wife gave birth to a daughter who died at 20 months after being accidentally scalded.

Revenge, abduction, a murder, mysterious disappearances... Stephen King might have concocted the true-life tales revolving around this unhappy lighthouse. As it happens, lightkeeper-turned-author Stuart Buchanan has beaten him to it. Buchanan now resides in one of the lighthouse keeper's cottages (the other has been restored as a museum), where he acts as caretaker and sells signed copies of his book, *Lighthouse of Tragedy*.

BELOW: reef-combing, Heron Island.

accesses the Bustard Beach camping area at the mouth of Eurimbula Creek. Camping permits may be obtained from the self-registration stand at the campground. To ensure a site during school holidays and long weekends, book in advance at Bundaberg QPWS office, 46 Quay Street, Bundaberg, tel: 4131 1600.

Another area of outstanding beauty is the 4,600-hectare (11,400-acre) **Deepwater National Park ❹**, 8 km (5 miles) to the south of Agnes Water. Here you'll encounter a mosaic of coastal vegetation, heathland fringed with dunes and sweeping beaches studded with freshwater creeks. The park is used as a breeding ground for loggerhead turtles; you can see hatchlings emerging at night between January and April (follow the precautions recommended by the QPWS park brochure). Access to the park is 4WD only. As with Eurimbula National Park, permits may be obtained at the campground, with advance bookings recommended for busy times (visit www.epa.qld.gov.au for maps of both parks).

Gladstone

Gladstone ❺, 175 km (109 miles) north of Bundaberg, is one of the biggest ports in Australia, with more than 60 million tons of cargo passing through each year. About two-thirds of this is coal from open-cut mines in the Bowen Basin reserve. Queensland Alumina Limited's refinery is the biggest in the world, processing 8.5 million tons of bauxite to produce 3.7 million tons of top-quality alumina (aluminium oxide), while Gladstone Power House produces 15 percent of the state's electricity. There are also cement plants, chemical plants and oil-exploration companies.

But it's not all industrial. Beyond the wharves and smokestacks lies the clear blue of the ocean, where turtles laze in the crystal-clear water, and further afield lie the coral cays on the southern Great Barrier Reef.

Gladstone's comparatively recent development means there's little history. A National Trust-listed fig tree in Roseberry Street is all that survives of the gracious 19th-century residence to which it belonged.

A Load of Bull

A colourful local personality and former mayor of Rockhampton, Rex Pilbeam had a baggy-necked Brahman bull cast in concrete and erected at the northern entrance to the city (the Brahman is the breed favoured by cattlemen to the north), and a similar sculpture of a Hereford (the British breed favoured by farmers in the south) at the southern end. Anticipating playfulness by local lads, Pilbeam had several spare sets of testicles for each animal placed in storage. Souvenir-hunters struck the Brahman almost immediately. They were dumbfounded when the mayor ordered his workmen to bolt on a replacement appendage the very same day.

The **Commonwealth Bank** (1929), the former **Gladstone Post Office** (1932) and the **Council Chambers** (1934) are interesting insofar as they reflect the then government's attempts to generate employment via public works programmes.

Amid thrusting industrial prosperity are Gladstone's **Tondoon Botanic Gardens** (Glenlyon Road; Oct–Mar Mon–Fri 7am–6pm, Sat–Sun 9am–6pm; Apr–Sept Mon–Fri 7am–5.30pm, Sat–Sun 8.30am–5.30pm; tel: 4971 4444). This magnificent 83-hectare (205-acre) site comprises rainforest and Australian native plants with good walking trails and lakes.

Heron Island

Heron Island ❻, 70 km (43 miles) northeast of Gladstone, is accessed by plane or fast catamaran (contact Gladstone Tourist Information Centre, Bryan Jordan Drive, The Marina; tel: 4972 9000 for details). This beautiful coral cay buzzes with diving enthusiasts, who stay at the Heron Island Resort, marine boffins who inhabit the university research station, and a noisy population of mutton birds, noddy terns, herons and silver eyes who go where they please.

One of only two resort islands positioned on the Great Barrier Reef itself (the other is Green Island off Cairns, *see page 187*), Heron Island offers spectacular snorkelling and diving, and the opportunity, between October and March, to see green turtles nesting.

Rockhampton

Only a few kilometres north of the Tropic of Capricorn (which is marked by a roadside spire), **Rockhampton ❼** is the commercial heart of central Queensland and the centre of the state's beef industry.

A sprawling city, with modern pubs and office blocks interspersed with older buildings, Rockhampton is a commercial centre for thousands of square kilometres of rich grazing country to its west, where heat, drought, floods and fires have shaped a hardy breed of survivors on the large, scattered cattle stations of the Dawson and Fitzroy River Valleys.

Rockhampton has some stunningly well-preserved old hotels and warehouses down by the river. You can pick up heritage trail brochures from any visitor centre in town.

BELOW: Gladstone.

BELOW: Long Beach, Great Keppel Island.

There's a wide range of attractions in "Rocky" and the **Customs House** in Quay Street (Mon–Fri 8.30am–4.30pm, Sat–Sun 9am–4pm; tel: 4922 5625) is a good place to start. Constructed in 1899, this gracious sandstone structure houses the Rockhampton Tourist and Business Information Centre and is a mine of information about the city's heritage and attractions. Here you can learn how brothers Charles and William Archer, on an expedition to the district in 1853, became the first Europeans to record and chart the Fitzroy River. The Archers built a wharf to transport wool from their property, Gracemere Station. The wharf site, dictated by rocks blocking further movement upstream, eventually became the port of Rockhampton.

Although Rockhampton's economy is agriculture-based, gold discoveries in the hinterland, notably at Canoona in the 1860s and Mount Morgan during the 1880s, furnished the wealth for its stately buildings. The National Estate lists an entire street – **Quay Street** – on its heritage register, and some of the state's finest colonial homes are found in **Agnes Street**.

The town also owns a superb **Art Gallery** (62 Victoria Parade; Tues–Fri 10am–4pm, Sat–Sun 11am–4pm; free; tel: 4927 7129) with a collection of 20th-century works by prominent Australian artists, and an enchanting green oasis in the **Botanical Gardens**, Spencer Street, The Range (daily 6am–6pm; tel: 4922 1654), with a Japanese garden, lagoons and small zoo with koalas and other native species.

Another worthwhile stop is the **Archer Park Station and Steam Tram Museum** (corner of Denison and Cambridge Streets; Sun–Fri 10am– 4pm; admission charge; free tram rides Sun 10am–1pm; tel: 4922 2774). The station – an ornate 19th-century edifice – houses a restored steam tram salvaged from a fleet of four built by Monsieur Valentin Purrey of Bordeaux, France, in 1908 to provide Rockhampton with public transport. These four-wheeled passenger "toastrack" trams, each powered by an underfloor steam engine,

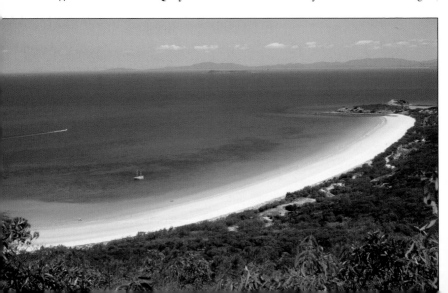

with the boiler and driver on a front platform and trailers behind, carried passengers in and around the town.

Other Rockhampton attractions include an excellent 18-hole golf course and a modern theatre.

"Rocky" itself can be insufferably hot, but don't let this bother you. Just slip quietly away on a 40-km (25-mile) detour to **Yeppoon** on the coast for a dip and some excellent local seafood.

Great Keppel Island

It's a 40-minute catamaran ride from Roslyn Bay, 7 km (4.5 miles) south of Yeppoon, to **Great Keppel Island ❽**. The island's main resort, operated by the Mercure group, offers free accommodation for children as part of an ongoing campaign to hose down the island's entrenched "get wrecked" image of teenage abandon. You could be forgiven for thinking the resort *is* the island. In fact, there are many alternatives – rental beach shacks, motel-style rooms, cabins, bunkhouses, floored tents and even an offshore houseboat (*see page 256*).

The island's coast is blessed with astounding rock formations, piratical caves and picture-postcard beaches. Great Keppel is not directly on the reef (although there is coral in most of the bays), so short cruises run out for divers.

Catamarans to the island depart from Roslyn Bay Marina three times daily. Charter flights operate from Rockhampton Airport. Contact Rockhampton Tourist and Business Information (208 Quay Street; tel: 4922 5625; www.rockhampton-info.com) for details.

Inland from Rockhampton

The historic mining town of **Mount Morgan ❾** is interesting, not so much for what it is, as for what it was. A stockman named William Mackinlay discovered gold 40 km (25 miles) inland from Rockhampton, but did nothing about it because the gold was mixed not with quartz, but with ironstone. In 1882, one of Mackinlay's daughters persuaded mining expert Thomas Morgan to assess the find. Morgan realised its worth, pegged 260 hectares (640

Map on page 134

A steam pressure valve on an exhibit outside the Mount Morgan Museum.

BELOW: the old railway station at Mount Morgan houses the visitor information centre.

Aboriginal art decorates the walls of some of the municipal buildings in Mount Morgan.

acres) and, with borrowed capital, rushed in a crusher. Morgan and Mackinlay became wealthy and sold out. Next came a syndicate that amassed an even greater fortune. By 1889, Mount Morgan's population had reached 5,800. When gold yields diminished, they mined copper. So it went until the 1920s, when a new company returned the mine to production as an open cut. Abandoned in the 1980s, the open cut has since filled with water, poisoned by waste from the mines.

A wealth of mining memorabilia is enshrined within the **Mount Morgan Museum** (Mon–Sat 10am–1pm, Sun 10am–4pm; admission charge; tel: 4938 2122). New museum operators expect to resume mine tours curtailed in 2004. Of special interest are dinosaur footprints unearthed by brickmakers excavating clay. Clearly visible in the roof of a cave, the tracks were formed 150 million years ago.

The Mount Morgan Tourist Information Centre is housed in the Historic Rail Complex (1 Railway Parade; tel: 4938 2312).

BELOW: fossicking for gems.

Emerald

Emerald ⑩, 263 km (163 miles) west of Rockhampton, is a rural community of about 13,000 people who busy themselves with coal mining, grazing, agriculture (grain and cotton) and horticulture (grapes and citrus). Emerald's focus shifted from grazing to agriculture in the late 1940s, a move hastened by the completion of the Fairbairn Dam across **Lake Maraboon** in 1972, creating a watery expanse three times the size of Sydney Harbour.

Tourism is a relatively low priority, though Emerald does possess a fine National Trust-listed **Railway Station** (*c.*1900) and, outside the town hall, two lumps of fossilised wood that are said to be 250 million years old. Beside the information centre on the Capricorn Highway stands **Emerald Pioneer Cottage and Museum**, a small historical village where exhibits include a cottage (1880), the former lock-up (1910), St Mark's Church (1884) and a vintage printing press (Mon–Fri 2–4pm; admission charge).

Emerald's most arresting attraction

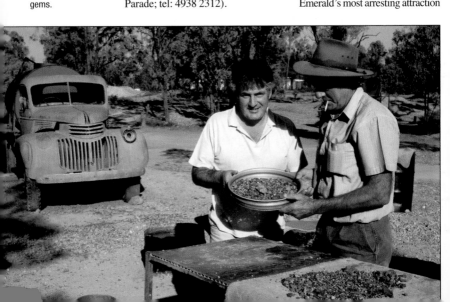

is an enormous reproduction of Van Gogh's painting, *Sunflowers*, resting on a 25-metre (82-ft) easel in **Morton Park**, a reference to the Easter Sunflower Festival.

Also in Morton Park is the **Federation Footpath**, a 100-metre (330-ft) mosaic pieced together by Emerald artists Maxine Wild and Daryl Black in 2001 to commemorate the centenary of Federation. (Central Highlands Visitor Information Centre, Clermont Street; Mon–Sat 9am–5pm, Sun 10am–2pm; tel: 4982 4142; www.central-highlandstourism.org.au).

The Sapphire Gemfields

Emerald is also a gateway to the central Queensland **gemfields ⓫**, the largest sapphire fields in the world. Fortunes were made during the 1970s and 1980s, and the region still yields enough precious stone to sustain communities at Rubyale, Sapphire, Anakie and Willows Gemfield – as well as on the gemfields themselves. There are several fossicking parks that sell buckets of "wash" that you sift through yourself – the gemfields' version of a lottery ticket. You'll need a licence to go fossicking, and a separate bush-camping permit if you want to camp. Contact the Central Highlands Visitor Information Centre (*see Emerald above*) for details.

Carnarvon Gorge

Lying between Emerald and Roma, in the middle of the Great Dividing Range, **Carnarvon Gorge ⓬** is a stunning oasis in an arid landscape. Towering sandstone cliffs form a steep-sided gorge with lush, vibrantly coloured side gorges. Cabbage tree palms, ancient cycads, ferns, flowering shrubs and gums line the main gorge. Well maintained walking trails allow you to explore this majestic gorge, with rare plants, wildlife and poignant

Aboriginal art; the rich indigenous culture can be found under several rocky overhands, with engravings, ochre stencils and freehand paintings at **Cathedral Cave**, **Balloon Cave** and the **Art Gallery**.

Camping is permitted during the Easter, June/July and September/October Queensland school holidays. Alternatively, you can stay at one of the bush resorts or lodges. Contact QPWS, tel: 4984 4505, for details.

Clermont

Clermont ⓭, 106 km (66 miles) north of Emerald, is a quiet country town with a colourful past. Explored by Ludwig Leichardt in 1845, Clermont became the first inland settlement north of the Tropic of Capricorn, founded on gold, copper, sheep and cattle.

In 1916, a flood swept through, killing 65 people – and convincing those who remained to drag the entire town to higher ground (where it still stands). A concrete "tree" at the southern entrance to Clermont marks the 1916 flood level. ❑

Map on page 134

In 2000, some Bundaberg tourists in the Sapphire Gemfields stumbled upon the 221-carat Millennium Sapphire, which sold for a cool $87,000.

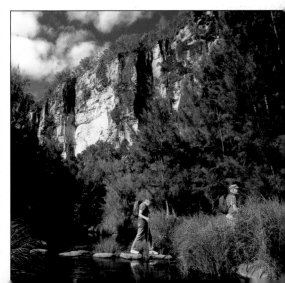

BELOW: one of the must-see destinations in Queensland is Carnarvon Gorge.

RESTAURANTS, CAFÉS & BARS

Agnes Waters and Town of 1770

Aggie's at the Agnes Water Tavern
Tavern Road, Agnes Waters
Tel: 4974 9469
Open: L & D daily. **$**
Informal dining in a tropical beer garden and atrium. Nothing fancy, just good steak and seafood dishes. Salad bar for lunch, vegetable bar for dinner.

The Deck Bar and Restaurant
Captain Cook Holiday Village, Captain Cook Drive, 1770
Tel: 4974 9157
Open: L Thur–Sun, D Wed–Mon. **$$**
Belgian chef Fred Gabriels gives fresh local seafood a European twist. The varied menu includes such Belgian specialities as *waterzooi* (a Flemish-style chowder), prawn croquettes and an irresistible chocolate fondue.

The Tree Bar
Captain Cook Drive, 1770
Tel: 4974 9599
Open: L Tues–Sun, D daily. **$**
Unpretentious and reasonably priced Aussie tucker. Steaks and seafood by day, supplemented by pizza dishes in the evening. Great views across Bustard Bay to the lighthouse.

Yok Attack Agnes Waters
Endeavour Plaza, Captain Cook Drive, Agnes Waters
Tel: 4974 7454
Open: L & D Thur–Tues. **$**
Authentic Thai food – good-value soups, noodles, stir fries and seafood curries.

Bargara

Bargara Berries Café
100 Hughes Road
Tel: 4159 1245
Open: 8am–5pm daily. **$**
There's nowhere better for strawberry dishes between July and October, when owner Lynn Hay prepares fresh strawberry pancakes, parfaits and pavlovas. The rest of the year, frozen strawberries are mixed with orange, mango and banana sauces. There's also good seafood, pasta, pizza and salads.

Bundaberg

Alexandra's New Orleans Cafe and Bar
66 Quay Street
Tel: 4152 7744
Open: D daily. **$$**
The in-crowd descends at weekends, drawn by inexpensive cocktails, Creole chicken and Cajun-spiced beef. Occupies a historic Queenslander decorated with New Orleans memorabilia.

Ann's Kiosk
Hinkler Rose Garden, Botanical Gardens, Young Street, North Bundaberg
Tel: 4153 1477
Open: L daily. **$**
Old-fashioned and family-oriented, Ann's Kiosk dishes up fish and chips, quiche, salads and Devonshire teas in a lovely outdoor setting overlooking the manicured lawns and garden of Bert Hinkler's House. A restored cane train trundles around the park at weekends. Lovely lunch spot.

H2O Bar and Bistro
Burnett Riverside Motel, 7 Quay Street
Tel: 4155 8777
Open: L & D Mon–Sat. **$$$**
Modern bistro fare – pasta, stir-fries, juicy steaks and locally caught fish.

Rendezvous Restaurant
220 Bourbong Street
Tel: 4153 1747
Open: D Mon–Sat. **$$**
Well-regarded and long-established à la carte restaurant serving modern Australian cuisine.

Spinnaker Bar and Bistro
1a Quay Street
Tel: 4152 8033
Open: L Tues–Fri, D Tues–Sat. **$$**
A Bundaberg institution and arguably the smartest restaurant in town. Emphasis is on seafood dishes such as Moreton Bay bugs with lemon risotto. The deck overlooks the Burnett River.

Thai Tulips Restaurant
47 Takalvan Street
Tel: 4153 1881
Open: L Tues–Fri, D Tues–Sun. **$**

LEFT: the dark rum affectionately known as "Bundy" is often served (in generous quantities) with coke.

Standard Thai dishes such as tom yum, stir-fries and curries.

Clermont

Peppercorn Motel
Capricorn Street
Tel: 4983 1033
Open: D daily Mon–Sat. $$
A la carte menu mainly based on steak and seafood, served in the restaurant or at the poolside.

Emerald

The Capricornian Restaurant
17 Esmond Street
Tel: 4982 1113
Open: D Mon–Sat. $$
Emerald's only stand-alone restaurant dishes up more exotic Queensland dishes such as crocodile, swordfish and soft-shell crab alongside more familiar dishes.

Emerald Explorer's Inn
Springsure Road
Tel: 4982 2822
Open: D Mon–Sat. $$
Fine dining and an extensive menu that reflects the prosperity of the region.

Gladstone

Kapers BYO Restaurant
124b Goondoon Street
Tel: 4972 7902
Open: D Mon–Sat. $$
Mediterranean-based fare that includes such dishes as cuttlefish in beer batter with chilli plum dipping sauce, as well as traditional favourites like Beef Wellington. Some vegetarian and coeliac-friendly dishes.

Scotties Bar and Restaurant
46 Goondoon Street,
Tel: 4972 9999
Open: D Mon–Sat. $$
Gladstone's young crowd and professional classes mingle at the bar. Menu runs the gamut from linguine with smoked rainbow trout to local grain-fed rump.

Thai Classic
100 Goondoon Street
Tel: 4972 1647
Open: L Mon–Fri, D daily. $
A predictable but tasty menu of Thai curries and stir-fries.

Vino Vino
76 Goondoon Street
Tel: 4972 7555
Open: L Mon–Fri, D Mon–Sat. $$
Coffee shop by day, à la carte restaurant by night. Well-known Gladstone chef Eddie Moller delivers an evening menu that relies on reef and beef dishes, supplemented by tapas and pasta. Wine list includes some premiums.

Yachties Bistro
Gladstone Yacht Club, 1 Goondoon Street
Tel: 4972 2294
Open: L & D daily. $
Stunning views of Auckland Inlet through to Gladstone Harbour and a menu that encompasses à la carte service and a nightly buffet. Seafood, pasta and meat dishes.

Mount Morgan

Leichardt Hotel
52 Morgan Street
Tel: 4938 1851
Open: L & D daily. $

Famous for its pizzas, this 1891 hotel includes a well-presented restaurant serving a wide range of traditional pub grub.

Lucky Strike
11 Central Street
Tel: 4938 2154
Open: D Wed–Mon. $$
George and Barbara Friesacher's restaurant is noted for fresh homemade pasta and award-winning pizzas. Tasty, unpretentious fare beneath the pressed metal ceiling of historic 19th-century premises. BYO.

Rockhampton

The Allenstown Hotel
8 Upper Dawson Road,
Tel: 4922 1853
Open: L & D daily. $$
The hotel's recently refurbished restaurant serves such sophisticated dishes as double-roasted duck and spiced pork belly with blue swimmer crab salad. Lounge and public bar feature traditional pub food with cheap specials. Live entertainment at weekends.

The Brunswick Hotel
Archer and West Street
Tel: 4922 1389
Open: L & D daily. $
Value for money at around A$6 for an overflowing plate piled with steak or seafood served with chips and salad or vegetables. Eat in the bar, the beer garden or restaurant.

The Cambridge Hotel
Cambridge and Bolsover Streets
Tel: 4922 3006

The hotel contains two restaurants – one for corporate types on expense accounts, another for the more budget-conscious. The Flame Char Grill specialises in prime steaks (open: L Mon–Fri, D Mon–Sat. $$). The Overflow Restaurant is an all-you-can-eat family bistro (open: L & D daily. $).

The Coffee House
William and Bolsover Streets
Tel: 4927 5722
Open: L & D daily. $$$
Owners Grant and Rebecca Cassidy deliver gourmet fare in contemporary surroundings. Signature dish is flash-seared grass-fed rib fillet with mushroom ragout.

Da Berto
62 Victoria Parade
Tel: 4922 3060
Open: L & D Tues–Sat. $$
Fresh Italian/Mediterranean fare. Typical dishes include gremola scallops, spice-dusted sweetlip and traditional pannacotta.

Thai Taste
635 Norman Road North
Tel: 4926 7788
Open: D Tues–Sun. $
Bangkok-style and Lao-style Thai dishes. Special Thai fried rice is a favourite with locals. Good value.

PRICE CATEGORIES

Prices are for a three-course meal per person with house wine:
$ = A$60 and under
$$ = A$60–100
$$$ = A$100 and over

SOUTHERN REEF AND THE WHITSUNDAYS

Heritage is sweet in the elegant sugar cane-producing town of Mackay, but the big attraction in this part of the state are the Whitsundays. Spectacular island idylls with pristine beaches and clear blue waters, they show nature at its very best

Brisbane ●

The area from Mackay north to the town of Bowen is a prosperous one thanks to the agriculture, mining and, increasingly, tourism industries. The coastal stretch is a convenient springboard for the Whitsundays, an archipelago of 74 jaw-droppingly beautiful islands in the southern Great Barrier Reef. Many of the islands now house tropical island resorts, with options to suit all tastes, whether family-friendly, sports-orientated or simply that perfect island hideaway.

ness District (CBD), but the flavour of modern Mackay is more cogently expressed by the waterfront developments north of the river such as **Marina Village**, adjacent to Mackay Harbour, and **Harbour Beach**, which looks across the Coral Sea to the Whitsunday Islands of Brampton, Keswick, St Bees and Scawfell.

In common with other coastal towns that rose to prominence during the sugar boom of the late 1800s and early 1900s, Mackay's CBD is blessed with imposing banks and

Map on page 148

LEFT: sail the Whitsundays... **BELOW:** ...or take the ferry.

Mackay

Fanned by fresh breezes and surrounded by a gentle rustling sea of sugar cane, **Mackay ❶**, 975 km (605 miles) north of Brisbane, is an attractive city distinguished by wide streets, tropical palms, elegant buildings and flocks of raucous rainbow lorikeets that appear around dusk. It exudes an air of prosperity – partly deriving from mining and sugar production (the Mackay region supplies about half of Queensland's coal and about one-fifth of Australia's raw sugar), partly from the tourism generated by its close proximity to the Great Barrier Reef.

Mackay's main centre is on the southern bank of the wide Pioneer River, where a number of heritage buildings survive in the Central Busi-

Mackay's Customs House (1902) is one of the few structures remaining in the once-busy precinct by the Pioneer River.

ornate art deco public buildings. The most efficient way to see them is by obtaining a copy of the *Heritage Walk* booklet, which covers 22 sites, from the **Mackay Visitor Information Centre** to the south of the town (320 Nebo Road; Mon–Fri 8.30am–5pm, Sat–Sun 9am–4pm; tel: 4944 5888) or the Town Hall (63 Sydney Road; Mon–Fri 9am–5pm, Sat–Sun 10am–3pm; tel: 4951 4803).

Listed by the National Trust, the formal façade and elegant clock tower of the old **Town Hall** (1912) speak volumes about Mackay's optimism and confidence at that time. One of the few structures to weather a devastating cyclone in 1918, the Town Hall continues to dominate the streetscape, though the council has long since shifted operations to the Mackay Civic Centre. Mackay gained many art deco buildings in the rebuilding programme that followed the 1918 cyclone.

The city's oldest commercial edifice, the **Commonwealth Bank** (1880; 63 Victoria Street) is marked by a masonry colonnade at street level with cast-iron columns supporting an iron "lace" balustrade and veranda roof on the upper storey.

Two other venerable sites are the **Customs House** *(see left)* and the **Courthouse and Police Station** complex at the corner of Victoria and Brisbane Streets.

Lending a contemporary edge to the streetscape is **Artspace Mackay** (Civic Centre Precinct, Gordon Street; Tues–Sun 10am–5pm, closed Mon; tel: 4968 4444 Mon–Fri and 4957 1775 weekends; www. artspacemackay. com.au). On offer here are workshops and masterclasses by visiting artists, exhibitions and installations.

The **Mackay Regional Botanic Gardens** (Lagoon Street; daily in daylight; tel: 4952 7300; www. mackayregionalbotanicgardens.com

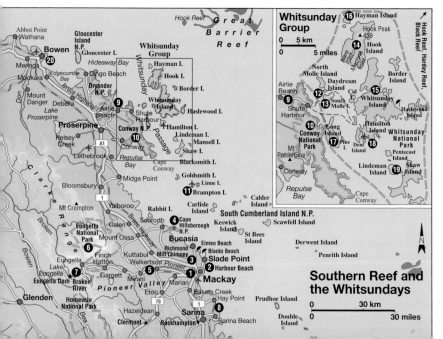

Southern Reef and the Whitsundays

.au), 3 km (2 miles) south of the city centre and very close to the Mackay Visitor Information Centre, are definitely worth a visit. Part of a 20-year project involving Mackay City Council and the State Government, these gardens promise to be truly amazing when completed. Stage one opened in 2003, stage two in 2006. Set beside the banks of Eulamere Lagoon, the park's gardens are accessed by pathways, ramps and bridges – heralded by a spectacular display at the main approach to the Visitor Centre. Exhibits include a tropical shade garden (daily 9am–5pm) and an elevated deck from which to observe wetland flora and fauna. Stage two has new exhibits to explain the evolution of plant life and presents displays of flora unique to the region.

Around Mackay Marina

North Mackay is blessed with excellent beaches, unfortunately blighted by box jellyfish from November to April. Public pools offer free admission on days when beaches are closed due to stingers. **Harbour Beach** , 6 km (4 miles) north of the centre, is patrolled throughout the year, and during holiday periods surf life-savers also patrol **Lamberts**, **Eimeo** and **Blacks Beaches** further up the coast. Town and Illawong Beaches, to the south of Mackay, are unsuitable for swimming but remain popular with locals for picnics.

Thanks to its ease of access to surrounding islands, prosperous Mackay enjoys an unusually high rate of boat ownership. **Marina Village** (at the northern end of Harbour Beach) is something of a jaw dropper, with 500 berths – six of them designed for 60-metre (196-ft) mega-yachts. Small boats are available for hire. A pleasant activity is to sail to a nearby island or follow the course of the Pioneer River through the city.

While in the vicinity of Harbour Beach, look for the white tower and red roof of the **Pine Islet Lighthouse** (1885) on the esplanade in Mulherin Drive. The lighthouse remained operational until 27 August 1985, when it was placed in storage. Reassembled on its present

Map on page 148

TIP

Among the more than 350 businesses operating within Mackay's CBD is the familiar mix of clubs, bars, alfresco coffee shops and brasseries. The largest concentration is on the busy main thoroughfare of Victoria Street.

BELOW: Mackay Marina.

TIP

If you're interested in
learning more about
how sugar is made,
the Farleigh Mill,
10 km (6 miles) north
of Mackay, on the
Bruce Highway, offers
tours of its sugar mill
during the crushing
season (July–Nov
Mon–Fri 1pm; admis-
sion charge; booking
essential; tel: 4963
2700).

BELOW: sugar cane
fields, Pioneer Valley.

site in 1992, the lighthouse now
enjoys National Trust listing and is
in close proximity to several upmarket restaurants.

The Mackay Visitor Information
Centre to the south of town *(see page
148)* is marked by a replica of the tall
brick chimney of the old Richmond
Sugar Mill, making it easy to spot.
The actual **Richmond Mill Chimney** ❸ (1881) – one of the last remaining stacks from the early sugar
boom – stands in Habana Road, 14
km (9 miles) north of Mackay. Richmond Mill was the district's first central mill, and became renowned for
the quality of its sugar and golden
syrup, but falling prices, coupled
with a ban on South Sea Islands
labour, led to its closure in 1895. The
ruins stand on private property surrounded by canefields, but the 20-
metre (65-ft) tapered chimney stack
is clearly visible from the road.

The **Mackay Bulk Sugar Terminal** in Mackay Harbour, reputedly
Australia's largest facility of this
type, represents a more modern
monument to the sugar industry –
but there are no tours.

The wild green yonder

For a coastal excursion, head 50 km
(31 miles) north along the Bruce
Highway, past pawpaw plantations
and cane farms, to the sandy beaches,
subtropical rainforest and mangrove-
fringed wetlands of **Cape Hillsborough National Park** ❹. Kangaroos
are often seen on these beaches. Fishing is allowed, but swimming is not.
Estuarine crocodiles populate the
waters, and box jellyfish are present
from October to May.

For a glimpse of quintessential
north Queensland scenery, head
along the Peak Downs Highway to
Walkerston ❺, 15 km (9 miles)
west of Mackay, where, in 1915,
grazier Albert Cook built **Greenmount Historic Homestead** (Greenmount Road; Mon–Fri, Sun 9.30am–
12.30pm; admission charge; tel:
4959 2250). This gracious family
home stands on land that belonged
originally to the city's founder, John
Mackay, but he was later forced to
sell it. The house retains original fur-
niture and fittings that belonged to
the Cook family, providing a real
insight into the life of a prosperous

grazier during the early 19th century.

From Walkerston, continue west for 65 km (40 miles) along the Mackay–Eungella Road, through the townships of Mirani (where opera singer Dame Nellie Melba once lived as the unhappy wife of a local sugar- mill manager), Gargett and Finch Hatton to **Eungella National Park 6** (tel: 4958 4552 or QPWS Mackay, tel: 4944 7800; www.epa.qld.gov. au/project/park). Here, if you're lucky, you may glimpse a platypus.

Essentially the road follows the course of the Pioneer River towards its source – a journey through cane fields, roadside mango trees, neat one-pub settlements, green fields and cane-train crossings. From **Finch Hatton**, at the base of the Clarke Range, a tortuous 18-km (11-mile) uphill road through the Great Dividing Range leads to **Eungella** township. Here you can enjoy the surreal experience of taking refreshment at the chalet while, a few metres away, hang-gliding daredevils launch themselves into the clear blue yonder.

The best spot to spy on platypuses is from a purpose-built viewing platform at **Broken River 7**. Reportedly, as many as eight of these duck-billed, otter-tailed, spur-legged marsupials have been seen here at one time, though sightings are not guaranteed.

Among the other weird and wonderful creatures that inhabit Eungella's mist-shrouded mountains are the Eungella gastric brooding frog, the Eungella spiny cray and Eungella honeyeater. Eungella has over 20 km (12½ miles) of walking tracks, the easiest being the Sky Window circuit which affords spectacular views of the Pioneer Valley.

Hay Point

Located 38 km (24 miles) south of Mackay, **Hay Point 8** is one of the largest coal-export ports in the world, comprising two separate terminals – the Dalrymple Bay Coal Terminal and the Hay Point Services Coal Terminal. The DBCT wharf stretches 3.8 km (2½ miles) out to sea, the Hay Point Services Terminal 1.8 km (1 mile). The terminals

Map on page 148

Evenings or early morning are the best times to spot platypus in the water at Eungella National Park.

BELOW: the coal terminal at Hay Point.

Mackay: Sugar Central

The city is named after John Mackay, who established a pastoral run in the river valley in 1861. By 1863, the first lots of land sold. Sugar cane was planted in 1865 and quickly eclipsed pastoralism as the district's foremost activity. Plantation owners turned to Kanaka indentured labour, but the dubious methods used to recruit the South Sea Islanders, akin to kidnapping, drew fierce criticism, and the practice was banned. Subsequently, Europeans, particularly Italians, provided the labour, forming their own settlements. Improved railway access from 1924 boosted the industry. By the 1920s, Mackay had become the fastest-growing town in Queensland.

The Great Barrier Reef is one of the last remaining habitats of the dugong or sea cow but this statue at Airlie Beach is the closest that most visitors will get to seeing one.

BELOW: sunset at Airlie.

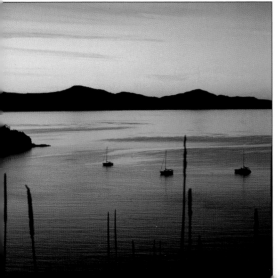

have a combined throughput capacity of around 100 million tons per annum – delivered from coal mines in the northern Bowen Basin by trains 2 km (1¼ miles) long and drawn by four locomotives. An open-air viewing platform affording an overview of this remarkable operation can be accessed in the Port Administration building, Horyu Maru Drive off Hay Point Road as you enter Hay Point township.

Airlie Beach

Airlie Beach ❾, about 140 km (87 miles) north of Mackay, is the principal gateway to the Whitsunday Islands. The antics of youthful international travellers endow the place with a sense of *joie de vivre*, while the trappings of the town's plutocracy lend an air of elegance and cosmopolitanism.

Airlie's location overlooking Pioneer Bay and the Whitsunday Passage has long marked it as a prime holiday destination. Tall resort apartments occupy the streets behind the Central Business District (CBD). The CBD itself is wall-to-wall with

bars, restaurants, nightclubs and souvenir shops. Shops open seven days a week, and traders at the Saturday market sell fruit and vegetables, arts and crafts and assorted gewgaws under the coconut palms on the foreshore.

A profusion of BMWs and Mercedes line the streets, and luxury yachts fill the **Abel Point Marina**. Berths have trebled to 500 at Abel Point, and a new mega-marina is under construction at the nearby Port of Airlie. Abel Point and **Shute Harbour**, 8 km (5 miles) away, serve as departure points for islands in the Whitsunday group and provide a base for charter operators offering both skippered and bareboat yachts.

Between Airlie Beach and Shute Harbour is the 22,500-hectare (55,600-acre) **Conway National Park ❿**, where the landscape closely resembles that of the Whitsunday Islands. This is because the islands were part of the mainland until rising sea levels drowned the coastal valleys thousands of years ago. The park's rocky cliffs provide a spectacular 35-km (22-mile) backdrop to the Whitsunday Passage and its islands.

To get to the national park from Airlie Beach, follow the Shute Harbour Road 2.5 km (1½ miles) southeast to the QPWS Whitsunday Information Centre (tel: 4946 7022). The entrance to the park is a further 4 km (2½ miles). A pleasant camping ground, complete with pebbly beach and million-dollar views, is located at the end of a 20-minute hike from the Swamp Bay/Mount Rooper car park. Pit toilets, picnic tables and a shelter shed are provided. Take a fuel stove and ensure you have a camping permit.

The Islands and Great Barrier Reef

The world's largest coral reef consists of over 2,500 separate, interconnected reefs stretching over

2,300 km (1,430 miles). The Great Barrier Reef Marine Park was established in the 1970s to help protect this magnificent but fragile ecosystem. The 20 or so resort islands inside the marine park offer many attractions: lodging varies from five-star resorts to backpacker hostels and campgrounds. Some are dry, barren and windy, others are lush and covered with rainforest. Many islands can be reached by seaplane, light plane or helicopter. The islands covered in this chapter are in the Southern Reef, mostly in the Whitsunday group.

Brampton and Carlisle Islands

Brampton Island ⓫, 32 km (20 miles) northeast of Mackay, is a beautiful island with rocky headlands dotted with hoop pines, sheltered bays and long sandy beaches. A 7-km (4-mile) walking track through the **Brampton Islands National Park** rises from sea level to 214 metres (700 ft) at Brampton Peak, offering views over nearby islands and the mainland. At low tide, you can walk across a sand spit to neighbouring **Carlisle Island**, in whose waters turtles feed.

The waters surrounding both islands are good for snorkelling and offer some excellent dive sites. There is also sailing and water-skiing in the bay. Brampton's resort is set in a tropical garden surrounded by coral and calm seas *(see page 257)*.

Direct flights to the island are available from Mackay and Hamilton Island. For more information contact Voyages (tel: 1300 134 044; www.voyages.com.au) or Brampton Island Resort (tel: 4951 4499; www.brampton-island.com). Day trips to the resort ceased in 1998, and non-resort guests wishing to visit Brampton Islands National Park should contact Reef Goddess (tel: 1300 760 846; www.islandreefcruises.com). Access to QPWS campsites on Brampton or Carlisle Islands is by charter flight or private boat (QPWS Mackay; tel: 4944 7800; www.epa.qld.gov.au).

Daydream Island

Daydream Island ⓬, located 5 km (3 miles) northeast of Shute Harbour,

Map on page 148

Brampton and Carlisle Islands are part of the Cumberland Island group. Like most of the islands off the Queensland coast, they were sighted by Captain Cook in 1770. Cook named the group after the Duke of Cumberland. The island itself was named simply "M" – until 1879, when a British Royal Navy commander named each of the islands in the group after a town in England's Lake District.

BELOW: Daydream Island, the antidote to summer in the city.

The "putt your way around Australia" mini golf course on Daydream Island is reputed to have cost over a million dollars.

BELOW: there are resorts across every price bracket in the Whitsundays .

is distinguished by something that you don't see very often these days – a minigolf course (or "putt putt", as it is sometimes known). This is no ordinary golf course, taking the form of a relief map of the Whitsundays (with Daydream as the last hole). The hazards have a political edge. At the Parliament House hole, John Howard's head protrudes from the green. When you reach the end, the likeness of resort owner Vaughan Bullivant delivers a prerecorded greeting.

A shoreline boardwalk and a rainforest walk link the 17-hectare (42-acre) island's two main centres of activity. If you tire of walking, you can hitch a ride on a motorised buggy. Live-in guests inhabit a 296-room facility set in manicured gardens on the northeast of the island. The southern end is mainly for day trippers. It has a tavern, souvenir shops, swimming pool, minigolf and an outdoor cinema in a spectacular setting. Yachties cruise in to see new releases. The resort's A\$3 million spa is reason enough to visit Daydream. The facility has 16 rooms and comes with its own

naturopath *(for more information on accommodation see page 257).*

To get there, fly to Hamilton Island's Great Barrier Reef Airport, then catch a ferry. Alternatively, fly to Proserpine Airport (Lascelles Avenue; tel: 4945 0200. www.whitsunday.qld.gov.au) for a bus/ferry connection.

South Molle Island

Southeast of Daydream Island is **South Molle Island** ⓭. The self-contained resort on a large, hilly island is popular with families; diving, swimming, sailing, golf, fishing and shops are all offered, but, as usual, Mother Nature steals the show. In all, there are 16 km (10 miles) of walking tracks. If time is limited, an easy 15-minute stroll from the resort through rainforest and grassland to Paddle Bay gives an accurate overall impression. The view from **Spion Kop** (154 metres/505 ft) is spectacular, and, on the way, you'll see the remains of a quarry where local Aboriginal people, belonging to the Ngaro tribe, dug up basaltic stones for axes and cutting tools. **Mount**

Jeffreys (194 metres/635 ft) and **Lamond Hill** (133 metres/435 ft) also afford good views.

The island is 45 minutes by launch from Shute Harbour and 90 minutes from Hamilton Island. People wishing to bush camp on South Molle will find QPWS sites at Sandy Bay and Paddle Bays. There are other sites on North Molle, Long, Tancred, Planton and Denman Islands. (South Molle Island Resort, tel: 1800 075 080; www.southmolleisland.com.au; QPWS, tel: 4946 7022.)

Hook Island

A good way to see the Whitsundays is by boat, and charter operators in Airlie Beach offer a tantalising range of vessels, both skippered and self-sail. For many Whitsunday seafarers, the first stop is **Nara Inlet** on the southern side of **Hook Island** ⓮, where Aboriginal cave paintings can be found at the far extreme of the inlet. Faded graffiti on rocks overlooking the inlet record a visit by actor Errol Flynn, who sailed his ketch *Sirocco* there in 1930.

The island's highest point is **Hook Peak** at 459 metres (1,500 ft). Another view, provided that the water is clear, is from an underwater observatory submerged 9 metres (30 ft) below the surface of the narrow passage between Hook Island and Whitsunday Island. Just north of the observatory is the low-key Hook Island Wilderness Resort (tel: 4946 9380; www.hookislandresort.com). Ferries depart Shute Harbour daily at 9am.

Whitsunday Island

Across Hook Passage is **Whitsunday Island** ⓯, at 109 sq. km (42 sq. miles) the biggest of the 74 Whitsunday Islands. It is notable for **Whitehaven Beach** – a pristine expanse of white sand that stretches 6 km (3½ miles) along the island's eastern side. As beaches go, Whitehaven is pretty

unbeatable. A popular destination for yachtsmen, day trippers and guests on excursions from nearby resort islands, the beautiful beach is so vast that you scarcely notice the presence of others. A boardwalk leads to a lookout high on **Tongue Point**, providing a sweeping view of Whitehaven Beach and Hill Inlet.

There is no resort on Whitsunday Island. However, the QPWS maintains six camping grounds. One of these is at **Sawmill Beach** on the western side where, in 1888, James Withnall set up a sawmill to provide timber for the mainland settlements of Bowen and Proserpine. A short walking track follows the coastline from Sawmill to Dugong Beach. Campers will need a QPWS permit.

Hayman Island

The Whitsunday group's most exclusive resort is **Hayman** ⓰ (tel: 4940 1234; www.hayman.com.au), a shimmering monument to 1980s entrepreneurial optimism. Sir Peter Abeles spent A$300 million creating his fantasy island, and, although the corporate high-flying market he

Map on page 148

A plaque explains how the Whitsundays got their name.

BELOW: kayaks for hire.

imagined he would cater for never quite materialised, the high standards (and prices) prevail. Today, the five-star resort is a big favourite with Australian honeymooners (*for further details see page 257*).

Located 33 km (20 miles) from the mainland, close to the Outer Reef, the island is circumnavigated by an 8-km (5-mile) bush circuit that takes around 2½ hours to complete. The sheltered waters between Hayman's sandy beach and the northern shores of Hook Island form a tranquil coral-trimmed lagoon, while Hook Island's blue-green mountains make a picture-perfect backdrop.

Day visitors are tolerated, provided they call ahead. Yachties who find it impossible to tear themselves away by dusk are expected to check in for the night.

Long Island

As its name suggests, **Long Island** ⑰ is long and thin – about 9 km (5½ miles) from end to end, narrowing at one point to only a few hundred metres. This narrow point is the location for the secluded four-and-

a-half star **Peppers Palm Bay**, one of three very different resorts on the island. Its sheltered lagoon is also a favoured overnight anchorage for bareboat yachtsmen, who can tie up to the palm trees lining the beach.

Club Crocodile in Happy Bay is a resort for all ages, but it's particularly popular for families with young children, with plenty of activities to keep them amused. Both resorts are just a short boat trip from Shute Harbour on the mainland.

The **South Long Island Nature Lodge** (tel: 4946 9777) in Paradise Bay is the smallest and most unusual of the island's resorts. It is largely self-sufficient – using solar power and natural gas where possible. Owner David Macfarlane, who designed and built the resort in the 1990s, says the entire complex consumes less energy than an average suburban house.

Hamilton Island

The Whitsunday group's largest, most aggressively marketed resort, **Hamilton Island** ⑱ (tel: 137 333; www.hamiltonisland.com.au) is

Electric buggies are the popular way for tourists to get around Hamilton Island. They are available for rent by the ferry terminal.

BELOW: diving and snorkelling are well-catered for on all the islands.

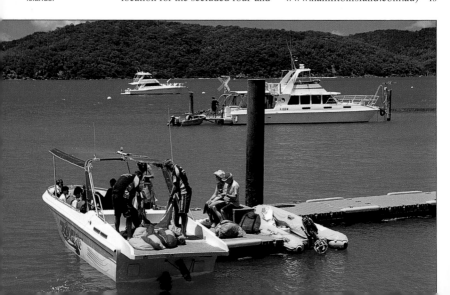

more akin to a Gold Coast development than a traditional Whitsundays resort. The island has become the region's major transport hub, providing both a convenient airport for travellers heading to resort islands and a safe harbour for boaties seeking provisions and/or running repairs. The island's centrepiece – the 19-storey **Reef View Hotel** *(see page 257)* – is distinguished by transparent lifts that run up and down the building's exterior.

Located 13 km (8 miles) southeast of Shute Harbour, Hamilton Island has everything: hotel suites, luxury apartments, private villas, self-contained suites and bures. The largest tourist facility in the Whitsundays, its four hotels provide 750 rooms and more than 200 apartments. There are 10 restaurants, six bars, more than 50 shops and an array of operators covering every conceivable holiday need.

Activities include snorkelling, reef fishing, sailboard riding, tennis and squash. A fauna park is home to koalas, kangaroos, emus, wombats and various bird life. There is a network of walking trails to Coral Cove, Passage Peak and Escape Beach.

Lindeman Island

At the southern end of the Whitsunday archipelago, **Lindeman Island** ⑲ is home to Australia's first Club Med (tel: 1300 855 052; www. clubmed.com.au/lindeman). Beyond the resort buildings, the island has retained the beauty of its natural setting. There is tennis, swimming and fishing, and the 690-hectare (1,700-acre) **Lindeman Islands National Park** offers lovely walks to secluded beaches, while the summit of **Mount Oldfield** is a fine place to watch the sun set.

Lindeman is 30 minutes by launch from Hamilton Island, and can also be reached from Mackay and Proserpine.

Bowen

Back on the mainland, **Bowen** ⑳ marks the halfway point between Mackay and Townsville, covered in the next chapter. The focus here is on agriculture. The area is well known for tomatoes, producing about half the Queensland output, and mangoes. Other major industries include cattle raising, coal mining and fish processing. The visitor centre near the Big Mango *(see right)* can provide directions to the beach at **Horseshoe Bay**, north of Bowen, where reef fish and coral come to within a couple of metres of the shoreline.

For panoramic views to Edgecumbe Bay and the Gloucester Passage, drive to the summit of **Flagstaff Hill**, just beyond the Bowen Boat Harbour. The centre can also point you towards attractions such as the **Bowen Historical Museum** (22 Gordon Street; Mon–Fri; tel: 4786 4333) and the **Courthouse** (1883) in Herbert Street, Bowen's main thoroughfare. They'll also clue you in about events such as the Bowen Family Fishing Classic held every September. ❑

Map on page 148

The Big Mango, proudly erected on the Bruce Highway in South Bowen, illustrates the importance of the annual crop (pictured on page 130). For information, contact the visitor centre (daily 8.30am–5pm; tel: 4786 4222).

BELOW: one of the key venues for Hamilton Island's thriving wedding industry.

RESTAURANTS, CAFÉS & BARS

Airlie Beach

Banjo's Bar and Bistro
Shute Harbour Road,
Whitsunday Shopping
Centre, Cannonvale
Tel: 4946 7220
Open: L & D daily. **$$**
Reasonably priced
steak, seafood, pasta
and salad dishes.

Mangrove Jacks Café
Shute Harbour Road
Tel: 4964 1888
Open: L & D daily. **$$**
Relaxed pub-style dining.
Everything from Thai
beef salads through to
rib fillet. Wood-fired
pizzas a speciality.

Panache on the Beach
263 Shute Harbour Road
Tel: 4946 6337
Open: L & D daily. **$$**
Cosmopolitan Italian
and other Mediterranean
fare. Attracts back-

packers by day and a
more affluent crowd in
the evening. Overlooks
the lagoon.

**Pescatori's Italian
Restaurant**
Water's Edge Resort
4 Golden Orchid Drive
Tel: 4948 4309
Open: L & D Wed–Mon. **$$$**
Elegant poolside dining
with lovely sea views.
Italian-based menu with
a seafood bias.

Terraces Restaurant
Golden Orchid Drive,
Terraces Resort
Tel: 4946 6678
Open: D daily. **$$**
Innovative Spanish and
Greek cuisine served
poolside with sea views
to boot. A choice of
seafood, lamb, beef,
chicken and quail
dishes.

Bowen

**Gilligan's Restaurant
at Whitsunday
Sands Resort**
Tel: 4786 5565
Open: L Sat–Sun, D daily. **$$**
Mainly seafood but with
steak and curry dishes.
International breakfast
includes devilled kidneys
and kippers. Ocean views.

Horseshoe Bay Café
Horseshoe Bay Road
Tel: 4786 3280
Open: L & D Tues–Sun. **$$**
Well-reviewed café. Self-
service by day, table ser-
vice by night. Good views
over the bay too.

Three Sixty on the Hill
Flagstaff Hill
Tel: 4786 6360
Open: L & D Wed–Mon. **$$**
Fantastic location on the
highest point in Bowen.
And the food more than

matches the splendour
of the outlook.

Cape Hillsborough
National Park

**Cape Hillsborough
Nature Resort**
Tel: 4959 0152
Open: L & D daily. **$**
www.capehillsboroughresort.
com.au
Located 50 km (30 miles)
north of Mackay, the
resort café offers fishermen's baskets, pizzas
and assorted snacks.

Eungella
National Park

**Platypus Lodge
Restaurant**
Broken River
Mountain Resort
Tel: 4958 4000
Open: D daily. **$**
Themed dishes designed
to express regional pro-
duce and culture. Rain-
forest setting.

Mackay

Fast-food and budget
outlets in Mackay are
clustered at Café Court,
Caneland Central, Man-
grove Road (tel: 4944
7111), and at the food
court within the Mount
Pleasant Shopping
Centre (tel: 4969 2400).

Church on Palmer Street
15a Palmer Street,
North Mackay
Tel: 4944 1477
Open: D Mon–Sat. **$$**
Stylish restaurant spe-
cialising in steak and
seafood. Modern Aus-

tralian dishes with a French influence.

Citron Brasserie
Seabreeze Resort Hotel,
72 Pacific Esplanade,
Lambert's Beach
Tel: 4955 1644
Open: L & D daily. $$
Well-presented reef and beef dishes.

Covers Bistro
Harrup Park Country Club,
Juliet Street
Tel: 4944 0000
Open: L & D daily. $
Reasonably priced char-grilled dishes, seafood and pasta, with vegetarian options.

Fifth Floor Training Restaurant
Central Queensland Institute of TAFE, Sydney and Shakespeare Streets
Tel: 4940 3281
Open: L Tues–Wed, Fri; D Thur; closed school hols. $
Supervised students prepare à la carte cuisine. An inexpensive way to experience fine dining, with great views too.

Galleon's Restaurant
Ocean International Hotel,
1 Bridge Road
Tel: 4957 2044
Open: B, L & D daily. $$$
Locally farmed barramundi, crocodile and kangaroo. House speciality is the ubiquitous seafood platter (A$175 for two).

The Galley
Mackay Yacht Club, 9–19 Breakwater Access Road, Outer Harbour
Tel: 4955 4950
Open: L & D daily; Sun B. $$
Upmarket modern cuisine.

LEFT: fish and chips on the beach.

Grinders Theatre Café
Mackay Entertainment Centre, Gordon Street
Tel: 4957 1750
Open: L & D daily. $
For good-value café and à la carte meals.

Latitude 21
Clarion Hotel, Mackay Marina
Tel: 4955 9400
Open: L & D daily. $$
Intelligent blending of Asian, African and European food served alfresco, with pleasant views over the marina.

Lighthouse Seafood Restaurant
Mackay Marina
Tel: 4955 5022
Open: L & D daily. $$
A la carte dining. Good wood-fired pizzas too.

Melaleucas
Comfort Resort Blue Pacific,
26 Bourke Street,
Blacks Beach
Tel: 4954 9090
Open: 5.30pm–late Mon–Sat. $$$
Russo-Ukrainian chef Sarrokh Sacidnia dishes up seasonal fare in casual style, including mains such as crayfish risotto, lamb shanks and kangaroo fillet steaks.

Muddies
Illawong Drive
Illawong Beach Resort
Tel: 4957 8427
Open: D daily, L Sat only. $$$
As the name suggests, this restaurant specialises in mudcrabs. Chef Kim Lee sources local crustaceans and delivers such dishes as chilli mudcrab and seafood platters.

Pacino's on the Waterfront
8 River Street
Tel: 4957 8131
Open: L & D Mon–Sat. $$
Cosmopolitan menu served in a delightful location on the bank of the Pioneer River. Pastas and wood-fired pizzas a speciality.

Satchmo's at the Reef
Mackay Marina
Tel: 4955 6055
Open: L & D daily. $
Tapas-style menu includes such dishes as tamarind-, chilli-and-coconut-marinated lamb cutlets and Singapore coconut noodle cakes.

Sorbello's Italian Restaurant
166 Victoria Street
Tel: 4957 8300
Open: L & D daily. $$
Speciality pastas and wood-fired pizzas. Traditional Italian decor.

Toong Tong Thai Restaurant
10 Sydney Street
Tel: 4957 8051
Open: L Mon–Fri, D daily. $
Curries and stir-fried dishes from Central Thailand. BYO.

The Islands
Most island resorts welcome day guests for lunch, though it is prudent to book ahead.

Hamilton Island (tel: 4946 9999) offers everything from wood-fired pizza to fine dining. The Beach House restaurant has an atmosphere of laid-back luxury (average main A$39–$49). Away from the bustling

harbour, the Outrigger Restaurant delivers modern cuisine with French and Japanese overtones (average main A$27–$37). For cheap eats and live music, young travellers head for Toucan Tango overlooking Catseye Beach. The island has a Kids Eat Free programme, offering free meals to kids 14 and under when dining with parents. Most places offer this service, but not all.

On **South Molle Island** (tel: 1800 075 080), day trippers can join resort guests for the buffet lunch (A$19).

Mermaids Restaurant on **Daydream Island** (tel: 4948 8488) is open for lunch daily, offering café-style fare such as tropical open grilled sandwiches and salt-and-pepper calamari (average spend A$20).

Hayman Island has five restaurants but only two are open for lunch. The Hayman Pool Bar and Beach Pavilion serves light lunches daily noon-5.30pm, including fish and chips, burgers and tapas (A$26–$35).

AROUND TOWNSVILLE

From gold rush to tourist boom, the area in and around Queensland's second-largest city is rich with attractions. There's architectural heritage in Townsville, Ravenswood and Charters Towers, plus natural wonders on the doorstep – from vast waterfalls to spectacular gorges, tropical rainforest and unspoilt island beaches

Brisbane ●

A dministrative headquarters for Queensland's far north and the state's second biggest city, Townsville is the hub of a thriving tourism industry as well as a prosperous service centre for the mineral-rich hinterland. A diverse, mostly youthful mix of people keep the city's casino, nightclubs and restaurants humming. Inland lie the gold-rush towns of Ravenswood and Charters Towers. The region also offers mountainous rainforests, pretty creeks, cane and banana plantations and, at Wallaman Falls, Australia's longest single-drop waterfall. Off the coast lie some of Far North Queensland's most spectacular islands – among them Hinchinbrook Island, Australia's biggest national park island.

Townsville

Townsville ❶ has never looked better – thanks, ironically, to two destructive cyclones that ripped the foreshore apart in 1997 and 1998, prompting a A$29 million restoration along The Strand. (Thankfully, Cyclone Larry in 2006 had no impact on the town.) Four man-made headlands jut into the sea, breaking the waves; thousands of palms and shrubs line the foreshore; and netted enclosures keep stingers at bay from November to May. Now, this 2-km (1¼-mile) stretch of

white sand, swaying palms and casual restaurants has redefined Townsville as a tropical resort of considerable appeal.

History and heritage

The city takes its name from Robert Towns, the entrepreneur widely credited with instigating the dubious system of importing indentured South Seas labourers to accomplish the hard work white men could not, or would not, do. Towns spent just three days in the city that bears his

Map on page 162

LEFT: the swimming hole at Little Crystal Creek, near Paluma.
BELOW: the water park on Townsville's Strand.

TIP

Dominating the cityscape of Townsville is the silhouette of 286-metre (940-ft) Castle Hill. Fine views of the city are to be had from the top. For the less energetic, the panoramic point at the top of 585-metre (1,920-ft) Mount Stuart is accessed by road 2 km (1¼ miles) south of Townsville.

BELOW: Townsville tower. The town centre has some impressive Art Deco buildings to go with the usual Victoriana.

name. Fortuitously, the establishment of the port of Townsville coincided with the discovery of gold at Ravenswood *(see below)*, the sugar-growing boom and the expansion of pastoral industries.

Townsville has a profusion of heritage buildings, 58 of which are listed by the National Trust. The City Council has mapped out a series of walks which highlight the older buildings. Contact the Townsville Visitor Information Centre (tel: 1800 801 902).

The city's picturesque, yacht-filled Ross River was named after William Ross, who opened the city's first pub, **The Criterion Hotel**, on The Strand. The splendid old **Post Office** (1861), on the corner of Flinders and Denham Streets, now houses an entertainment venue called The Brewery. Opposite is the **Perc Tucker Regional Gallery** (Mon–Fri 10am–5pm, Sat and Sun 10am–2pm; tel: 4727 9011; www.townsville.qld.gov.au/perctucker; free), formerly

the Union Bank of Australia, built in 1881. The gallery showcases a collection of north Queensland art and also puts on a programme of music, theatre, dance and talks.

Merely to glance at the city's **Railway Station** (1903) is to comprehend the importance of rail transport in Queensland at the turn of the 20th century. At the terminus of a track connecting the inland gold-mining centres of Ravenswood and Charters Towers, this commanding building represents 19th-century railway architecture at its most eloquent.

Modern Townsville has a cosmopolitan edge that suits the elegance of its colonial backdrop. There's a casino overlooking Cleveland Bay, and a dozen or so eating places jostle for attention in **Palmer Street**.

Wildlife watching

In and around Townsville are various places to enjoy the weird and wonderful world of native Australian

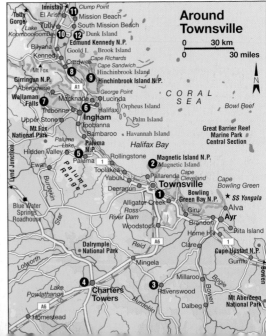

Map on page 162

fauna and flora. If you can't find time to snorkel or dive on the Great Barrier Reef, pay a visit to **Reef HQ** (Flinders Street East; daily 9.30am– 5pm; admission charge; tel: 4750 0800; www.reefhq.com.au). The world's biggest coral-reef aquarium, it contains 130 coral species, 120 fish species, plus myriad sea stars, sea urchins, sea cucumbers, sponges and assorted reef organisms. A predator tank contains reef sharks, stingrays, sea turtles and large predatory fish. There is also a replica of the bow section of the SS *Yongala*, sunk during a tropical cyclone in 1911 with 120 people on board.

At the nearby **Museum of Tropical Queensland** (daily 9.30am– 5pm; admission charge; tel: 4726 0603; www.mtq.qld.gov.au), the gallery space is taken up by a full-size reconstruction of the bow of HMS *Pandora*, the frigate dispatched from England to track down the mutinous crew of HMS *Bounty (see box below)*.

Just 17 km (10 miles) south of Townsville down the Bruce Highway is the **Billabong Sanctuary** (daily except Christmas Day 8am– 5pm;

admission charge; tel: 4778 8344; www.billabongsanctuary.com.au), a great wildlife park where you can cuddle a koala or feed a croc.

Magnetic Island

Backpacker-friendly **Magnetic Island ❷** remains an inexpensive destination – blessed by a string of stunning beaches, a resilient wildlife population and an average of 300 sunny days per year.

Within sight of Townsville, the island covers 5,200 hectares (12,850 acres) and rises to almost 500 metres (1,630 ft) at Mount Cook. It is 11 km (7 miles) at its widest point and fringed by 40 km (25 miles) of coastline. Despite increased tourism numbers, "Maggie" retains its laid-back atmosphere.

A national park, crossed by 25 km (15½ miles) of walking track, occupies over half the island. An 8-km (5-mile) hike from Picnic Bay to West Point takes in tidal wetlands, mangroves, saltwater swamps and creeks. Also starting from Picnic Bay is a 600-metre (2,000-ft) walking track to **Hawkings Point**, with views to

HMS Pandora *was sent in 1790–1 from England to find HMS* Bounty. *The* Bounty *was not discovered until 1977.*

BELOW: reef life in the aquariums at Reef HQ.

Search for the Mutineers

The English sent the naval frigate HMS *Pandora* to the South Pacific in search of mutineers from HMS *Bounty*, led by the legendary Fletcher Christian. Although the *Pandora's* captain Edward Edwards was unable to find Christian, he did manage to apprehend 14 of the *Bounty* crewmen in Tahiti. He was returning to England when his ship went down east of Cape York. Christian, immortalised by Marlon Brando in the 1962 film *Mutiny on the Bounty*, is thought by some to have been killed in 1793 by a Tahitian who accompanied him to then uncharted Pitcairn Island. A more romantic theory suggests that he slipped back to England, living undetected with his lover.

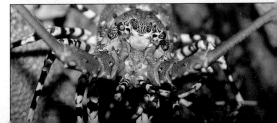

Captain Cook christened Magnetic Island in the mistaken belief that something in its geological composition had affected his compass.

Paragliding at sunset - just one of the activities available on Magnetic Island.

Townsville, Rocky Bay and Arcadia.

Fast catamaran and barge services connect Townsville Marina with Magnetic Island's Nelly Bay. Book passenger tickets through Sunferries (tel: 4771 3855; www.sunferries.com.au), vehicular barges through Magnetic Island Passenger and Car Ferry (tel: 4772 5422; www.magneticislandferry.com.au).

Off Cape Bowling Green is the wreck of the SS *Yongala*. The 90-metre (300-ft) vessel rests in about 30 metres (100 ft) of water, where it has become home to a bewildering variety of marine life. (Yongala Dives, tel: 1800 635 334; www.yongaladive.com.au; Adrenalin Dives, tel: 4724 0600; www.adrenalindive.com.au; Pro Dive Townsville, tel: 4724 0600; www.prodivetownsville.)

Ravenswood

It takes a stretch of the imagination to envisage former gold-rush town of **Ravenswood** ❸, 130 km (80 miles) south of Townsville, in 1871, when 30 hotels served a shanty town of about 1,000 fossickers. That was just three years after stockman Mar-

maduke Curr noticed specks of alluvial gold in the bottom of his pannikin after scooping up a drink of water from Elphingstone Creek.

Ravenswood's population peaked at 4,700 in 1903. After 1908 the town fell into slow decline, leaving a legacy of 19th-century buildings amid mullock heaps, tall chimneys and derelict machinery. During the 1920s many of the remaining residents walked out. Technology enabled a modest revival in the 1930s, but by the 1960s the population had fallen to 70. It is now 300.

An open-cut gold mine opened in 1987, but Ravenswood has been saved mainly by tourism. Everything that remains of the town has been listed by the Australian Heritage Commission and the National Trust of Queensland – to order a beer in the bar of **The Imperial Hotel**, Macrossan Street, is to understand why. Virtually nothing in this bar has changed since the early 1900s, down to the cedar-and-glass fittings, beer engines and ceramic taps. One of only two hotels remaining in Ravenswood – the other is **The**

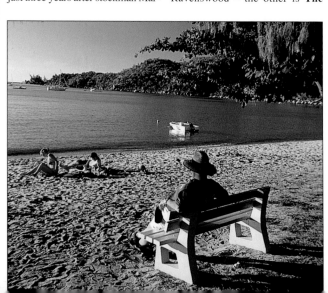

RIGHT: Alma Bay on Magnetic Island.

Railway Hotel in Barton Street – the Imperial was owned and operated by members of the Delaney family for over 90 years until 1994.

Charters Towers

During a gold boom that lasted almost three decades, **Charters Towers** ❹, 135 km (84 miles) south-west of Townsville, became Queensland's second-largest city, after Brisbane. With a population of 27,000 at its zenith, the city operated its own Stock Exchange and was known to its residents as "the World", because there was nothing that couldn't be obtained there.

Gold was discovered in 1871 by an Aboriginal youth named Jupiter, in company with three European prospectors. By the end of 1872, 3,000 hopeful prospectors had arrived, though many soon relocated to the Palmer River fields. When alluvial gold petered out, crushing machinery extracted reef gold. After 1899 yields gradually diminished, and, when the mine was declared unprofitable in 1912, many people left the city.

Private boarding schools were established in vacant heritage buildings from 1912, giving the city its second wind, and in the late 1960s tourists began to take an interest in this world-famous goldfield. Then, as now, visitors were fascinated by the **Stock Exchange** (1888), with its glazed vault supported by ornate steel trusses above a central court. Restored in the 1970s, it is now owned by the National Trust. The ground floor, where financial business was conducted, is occupied by a café, beauty salon and gift shop.

Other National Trust-listed sites include the impressive **Courthouse** (1886), at 28 Hodgkinson Street, and **Thornburgh House** (1890), at 57–59 King Street, formerly the residence of mining magnate, EHT Plant, but now a boarding school.

Behind its somewhat residential exterior, the **Civic Club**, at 36 Ryan Street, offers an intriguing insight into what it was to be a member of the Charters Towers elite in Victorian times. It was built in 1900 as the headquarters for a gentleman's club, where the wealthy and influential

Map on page 162

TIP

Exhibits in Ravenswood's Court-house Museum (Macrossan Street; daily 11am–1pm; tel: 4770 2047) trace the town's history. Ask for a map and a descriptive brochure.

BELOW: only one kind of train still comes to Ravenswood.

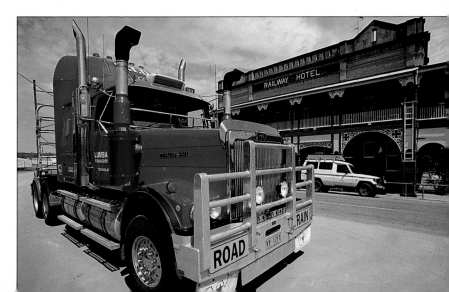

might congregate to play cards or engage in billiards. These days, the club has abandoned pretensions of all-male snootiness, and visitors are encouraged to drop by to meet the locals. Reportedly, the Friday night steak and sausage sizzle is a blast.

Pains have been taken to preserve Charters Towers' 19th-century streetscape. In some cases, heritage façades hide new buildings; the Visitor Information Centre (74 Mosman Street; daily 9am–5pm; www.charterstowers.qld.gov.au) is an example of this.

Paluma

About 60 km (37 miles) north of Townsville, the historic **Mount Spec Tourist Road** leaves the Bruce Highway, turning inland towards the mountains of the Paluma Range. This scenic road was built mostly by hand during the depression of the 1930s and forms the southern gateway to the **Wet Tropics World Heritage Area**, **Mount Spec National Park** and the tiny mountain village of **Paluma ⑤**.

Along its tortuous bends are many fine examples of stonework, the most striking of which is the much-

photographed masonry bridge over **Little Crystal Creek**, a popular swimming hole fed by icy, crystal-clear water from the gorge.

From Paluma, walking tracks access the Mount Spec area of **Paluma Range National Park**, home to the Herbert River ringtail possum and the northern bettong. About 120 avian species are found here, including all four types of bowerbird.

One of north Queensland's spectacular drives is the 15-km (9-mile) road connecting Paluma village with **Lake Paluma** (actually a large dam). The road, part gravel, passes through dense rainforest where cassowaries are sometimes seen.

Cottage accommodation is available in Paluma Rainforest Village (tel: 4770 8520; www.palumarainforest.com.au). Queensland Parks and Wildlife Service issues camping permits for Paradise Waterhole on Big Crystal Creek, at the foot of the range (tel: 4777 3112; www.epa.qld.gov.au), and NQ Water issues camping permits for Lake Paluma (tel: 4759 4759; www.nqwater.com.au).

Charters Towers is rich in grand colonial structures built on the strength of the early gold discoveries.

BELOW: the Civic Club appears unchanged since its Victorian heyday.

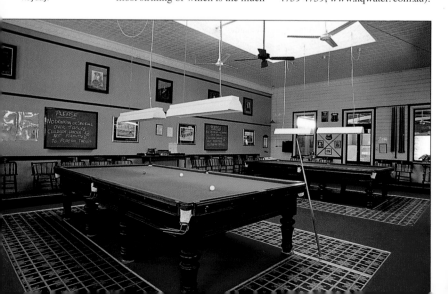

Ingham

Around 60 percent of the 5,500 citizens of **Ingham ❻** are of Italian descent, giving this northern sugar town a touch of European zest. Along the main street, older Italians talk in their native tongue and read the town's Italian-language newspaper.

Italians began arriving here in the 1890s, filling the labour shortage in the sugar fields left by Kanaka cane cutters, who were, by this time, being repatriated to their South Seas homelands. The Italian community helped each other to buy farms and bring family members to Australia, until, by the mid-1920s, Italian farmers outnumbered Anglo-Saxons – a source of deep resentment to farmers of British descent at the time. During World War II, many Italian cane workers were interned as a consequence of Mussolini's alliance with Nazi Germany.

Located 110 km (68 miles) north of Townsville, Ingham's appeal lies in its proximity to secluded beaches, fishing grounds and national parks, including one at **Orpheus Island**, 20 km (12½ miles) offshore. Anglers can fish from the shore or launch boats at **Lucinda**, a port town with a jetty nearly 6 km (4 miles) long, or at Dungeness, Forrest Beach and Taylor's Beach. Other boat ramps are at Mona Landing and Cassady Creek.

Beware of crocodiles in these parts. Do not clean fish at the water's edge, stand on floating logs (they might be crocodiles) or dangle arms and legs in the water. The man after whom Ingham was named – Oxford-educated adventurer William Ingham – paid little heed to these precautions. In the 1870s he made news in the London *Times* after wrestling and stabbing to death a 4-metre (13-ft) crocodile. Fearless to the end, Ingham met his demise in New Guinea in 1878, when cannibals boarded his boat, chopped off his hands, then roasted and devoured him.

Wallaman Falls

It's well worth the 51-km (32-mile) drive northwest to the spectacular **Wallaman Falls ❼** in **Girringun National Park**. This is Australia's longest waterfall with a single drop and is at its best following the wet-

Map on page 162

TIP

Ingham's Australian Italian Festival in May celebrates the cultural *rapprochement* between new and old Australians. It's country fun – with greasy-pole competitions, mud crab-tying events and spaghetti-eating contests. A vintage cane train is dusted off to carry children along the narrow-gauge track at Ingham's Victoria Mill, and there's a procession with Italian songs.

BELOW: beneath the canopy of Paluma's dense rainforest.

Statue gracing the the streets of laid- back Ingham, in the heart of the sugar- cane district.

BELOW: the cemetery at Ingham reflects the presence of early settlers from Italy and Spain.

season rains. You can swim at the base of the falls. However, resist the temptation to climb Mount Fox, an extinct volcano within the park, as the views from the top are disappointing. For further information, contact the Hinchinbrook Visitor Information Centre (corner of Bruce Highway and Lannercost Street, Ingham; Mon–Fri 8.45am–5pm, Sat–Sun 9am–2pm; tel: 4776 5211; www. townsvilleonline.com.au).

Cardwell

First settled in 1864, **Cardwell ❽**, located 160 km (100 miles) north of Townsville, was envisaged as the main port for north Queensland. However, mountain ranges to the west made access difficult, and the discovery of gold at Charters Towers gave Townsville the advantage. Virtually unnoticed for most of its existence, Cardwell grabbed the headlines in the late 1990s due to a controversial development by entrepreneur Keith Williams. Environmentalists greeted Williams's Port Hinchinbrook scheme with deep dismay, engaging in a war of words

over the impact of a mega-resort on the nearby World Heritage-listed Hinchinbrook Island *(see opposite)*.

Green arguments fell on deaf ears. Today, a palm-lined drive leads to a massive marina, where pleasure boats bob and lavish apartments overlook one of the most beautiful islands on the planet. When completed, **Port Hinchinbrook** will contain over 600 private residences, apartments and villas, a hotel, a 250-berth marina, an 18-hole golf course, a health club and associated recreational facilities.

Edmund Kennedy National Park, 4 km (2½ miles) north of Cardwell, was named after explorer Edmund Kennedy, who passed this way in 1848 while attempting to travel overland from Rockingham Bay to Cape York *(see page 21)*. A network of walking tracks passes through and over tropical rainforest and mangroves.

There's a spectacular lookout 2.5 km (1½ miles) west of Cardwell. A 20-km (12½-mile) scenic drive takes in swimming holes at **Attie Creek Falls**, **Dead Horse Creek** and the

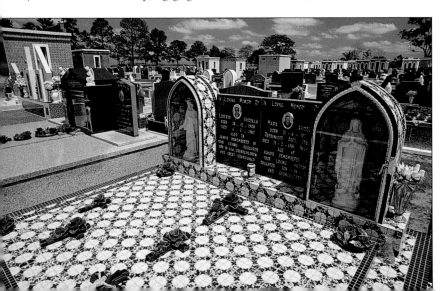

Spa Pool, finishing near Edmund Kennedy National Park. For further information, contact the Rainforest and Reef Visitor Centre (142 Victoria Street, Cardwell; daily 8am–4.30pm; tel: 4066 8601; www. epa.qld.gov.au).

Hinchinbrook Island

Hinchinbrook Island ❾, 160 km (100 miles) north of Townsville, is Australia's biggest national park island, with no human presence save for a small resort at Cape Richards (tel: 4066 8270; www.hinchinbrookresort.com) and assorted bushwalkers. Within the island's 39,900 hectares (98,500 acres) are lush rainforests, heath-covered mountains, sweeping sandy beaches, rocky headlands, paperbark and palm wetlands, mangrove-fringed shores and open woodlands.

The best time to follow the 32-km (20-mile) trail along the island's east coast is during the cooler months, from April to September. Camping grounds have been established along the route. Allow three days to complete the journey and note that this

trek is for fit and experienced bushwalkers *(see page 269)*. Limits apply to the number of walkers allowed on the trail at any one time, and bookings are required at least six months in advance.

Water taxis from Cardwell and Lucinda transfer campers and walkers to the island. Ingham Travel operates a shuttle bus between Cardwell, Ingham and Lucinda. For details on walks or access, contact the Rainforest and Reef Visitor Centre.

Tully

The highway north of Cardwell passes through cane farms and banana plantations interspersed with pretty creeks and swathes of rainforest. It's picturesque country, made luxuriant by tropical rainstorms. The road passes Kennedy, a tiny town with a store and a school, before crossing the Tully River and leading into the main street of **Tully** ❿.

Other Queensland cities make much of their sunny weather. Tully, about 240 km (150 miles) north of Townsville, celebrates the rain. Indeed, the first thing you notice on

Map on page 162

Tully's 3,500 citizens compete with Babinda and Innisfail for the Golden Gumboot award for highest rainfall. It's tongue-in-cheek stuff, but rivals take genuine pleasure in sinking in the boot when Tully falls behind. Undeterred, Tully hosts the annual Golden Gumboot Festival every September, when events include a gumboot throwing competition.

BELOW: Hinchinbrook Island seen from the jetty at Cardwell.

entering the main street is a huge **Gumboot**. The boot stands 7.93 metres (26 ft) high – the height the rain reached during Tully's record-breaking deluge in 1950 *(see page 130)*. Inside, a spiral staircase accesses a viewing platform with views to the Tully Sugar Mill and Mount Tyson.

Originally known as Banyan, Tully was surveyed in 1883, but little happened until 1925 when the government built the (then) biggest sugar mill in Australia – now the heart of Tully. Massive areas of sugar cane are under cultivation, and, during harvest from June to November, the mill operates day and night, crushing over 2.4 million tons. Banana production is also thriving.

Guided tours of the mill are more or less mandatory during the harvest, and hardy visitors can undertake a three-hour hike to the Mount Tyson lookout for an overview of Tully and the surrounding farms.

The main tourist attraction is the **Tully Gorge**, which descends from an escarpment to form more than 45 rapids that thunder in spectacular style through steep gorges amid World Heritage-listed rainforest.

The lure of adventure draws thousands of white-water rafters annually. The experience is open to beginners as well as more experienced rafters, under the supervision of qualified river guides. The Flip Wilson Lookout downriver from the Cardstone Weir offers a good observation point for watching the rafters as they plummet past, wide-eyed and charged with adrenalin. For information about rafting and bushwalks, contact Tully Visitor and Heritage Centre, Bruce Highway, Tully; tel: 4068 2288; www.csc.com.au.

Misty Mountains

Inland from Tully and Innisfail is Australia's first network of long-distance wilderness walks in high-altitude rainforest – the Misty Mountains (tel: 4046 6600; www.misty-mountains.com.au), which can also be accessed from Cairns *(see page 185)*. More than 130 km (81 miles) of tracks have been constructed along old logging trails, often following the ridgelines used by the traditional

Tully Gorge rafting operators will arange pickups from Mission Beach and Cairns.

BELOW: Sunday afternoon in Tully.

Aboriginal owners. One of the more appealing walks is the five-hour return trek through pristine rainforest to the rarely visited but serenely beautiful **Elizabeth Grant Falls**, cascading 300 metres (1,000 ft) into Koolmoon Creek. The start of the walk is 40 km (25 miles) from Tully along Tully Gorge Road (also known as Cardstone Road). Follow the signs and turn right into Cochable Creek campground. To book, tel: 13 13 04 or contact: www.qld.gov.au/camping.

Mission Beach

Turn right north of Tully for the 20-km (12½-mile) drive to **Mission Beach ⓫** – the generic name for a string of small seaside communities set amid rainforest. Mission Beach is a chic resort village with decent restaurants and an atmosphere that hovers between upmarket exclusivity and backpacker *joie de vivre*.

The name derives from the Aboriginal mission established in 1914 but destroyed by a cyclone four years later. The strip runs north from Tam O'Shanter Point to South Mission Beach, Wongaling, Mission Beach, Clump Point and Bingil Bay. **Clump Point** is the departure point for cruises to the Great Barrier Reef and Dunk Island. The area has well-marked rainforest walks where cassowary sightings are not uncommon.

The Mission Beach Visitors Information Centre (Porter Promenade; tel: 4068 7099; www.mission beachtourism.com) can provide details of the region.

Dunk Island

A regular ferry service connects Mission Beach with **Dunk Island ⓬**, the island chronicled by Edmund James Banfield in his book *Confessions of a Beachcomber*. Only 6 km (4 miles) long and 2 km (1¼ miles) wide, the island is small enough to feel intimate, big enough to permit moments of solitude. A four-star, family-orientated resort (tel: 612 8296 8010; www.dunk-island.com) occupies the northwestern end. The rest of the island is national park. Views over the island and the mainland, 4.5 km (3 miles) away, can be had from the 271-metre (890-ft) **Mount Koo-tal-oo**. ❏

Map on page 162

Dunk Island is open to day-trippers who can catch the regular ferry across from Mission Beach.

BELOW: any afternoon on Mission Beach.

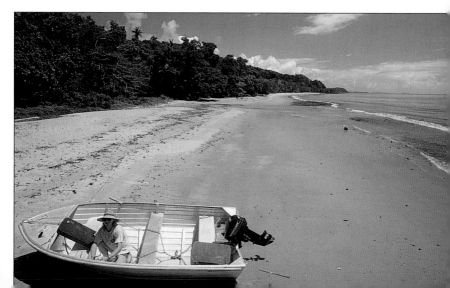

RESTAURANTS, CAFÉS & BARS

Cardwell

Portside
Port Hinchinbrook Marina
Tel: 4066 4007
Open: L & D daily. **$$**
Portside offers a modern menu based on steak, wild-caught barramundi and local mud crab. Tables spill onto a deck with great views overlooking the marina and Hinchinbrook Island. The wine list covers all bases from Laurent-Perrier champagne downwards.

Charters Towers

Henry's Café and Restaurant
82 Mosman Street
Tel: 4787 4333
Open: L & D Tues–Sat. **$$**
Henry's comes as something of a surprise, with

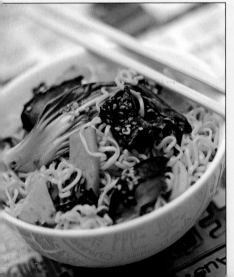

a Mod Oz menu incorporating Indian, Japanese and Thai influences. High ceilings, cream walls and slatted blinds lend this heritage-listed restaurant a delightfully cool ambience.

Redz
32 Gill Street
Tel: 4787 8044
Open: L daily. **$**
A good place to while away a few hours, as it combines a café with a bookstore. Excellent coffee, juices, bruschetta, baguettes and quiches. Interesting selection of books, too.

Dunk Island

Beachcombers
Dunk Island Resort
Tel: 4068 8199
Open: D daily. **$**

The island's main resort restaurant, specialising in tropical cuisine with a predilection for buffets.

Hinchinbrook Island

Hinchinbrook Island Wilderness Lodge Restaurant
Cape Richards
Tel: 4066 8725
Open: Apr–Jan L & D daily.
Phone ahead. **$$**
The lodge restaurant welcomes visitors and offers well-presented à la carte cuisine.

Ingham

Lou's Emporium
Lannercost Street
Tel: 4776 1587
Open: L daily. **$**
Lou's is a delicatessen, not a restaurant, but the shelves display a remarkable array of items, all connected with Italy – reflecting the substantial Italian community in Ingham. Owner Venero Cavallaro stocks everything from cutlery through to condiments.

The Olive Tree Coffee Lounge
45 Lannercost Street
Tel: 4776 5166
Open: L daily, D Fri–Sun. **$**
This is about as close as it gets to a full-on Italian restaurant in Ingham. Good coffee and Sicilian fare prepared in the traditional manner make it popular with locals, too.

Magnetic Island

Barefoot Art Food Wine
5 Pacific Drive,
Horseshoe Bay
Tel: 4758 1170
Open: L & D Thur–Mon. **$$**
There's a bit of everything here. The wine list has more than 100 entries, and the food is Mod Oz with Asian touches. Sit in a tropical garden or on the deck overlooking the sea. The art gallery is an added bonus.

Geckos
Maggie's Beach House,
Pacific Drive, Horseshoe Bay
Tel: 4778 5144
Open: L & D daily. **$**
Café and bar with a beach location, so it's a great place to watch the sun set. Geared towards budget travellers.

Sandbar Restaurant
1/7 Pacific Drive,
Horseshoe Bay
Tel: 4778 5477
Open: L daily, D Tues–Sun. **$$**
Features bistro-style food with an emphasis on seafood. Located on the beach, it's a pleasant place to chill out and people-watch.

Mission Beach

Blarney's by the Beach
10 Wongaling Beach Road
Tel: 4068 8472
Open: D Mon–Sat. **$$**
Main courses at Blarney's include crispy roast duck and grain-fed

LEFT: chop chop. Fast food takes many forms.

beef steak served with king prawns. Established in 1994, the place is popular with locals as well as tourists.

Zestivale
Castaway at the Beach Resort, Pacific Parade
Tel: 4068 7810
Open: B, L & D daily. **$$$**
Melbourne expatriate chef Peter Mcleod delivers a wide-ranging menu that includes such dishes as prime eye fillet beef with prawns and red claw in creamed garlic sauce.

Paluma

Ivy Cottage
Mount Spec Road
Tel: 4770 8533
Open: varies – phone. **$**
This is Paluma's oldest house. It's in a great location backing onto the rainforest and serves light meals and traditional treats such as Devonshire teas and coffee made the old-fashioned way.

Townsville

Bennys Hot Wok Café
17–29 Palmer Street
Tel: 4721 1474
Open: L Thur–Fri, Sun, D Tues–Sun. **$$**
The food here is a modern fusion of Thai, Japanese and Chinese. Sushi, traditional soups, Asian salads, Thai curries and stir-fries.

Bistro One
30–34 Palmer Street
Tel: 4771 6333
Open: B, L & D daily. **$$**

Chic modern Australian fare with a Mediterranean influence, using very fresh ingredients. Separate menus for breakfast, lunch and dinner.

Cactus Jack's Bar and Grill
21 Palmer Street
Tel: 4771 4511
Open: D daily. **$**
If you feel like a change, try the Tex-Mex food here – fajitas, tortillas, enchiladas, nachos et al – served along with the more familiar Ozzie fare.

C Bar Café
Gregory Street Headland, The Strand
Tel: 4724 0333
Open: L & D daily. **$$**
Attractively situated on an artificial headland, right on the beachfront, offering alfresco dining with marvellous sea views. There's a café menu by day, and more upmarket restaurant-style dining by night.

Ladah
Shop 1/157 Stanley Street
Tel: 4724 0402
Open: L daily. **$**
Gourmet café cuisine. Good breakfast menu and lunch snacks such as smoked cod and potato pie.

Michel's Café and Bar
7 Palmer Street
Tel: 4724 1460
Open: L Tues–Fri, D Tues–Sun. **$$**
Multi award-winning restaurant. Seafoods, pastas and salads served within the

restaurant or on the terrace.

Naked Fish
60 The Strand
Tel: 4724 4623
Open: D daily. **$$**
As the names implies, the emphasis here is on seafood. Pleasant location, friendly staff and an appealing menu.

The Point
The Rockpool, The Strand
Tel: 4771 6916
www.thepointtownsville.com
Open: L Fri–Sat, D Tues–Sun. **$$**
Stunning location and East-West cuisine blending a burst of flavours from China, Malaysia, Thailand and Japan.

Rhino Bar
3 Palmer Street
Tel: 4771 6322
Open: L Fri, Sun; D daily. **$$**
Tapas, steaks, draught beers and cocktails. The décor is fashionable; the crowd likewise.

Table 51
51 Palmer Street
Tel: 4721 0642
Open: L & D Wed–Sun. **$$**
Stylish upmarket restaurant with an appealing modern Australian menu. Winner of the Best New Restaurant in the RACQ awards 2005.

Wayne and Adeles Garden of Eating
11 Allen Street
Tel: 4772 2984
Open: L Sun, D Wed–Mon. **$$**
This homely restaurant has won awards annually since 1994, including Best BYO in Queensland.

PRICE CATEGORIES

Prices are for a three-course meal per person with house wine:
$ = A$60 and under
$$ = A$60–100
$$$ = A$100 and over

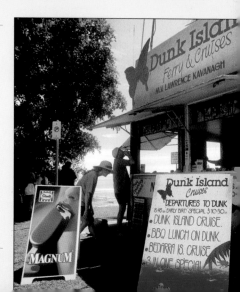

RIGHT: head to Dunk Island for a BBQ lunch.

AGRICULTURE

Go into any supermarket in Australia and there will be produce from Queensland on the shelves. It seems that the state is one giant farm, even where the land is at its most arid

Agriculture is absolutely central to the Queensland economy, with bananas, pineapples and peanuts leading the way and then a whole host of other produce following on, including cattle, sugar, cotton, wool and countless fruit and vegetables, some tropical, some temperate. It is almost impossible to travel within the state without seeing evidence of one of these, whether it's the banana fields of the tropical north, the quaint narrow-gauge trains holding up traffic as they transport sugar cane to the mills, or cattle wandering across the road in the dusty Outback.

You can visit a sugar mill during the processing season, or even stay on a farm or cattle station if you want the full hands-on experience. Most visitors, however, are happy simply to make the most of the produce further down the line, whether picking up a box of mangoes at a roadside stall, or a range of goodies at one of the markets. Better still, follow the process one step further and seek out, with the help of the dedicated sections in this book, one of the many fine restaurants that make the most of seasonal produce in season to create dizzy pleasures for the gourmand.

LEFT: Furphy's water cart was found on farms from the 1870s onwards. They were also used in World War I, and it's believed the colloquial term for a lie or rumour derives from this early equivalent of watercooler gossip.

ABOVE: pineapples, along with other tropical fruit such as mangoes and pawpaws, are shipped across Australia but tend to be cheaper locally.
LEFT: inland is cattle country, where drovers have to muster stock on huge stations that can occupy thousands and thousands of square kilometres. Eventually they will be sold at market, as here at Cloncurry.

ABOVE: in June to December sugar-cane is harvested in northern Queensland and loaded onto railtrucks which trundle slowly along narrow-gauge lines to the nearest mill. In this period it's pretty much certain that if you're driving, you will get held up at some point as the trains meander backwards and forwards across the roads.

RIGHT: rich soil and a generally predictable climate means that Queensland's farmers are producing fruit and vegetables for the rest of the country year-round.

ABOVE: bananas are a key product, and, with imports barred, Australia is dependent on northern Queensland for them. This became only too evident in 2006 when Cyclone Larry devastated the crop and within weeks none could be found.

MILL TOURS

Anyone travelling through Queensland, particularly the north, at the height of the sugar season will find it hard to avoid its sweet, sticky presence. Visit Gordonvale on the coast just south of Cairns, and the smoke billowing out from the factory chimney just beyond the town square imbues the air with a pungent syrupy fragrance that is impossible to avoid. There are no tours of this mill, but visitors to Tully, a few kilometres further south, can join a tour of the mill there and, in an hour-and-a-half with a guide, gain a basic knowledge of the crushing and processing of sugarcane. The mill works round the clock during the season and has a throughput of over 2 million tons of cane. Sugar is Queensland's largest agricultural product and the country's

second largest export crop. Most of the farms are family owned and average about 75 hectares (185 acres).

BELOW: a small but successful coffee industry feeds the booming café market. Specialist flavours include this example, featuring the de facto national nut of Australia.

CAIRNS TO CAPE TRIBULATION

Cairns is perfectly placed for exploring everything the tropical north has to offer, both on and offshore. It's the gateway to the Great Barrier Reef and the Wet Tropics rainforest, and is backed by the lush, cool plateau of the Atherton Tableland

All roads lead to Rome, but for Cairns the reverse is also true. With its own international airport, the premier city of tropical Far North Queensland attracts visitors from all over the world – only to wave them goodbye as they head off to the myriad attractions on the Great Barrier Reef, the coastal beaches and Atherton Tableland. Choppers and catamarans speed to reef platforms. Cable cars and a scenic railway connect with Kuranda's souvenir shops in the mountains beyond. There are reef excursions, journeys aboard underwater contraptions, hair-raising experiences on rapids, sybaritic champagne sessions aboard charter yachts. Visitors join 4WD safaris to Cape York, tackle marlin in the Coral Sea or embark on bushwalking expeditions. Even the food trail veers away from Cairns, plunging deep into the wilds of the Atherton Tableland. It's admirable to find operators so selflessly engaged in redirecting new arrivals to other destinations (hoping, no doubt, that they will one day return to Mother Cairns).

Gateway to Paradise

The reputation of **Cairns ❶** as a "tropical gateway" deters many visitors from devoting any length of time to exploring the city itself. Yet there is much of interest in this cosmopolitan hub. Restaurants and clubs are kept busy by a passing parade of mature travellers and fun-seeking backpackers. So much is happening that it's hard to believe that when the late Hollywood actor and game-fishing enthusiast Lee Marvin "discovered" Cairns in the 1970s, it was a sleepy backwater with ramshackle pubs, colourful characters and plenty of marlin swimming off the coast.

Change was slow until the development boom of the 1980s intro-

Map on page 178

LEFT: tourists on a glass bottomed-boat.
BELOW: taking it easy in Marlin Marina.

Drop in at the century-old Cairns Yacht Club and rub shoulders with barnacled locals while washing down prawns with beer. Hemmed in on all sides by high-rises, the club has been assured that its two-storey weatherboard headquarters will remain unmolested by developers – for the time being at least. Its veranda is a fine place to sip a beer.

BELOW: the Esplanade at Cairns.

duced modern hotels and high-rise blocks. These days, Cairns presents a sophisticated face while still exuding a sense of tropical ease from the shady verandas of its old-fashioned pubs and timber-and-tin stilt houses. The mosquito-infested swamps that blighted pioneers in the gold-and-tin rush eras have long since been reclaimed – but you can still see how Cairns used to be as you pass through steamy mangroves and verdant cane fields on the short drive from Cairns International Airport to the city centre.

With a population of 120,000, modern Cairns enjoys the benefits of air-conditioned shopping malls and international tourism. Japanese signage adorns opal stores, boutiques and gift shops; hotel clocks are set to London, New York and Tokyo time. Along The Esplanade, backpackers congregate in cafés and bars lining the strip or sunbake, minimally clad, on the lawns of an artificial lagoon –

somewhat incongruous amid locals picnicking beneath the Moreton Bay figs and palm trees. Nearby, a cluster of ritzy hotels dominates the waterfront. Completing the picture of tropical languor is The Pier Marketplace shopping complex, open daily, with weekend markets, and a marina for Cairns's marlin fishing fleet and pleasure boats.

At high tide, the ocean laps the narrow beach along the shoreline. At low tide, primeval mudflats extend to the distant blue of the sea. Cairns's affection for its mudflats became apparent some years ago when environmentalists successfully fought a scheme to inundate them.

History, art and botany

Much of the city's original architecture has been demolished, but enough remains to give an idea of how it used to be, particularly around the Wharf Road, Abbott Street and Lake Street precincts.

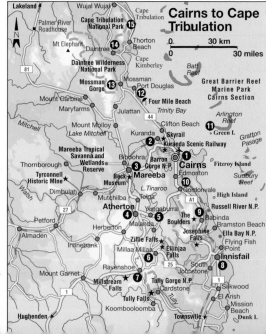

Cairns to Cape Tribulation

The row of rough-and-ready pubs that once made up the Barbary Coast Wharf precinct has been reduced to just one – the much sanitised Reef Hotel (35–41 Wharf Street), which houses a casino and, in its glass rooftop dome, an enchanting zoo (Cairns Rainforest Dome; daily 8am–6pm; admission charge; tel: 4031 7250; www.cairns dome.com.au), with the usual kookaburras and koalas, and a giant croc called Goliath.

Hides Hotel in Lake Street dates from the 1920s, when it was the epitome of tropical elegance. Opposite is the splendid School of Arts, built in 1907, now home to the **Cairns Historical Museum** (Mon–Sat 10am–4pm; admission charge; tel: 4051 5582; www.cairnsmuseum.org.au). The museum traces the city's genesis from mosquito-infested swamp to sugar town, railway terminus, port and international tourist destination.

Also on Lake Street, at no. 37, stands the former headquarters of the **Adelaide Steamship Company** (1910), still adorned by a sculpture of one of the company's vessels.

The elegant **Regional Art Gallery** (corner of Abbott and Shield Streets; Mon–Sat 10am–5pm, Sun 1pm–5pm; admission charge; tel: 4046 4800 www.cairnsregional-gallery.com.au) presents interstate and international exhibitions as well as showing works by internationally respected local artists like Ray Crooke and Rosella Namok.

One of Cairns's less visited treasures is the **Flecker Botanic Gardens** (Collins Avenue, Edge Hill; Mon–Fri 7.30am–5.30pm, Sat–Sun 8.30am–5.30pm; tel: 4044 3398). About five minutes' drive from the city centre, the main gardens are a rainforest in miniature, with tall trees and palms covered by lianas and tropical climbers, orchids, bromeliads and ferns. Boardwalks weave through lowland swamp forest and melaleuca wetland. Within the gardens is a section devoted to flora used by local Aborigines for medicine, food, weapons and shelter.

While you're in the Botanic cultural precinct, the **Tank Arts Centre** (Collins Avenue; Mon–Fri 8.30am–5pm; tel: 4032 2349) is worth a visit.

Map on page 178

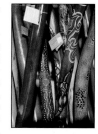

Didgeridoos for sale in Cairns.

BELOW: playing the didgeridoo at Tjapukai Cultural Park.

Aboriginal Culture Park

On the outskirts of Cairns, at Caravonica, is the **Tjapukai Aboriginal Cultural Park** (daily 9am– 5pm; www.tjapukai.com.au). Here the history and culture of the rainforest people of Tropical North Queensland is showcased through high-tech theatrical performances full of dazzling special effects. As you might expect of a show that has been in continuous performance since the mid-'80s (with an entry in the Guinness Book of Records to prove it), it runs smoothly, if routinely. A cinema within the complex screens archival footage of life on an Aboriginal mission in the 1950s, with sobering depictions of massacres and photographs of Aboriginal people in chains.

Barron Falls is one of the main stops on the trip up to Kuranda. The falls can also be seen from the Skyrail cableway.

BELOW: Kuranda scenic railway.

Ingenious use of converted World War II fuel tanks has created space for art and photography exhibitions, jazz concerts and markets.

Walk along Collins Avenue to a small off-street parking bay, which is the beginning of the **Red Arrow Walk**. A well-made but steep walking track leads you to tranquil gullies, through virgin rainforest, and to sweeping viewpoints that look out over the town centre, Trinity Bay, the airport, and the mangrove creeks and swamps along the coast.

Palm Cove

North of Cairns is a string of pretty laid-back beaches, all clearly indicated on the Captain Cook Highway. Upmarket **Palm Cove** is the largest of these northern beach resort areas before reaching Port Douglas, and is where many visitors base themselves. Once a secluded playground for Cairns dwellers, Palm Cove has attracted low-rise development that conspires to enhance rather than diminish this esplanade of subtle resorts, tall palms and towering melaleucas.

Unlike Cairns, it has a beach, with waters that are deeper than at other beaches further south, making it clearer in choppy weather.

Kuranda

These days, most tourists split the pleasant 44-km (27-mile) return trip from Cairns to **Kuranda ❷** (pop. 600) into two experiences (both more enjoyable than the visit to Kuranda itself). A train, with vintage coaches, takes you in one direction, climbing tortuously amid spectacular scenery, through tunnels and past impressive waterfalls; the other half of the journey is by **Skyrail**, a 7.5-km (4½-mile) aerial tramway that glides over the treetops of the **Barron Gorge National Park**. This ingenious piece of engineering allows you to see the gorge's eucalyptus woodlands and vine-clad rainforests without the inconvenience of skinned shins or tick bites. The journey takes 90 minutes and includes stops at Red Peak, where a boardwalk ventures into the rainforest, and Barron Falls, where you can see the remains of a 1930s hydroelectricity plant.

At ground level, the **Scenic Railway** winds through the gorge to the flower-decked Kuranda Railway Station, a listed building. Between 1887 and 1891, a workforce of 1,500 men built the 24 km (15 miles) of track between Redlynch and Kuranda, which entailed the construction of no fewer than 15 tunnels and 40 bridges – all by hand. The Christmas Creek railway bridge is a rare example of wrought-iron construction.

At the Kuranda Railway Station, there's a free bus to the village, where tourism has taken over. Among Kuranda's attractions are the **Heritage Markets** (Rob Veiver's Drive; daily 10am–4pm), selling a cheerful jumble of local and imported arts and crafts and produce. Near by is a butterfly sanctuary, a koala park and an aviary (complete with resident cassowary).

A third way to reach Kuranda is by bus from the terminus in Lake Street, Cairns. Contact White Car Coaches (tel: 4091 1855) for schedules. For more information, contact the Kuranda Information Centre (daily 10am–4pm; tel: 4093 9311; www.kuranda.org).

Mareeba

It's a 64-km (40-mile) drive from Cairns to **Mareeba ❸** – famous as a tobacco town until anti-smoking campaigns rendered the crop unviable, now better known for sugar, coffee, mangoes and tropical fruits. It's possible to sample coffee and tropical fruit wines at local plantations. One of the biggest operations is the Nastasi family's Golden Drop Winery (227 Bilwon Road; daily 8am–6.30pm; tel: 4093 2750) which specialises in mango wine. More diverse is the **Mount Uncle Distillery** (1819 Chewko Road, Walkamin; daily 10am–5pm; tel: 4086 8008), a working banana, avocado and macadamia nut farm where visitors are invited to taste home-made

banana, coffee, mulberry and mango liqueurs. North Queensland Gold Coffee Plantation (Dimbulah Road, via Mareeba; tel: 4093 2269) offers plantation tours and coffee tastings. Another "food trail" stop is **The Coffee Works** (136 Mason Street, Mareeba; tel: 4092 4101), where visitors are shown through the blending factory before being invited to sample house specialities like macadamia-flavoured coffee, coffee liqueur and chocolate-coated macadamia nuts.

North of Mareeba, at the end of an unsealed road which winds for 7.5 km (4½ miles) through sugarcane fields, is the **Mareeba Tropical Savannah and Wetland Reserve** (Pickford Road; April–Dec, Wed–Sun, 10am–4pm; free; tel: 4093 2514; www.mareebawetlands.com). This is a gateway to the Cape York peninsula and the Gulf Savannah region, presenting a superb introduction to the wonderful biodiversity along the Savannah Way, the route that stretches across the top of Australia from Mareeba to Broome 3,200 km (2,000 miles) away *(see*

Mareeba is a service centre for the Cape York and Gulf Country cattle stations. Huge road trains bring beasts from outlying stations each week to be auctioned. Every July, ringers and stockmen converge for Mareeba's rodeo.

BELOW: mango grower in Mareeba.

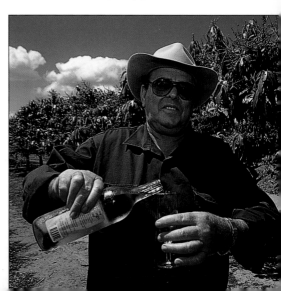

Chillagoe

The former mining settlement of Chillagoe is an archetypal Outback town. The ruins and relics of boilers, steam engines and tall chimney stacks set against jagged limestone outcrops, chiaroscuro caves and ancient Aboriginal rock paintings present a surreal and captivating landscape. Located 215 km (134 miles) west of Cairns, via Mareeba and Dimbulah, Chillagoe can be visited on a day trip from Cairns, but an overnight stay will give you more time to absorb this fascinating place. The Hub Interpretive Centre (Queen Street; tel: 4094 7111) is a good place to get your bearings, and provides an overview of Chillagoe's mining history.

Chillagoe's life as a mining town began in 1887, when magnate John Moffat pegged claims in the area and built a private railway between Chillagoe and Mareeba. Construction of his Chillagoe smelter began in 1900, setting the scene for a sorry saga of ineptitude, scandal and plain bad luck. First, a series of mishaps resulted in the smelter standing idle for the duration of the World War I metals boom. Allegations of corruption at the smelters in the 1920s led to a Royal Commission which sank the career of Federal Treasurer "Red" Ted Theodore. Through the 1930s, the then state-owned smelters made

stupendous losses in a noble but futile bid to alleviate the Great Depression. In 1943, the works closed for the fourth and final time. In all its history, the Chillagoe smelters never once turned a profit. Today, the main chimney still dominates the township.

There are about 150 derelict copper and lead mines in the area, but the township's main attraction are the limestone caves that surround it. The Chillagoe caves were formed 400 million years ago when receding sea levels exposed ancient coral reefs. Today stalactites, stalagmites and flowstones embellish the caverns and passages. Several species of bat have colonised the caves, which also provide one of only five known nesting places for the white-rumped swiftlet, an avian species that shares the bat's ability to navigate in darkness.

Above ground, a belt of soaring limestone pinnacles 45 km (28 miles) long and 5 km (3 miles) wide extends to the south and northwest. Up to 70 metres (230 ft) high, these eerie towers are an unforgettable sight. Flora has a tough time of it around Chillagoe but the harshness of the terrain creates interesting variants – notably the brilliant red blossoms of bat's-wing coral trees and the bulbous trunks of bottle trees.

Among the most impressive caves in the Chillagoe–Mungana National Park is Royal Arch Cave, a 1.5-km (1-mile) passage punctuated by 13 side chambers, random tree roots and intermittent shafts of light. Walking paths connect Royal Arch with Donna, Pompeii, Bauhinia and Trezkinn Caves – and also join with another marvel called Balancing Rock, a gravity-defying boulder balanced on its end. Another absorbing cave is The Archways, 16 km (10 miles) northwest of Chillagoe, where daylight filters through passages edged with maiden hair fern, and Aboriginal art adorns the smaller galleries.

It is permissible to explore The Archways, Pompeii and Bauhinia Caves without a guide. However, if you do go it alone QPWS advises you to take at least two torches and always to go accompanied. For self-guided maps and/or a copy of *Rocks and Landscapes of the Chillagoe District*, contact Chillagoe–Mungana Caves National Park (Queen Street, Chillagoe; tel: 4094 7163). Guided tours of the Royal Arch, Trezkinn and Donna Caves can be booked at The Hub. ❏

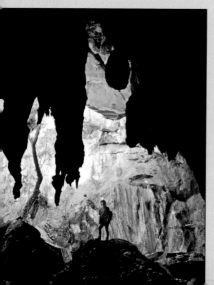

LEFT: impressive rock formations.

page 209). **Clancy's Lagoon**, fed by excess irrigation water, attracts a high concentration of regional wildlife such as brolgas, sarus, cranes, red-tailed black cockatoos and the strikingly elegant jabiru, Australia's only stork. The facility is staffed by rangers. You can do several walks on your own, but guided boat tours and twilight wildlife safaris are available (advance booking required).

Military hardware enthusiasts will enjoy the **Beck Museum** (Kennedy Highway; daily 10am–5pm; admission charge; tel: 4092 3979) on the southern edge of Mareeba. Its extensive collection includes 1940s aircraft, vehicles and weaponry, most of it housed in a huge hangar.

Head south on the highway for the township of Tolga and the **Big Peanut**, where you can sample hot, freshly roasted peanuts right beside the plantation *(see page 130).*

Tyrconnell

Southwest of Mareeba lies Dimbulah and the **Tyrconnell Historic Mine** (tel: 4093 5177; www.tyrconnell.com.au), a well-preserved rem-nant of 19th-century gold fever. The highlight of the mine site tour, taken either on a day trip or during an overnight stay in one of the cabins *(see right),* is the firing up of the quartz-crushing machine. Despite a century of neglect, this steam-age antique clatters into action, with a great whirring of flywheels and the crack of mechanical hammers.

A few kilometres away is **Thornborough**, a once roistering gold town of 22 hotels and 10,000 souls, now reduced to a decayed scattering of rusty tin shacks and a cemetery where early settlers are buried.

Atherton and Yungaburra

Sandwiched between the Cairns coast and the Outback at the edge of the Great Dividing Range is the lush and elevated sweep of the Atherton Tableland. It's a rain-soaked area of fertile pastures, dairy farms, country towns, scenic lakes, tropical forests and waterfalls. Handy to local attractions is the country town of **Atherton ❹**, where the Atherton Tableland Information Centre (corner of Main Street and Silo Road; daily 9am–

For a taste of bush life, the Tyrconnell Outback Experience (www.tyrconnell.com.au), run by mine owners Andy Bell and Cate Harley, offers accommodation in cottages and camp-grounds. Gold-panning, bushwalking, stargazing and horse-riding are among the activities laid on for guests.

BELOW: historic church in Yungaburra.

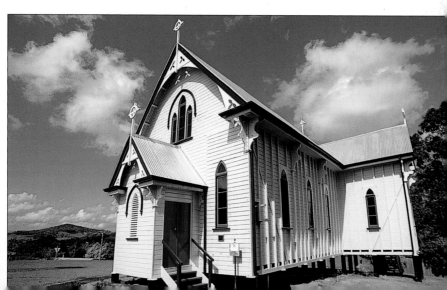

TIP

Spend a tranquil afternoon at Lake Eacham, a volcanic crater lake in the rainforest, not far from Yungaburra. You can swim in the placid water or follow signs to the ranger station to pick up trail maps. There is a 3-km (2-mile) circuit around the lake, which is a cassowary habitat, and you're also likely to see scrub turkeys, yellow robins and a range of water-birds.

BELOW: Millstream Falls.

5pm; tel: 4091 4022; www.athertonsc.qld.gov.au) provides maps and brochures and makes bookings.

The main point of interest in the town itself is the **Hou Wang Temple** (Herberton Road; 10am–4pm; www.houwang.org.au). Built in 1903, it was once the spiritual heart of a thriving Chinatown. When tin was discovered on the Wild River in 1880, Chinese labourers established a separate settlement across the creek from the Europeans at Prior's Pocket, later renamed after prospector John Atherton. At its height, in 1909, Chinatown comprised a short main street lined with 100 shops and houses. Commercial enterprises included a herbalist, two gambling dens, a live-music venue and several general stores. After World War I, when Chinese farm leases were made over to soldier-settlers, the Chinese population dwindled to a handful of elderly men who used the temple intermittently until the 1970s. Restored by the National Trust, the temple is lined with cedarwood and decorated with ornate carvings embellished with vermilion and gold.

Another of Atherton's attractions are the **Crystal Caves** (69 Main Street; Mon–Fri 8.30am–5pm, Sat 8.30am–4pm, Sun 10am–4pm; admission charge; tel: 4091 2365; www.crystalcaves.com.au), where the owner has built a substantial artificial cave to house his collection of crystals, fossils and gems.

Yungaburra ❺, 12 km (7½ miles) east of Atherton, is a cheerful town renowned for its heritage houses (the National Trust has listed 23 sites), picturesque crater lake (*see left*) and the 500-year-old Curtain Fig Tree, an amazing natural sculpture with long aerial roots resembling a hanging curtain. The town has a range of decent restaurants, and the Tableland's biggest market is held here on the fourth Saturday of every month, where a wide range of food and quality arts and crafts are sold. A lively two-day folk festival is held every October (www.yungaburrafolkfestival.org).

The Waterfalls Circuit

A 15-km (9-mile) drive southeast of Yungaburra through lush green hillside pastures dotted with black-and-white friesian cows, leads to **Malanda**, where dairying has been the town's main occupation since the early 1900s. Neighbouring **Millaa Millaa** ❻, 25 km (15 miles) to the south, is another dairy town – memorable because it is ringed by some of the Tableland's most spectacular waterfalls. Enter the waterfall circuit by taking the Theresa Creek Road, 1 km (⅔ mile) east of Millaa Millaa on the Palmerston Highway. **Millaa Millaa Falls** is the most photogenic, with the best swimming hole, a picnic area and teahouse. But **Zillie Falls** and **Ellinjaa Falls** are also attractive (the latter also has a swimming hole). Back on the Palmerston Highway, 5 km (3 miles) towards Innisfail, there's a turn-off to the **Mungalli Falls**.

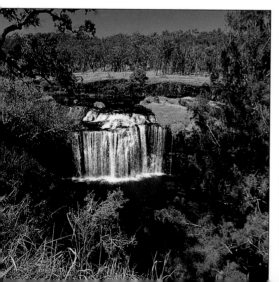

Ravenshoe

At 920 metres (3,000 ft) above sea level, **Ravenshoe** ❼, 25 km (15 miles) southwest of Millaa Millaa, is the highest town in Queensland. The town at the top of the Great Dividing Range came into being around 1900 as a centre for the timber industry. Logging was outlawed in the 1980s when the surrounding 2.2 million acres (880,000 hectares) of rainforest were declared a World Heritage site.

Today Ravenshoe provides a more sustainable resource in the form of wind-generated power. About 5 km (3miles) outside town, the 20 graceful turbines of Windy Hill Wind Farm swish musically in the breeze, generating enough electricity to supply about 3,500 homes.

Today Ravenshoe is the main entry point for the Millstream Falls and the Misty Mountains trails. **Millstream Falls** are the widest falls in Australia, spilling over an ancient lava flow. In the rain shadow of the eastern dividing ranges, the dry, open woodland offers stark contrast to the nearby rainforest. To get there,

drive 3.5 km (2 miles) past Ravenshoe on the Kennedy Highway towards Mount Garnet and look for the sign. A 400-metre (440-yard) track descends from the car park through eucalypt forest to the falls.

The **Misty Mountains Trails**, a network of long-distance walking tracks through high-altitude rainforest, and the **Tully Gorge National Park** are within easy reach *(see page 170)*. For detailed information and maps of all these natural attractions, visit the **Ravenshoe Visitor Centre** (24 Moore Street; daily 9am–4pm; tel: 4097 7700; www.ravenshoevisitorcentre.com.au).

Innisfail

Cyclones are a fact of life in Queensland's far north, but few have matched the fury of Cyclone Larry, which swept through the town of **Innisfail** ❽, 85 km (53 miles) south of Cairns, on 20 March, 2006, smashing houses and destroying crops *(see box below)*.

Innisfail, a sugar town with a strong Italian presence, has seen it all before. The ferocious Cyclone

Map on page 178

Railco, or the Ravenshoe and Atherton Insteam Locomotion Company, runs trains along a 7 km (4 mile) section of track every Saturday and Sunday.

BELOW: the aftermath of Cyclone Larry.

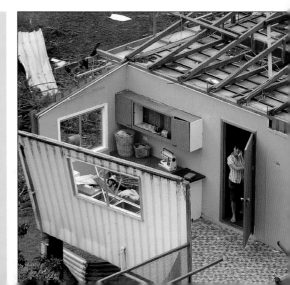

Cyclone Larry

It's impossible to comprehend the power of a tropical cyclone unless you have experienced one: according to witnesses, Larry's 250km/hour winds wrenched huge trees from the ground by the roots, then hurled them down. Innisfail absorbed the brunt, but Silkwood, Babinda, Tully, Atherton and Yungaburra also took a pounding. When the cyclone was spent, its swathe of destruction stretched from north of Cairns to Hinchinbrook Island, and as far west as Chillagoe. With overall damage estimated at A$1.5 billion, it will take time for local communities to reconstruct their towns and lives, but the people of Far North Queensland are nothing if not resilient.

This mosaic plaque in Gordonvale bemoans the blight of the cane toad, introduced from Hawaii in 1935 in the mistaken belief that it would eat the beetles that were destroying the cane crop: "Cane toads have become an economic and social liability... To date, no effective method has been found to eliminate them."

BELOW: following a rainforest trail.

Winifred which swept through in 1986 left three dead – a tragedy which, if anything, drew this 20,000-strong community closer together. Successive waves of Italian immigrants settled in Innisfail from 1907 onwards. Hard-working and frugal, the first Italians helped one another to progress from cutting cane to owning their farms.

Throughout the last century, immigrants from other countries joined the community. Today, Innisfail's population is a cosmopolitan mix of Spanish, Greek, Yugoslav, Maltese and Chinese.

The district's most romantic landmark is the ruin of **Paronella Park** (daily 9am–9.30pm; tel: 4065 3225; www.paronellapark.com.au), 20 km (12 miles) southwest of Innisfail, where, in the 1930s, a Spanish dreamer named José Paronella built a "Spanish-style castillo". Inspired by the Moorish architecture and gardens of Spain, Paronella Park was one of north Queensland's earliest tourist attractions – a pleasure palace where visitors sipped tea, played tennis or danced in the ballroom.

Despite flood, fire and weathering, you can see what it used to be. If anything, the place is more successful as a ruin than in its heyday. It now offers guided walks, bush-tucker lectures and Aboriginal dancing.

For more information about what to see and do in the region, visit the **Innisfail Information Centre** in Mourilyan, 6 km (4 miles) south of Innisfail on the Bruce Highway (open Mon–Fri 9am–4pm, Sat–Sun 10am–3pm; tel: 4063 2655; www.innisfailtourism.com.au).

Babinda and the Josephine Falls

Motoring north from Innisfail along a scenic stretch of the Bruce Highway, the next town is **Babinda** ❾. Before you get there, look for the turn-off that leads to **Josephine Falls** (20 km/12 miles from Innisfail), at the eastern approach to Mount Bartle Frere, Queensland's highest mountain. This is rugged country. Rainfall often tops 10,000 mm (395 inches), sending rivers and creeks plunging through the lush, dense rainforest that covers the landscape. It's unusual to find so much natural beauty concentrated in a rural community so close to a major centre. (Cairns is just 50 km/31 miles to the north.)

The falls are 8 km (5 miles) off the main highway and exceedingly beautiful, with tumbling cascades of water splashing over rocks amid luxuriant tropical rainforest. You can swim in the natural pools, but the rocks are slippery and flash flooding is an ever-present possibility; there have been instances of fatality and serious injury. The safe option is to observe Josephine Creek from one of the viewing platforms accessed via a 600-metre (1,950-ft) walking track leading from the car park through tropical rainforest.

The Boulders, 7 km (4 miles) west of Babinda, is another stunning location – a Wet Tropics World Heri-

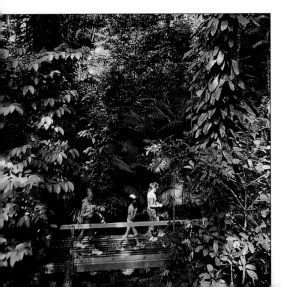

tage area with a nature reserve, visitor facilities and well-marked trails. At the time of writing, however, parts of the park were closed due to cyclone damage to bridges and walkways, so find out the latest news at Babinda before you set off.

Babinda itself is a tidy town of 1,200 people mostly engaged in the sugar industry. Its best-loved landmark is the Babinda Hotel. Built by the government in 1917 to supply lodgings for the hundreds of itinerant sugar workers, it was Queensland's only state-owned hotel. In an attempt to control alcohol consumption, the sale of liquor had been banned in all sugar-growing areas. The hotel was the only legal watering hole in the district. It would certainly have been a lively place at the end of the cane-cutters' back-breaking day.

Gordonvale

Gordonvale ⑩, 24 km (15 miles) south of Cairns, is a benign, solid town of old-fashioned shops, well-preserved streetscapes, historic buildings and a huge sugar mill, all overlooked by **Walsh's Pyramid**, the highest free-standing peak in the world. Rising 922 metres (3,000 ft), this symmetrical mountain is the venue of the Great Pyramid Race held in Gordonvale every August, when competitors clamber to the summit and back for a trophy.

Gordonvale's other claim to fame is that it was the first town to release cane toads into the wild, in the ill-conceived plan to rid the sugar crops of beetles. The toads devoured everything but beetles, and being toxic, inflicted death on native species. Even worse, they proved to be prolific breeders *(see left and page 131)*.

The route from Gordonvale to Cairns takes the Bruce Highway for 23 km (14 miles), an easy but sometimes busy road.

Green Island

Cairns is the gateway to some of the most popular destinations on the Great Barrier Reef. The 2,300-km (1,430-mile) stretch of reefs, coral cays and islands comes closest to the shore up here in the tropical north. Diving is extremely popular, but it's not the only way to experience the beauty of the reef. There are plenty of day cruises to the islands, with opportunities to go snorkelling or view the marine life from the comfort of a glass-bottomed boat.

The closest island to Cairns, lying 27 km (17 miles) offshore, is **Green Island ⑪**, an alluring place edged with white sand and ringed by reefs. Somewhat overrun by trippers during the day, the island's population shrinks dramatically at nightfall when it becomes the preserve of guests staying at the upmarket resort and a handful of residents. Old timers will tell you that the reef at Green Island isn't what it used to be. Others say it's never been better. Either way, it's worth going for a snorkel or taking a trip on one of the glass-bottomed boats operating by the pier.

Map on page 178

TIP

For those who can't see a mountain without wanting to climb it, the track up 1,622-metre (5,322-ft) Mount Bartle Frere is irresistible. Provided the summit is not shrouded in cloud (as often happens), your efforts will be rewarded with panoramic views of the Bellenden Ker Range, the coastal lowlands and the Tableland.

BELOW: narrow-gauge sugar trains crisscross the roads.

Visiting the Reef

Regardless of your reason for visiting the Great Barrier Reef, weather will play an important part in your enjoyment of its scenic attractions. From late April through to October it's at its best, the clear skies and moderate breezes offering perfect conditions for coral-viewing, diving, swimming, fishing and sunning. In November the first signs of the approaching "Wet" appear: variable winds, increasing cloud and showers. By January it rains at least once most days.

The easiest way to visit the reef is not to stay on an offshore island but to take a day trip from **Cairns** or **Port Douglas**. Every morning dozens of fully equipped diveboats and catamarans head out from the two centres to various preselected sites. You can also take reef trips from **Cape Tribulation**. About an hour later, wherever you leave from, you'll be moored by the coral. Because the water is so shallow, snorkelling is perfectly satisfactory for seeing the marine life (in fact, many people prefer it to scuba diving; even so, most boats offer tanks for experienced divers and "resort dives" for people who have never dived before).

Above the waves, the turquoise void might be broken only by a sand cay crowded with sea-

birds, but as soon as you poke your mask underwater, the world erupts. It's almost sensory overload: there are vast forests of staghorn coral, whose tips glow purple like electric Christmas-tree lights; brilliant blue clumps of mushroom coral; layers of pink plate coral; bulbous green brain coral. Tropical fish with exotic names slip about as if showing off their fluorescent patterns: painted flutemouth, long-finned batfish, crimson squirrel fish, hump-headed Maori wrasse, cornflower sergeant-major. Thrown into the mix are scarlet starfish and black sea cucumbers (phallic objects that you could pick up and squeeze, squirting water out of their ends). You definitely don't pick up the sleek conus textile shells – they shoot darts into anything that touches them, each with enough venom to kill 300 people.

Almost all reef trips follow a more or less similar format. There's a morning dive, followed by a buffet lunch; then, assuming you haven't eaten too much or partaken excessively of free beer, an afternoon dive. There should be a marine biologist on board, who will explain the reef's ecology. Before you book, ask about the number of passengers the boat takes: they vary from several hundred on the famous Quicksilver fleet of catamarans to fewer than a dozen on smaller craft.

One of the good things about the Quicksilver experience is the opportunity it affords for novices to try their hand at scuba diving. After an induction session, beginners descend into an underwater coral garden, strung with wire ropes to guide their way and marked with signs explaining what they're seeing. Friendly reef fish swim within touching distance. It's non-threatening and totally enjoyable.

As a general rule, the further out the boat heads, the more pristine the diving (the Low Isles, for example, near Port Douglas, have suffered). But don't be conned by hype about the "Outer Reef" – as the edge of the continental shelf it may be the "real" reef, but it looks exactly the same as other parts.

Even in the winter months, the water here is never cold, but it is worth paying a couple of dollars extra to hire a wetsuit anyway; most people find it hard not to go on snorkelling for hours in this extraordinary environment. ❏

LEFT: fusiliers schooling over coral reef.

In the middle of the island is a reptile park and tribal-art museum, **Marineland Melanesia** (tel: 4051 4032 for times; admission charge; www.marinelandgreenisland.com). The museum is owned by retired crocodile hunter George Craig, who spent 20 years in the Northern Territory and Papua New Guinea gathering his collection of reptiles, rare fish and primitive art. George's crocs earn their keep with twice-daily performances. The brute power of the 5.5-metre (18-ft) Cassius, 100 years of age and arguably the biggest croc in captivity, should be seen by anyone tempted to swim in crocodile habitat.

Port Douglas

A scenic coastal road heads 80 km (50 miles) north from Cairns to **Port Douglas** ⑫, a chic resort notable for its great restaurants and its proximity to the northern end of the Great Barrier Reef. Like most of the coastal settlements, it was founded after a gold rush in the 1870s, when the Gugu-Yulangi people were forced from their land. What began as a tent city of grog shops, boarding houses

and providores burgeoned into a boomtown of 8,000 residents with 20 permanent hotels, an unrecorded number of brothels, a regular postal service and a local newspaper. By 1886, gold was on the wane and miners moved to new fields in Papua New Guinea. When Cairns became the regional railhead, Port Douglas drifted into the long hibernation that prevailed until a couple of decades ago. These days it's a vibrant place, surrounded by glitzy resorts.

The approach from the main road is an early clue to the town's evolution. It is lined by an avenue of about 450 huge African oil palms, and as many again are planted around the Sheraton Mirage Resort and the Marina Mirage – part of the extravagant vision of former multi-millionaire Christopher Skase, who went spectacularly bust in a series of media and leisure ventures.

A casually elegant throng promenades along Macrossan Street's lushly landscaped boulevard of ritzy restaurants and swanky boutiques. Buildings from Port Douglas's frontier days remain. On the foreshore

Map on page 178

TIP

Food is an integral part of the experience in Port Douglas. At least 40 restaurants compete for your custom. The Nautilus Restaurant is an institution. So is the Salsa Bar and Grill. But the most interesting of them – Flames of the Forest – has no known address, appearing and disappearing like a conjurer's rabbit (see page 193).

BELOW: the upmarket Marina Mirage Resort in Port Douglas.

TIP

Heading north from Port Douglas, travellers pass cane farms and exotic fruit plantations to Miallo, famous as the place where actress Diane Cilento established her 500-seat Karnak Playhouse (tel: 4098 8111; www.karnakplay-house.com.au) with late husband, playwright Anthony Shaffer. It's worth a look for the setting alone.

stands the **Courthouse** (1879), now a museum, and near by is historic **St Mary's by the Sea** church with its dramatic open window to the sea.

The **Four Mile Beach** is among the region's most beautiful. Once backed by nothing but hinterland swamp, it retains an air of spacious solitude (the southern end is the least crowded part – or you could stroll the 4 km/2½ miles to the northern end). Avoid swimming during the stinger season (October–May) when venomous box jellyfish infest the waters. If the water proves irresistible, swim inside the nets, designed to minimise exposure to the box jellyfish's potentially fatal sting.

Every morning dozens of boats head out for day trips on the reef: just offshore are the highly popular Low Isles, while a string of excellent snorkelling spots is only an hour away. Operators range from tiny sailships catering for only a dozen passengers to the massive Quicksilver catamarans that can shuttle several hundred people at a time to a well-equipped pontoon moored on the Outer Reef (see page 188).

The Mossman Gorge

Heading north on the Captain Cook Highway, about 10 km (6 miles) beyond the turnoff to Port Douglas you'll pick up signs to **Mossman Gorge** ⑬ (about 5 km/3 miles west of the pleasant town of Mossman) at the southeastern edge of Daintree Wilderness National Park. From the car park you can access the swimming area a little way upstream. Exercise caution if you decide to swim among the rocks, especially after it's rained. Just a little further up the path is a suspension bridge leading to a 3-km (2-mile) walking circuit past mountain streams and lush, dripping foliage.

Daintree

Slightly further north, past rich sugar-cane country, is the village of **Daintree** ⑭ (55 km/34 miles from Port Douglas). For those with the time for exploratory detours on the way, side roads lead to small seaside communities at **Newell Beach** and **Wonga Beach**.

Daintree stands on the southern bank of the Daintree River, framed

BELOW: Daintree River cruise boats.

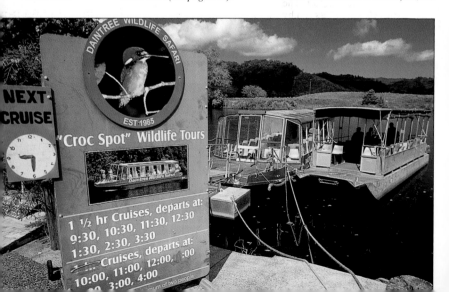

by rainforested mountains and an undulating landscape of lush farmland and cattle properties. Settled in the late-1870s by cedar fellers, Daintree enjoyed a brief incarnation as an inland port. Today, its small community thrives on tourism, offering guided walks, eco-tours and, most successfully, river cruises. The tours take you up- or downstream, depending on weather and tide, through narrow reaches lined with mangroves or rainforests that are rich in wildlife. It's unusual not to spot a crocodile at a safe distance, especially in the cooler months when the huge reptiles come out of the water to sun themselves on the river banks.

Cape Tribulation

The rainforested mountains and long sandy beaches of **Cape Tribulation ⑮** are accessed via ferry at the Daintree River Crossing, about 15 km (9 miles) back from Daintree Village. Beyond the ferry, conventional two-wheel-drive access is possible as far as Cape Tribulation. High clearance is useful, and caravans are not recommended since the road is narrow and winding. The imperfect road is compensated by one of the most beautiful and biologically diverse areas in the world, where ancient plants and animals thrive in forest-covered mountains that rise steeply from the coast. Part of the Wet Tropics World Heritage Area, this is one of Australia's last extensive areas of tropical lowland rainforest. No matter what the weather, it's an awe-inspiring sight.

The Cape Tribulation Road area is scattered with lovely places to eat and sleep – high-quality eco-lodges nestle in the forested hills and beaches. Before proceeding north, it's worth stopping at the **Alexandra Range Lookout** for sweeping views back across the wide mouth of the Daintree River, Snapper Island and the cane fields and ranges beyond.

Near by, the **Daintree Discovery Centre** (daily 8.30am–5pm; tel: 4098 9171; www.daintree-rec.com. au) provides ample information. An aerial walkway leads up to the 23-m (76-ft) Canopy Tower for a bird's-eye view of the forest floor.

Other worthwhile stop-offs are the picturesque **Cow Bay Beach** and **Thornton Beach**.

At the end of the road, **Cape Tribulation** itself has a host of accommodation and dining options from the rustic to the chic, but the focus is on the glorious mangrove-fringed **Myall Beach**.

Beyond the headland, at the southern end of Emmegen Beach, is the beginning of the **Mount Sorrow Trail**, a challenging climb to the ridge of Mount Sorrow. Less demanding is the Dubuji Boardwalk through mangroves by Myall Beach. Contacts: Tourism Tropical North Queensland (tel: 4051 3588) for general information; QPWS (tel: 4098 0052) regarding walking trails and permits. The Daintree Cape Tribulation website www.daintreecoast.com is a useful resource. ❑

Map on page 178

Cape Tribulation is an incongruous name for one of Australia's most serene corners, but then Captain Cook was in a poor mood after his ship, Endeavour, was holed on a reef in 1770: "I named...the north point Cape Tribulation because here began all our troubles." His choices for Mount Misery, Cape Sorrow and the like confirm that he wasn't having a relaxing voyage.

BELOW: Cape Tribulation beach.

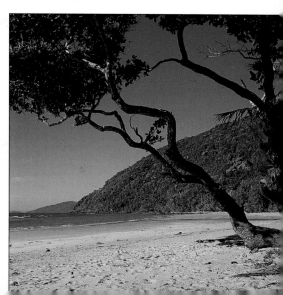

RESTAURANTS, CAFÉS & BARS

Cairns

Beethoven Café
105 Grafton Street
Tel: 4051 0292
Open: L Mon–Fri. $
Bread of all descriptions
with interesting fillings
and, the clincher, spec-
tacularly good cakes.

**Botanic Gardens Café
and Restaurant**
Flecker Botanic Gardens,
Collins Avenue, Edge Hill
Tel: 4053 7087
Open: B and L daily. $
All-day breakfasts; light
lunch until 3pm (anything
from Greek salad to
smoked salmon). Cheap
and cheerful fare in a
magnificent setting.

Café China
Rydges Plaza Hotel, corner
Grafton and Spence Streets
Tel: 4041 2828
Open: L Sun–Fri, D daily. $$
Mainly Hong Kong-style
cuisine with some
Szechuan menu entries.
House specialties
include salt-and-pepper
mud crab, Peking duck
and steamed coral trout.

Coral Hedge Brasserie
The Esplanade
Tel: 4031 2211
Open: D Tues–Sat. $$
The signature restaurant
of Rydges Esplanade
Resort. Well-presented
international cuisine is
complemented by a
seafood buffet and steak
cooked before your eyes.

Donnini's Ciao Italia
Marina at the Pier
Tel: 4051 1133
Open: L & D daily. $

Known for its excellent
pizzas, but other Italian
classics are also on
offer. Boardwalk location
with views over the
marina. Good value.

Fusion Organics
135 Grafton Street
Tel: 4051 1388
Open: L Mon–Sat. $
Health-conscious eatery,
which uses organic and
local produce. Good
coffee, juices and gluten-
free cakes.

Lemongrass
Kamerunga Road, Stratford
Tel: 4055 2707
Open: D Tues–Sat. $
Innovative mingling of
modern flavours with
eastern influences. Rea-
sonable prices too. BYO.

Mondo Café Bar & Grill
Cairns Hilton,
34 The Esplanade
Tel: 4052 6780
Open: L & D daily. $
A popular meeting place
for locals and tourists –
both for its stunning
views across the inlet
and its well-designed
menu. Just the spot for a
late-afternoon drink.

Perrotta's at the Gallery
38 Abbott Street
Tel: 4031 5899
Open: L & D daily. $
Outside the Cairns
Regional Gallery and
noted for its coffee, Perrotta's is the place to
see and be seen. Good
food. Wine by the glass.

Pesci's on the Water
C1 Pier Marketplace,
The Esplanade

Tel: 4041 1133
Open: L & D daily. $$
A fine place to watch
boats on the inlet while
enjoying very good
Mediterranean cuisine.

The Red Ochre Grill
43 Shields Street
Tel: 4051 0100
Open: L Mon–Fri, D daily. $$$
Renowned for innovative
handling of bush-tucker
flavours and native
species. Examples
include smoked wild
spice-crusted kangaroo,
crocodile wonton and
emu paté.

Tandoori Oven
62B Shields Street
Tel: 4031 0043
Open: D Mon–Sat. $
This pleasant café serves
mostly North Indian food.
The curries and breads
are good but the dishes
from the tandoori oven
are special. BYO.

Yamagen
Lake Street
Tel: 4031 6688
Open: D daily. $$$
A classy Japanese
restaurant attached to
the Cairns International
Hotel. Food and decor are
top quality. Not cheap.

Cape Tribulation

Café-on-Sea
Thornton Beach
Tel: 4098 9118
www.cafeonsea.com
Open: L & D daily. $
Casual café about 24 km
(15 miles) north of the
Daintree River ferry
offering fresh salad-

based meals. Beachfront
location makes it a fine
place for a light, afford-
able lunch – anything
from ham, cheese and
tomato baguette to wild
grilled barramundi.

**Heritage Lodge
Restaurant**
Turpentine Road, Diwan
Tel: 4098 9138
www.heritagelodge.net.au
Open: L and D daily. $$
Heritage Lodge is about
19 km (11 miles) north
of the Daintree River
ferry. Bordered by Cooper
Creek and set in pristine
rainforest, this airy
restaurant occasionally
hosts unscheduled
appearances by cas-
sowaries searching for
the bush plums growing
in the grounds. Evening
meals focus on game
dishes such as crocodile,
kangaroo and wild boar.

Chillagoe

**Chillagoe Observatory
and Eco-Lodge**
1 Hospital Avenue
Tel: 4094 7155
Open: D daily. $
Owner Susan Present
offers a good standard
of menu served within a
covered open space
surrounded by greenery
and birdlife.

Post Office Hotel
17 Queen Street
Tel: 4094 7119
Open: L daily, D Mon–Sat. $
Country-style pub grub
served at the bar or in
the beer garden.

Daintree

Julaymba Restaurant and Gallery

20 Daintree Road
Tel: 4098 6100
Open: L & D daily. **$$$**
Overlooks a peaceful freshwater lagoon within the rainforest. The menu incorporates bush-tucker flavours; typical of the dishes are red claw wok tossed in fresh ginger and garlic, or crocodile tortellini in a saffron and fennel sauce, served with rocket and munthari berries. Named after the local Kuku Yalanji word for Daintree River, Julaymba Restaurant is part of the Daintree Eco-Lodge and Spa.

Green Island

Emerald Restaurant

Green Island Resort
Tel: 4031 3300
Open: L & D daily. **$$$**
This restaurant leaves no stone unturned in its effort to present fabulously luxurious cuisine. Service is flawless, the setting superb.

Millaa Millaa

Out of the Whey Café

Brooks Road, Mungalli (near Millaa Millaa)
Open: L daily. **$**
This isn't a restaurant in the strict sense. it's a farmhouse veranda where farmers Rob and Sally Watson serve light refreshments to visitors who've come to see cheese and yoghurt being made. The Mungalli Creek Dairy is 10 km (6 miles) from Millaa Millaa.

Palm Cove

Far Horizons Restaurant

Angsana Resort,
1 Veivers Road
Tel: 4055 3000
Open: B, L & D daily. **$$**
Well-reviewed restaurant in a beautiful location featuring international cuisine with an Asian influence. Dine alfresco by the beach or indoors.

Nu Nu's

Outrigger Beach Club,
123 Williams Esplanade
Tel: 4059 1880
Open: L & D daily. **$$$**
Nu Nu's is owned by Nick Holloway (formerly head chef at Melbourne's Pearl Restaurant). Cairns foodies go into raptures about his use of Asian and Mediterranean flavours. Everything is made from scratch – from breads and jams through to coconut creams.

Palm Cove Tavern

Veivers Road
Tel: 4059 1339
Open: L & D daily. **$**
Good quality pub grub in this busy establishment where service just fails to keep up with the demands of the diners.

Sebel Reef House Restaurant

99 Williams Esplanade
Tel: 4055 3633
Open: L & D daily. **$$$**
Renowned chef Philip Mitchell's fare exhibits deceptive simplicity. By day, he tempts with meze plates of hummus, ground feta and olive, aubergine salsa and roti bread. By night, he serves entrées such as crispy fried ocean prawns

with lime, coconut, mango, soy and ginger.

Port Douglas

Flames of the Forest

Bus begins picking up diners from 6pm.
Tel: 4098 2755
www.flamesoftheforest.com.au
Open: D Thur–Sat. **$$$**
Dine in the rainforest and listen to Aboriginal stories: guests are picked up from their hotels and transported to the Mowbray Valley, where flames light a path to a clearing and candles flicker beside a stream. More candles illuminate tables, immaculately set. It's *Lord of the Rings* meets *Alice in Wonderland* – an original and magical experience.

Nautilus Restaurant

17 Murphy Street
Tel: 4099 5330
www.nautilus-restaurant.com.au
Open: D daily. **$$$**
Everybody in Port Douglas goes to the Nautilus at least once. Bill and Hilary Clinton, Rod Stewart and Mick Jagger have been – along with many thousands of less celebrated diners, who soak up the tropical ambience while sampling such culinary offerings as wok-tossed squid with vegetables, tatsoi and lychees.

Salsa Bar and Grill

26 Wharf Street
Tel: 4099 4922
www.salsa-port-douglas.com.au
Open: L & D daily. **$$**
If any one dish exemplifies Port Douglas, it's the chilli mud crab,

and this is the best place to try it: the house speciality is fat, fresh crab with richly flavoured sauce. The restaurant itself is airy with an open deck and a view across Wharf Street to St Mary's and Dickson's Inlet.

Yungaburra

Eden House Heritage Restaurant

20 Gillies Highway
Tel: 4095 3355
www.edenhouse.com.au
Open: L Sun, D Thur–Mon. **$$$**
Highly regarded French chef Laurent Pedemay wields the skillet, delivering a menu based on locally sourced produce. Pedemay handles Gallic cuisine with authority, with added Asian and now Australian flavours.

Nick's Swiss Italian Restaurant

33 Gillies Highway
Tel: 4095 3330
Open: L Wed, Fri–Sun, D Tues–Sun. **$$**
Nick has been serving Italian-Swiss cuisine and modern Australian dishes since 1986. The Alpine theme does seem a little at odds with his prize-winning tropical garden – but after a few beverages from the Yodeller's Bar, who cares?

PRICE CATEGORIES

Prices are for a three-course meal per person with house wine:
$ = under A$60
$$ = A$60–90
$$$ = A$90–120
$$$$ = A$120 +

RAINFOREST

Tropical or temperate, rainforest is one of Queensland's defining characteristics, as well as a key tourist attraction

High rainfall – at least 2 metres (6 ½ ft) – is a prerequisite for rainforest, and then it's generally a matter of latitude and proximity to the ocean which defines it as tropical or temperate. Queensland is big enough to have both. Rainforests are nature *in extremis*. Two-thirds of all the earth's plant and animal species can be found within them, and in north Queensland the highest diversity of local endemic species in the world is present. It is the last bastion for some of them, while others are still being discovered, particularly in the upper regions under the canopy, an area only recently appreciated for the richness of its various flora and fauna.

It is estimated that the tropical rainforest stretching from just north of Cairns to Cape Tribulation and on to Cooktown is in the region of 110 million years old, and constitutes the last remnant of the forest that used to cover all of Australia and, before that, Gondwanaland. Now protected as an element of the Wet Tropics World Heritage Area, it is a key attraction for monied tourists, and so the economic rationale that has seen the destruction of forests elsewhere in Australia and round the world, would probably now protect it, irrespective of the heritage listing.

LEFT: the cassowary can still be found in small pockets of dense rainforest, but you're more likely to see the road sign than the real thing.
BELOW: one of the best places to spot platypus is in the rivers and streams of the Atherton Tableland where the climate is temperate. Try looking beside the bridge in Yungaburra, in early morning or at dusk.

LEFT: the frill-necked lizard may be seen on the ground and sometimes in the trees searching for insects. The ruff normally only fans out (and its jaws will be agape for extra effect) when the lizard is frightened; the rest of the time it lies streamlined against its neck and shoulders.

THE DAINTREE

Some of the most easily accessible rainforest, and therefore most visited, is in the Daintree National Park. There's a well-worn route from Cairns or Port Douglas up to Cape Tribulation, and every tour bus or expedition will stop at least once for a walk in the woods. In several places there are short boardwalk circuits from handy parking spots, and the way is marked by a series of interpretive boards. This makes it easy for the visitor and also helps in managing the forest by keeping tourists away from more pristine areas.

The complete packaged rainforest experience can be enjoyed at the Daintree Discovery Centre, a short distance north of the Daintree Ferry. Boardwalks wend along the forest floor, and a steel walkway through the canopy allows an entirely different perspective on life as the birds see it. Audio guides are available and there are more of the ubiquitous interpretive boards. The cassowaries here seem used to visitors.

ABOVE: treefrog.
LEFT: brolgas can be found in most of northern and eastern Australia, especially where there is marshland or shallow water, which they favour as a nesting site.
RIGHT: temperate rainforest carpets the hills in Springbrook National Park to the west of the Gold Coast in the state's south.

RIGHT: smaller breeds of marsupial, such as this pademelon, spend their time scurrying around the forest floor, mostly at night. Being the smallest in the wallaby family, they tend to be susceptible to introduced predators such as cats and foxes.

RIGHT: tropical rainforest tends to have so much rain that bushfires rarely affect it. However, in more temperate areas woodland can be susceptible, particularly in the dry season, and restrictions are introduced on camp fires, barbecues and the use of some machinery in times of high to extreme fire danger.

SPRINGBROOK RURAL FIRE BRIGADE

LOW   MODERATE   HIGH   VERY HIGH   EXTREME

TODAY'S FIRE DANGER

COOKTOWN AND THE CAPE YORK PENINSULA

Historic Cooktown is the final frontier beyond which sprawls the Cape York Peninsula, a popular destination for four-wheel drive expeditions to the remote Outback and the continent's northernmost tip. It's an amazing, eye-opening journey, but not one to be undertaken lightly

Brisbane ●

L ocated 350 km (217 miles) by the inland route from Cairns, **Cooktown** stands at the mouth of the Endeavour River, where Captain Cook spent 48 days repairing his ship after coming to grief on the corals. Beyond lies the Cape York Peninsula, where swamps, rivers and rainforest offer sanctuary to rare wildlife species, and the vast plains, giant termite mounds and woodlands lend the intrepid traveller a delicious sense of freedom. Almost 10 percent of the Cape has been dedicated as national park. Offshore lies the Great Barrier Reef Marine Park, creating a rare confluence of protected zones on both land and sea.

Cooktown

Cooktown ❶ can be reached from the south by two roads: an inland road and a coastal road. The inland route from Cairns follows the highway via Mareeba, Mount Molloy, Mount Carbine, the Palmer River and Lakeland, and is fully paved, with year-round access to conventional vehicles. The coastal route is shorter but you'll need a 4WD for the stretch from Cape Tribulation to Cooktown. It's highly inadvisable to attempt this route during the wet season, but, if you must be gung-ho, watch the tide at Bloomfield River – unless you want to contribute to the

crocodiles' diet as you swim downstream after your retreating vehicle.

About 25 km (15 miles) from Cooktown, the inland road and the coastal route converge. Whichever route you take, be sure to call into the **Lion's Den** at Helenvale, on the coastal road near the junction. One of the oldest pubs in north Queensland, it features the original wooden bar, a piano, an array of pickled snakes and some equally pickled locals.

Cooktown is one of Far North Queensland's unspoiled outposts,

Map on page 198

LEFT: Aboriginal rock art at Laura with guide, Fred Coleman. **BELOW:** one of a clutch of old hotels in Cooktown.

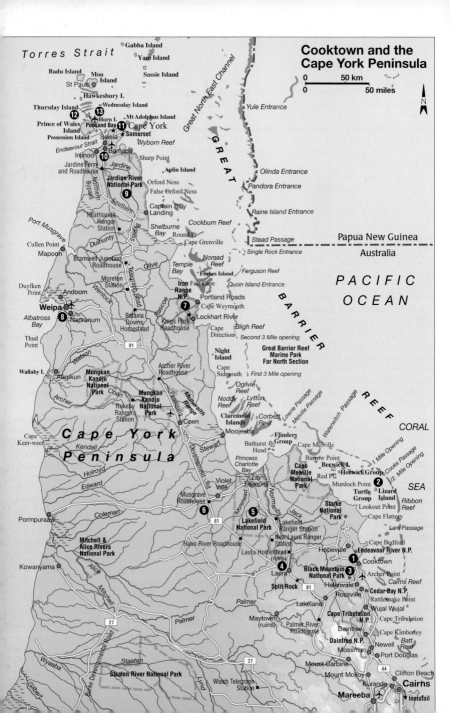

Torres Strait

Gabba Island
Yam Island

Badu Island
Moa Island
Sassie Island
St Pauls
Hawkesbury I.

Thursday Island
Wednesday Island
Mt Adolphus Island
13
Horn I.
Prince of Wales Island
Punsand Bay **11** Cape York
Possession Island
Seisia ★ Somerset
Injinoo
Endeavour Strait
Jardine Ferry
and Roadhouse **10** Bamaga
Jardine

Cooktown and the Cape York Peninsula

0   50 km
0   50 miles

N

Yule Entrance

GREAT

Wyborn Reef

Sharp Point

Aplin Island

Orford Ness
False Orford Ness

Olinda Entrance

Pandora Entrance

Jardine River National Park **9**

Heathlands Ranger Station

Captain Billy Landing

Raine Island Entrance

Cullen Point
Mapoon

Bramwell Junction Roadhouse

Port Musgrave

Dulhunty

Shelburne Bay
Round Pt
Cape Grenville

Stead Passage

Single Rock Entrance

Papua New Guinea
Australia

Moreton Station
Batavia Downs Homestead

Nomad Reef

Temple Bay

Forbes Island

Ferguson Reef

PACIFIC OCEAN

Duyfken Point
Andoom

Weipa **8** Napranum

Albatross Bay

Iron Range N.P. **7**

Fair Cape

Quoin Island Entrance

Portland Roads
Cape Weymouth
Lockhart River

Bligh Reef
Second 3 Mile opening

BARRIER

Thud Point

Kings Park Roadhouse

Cape Direction

Wallaby I.
Aurukun

Mungkan Kandju National Park

Archer River Roadhouse

Night Island

Great Barrier Reef Marine Park Far North Section

First 3 Mile opening

REEF

Rokeby Rangers Station

Mungkan Kandju National Park

Coen

Ogilvie Reef

Noddy Reef
Lytton Reef

CORAL

Cape Keer-ween

Cape York Peninsula

Kendall

Holroyd

Claremont Islands

Corbett Reef

Moojeeba

Bathurst Head

Flinders Group

Cape Melville

Barrow Point
Red Pt.

Cape Melville National Park

Murdoch Point

Horwick Group

2
Turtle Group
Lizard Island

SEA

Lookout Point

Ribbon Reef

Lark Passage

Edward

Musgrave Roadhouse **6**

Violet Vale

Lily Lagoons

Starke National Park

Cape Flattery

Pormpuraaw

Coleman

5

Lakefield National Park

Lakefield Ranger Station
New Laura Ranger Station

Cape Bedford

Endeavour River N.P.

Mitchell & Alice Rivers National Park

Hann River Roadhouse

Laura Homestead (ruins)

Hopevale

1 Cooktown

Kowanyama

Laura

Black Mountain National Park **3**

Archer Point

Cairns Reef

Split Rock **4**

Helensvale
Rossville

Cedar Bay N.P.
Rattlesnake Point
Wujal Wujal

Palmer

Lakeland

Cape Tribulation N.P.

Cape Tribulation

Maytown (ruins)

Palmer River Roadhouse

Cape Kimberley

Daintree N.P.

Daintree

Cape Kimberley

Batt Reef

Mossman
Port Douglas

Mount Carbine

Staaten

Staaten River National Park

Walsh Telegraph Station

Mount Molloy

Kuranda

Clifton Beach

Cairns

Mareeba

Innisfail

shielded from crass development by its very isolation. In part, the appeal of Cooktown is bound up in its frontier flavour. Although many of the rough edges have been smoothed over, the town retains a colourful cast of characters – pub raconteurs, Aboriginal ringers, ageing hippies and rugged individualists.

Captain Cook's visit has inspired a profusion of monuments around the town, but your eye is mainly drawn to the swaggering architecture residual from Cooktown's shining moment as a gold-mining port. Most of this dates from the building boom that followed prospector James Mulligan's 1873 discovery of alluvial gold in the Palmer River – a wild and woolly era when Cooktown's notorious bordello keeper, Palmer Kate, vowed to feed rivals to the crocodiles and thirsty miners were relieved of hard-won gold after drinking spiked whiskey. At one point 35,000 prospectors were digging on the goldfields. By 1880, Cooktown itself contained 47 hotels, countless grog shops and a mind-boggling array of brothels, bakeries and breweries.

The town's population peaked at 4,000, but by the 1890s the Palmer River rush was over and people began to drift away. Next, a cyclone flattened the town. An enforced military evacuation during World War II completed the depletion to just a handful of people. Revival has been slow but steady.

Cooktown landmarks

Cooktown still thrives on the memories, and it has maintained a languid charm. Poking between palm trees on the wide main street are many late 19th-century buildings, including the former **Queensland National Bank** (1891), the former **Bank of North Queensland** (1890) and the former **Post Office**

(1876–7), all in Charlotte Street, and three surviving watering holes (to avoid confusion, known as the Top, Middle and Bottom pubs).

The **James Cook Historical Museum** (Helen and Furneaux Streets; daily 10am–4pm; admission charge; tel: 4069 5386), located in the former convent of St Mary, is one of the best in Australia. Exhibits include Cook's journals and the original anchor of the *Endeavour*, retrieved from the reef. The museum also covers the indigenous Guugu Yimithirr Bama culture, the gold rush and the Chinese presence.

At the end of Charlotte Street is a seafront park where Cook brought the *Endeavour* ashore. Like Cook, you can climb **Grassy Hill**, from where there is a fabulous view of the town, the river and the ocean. The Cooktown cemetery, just north of town, is full of its own stories of the old pioneers.

Information can be obtained from the **Visitors' Information Centre** (tel: 1800 174 895), part of a complex containing an environment

Map on page 198

TIP

Members of the local Guugu Yimithirr tribe offer Aboriginal experiences from bushtucker foraging to guided walks. The Visitors' Information Centre can arrange bookings. They also hand out a brochure called *Cooktown's Heritage and Scenic Rim*, which highlights the town's excellent walking trails.

BELOW: Cooktown on the Endeavour River, from Grassy Hill.

centre, two galleries, a bookstore and café, located within the 62-hectare (153-acre) **Botanic Gardens** in Finch Bay Road. Established in 1878, the gardens are crossed by stone paths leading to pretty beaches at Finch Bay and Cherry Tree Bay (beware of crocodiles and stingers).

Lizard Island

Lizard Island ❷, 27 km (19 miles) off the coast and about 100 km (62 miles) north of Cooktown, is a dry, rocky and mountainous island with some superb beaches for swimming and pristine reef which makes for great snorkelling and diving. The Lizard Island group became a national park in 1939, and the Australian Museum established a research station there in 1973.

The Lizard Island Resort (tel: 1300 134 044; www.lizardisland. com.au), a playground for the rich, opened in 1975. It's geared for high earners, but anyone with a QPWS permit can camp at Watson's Bay.

Captain Cook anchored in one of Lizard Island's bays in 1770, climbing the hill now known as **Cook's Look** to plot his passage through the treacherous reef. It's a pleasant walk to this, the island's highest point (359 m/1,178 ft). Cook named the island after one of 11 species of lizard that live here. Green and loggerhead turtles nest in late spring, and black flying foxes inhabit the mangroves. Birdlife includes pheasant coucals, yellow-bellied sunbirds, white-bellied sea eagles and terns.

Black Mountain National Park

Alarming tales are told of men and beasts disappearing into **Black Mountain**'s ❸ labyrinthine jumble of smooth black rocks, 30 km (19 miles) south of Cooktown. Entire herds of cattle have allegedly been swallowed up – presumably devoured by the carnivorous ghost bats within. To the Kuku Yalanji Aboriginal people, the mountain represents an important meeting place and is the source of a rich mythology. More prosaically, geologists describe the boulders as a molten mass that solidified below the earth's surface 260 million years

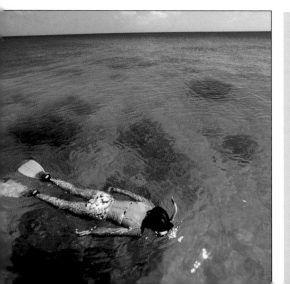

BELOW: snorkelling off Lizard Island.

Bloomfield Lodge

For a close-to-nature experience, stay at Peppers Bloomfield Lodge (tel: 4035 9166; www.peppers.com. au/bloomfield) in Weary Bay, south of Cooktown. Getting there is an adventure in itself; a bush airstrip has to be cleared of wallabies before the plane from Cairns can land. Then follows a two-hour odyssey along back roads and, finally, a punt journey down the Bloomfield River. Keep a sharp eye and you may spot a crocodile lazing in the mangroves. Civilisation seems aeons away. Bloomfield Lodge makes minimal imprint on this dramatic coastline – an old jetty, a patch of sand, a cluster of roofs peeping through the foliage – but the luxury of this retreat is unforgettable.

ago. The rocks appear black, but are actually light-grey covered with algae. On very hot days, rain can cause them to explode. The boulders shelter three creatures found nowhere else in the world – the Black Mountain skink, the Black Mountain gecko and the Black Mountain microhylid frog.

Laura

The journey from Cooktown to Australia's northernmost tip makes for an adventurous and memorable road trip, but if you would rather not go it alone there are plenty of tour companies that can take you.

The first leg of the journey goes via Lakeland through Quinkan Country, named after the Aboriginal spirits, or "Quinkans", who inhabit the sandstone bluffs. The first stop is **Split Rock**, 10 km (6 miles) south of the tiny township of Laura. Here you'll find some of the finest examples of Aboriginal rock art, dating back 14,000 years. They can be reached via two walking tracks. The easier path takes about half an hour, the other takes up to three hours. Contact the **Quinkan Regional Cultural Centre** (tel: 4060 3457) for information and to arrange local guides to some of the other, less accessible rock-painting galleries in the area. The centre itself has fascinating exhibits about the area and its people.

Laura ❹ (140 km/87 miles from Cooktown) has a mainly Aboriginal population of about 70. The Aboriginal Dance and Cultural Festival, held at the **Ang-gnarra Festival Ground**, 15 km (9 miles) south of Laura, every June in odd-numbered years, attracts up to 5,000 people.

Lakefield National Park

A right hand turn 2 km (1¼ miles) north of Laura leads to **Lakefield National Park ❺** – a 537,000-hectare (1.33-million acre) park characterised by mighty rivers, spec-

tacular wetlands, waterbirds, barramundi and estuarine and freshwater crocodiles. There are mangroves and mudflats to the north around Princess Charlotte Bay, grasslands and paperbark woodlands on floodplains and sandstone hills to the south. The park is home to several rare species, including the golden-shouldered parrot and the spectacled hare-wallaby. Traditional owners, the Lama Lama, Kuku Warra, Kuku Yamithi and Kuku Thaypan, take a hand in managing the park.

Several camping areas near rivers and waterholes are provided. Information about campsite locations is provided at the self-registration shelters throughout the park. Camping permits can be obtained from the shelters, or from the ranger station (tel: 4060 3271), 82 km (51 miles) along Lakefield Road towards Musgrave, below Kalpowar Crossing.

Lakefield's grazing history dates back to 1879, when a lease was granted for Laura cattle station. About 30 km (22 miles) north of Laura, the old **Laura Homestead** still stands, albeit slightly the worse

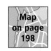
Map on page 198

The Aboriginal Dingaal people have viewed Jiigurru (Lizard Island) as a sacred place for 3,000 years – shell middens have been found dating back that far. It was used for initiation ceremonies and as a base for collecting shellfish, fish, turtles and dugongs.

BELOW: ancient painting on Mushroom Rock near Laura.

for wear. The Red and White Lily Lagoons, 8 km (5 miles) north of Lakefield Ranger Station, are lovely.

Musgrave to Archer River

Take the Marina Plains Road past Violet Vale to rejoin the Peninsula Development Road at **Musgrave Roadhouse** ❻ (tel: 4060 3229). Built as an overland telegraph station in 1887, the station was fitted with rifle ports and interior rainwater tanks in case of attack or siege. The building is now a licensed café and roadhouse selling fuel, groceries and takeaway food, and there are also basic rooms and camping facilities.

Next is the former gold town of **Coen**, 109 km (68 miles) north of Musgrave. The ruins of Coen's Great Northern Mine, established in 1892, stand on the edge of town. The town comprises a pub, two general stores, post office, hospital, school, police station, an airstrip and an Aboriginal cultural centre. The airport is about 22 km (14 miles) to the north. Skytrans (tel: 40 462 462; www.skytrans.com.au) flies from Cairns to Coen.

Here and there you'll see signs warning of "Road Trains", huge trucks with limited manoeuvrability. If you encounter one on an unsealed road, pull over as far as you can, stop the car and wind up the windows, because they raise a great deal of dust.

A little further on is the track to rugged **Mungkan Kandju National Park** (tel: 4060 1137; self-registration station within the park) where eucalypt woodlands and melaleuca (paperbark) swamps extend from the McIlwraith Range to the junction of the Archer and Coen Rivers. The Coen Information and Inspection Centre (tel: 4060 1135) stands opposite the airport turn-off.

The **Archer River Roadhouse** (tel: 4060 3266) lies 65 km (40 miles) north of Coen along a sandy track that is relatively smooth at the start of the dry season, becoming very rough as traffic intensifies. The roadhouse represents the last chance to stock up on fuel and provisions before the 200-km (124-mile) haul to Weipa.

If you have time for a detour, it's worth heading for the **Iron Range National Park** ❼; turn east off the Peninsula Development Road 22 km (14 miles) north of the Archer River Roadhouse; it's another 110 km (70 miles) to the ranger station (tel: 4060 7170) at King Park Homestead. This beautiful national park, where tropical rainforest meets the windy beaches of the Coral Sea, is the largest area of tropical lowland rainforest remaining in Australia, and is home to some rare flora and fauna, like the striking green eclectus parrot. William Bligh landed here after the *Bounty* mutiny, and explorer Edmund Kennedy left a party here during his ill-fated expedition in 1848 *(see page 21)*.

The park's several bush camps include one at Gordon Creek, where rusty mining relics remain from the 1930s and 1940s.

Weipa

The isolated mining town of **Weipa** ❽, 145 km (90 miles) northwest of the Archer River Roadhouse, was built to accommodate the mine workers; the town has the world's largest deposits of bauxite, the ore from

On the Road

Beyond Laura, you're in 4WD territory. Gung-ho drivers have been known to nurse conventional vehicles all the way to Weipa, but Coen, 108 km (67 miles) north of Musgrave, is the recommended extreme. For 4WD drivers, the best time to travel to Cape York is between June and December, in the drier months. Even then, caution should be exercised. For details about road closures, phone the Queensland Department of Main Roads on 1800 077 247, or the RACQ Road Reports (all hours), Brisbane: 3219 0900 or Cairns 4033 6711; www. racq. com.au.

For details of companies which hire 4WD vehicles, refer to *page 250*, where you'll also find advice on safe driving. Here are a few additional points to remember: when driving in dusty conditions, or in a convoy, especially in bulldust, clean your air filter daily. Move to the left when oncoming vehicles approach; most accidents in Cape York are head-on collisions. Be particularly understanding of road-train drivers hauling huge trailers. Before crossing a creek or river, check to see how deep it is. Make sure that it is not flowing too swiftly and that there are no holes in the bottom.

which aluminium is processed. In a dramatic location and with good amenities, Weipa prides itself on its great fishing and stunning sunsets.

This area was the first stretch of Australian coastline ever to be explored by Europeans. Dutch mariner Willem Janssen anchored the vessel *Duyfken* in Albatross Bay, off present-day Weipa, in March 1606. He was unimpressed, reporting that the indigenes knew little of metals and "and even less of nutmegs, cloves and pepper". Matthew Flinders noted the reddish hue of the cliffs around Albatross Bay during his circumnavigation of Australia in 1802 – but almost a century would pass before this redness would be identified as bauxite. In 1955 geologist Harry Evans, guided by Aborigines George Wilson and Old Matthew, realised the true potential of the find. Weipa is now the largest bauxite mine in the world. Mine tours are available April–Nov daily at 8.30am and 2.30pm (tel: 4069 7871; www.campweipa.com).

The huge shell mounds dotted along the rivers flowing into Albatross Bay contain an estimated 200,000 tons of shells – more than 9,000 million cockles. They are thought to have been formed between 2,000 and 400 years ago by successive generations of Aboriginal people, and they are now a protected archaeological site.

Map on page 198

To the Cape

Returning from Weipa, look for a short cut about 70 km (43 miles) out of town heading east to Batavia Downs Homestead and the Telegraph Road. This will slice 80 km (50 miles) off the journey to the tip of the Cape, though you run the risk of getting bogged after wet-season rains. Locals prefer to go the long way. Check with Weipa Police (tel: 4069 9119) or Batavia Downs Stations (tel: 4060 3272) before setting out.

The final 22 km (17 miles) to the Wenlock River is along a very rough road. There is now a concrete bridge over the river, but it still floods in the wet season. The 155 km (96 miles) from the Wenlock River to the Jardine River via the Telegraph Road take you across several challenging creek crossings, and are only for the

In 1928, two New Zealanders drove an Austin Seven from Sydney to the tip of Cape York – the first car to do so. Hector McQuarrie and Dick Matthews lashed their Austin Seven to makeshift rafts to cross swollen streams. The trip took a month.

BELOW: 4WD – the only way to travel in Cape York.

intrepid traveller. A newer and easier route is via the Southern and Northern Bypass Roads, which avoid most of the rivers and creeks (although drivers speed along these corrugated roads far too fast, so you have another hazard to deal with).

On the northern bank of the Wenlock, **Moreton Station** (tel: 4060 3360) provides accommodation but no fuel. Alternatively, continue 40 km (25 miles) from Moreton to **Bramwell Junction Roadhouse** (tel: 4060 3237), a popular stop where you'll find cabins, campsites and fuel. Here you can decide whether to take the scenic Telegraph Road with its many river crossings or to brave the corrugations of the Southern and Northern Bypass Roads. For advice and information, contact the **Heathlands Ranger Station**, midway along the Southern Bypass Road (tel: 4060 3241), which is the base for the **Jardine River National Park** .

This vast, remote wilderness, encompassing much of the catchment of the Jardine River, is the traditional country of several Aboriginal groups. At the time of writing the park was

BELOW: Cape York helicopter safari.

closed due to flooding and subsequent road damage sustained from Cyclone Monica in April 2006. Contact QPWS Information Centre in Cairns (tel: 4046 6600) for up-to-date information.

Popular detours from Telegraph Road include **Twin Falls** (where you can camp) and **Fruitbat Falls** (no camping). These falls, with their crystal-clear waters, are a delightful place to stop for a swim.

There are several challenging creeks to cross over the next 23 km (14 miles) to the Jardine River. If you prefer the safer route, take one of the tracks heading west to the Northern Bypass Road. At the **Jardine River Ferry and Roadhouse** you are advised to take the ferry crossing, run by the Injinoo community, since the ford crossing is treacherous. The fee includes a camping permit for the surrounding area.

Bamaga

Bamaga ⑩, about 70 km (43 miles) from the ferry crossing, is a small, laid-back community (pop. 2,000) mainly comprised of descendants of Saibai Islanders, who voluntarily relocated from their Torres Strait island following a tidal inundation in 1947. The town takes its name from the Saibai leader who ordered the evacuation. It has a shopping centre, a hospital, a police station and a well-equipped resort. Flights to Cairns, Horn Island and Weipa depart from Injinoo Airport, a 40-minute drive from town.

Seisia

Australia's northernmost town is **Seisia** (pronounced 'Say-sia'), 6 km (4 miles) up the road from Bamaga. It's a pleasant place to linger and wash off the dust of the Outback, with a small lodge, camping ground, garage, supermarket and laundry. Fast launches depart from Seisia Wharf for Thursday Island (Mon–Sat

during the tourist season, less frequently at other times; contact Peddells Thursday Island Tours, tel: 4069 1551). Seisia is the departure point for 4WD pilgrims who decide to make the return journey by sea. The cargo barge *Trinity Bay* will transport vehicles; it travels weekly between Seisia, Thursday Island and Cairns (contact Seaswift, tel: 1800 424 422).

Cape York and the Tip

The drive north to **Cape York** ⓫ is delightful, crossed by crystal-clear creeks and bordered by ferns. Heathland and savannah make this a birdwatchers' paradise. More than 250 species have been identified so far, some of them unique to the region.

Punsand Bay (tel: 4069 1722), a fishing resort 5 km (3 miles) west of the tip and 28 km (17 miles) from Bamaga, offers meals and accommodation in a beautiful setting. Rainforest grows to the edge of the beach, and the sunsets are striking.

Not far from here is the former British outpost of Somerset, where notorious adventurer Frank Jardine wreaked havoc on the Aboriginal population. Apart from the grave of Jardine and his wife there's not a lot to see.

From Pajinka Wilderness Lodge (closed after being damaged by fire), a few hundred metres from the tip of Cape York, follow the path from the old lodge through the rainforest and along Frangipani Bay. A sign on the rocks marks the end of the Australian continent. Behind you lies some of the most savagely beautiful landscape on the planet. Off the coast is Possession Island, where Captain Cook claimed the east coast of Australia for England.

Thursday Island and Horn Island

With little to do in Bamaga, most visitors take the ferry to **Thursday Island** ⓬, a multicultural island known affectionately as TI. The trip itself offers magnificent views of sheltered bays and golden beaches.

The island's rich history is evident in the older buildings; All Souls and St Bartholomew's Quetta Memorial Church in Douglas Street

TIP

The Seisia Resort and Campground (tel: 1800 653 243) is a popular campsite which also acts as a booking agent for local tours – guided fishing trips, pearl-farm tours, croc-spotting, 4WD drive tours of the Tip and scenic flights.

BELOW: giant termite mound on the coast of Cape York.

Map
on page
198

*Traditional Torres
Strait Island dances
are performed by
pupils from the
Thursday Island High
School during
festivals and for
special events.*

BELOW: playing on
the beach in front of
Thursday island's
town centre.

was built in 1893 in memory of the
victims of the Quetta shipwreck of
1890, one of Australia's worst maritime disasters. Another late 19th-
century ecclesiastical landmark is the
church of Our Lady of the Sacred
Heart, with timber spires and trompe
l'oeil murals by Thursday Island-born
artist David Sing. The Victorian
splendour of HM Customs stands
intact, albeit deprived of its harbour-
front prominence by a rusty warehouse. Other places to visit include
Green Hill Fort, built in the 1890s to
repel a feared Russian invasion, and
TI's cemetery, where the graves of
700 Japanese pearl divers rest beside
those of Torres Strait pilots, fortune
hunters, sailors and ships' passengers
drowned at sea, as well as generations
of islanders. A lively night out is usually guaranteed at the **Federal Hotel**
(Victoria Parade; tel: 4069 1569) – it's
smoky and noisy, with a band and
pool tables.

The airport for the Torres Strait is
located on **Horn Island** ⓭, a 10-
minute ferry ride from Thursday
Island. Horn Island, and its small
town of Wasaga, is quiet and un-

developed, its main point of interest
being the **Heritage Museum and
Gallery** (admission charge; tel: 4069
2222) within the Gateway Torres
Strait Resort, a couple of minutes,
walk from the wharf. The museum
explains pre-colonial culture in the
Torres Strait and traces outside intru-
sion from the 1860s and 1870s, when
bêche-de-mer crews, pearl-shellers,
Protestant missionaries and government officials began to arrive. The
pearl-shell industry came to a halt
during World War II when naval
authorities requisitioned the boats.
Horn Island became a battle zone,
suffering eight air raids by the Japanese. The museum addresses the
largely unrecognised contribution of
Torres Strait Islanders who joined
forces with 7,000 Australian and
United States military personnel during World War II.

You can visit other islands in the
Torres Strait, but there is virtually no
tourist infrastructure. Most inhabited islands have an airstrip for light
aircraft. Contact the Torres Strait
Regional Authority (tel: 4069 1247;
www.tsra.gov.au). ❏

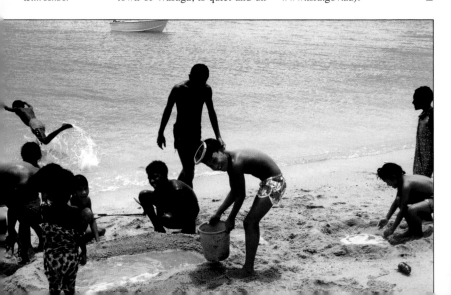

RESTAURANTS, CAFÉS & BARS

Bamaga

The Paper Bark Room
Resort Bamaga, corner Lui
and Adidi Streets
Tel: 4069 3050
Open: D daily. **$$**
Well-appointed restaurant
overlooking a tropical
garden. Menu includes
far north favourites such
as barramundi, crayfish
and steak.

Cooktown

The Balcony Restaurant
Sovereign Resort, corner
Charlotte and Green Street
Tel: 4069 5400
Open: L & D Apr–Nov. **$$**
Light tropical fare with a
Continental flavour.

Restaurant 1770
Fisherman's Wharf, Webber
Esplanade
Tel: 4069 5440
Open: L & D daily. **$$**
Stunning location and a
mainly seafood menu,
along with the usual reef
and beef dishes.

River of Gold
Hope Street
Tel: 4069 5222
Open: D daily. **$$**
Serves solid country-
style fare with nightly
specials.

Shadows of Mount Cook
Corner of Hope and
Burkitt Streets
Tel: 4069 5584
Open: D Tues–Sat. **$$**
A 20-seat restaurant
overlooking extensive
gardens within a rainfor-
est. Co-owner Peter Way

cooks locally sourced
game and seafood to his
own style. Best to book.

Veranda Café
Nature's Powerhouse, Botan-
ic Gardens, Walker Street
Tel: 4069 6004
Open: L daily. **$**
Healthy meals prepared
from fresh, pesticide-
free local ingredients.

Laura

Laura Roadhouse
Peninsula Development
Road
Tel: 4060 3419
Open: L & D daily. **$**
Hamburgers, fish and
chips, steaks and vege-
tables, fish and salad.

The Quinkin Hotel
Terminus Street
Tel: 4060 3393
Open: L & D daily. **$**
Traditional pub-counter
meals in a typical Out-
back pub environment.
Steak and barra dishes.

Musgrave

Barras Bar and Grill
Heritage Resort
Tel: 4069 8000
Open: D daily. **$$**
Grilled steaks and
seafood served poolside
or in the dining room.

Musgrave Roadhouse
Peninsula Development
Road. Tel: 4060 3229
Open: D daily. **$$**
Plain, mainly grilled fare.
Dishes such as T-bone
with egg and chips are
served at tables spread

under the historic tele-
graph station/fortress.

Torres Strait Islands

Jardine Restaurant
Corner Normanby and Victor-
ia Parade, Thursday Island
Tel: 4069 1555
Open: D daily. **$$**
Sophisticated food and
wine in an intimate
restaurant decorated with
island art and memora-
bilia. Also an open-air
bistro with an affordable
lunch and dinner menu.

**The Gateway Torres
Strait Resort**
24 Outie Street, Horn Island
Tel: 4069 2222
Open: D daily. **$**
Buffet menu changes
from night to night.

Wongai Hotel
2 Wees Street, Horn Island
Tel: 4069 1683

Open: L Mon–Sat, D daily. **$**
Traditional pub food. Torres Strait Island musical
legend Seaman Dan per-
forms Wednesday nights.

Weipa

Albatross Bay Resort
Duyfken Crescent
Tel: 4090 6666
Open: L & D daily. **$**
Wide range of dishes from
upper-end cuisine to pub
grub served on a spa-
cious deck overlooking
the sea. Great sunsets.

PRICE CATEGORIES
Prices are for a three-course meal per person with house wine: **$** = A$60 and under **$$** = A$60–100 **$$$** = A$100 and over

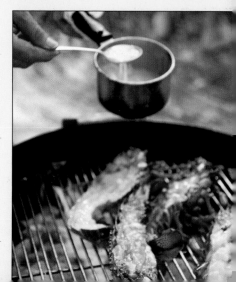

RIGHT: catch it, cook it, eat it.

SAVANNAH WAY

Vast distances, stark terrain and pockets of miraculous beauty mark the remarkable sweep of country that is the Savannah Way. Crossing the Gulf of Carpentaria from Cairns to Camooweal, this epic route follows the footsteps of explorers Ludwig Leichhardt and Burke and Wills. It is also very hot and, in summer, extremely wet

Brisbane ●

The Savannah Way is one of Australia's ultimate adventure drives, linking Cairns in tropical north Queensland with the historic pearling town of Broome in Western Australia. The Queensland section embraces the geological phenomenon of the Undara Lava Tubes at one end and the timeless beauty of Boodjamulla National Park (Lawn Hill) at the other. In between, there are lost mines, ghost towns, desert oases, curious limestone formations and busy gemfields. You'll meet laconic graziers, wild trawlermen and flinty fossickers. This is raw Outback, and care should be taken when driving *(see page 250)*.

Undara Lava Tubes

Undara is an Aboriginal word meaning "long way" – and it's an appropriate description for the geological phenomenon that is the **Undara Lava Tubes ❶**, 55 km (34 miles) east of Mount Surprise and 17 km (10 miles) from the start of the Gulf Developmental Road. The longest lava flow from a single volcano in modern geological times, Undara was formed 190,000 years ago when lava from the eruption spewed down the paths of ancient river beds. The lava at the surface cooled and hardened, forming a crust, while the

molten lava drained away – leaving a series of massive basalt tubes extending underground for 100 km (62 miles). Only nine of the 169 sections of the tube system can be visited. The rest are too toxic, too fragile or too difficult to enter.

The area falls under the protection of the Undara Volcanic National Park (tel: 4097 1485). The only way to explore the tubes is by signing up for a tour with one of the following: Undara Experience (tel: 1800 990 992, www.undara.com.au), Bedrock

Map on page 210

LEFT: dwarfed by the surroundings in Lawn Hill Gorge. **BELOW:** road hazard.

Visitors who stay at Undara's Lava Lodge site are invited to gather around the camp fire to be serenaded by a man with a ukelele .

Village (tel: 4062 3193; www.bed rockvillage.com.au), or Cape Trib Connections (tel: 1800 838 757; www.capetribconnections. com), based in Cairns, which specialises in guided tours throughout the far north.

To enter the tubes, some as big as train tunnels, is to embrace a subterranean wilderness that has sent entomologists and biologists into raptures – more than 40 new species have been identified in Undara's dark recesses, some of them inhabiting atmospheres with carbon dioxide levels 200 times higher than that on the surface.

Above the caves, the grassy open spaces of the savannah are interspersed with patches of dry rainforest where the tube ceilings have collapsed, forming shallow canyons.

Accommodation at Undara Lodge (booked through Undara Experience, *see above*) is in a set of restored antique railway carriages. There's also a central camping area. In summer, the lodge conducts sunset tours to the mouth of **Barker's Cave**, where brown tree snakes and pythons make short work of bats foolish enough to venture within striking range. The bat population of Barker's Cave has been conservatively estimated at 40,000. Those who have entered the bats' domain have likened the experience to being blindfolded in a wind tunnel filled with sonic guided missiles.

QPWS has cut a self-guided trail up and around the crater rim of Kalkarni, the volcano that started it all.

Mount Surprise

Located 55 km (34 miles) from the eastern end of the Gulf Developmental Road, **Mount Surprise** ❷ is a go-ahead little place with a pub, two cafés, a general store, a railway station, a service station and a handful of gem shops. Its economy mainly depends on cattle grazing, gemstones and tourism. During June,

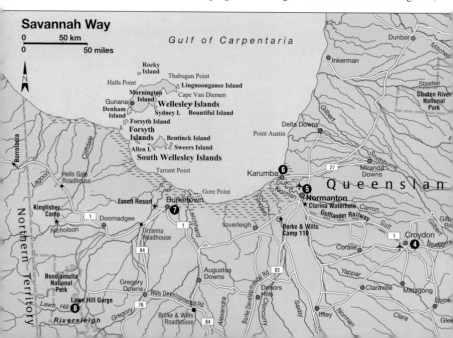

July and August the town's permanent population of 65 doubles, as recreational fossickers arrive in search of the local topaz, zircon, sapphire, aquamarine, smoky quartz and amethyst.

Mount Surprise Gems and Fossicking (Garland Street; tel: 4062 3055; www.mtsurprisegems.com. au) can supply mud maps, fossicking knowledge and equipment. Most fossickers head for the gemfield at O'Brien's Creek, renowned for its topaz. Fossickers' Licences may be obtained from the Mining Registrar in Georgetown, the BP Roadhouse, Mount Surprise or Mt Surprise Gems & Fossicking.

Georgetown

Georgetown ❸, about 100 km (62 miles) west of Mount Surprise, owes its existence to the gold fever that swept Queensland in the late 19th century. Initially it was just one of several shanty towns on the Etheridge Field in 1869. Within two years, however, the township had emerged as the region's administrative centre. Georgetown's fortunes fluctuated following discovery of gold at the Palmer River in 1873 and the Hodgkinson rush of 1876. Between 1880 and 1900, Georgetown's population hovered at around 300 – about the same as it is today. The glory days of mining are gone, but amateur prospectors continue to visit the area in the hope of stubbing their toe on a nugget.

National Trust-listed **Antbed House** in South Street was built in the boom years between 1880 and 1900. This former mine manager's residence was constructed of termite-mound adobe rather than the usual timber and iron. Other historic buildings include the Shire Hall (1908) in St George Street, the Masonic Temple on the corner of Haldane and Cumberland Streets and the Catholic Church (1913) in High Street.

Map on page 210

Map on page 210

TIP

The tourist information service in Georgetown, known as the **Terrestrial Centre** (Low Street; tel: 4062 1485; Apr–Sept daily 9am–5pm, Oct–Mar Mon–Fri 8.30am–4.30pm), includes a comprehensive display of the minerals, crystals and fossils which have shaped the history of the region.

BELOW: Undara Lava Tube.

BELOW: the Gulflander.

About 20 km (12½ miles) west along the Croydon Road stands the **Cumberland Chimney**, marking the site of an early gold-ore crush-ing plant. The dam built as part of the crushing plant has been colonised by waterbirds, making for a picturesque bush scene.

Forsayth, 40 km (25 miles) south of Georgetown, is popular with gold fossickers. **Agate Creek**, about 70 km (43 miles) further south, yields multicoloured agate formations known as "thunder eggs". Profes-sional miners and amateur "rock hounds" alike use hand tools to dig for this translucent quartz formed as a result of volcanic activity some 250 million years ago.

Conventional vehicles can tra-verse the gravel road that leads to Agate Creek May–September. At other times it's 4WD territory.

Even if you don't find gems, you'll have come to grips with one of the world's most unforgiving, yet hauntingly beautiful, landscapes.

Intending fossickers should call into the Queensland Department of Minerals and Energy office in Georgetown (weekdays 9am–5pm) for information and a Fossicker's Licence.

Croydon

Croydon ❹ is connected to Nor-manton by the *Gulflander*, a historic train that trundles between the two towns once a week. A journey on the *Gulflander* has long been de rigueur for travellers reaching the inland port of Normanton. For many the issue of destination is eclipsed by the romance of simply being aboard this beguiling old rattler *(for detailed information, see Tip left)*.

The railway line was completed in 1891 when Croydon was a boom-ing gold-mining town. Gold was discovered in 1885; a year later, 2,000 people were working the gold-fields, swiftly rising to 6,000. By the end of World War II, the gold had run out and Croydon had become a ghost town. More recently, as tourists arrived on the train and milled about looking for things to do, the citizens of Croydon set about creating a tourism indus-try. Buildings from the town's gold-

rush days have been retrieved from dereliction and rebuilt on Samwell Street, where guided tours are given.

Rating high among Croydon's 19th-century treasures is the Heritage-listed **Courthouse** (1887). Flanked by the old police station on one side and the old town hall on the other, the courthouse is distinguished by its iron cladding, and a clock tower to add gravitas. These three buildings form the core of a historic precinct that includes the surgeon's house, the mining warden's office, the general store, the old butcher's shop and the Croydon railway station. Croydon's **Visitor Information Centre** (daily 8.30am–5.30pm, closed Sat–Sun in wet season; tel: 4745 6125) is located in the old police sergeant's residence in Samwell Street.

Normanton

Being the terminus of the Normanton–Croydon railway, **Normanton** ❺ was accorded a more impressive station than Croydon – complete with a blacksmith's shed and carpenters' workshop. Today, the station's arched roof has become one of the far north's most photographed buildings, synonymous with Normanton's history and emblematic of the rich cast of characters among its population.

Actor Paul Hogan says he based *Crocodile Dundee* on the people he met around Normanton. At the **Purple Pub**, **Albion Hotel** or **Central Hotel**, you'll meet barracuda fishermen, stockmen, local Aborigines, kangaroo shooters, fossickers, assorted wild men and, increasingly, curious tourists. The frontier atmosphere is lent zest by historic buildings spread throughout the town – among them, the **Carpentaria Shire Offices**, the 1886 **Bank of New South Wales** (now Westpac), the notorious Normanton **Gaol** and the **Burns Philp Building**, now the library and visitor information centre (tel: 4745 1065).

The town is situated on the banks of the Norman River, 150 km (93 miles) west of Croydon. Explorer Frederick Walker discovered the river while looking for Burke and Wills *(see page 21)*. He was followed

Map on page 210

TIP

People come from miles around to the **Normanton Rodeo** (tel: 4745 1155), held annually during the Queen's birthday weekend in June, when hard men and women of the Outback do battle with bucking bulls and feisty horses. Another lively Outback event is the **Normanton Races** (tel: 4745 1580 for dates, which vary from year to year).

BELOW: Normanton's Purple Pub.

TIP

Norman River Fishing and Cruises (tel: 4745 1347) depart from Normanton Boat Ramp twice daily. Owner Dennis Taney is an accredited Savannah Guide who knows where to find the tidal water barramundi, exotic birdlife and local crocodiles. His punt, which seats 12 passengers, ranges up to 30 km (18 miles) upstream "depending on where the fish are biting". Fishing trips 7.30am; sunset cruises 5pm.

BELOW: croc on a rock, in Normanton.

by William Landsborough who, in 1867, chose the site for a port. Normanton's boom years were during the gold rush of the 1890s, when it was the port for nearby Croydon, but, as the gold petered out, the town went into slow decline – hitting an all-time low in the late 1940s when the population fell to about 200 (it's now 1,500). The revival is partly attributable to tourism, partly to the fishing industry at Karumba, 70 km (43 miles) to the north.

From mid-May to September, there are two short trips on the *Gulflander (see page 212)* which are both popular. On Saturday morning, the Morning Tea and Damper Trip departs from Normanton at 9am for Clarina Waterhole, and on Thursday afternoons, the Sunset Sizzle Trip leaves Normanton Station at 4pm and returns about 6.30pm. The barbecue is free, soft drinks are available for sale, and if you want a beer or a glass of wine, you can take your own.

Karumba

Karumba ❻ sits at the mouth of the Norman River, about 70 km (43 miles) northwest of Normanton on the Gulf of Carpentaria. It is a port of about 600 people mainly engaged, one way or another, with commercial prawn trawling and professional barramundi fishing. During the two prawn seasons, the fishing fleet quadruples. The rest of the time, Karumba basks quietly in the sun, uncertain if it's an Outback outpost or a fishing port. The only town on the Gulf Coast serviced by a bitumen road, it's linked via the Savannah Way from Cairns and the Matilda Highway from the south.

Older travellers, European backpackers and amateur fishermen turn up in force during the dry winter months, attracted by ripping yarns of suicidal barramundi, life-changing sunsets and the meteorological phenomenon known as "morning glories" (cigar-shaped cloud formations that roll out of the Gulf in lines of three or four at sunrise from late September to early November).

Other attractions include taking a cruise along the crocodile-infested **Norman River**, or a game-fishing expedition to the Gulf *(see Tip left)*.

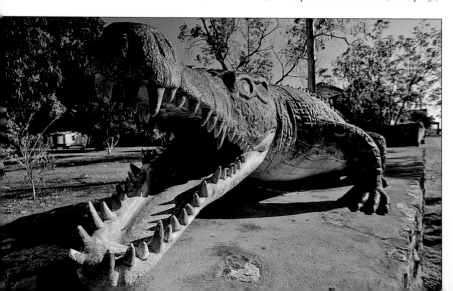

If you've ever wondered about the mysteries of piscatorial bisexuality, or just wanted to see some big fish close up, visit the **Karumba's Barramundi Discovery Centre** (148 Yappar Street; daily 1–4.30 pm; admission charge; tel: 4745 9359).

A fascinating insight into local culture can be had at Karumba's **Animal Bar**, adjacent to the main boat ramp, where tattooed prawn fishermen let off steam after protracted periods at sea. If the atmosphere becomes too boisterous, you can relocate to the lounge, known as the Suave Bar. Women are in short supply in Karumba (the ratio of men to women is around seven to three), so female visitors can expect to receive a more than usually warm welcome.

Burketown

Burketown ❼ (pop. 180) is a remote settlement 30 km (18 miles) from the Gulf of Carpentaria. It is named after Robert O'Hara Burke *(see page 21)*, and there is a sign about 50 km (31 miles) along the road from Normanton to Burketown indicating the doomed explorer's last camp – Camp 119. Few of Burketown's early structures have stood the test of time, but the former post office, built in 1887, is one of them. Restored, relocated and redefined as the **Visitor Information Centre** (tel: 4745 5111), it stands at the intersection of Musgrave and Burke Streets.

The **Burketown Hotel** (Beames Street; tel: 4745 5104), just to the east, is a friendly Outback pub; originally built as the customs house, it's the oldest building in Burketown. The **War Memorial** is directly outside, and the shire offices are next door.

The barramundi fishing is excellent, and this is what lures visitors to this tiny town on the flat plains of the Albert River. Burketown also happens to be an important access point for Lawn Hill National Park and the World Heritage-listed Riversleigh fossil field.

Lawn Hill Gorge

Lawn Hill Gorge ❽, southwest of Burketown in the remote northwest highlands, is the scenic centrepiece of **Boodjamulla National Park**'s magnificent array of limestone

Map on page 210

From Normanton, the Savannah Way (also known as the Gulf Track here) sweeps across the flat plains of the Gulf to Burketown. The road is unsealed, but is open to conventional vehicles during the dry season; don't attempt the journey during the wet season (November–April) as heavy rain can close the road.

BELOW: fired up for fishing in Karumba.

Map on page 210

Termite mounds are found in many parts of outback Queensland but there are subtle variations in size and shape. Compare this example with the one pictured on page 205.

BELOW: making the most of Lawn Hill Gorge.

escarpments, spring-fed creeks and tranquil waterholes. On Lawn Hill Creek, the gorge is a beautiful Outback oasis – a place where 60-metre (200-ft) red sandstone walls reflect in green waters inhabited by turtles and freshwater crocodiles. The park is intersected by walking trails with evocative names like Wild Dog Dreaming, Cascades and Island Stack. At sunrise the call of the sandstone shrike-thrush echoes through the gorge. Wallaroos, tiny bats and ringtail possums hide among the rocky outcrops. It's a far cry from the flat plains of the Gulf.

The main problem is getting there. Detailed directions are provided at www.epa.qld.gov.au (find Boodjamulla NP under Parks and Forests). Unsealed roads in the area provide unpredictable access, and precautionary steps should be taken before setting off *(see page 250)*, as there is limited communication and no mobile-phone reception. During the wet season (Nov–April) you should travel by 4WD and carry an over-supply of food in case you become stranded.

Formerly known as Lawn Hill National Park, the park has been renamed Boodjamulla in deference to its Aboriginal owners. Boodjamulla translates as "rainbow serpent country". Midden heaps, grinding stones and rock art scattered throughout the park offer testimony to the Waanyi people's 17,000-year occupancy. Two rock-art sites have been made accessible to visitors.

The southern section of the park is occupied by the World Heritage-listed **Riversleigh** area, where bones dating back 25 million years are preserved in lime-rich sediments. Most of the significant finds are displayed at the Riversleigh Fossils Centre in Mount Isa, but D-Site, where the first fossils were found, gives visitors an opportunity to view fossilised mammals and reptiles *in situ*. Climb to the top of the hill for striking views across the plains.

There are numerous trails of varying lengths and difficulty through the park, and canoeing through the gorge is wonderful. For more information, contact the park ranger (2pm–4pm; tel: 4748 5572). ❏

RESTAURANTS, CAFÉS & BARS

Croydon

Club Hotel
Corner Sircon and
Brown Streets
Tel: 4745 6184.
Open: D daily. **$**
Standard Outback pub
menu is enlivened by
specials such as lasagne
and shepherd's pie. Tra-
ditional Wednesday-night
roasts coincide with the
arrival of the *Gulflander*
from Normanton.

Croydon Café
Brown Street
Tel: 4745 6159
Open: 7am–7.30pm. **$**
Once every Australian
country town had a café
like this – cheap and
cheerful hamburgers,
sandwiches and fish and
chips, with groceries and
fishing tackle on the side.

Georgetown

Midway Caravan Park Restaurant
High Street
Tel: 4062 1219
Open: daily. **$**
Plain and simple country
fare served in an outdoor
setting – everything from
chips to chicken Kiev.

Karumba

Karumba Seafoods
Corner Yappar and
Massey Streets
Tel: 4745 9192
Open: L and D daily. Some-
times closed during the wet
season (Nov–Feb). **$**
Mick and Janice Jocelyn

run this bistro near the
Norman River, where you
can get a decent cup of
coffee and very fresh
seafood, all served on an
elevated deck amid tropi-
cal greenery. BYO.

The Sunset Tavern
2 Ward Street,
Karumba Point
Tel: 4745 9183
Open: L and D daily. **$**
This a great place to sip a
beer while watching the
sun set on the Gulf of Carpentaria. Bill of fare runs
from snacks through to
steaks and the ubiquitous
seafood platters.

Mount Surprise

Mt Surprise Café
Garland Street
Tel: 4062 3055
Open: B, L & D daily
Apr–Sept. **$**

Owners Pete and Pam
Blackburn serve real
coffee (as distinct from
the instant coffee so
prevalent in the Outback)
and also give gem-
faceting demonstrations.

Undara Iron Pot Bistro
Undara Lodge
Gulf Development Road via
Mount Surprise
Tel: 4097 1900
Open: L and D. **$$**
As well as buffet lunches
and three-course dinners,
the lodge puts on a slap-
up bush breakfast – a
round-the-campfire affair
that takes place about
200 metres (660 ft) away
from the main complex.

Normanton

Albion Hotel,
Haig Street
Tel: 4745 1218

Open: L and D. **$**
Country-style pub food
with few surprises but
easy on the pocket. Eat
at the bar or dine on the
deck.

The Purple Pub
94 Landsborough Highway
Tel: 4745 1324
Open: L & D Mon–Sat. **$**
Predictably, given the
pub's location near the
Gulf, the menu focuses
on barramundi served
with chips. Generous
helpings in a typical
Outback dining room.

PRICE CATEGORIES

Prices are for a three-
course meal per person
with house wine:
$ = A$60 and under
$$ = A$60–100
$$$ = A$100 and over

RIGHT: bush tucker

MOUNT ISA AND THE WEST

For true Outback grit, the region around Mount Isa has it all: Aboriginal bravery in the face of incredible odds; the rise of a desert city of silver and copper; the humble beginnings of that most Australian of institutions, the Royal Flying Doctor Service, and the murky origins of the nation's unofficial national anthem, *Waltzing Matilda*

Brisbane ●

The mining city of **Mount Isa** ❶ erupts like a post-Apocalyptic mirage from the stony plateaux and escarpments of the Selwyn Range, leaving a powerful, almost surreal, first impression. Once in the city, you'll discover a prosperous, down-to-earth community that takes work and relaxation seriously.

While Mount Isa functions as a service centre for surrounding districts, it's a mining community at core, owing its existence to the rich deposits of lead, zinc, silver and copper ore to the west of the city. A high proportion of the 23,000 inhabitants earn their living from the mine in one way or another – making for an intriguing combination of professions and nationalities. Add several cosmopolitan social clubs, around 20 restaurants and a couple of man-made lakes to the mix and you have a desert metropolis like no other.

The **Mount Isa Mine** (owned and operated by Swiss company Xstrata since 2003) continues as one of the most highly mechanised and cost-effective mines on the planet. At 2,000 metres (6,560 ft) beneath the surface, the Enterprise copper mine is the deepest in Australia. For an idea of the sheer scale of operations, you can take a surface tour (Mon–Sat 11am; admission charge; tel: 4743 2006; www.campbellstravel.com.au).

Around the town

Most of the city's attractions are grouped at the **Outback at Isa** complex in Marian Street (tel: 1300 659 660; www.outbackatisa.com.au), where you'll find the Visitor Information Centre, the Hard Times Mine, the Isa Experience Gallery, the Riversleigh Fossil Centre and a land-scaped park that mimics Lawn Hill Gorge *(see page 215)*.

Exhibits at the complex cover a wide spectrum of historical, cultural and social issues. Set aside at least

Map on page 220

LEFT: the Ernest Henry Mine near Cloncurry.
BELOW: the public viewing area.

The detour across dusty plains from Hughenden is amply rewarded by views over Porcupine Gorge (see page 224).

two hours to complete a circuit of the **Hard Times Mine** (named after the horse ridden by prospector John Campbell Miles, who discovered a rich lode of lead, silver, copper and zinc here in 1923). This A\$5 million mock-up of the real thing, comes complete with 1.2 km (¾ mile) of tunnels, hands-on drilling, massive machinery and a miner's "crib room". Expect to don overalls, boots, miner's cap, lamp and ear-muffs before descending in a shaft cage to the mine floor.

The **Isa Experience Gallery** uses a range of electronic media to illustrate the district's past and present, supplemented by historic photographs, illustrative dioramas and other exhibits. The **Riversleigh Fossil Centre** is a fascinating recreation of Australia's prehistoric fauna, with actual fossils and a working laboratory.

More recent history is enshrined at the nearby **Kalkadoon Tribal Council and Cultural Keeping Place** (Marion Street; Mon–Fri 9am–5pm; admission charge; tel: 4749 1001). The territory on which Mount Isa stands formerly belonged to the Kalkadoons, an Aboriginal tribe that resisted white settlement long after their brethren elsewhere had been demoralised or slain. The Kalkadoons engaged native police and squatters in wily guerrilla warfare for more than a decade, striking unexpectedly then melting into the hills. Lured into open conflict at Battle Mount, north of Cloncurry, in 1884, they were mown down by native police with carbines. Descendants of the Kalkadoons staff their brightly decorated building, telling stories and explaining the use and meaning of tribal artefacts.

The National Trust-listed **Tent House** (Fourth Avenue; Apr–Sept daily 10am–2pm; admission charge) is one of 200 such houses that provided inexpensive but comfortable

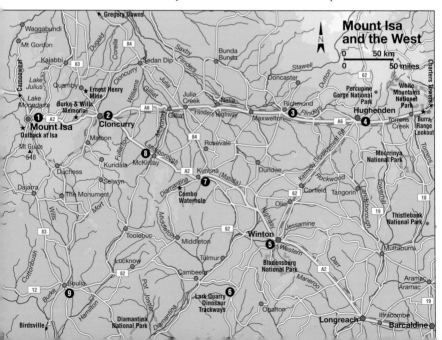

Map on page 220

miners' accommodation during the 1930s and 1940s. Designed for coolness in a harsh climate, these houses were built of hessian, canvas, wood and corrugated iron with a double roof to allow breezes through.

The **Underground Hospital Museum** (Joan Street; Apr–Sept daily 10am–2pm; admission charge; tel: 4743 3853) is a telling reminder of World War II. With the threat of bombing by the Japanese, Mount Isa hospital decided to go underground; it's been preserved much as it would have been in the 1940s.

Away from the mines, the people of Mount Isa relax at the artificial **Lake Moondarra**, 20 km (12½ miles) north of the town – a popular spot for swimming, boating, waterskiing, fishing and birdwatching.

For a fascinating insight into how children in remote communities are educated, visit the **School of the Air** (Kalkadoon High School, Abel Smith Parade; tours Mon–Fri 9am and 10am in term time; tel: 4744 9100), where qualified teachers educate Outback children via a digital network. In a similar vein, the

Royal Flying Doctor Service (11 Barkly Highway; Mon–Fri 9am–5pm; donations welcome; tel: 4657 4255) is worth a visit; guides show visitors through a small museum and display area illustrating this vital Outback service.

The town really comes alive on the second weekend in August, when the annual **Mount Isa Rodeo** (www.isarodeo.com.au) – the biggest rodeo in Australia – is held. The city centre shuts down for a Friday night Mardi Gras parade and fireworks. Accommodation is scarce to non-existent, and it pays to bring a tent.

Cloncurry

Cloncurry ❷, 125 km (78 miles) east of Mount Isa, is a pleasant Outback town of about 3,000 people, with several worthwhile attractions. Prominent among them is **John Flynn Place** (corner Daintree and King Streets; Mon–Fri 8am–4.30pm year round, Sat–Sun 9am–3pm May–Sept; tel: 4742 4125). This modern museum celebrates the visionary bush clergyman John Flynn, who began the Royal Flying

TIP

For a scenic overview of Mount Isa, head for the **City Lookout** (a short drive off Hilary Street), preferably at dusk when the mine lights up. You can see the whole city sprawled out across a flat valley, backed by low hills, and all dominated by the mine.

BELOW: sunset on Mount Isa.

The Flying Doctor Service was started in Cloncurry in 1928 by the Revd John Flynn to provide "a mantle of safety" over the Outback. Its first plane was supplied by the Queensland and Northern Territory Aerial Service (QANTAS).

BELOW: bareback riding in the Mount Isa rodeo.

Doctor Service here in 1928. Exhibits include the actual Traeger pedal wireless used by Flynn's aviators and medicos, plus a model of the *Victory*, the first RFDS aircraft. The museum forms part of a complex incorporating an art gallery, cultural centre and outdoor theatre. Flynn chose Cloncurry because of its location in a region where remote mining and grazing communities were poorly served by medical help.

Cloncurry was founded when Ernest Henry discovered copper in 1867. The **Post Office** (1895; 47 Scarr Street) and **Courthouse** (1897; 42 Daintree Street) reflect the prosperity of the era.

The pioneering prospector's name is honoured at the **Ernest Henry Mine** – a modern open-cut copper-and-gold mine 36 km (22 miles) north of Cloncurry – and there are good tours to it from the Mary Kathleen Museum *(see below)*. In fact, the mineral fields around Cloncurry contain several interesting old mine sites and towns – among them Kuridalla, Selwyn, Kajabbi, Duchess and Dobbyn.

About 20 km (12 miles) south of Cloncurry is the **Bower Bird Creek Battery**, listed by the National Trust. The battery, which is remarkably intact, stands near the ghost town of Bower Bird, which, in 1895, comprised three stores, two hotels and a post office. Located on a spinifex-covered hill, the site contains a number of early surface workings, and there's a camp site about 100 metres (330 ft) east of the battery. If you want to inspect the mine, first call into the Cloncurry Information Centre, McIlwraith Street (tel: 4742 1361) for directions and advice.

The **Mary Kathleen Memorial Museum and Park** (McIlwraith Street; Mon–Fri 8am–4.30pm, Sat–Sun 9am–3pm Feb–Sept; admission charge; tel: 4742 1361) has some interesting relics from the Burke and Wills expedition (the prize exhibit is a water bottle allegedly belonging to explorer Robert O'Hara Burke). Other displays include rare Aboriginal artefacts, a collection of old mining machinery and the Rail Ambulance

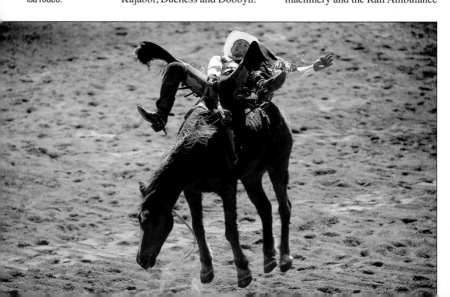

used from 1956 to 1971. The museum's information centre is an exhibit in itself, having been used as a police station in the early mining towns of Oona and Dobbyn, and, later, in Mary Kathleen. Now little more than a memory, Mary Kathleen, halfway between Mount Isa and Cloncurry, was constructed in 1954 by the Rio Tinto Mining Company to house its uranium miners.

More fragments of the past linger at the **Afghan and Chinese Cemeteries** though, unfortunately, most of the graves have been washed away by floods. Afghans helped build roads and railways in the Outback; accustomed to desert conditions, many then became traders and married Aboriginal women. The Chinese, who arrived en masse during the gold-rush era, also intermarried with the local population. The sole surviving headstone in the Muslim section marks the final resting place of Cloncurry mullah Syid O Mar who died in 1915, aged 45. Only one grave remains of the original 50 in the Chinese cemetery.

Richmond

Incredible though it may seem, Queensland's dry and dusty Outback was once a verdant flood plain. Huge winged reptiles glided in air currents. Sharks and lungfish swam in its lakes. Dinosaurs roamed its forests and shorelines. The proof resides in the small Outback town of **Richmond ❸**, 287 km (178 miles) east of Cloncurry, where a marine-fossil museum at **Kronosaurus Korner** (91–93 Goldring Street; daily 8.30am–4.45pm; admission charge; tel: 4741 3429; www.kro nosauruskorner.com.au) showcases 200 exhibits. The region has yielded several important finds – most recently in 1989, when a local grazier unearthed the skeleton of a Pliosaur, which swam in the inland sea 100 million years ago. Also

among the museum's exhibits is Australia's most complete and best-preserved dinosaur skeleton, the Minmi, unique because much of its fossilised skin remains.

Richmond was explored by William Landsborough in 1862 while searching for doomed expeditionists Burke and Wills. Pastoralists who read Landsborough's glowing reports soon followed. The **Pioneer Heritage Walk** traces the town's history through its landmarks, taking in the unusual Roman Catholic church, the corrugated-iron Strand Theatre and restored Cobb & Co. stage coach *(see right)*. In **Lions Park**, on Goldring Street, there's a monument made of "moonrocks" – variously shaped limestone rocks, which often contain fossilised remnants of fish and shells.

Hughenden

Hughenden ❹, about 100 km (62 miles) east of Richmond, is the centre of the large Flinders River pastoral district. Its main tourist draw is the Muttaburrasaurus – the replica of a virtually complete dinosaur skeleton.

Map on page 220

The 1880 discovery of gold at Woolgar, 113 km (70 miles) north of Richmond, led to the town becoming a staging post for Cobb & Co. – a link recalled by a beautifully restored coach in Goldring Street.

BELOW: one of the last Afghan gravestones in Cloncurry's cemetery.

At Kronosaurus Korner in Richmond, the Marine Fossil Museum displays some of the finest examples of local marine fossils from the long-gone Cretaceous Inland Sea. They also offer guidance on local sites to fossick for your own fossils.

BELOW: what put Hughenden on the map.

Measuring 7 metres (23 ft) from snout to tail, Muttaburrasaurus would have been a fearsome critter in his prime. He can be seen at the **Flinders Discovery Centre** (37 Gray Street; daily 9am–5pm; admission charge; tel: 4741 1021).

Among the centre's displays is an exhibit explaining the genesis of **Porcupine Gorge** – a spectacular national park, 61 km (38 miles) north of Hughenden, where towering sandstone cliffs and lush green vine forests fringe permanent waterholes lined with casuarinas and paperbarks. A permit is required to camp at the park's Pyramid Lookout (contact the QPWS; tel: 131304; www.epa.qld.gov.au). A scenic 1.2-km (¾-mile) walk leads into the gorge; however, anyone planning an extended excursion on foot should notify the ranger at Hughenden (tel: 4741 1113).

The same ranger fields enquiries about **White Mountains National Park**, 80 km (50 miles) northeast of Hughenden on the Flinders Highway. The park's name derives from its spectacular white sandstone bluffs and gorges, though the terrain varies widely from spinifex grasslands to sand dunes. Conventional access is possible to **Burra Range Lookout**, but a 4WD is recommended to reach the campground at Cann's Camp Creek. During the wet season between October and April the road can be closed.

Winton

Tourism has taken root in the Australian Outback – and in many ways **Winton ❺**, 1,400 km (870 miles) northwest of Brisbane, led the way. When the drought of the 1960s threatened to turn Outback centres into ghost towns, Winton pharmacist Peter Evert and his brother Vince opened an opal museum, revived Winton's historic open-air cinema and ran minibus tours to nearby stations to give city slickers a taste of rural life. Peter Evert helped found Winton's Outback Festival in 1972, and took tourist groups in his six-seater charter plane to historic sites and Outback places previously accessible only to 4WD vehicles.

Winton inspired a verse of Australia's most famous song, and in 1995 the Waltzing Matilda Centenary marked a turning point in its fortunes, when more than 14,000 people surged into the town for an eight-day festival. Businesses did roaring trade. Cattle stations opened up for homestays. Shopkeepers spruced up their acts. Now Winton is barely recognisable from the down-at-heel settlement of 30 years ago. Footpaths have been paved, streets landscaped, gaudy signage replaced.

Winton's **Waltzing Matilda Centre** (50 Elderslie Street; daily 8.30am–5pm; public holidays 10am–4pm; admission charge; tel: 4657 1466; www. matildacentre. com.au) is a high-tech museum, complete with a computer-generated swagman relating his role in Australia's most famous song.

Winton's other claim to fame is that it is where in 1920 QANTAS was born, and you'll find a number of displays on the first Australian airline at the Waltzing Matilda Centre.

Another Winton landmark is the **Corfield & Fitzmaurice Building** (63 Elderslie Street; tel: 4657 1486), a retail outlet that traded more or less continuously from 1878 to 1987. The present building, listed by the National Trust, was built in 1916 and houses a craft co-operative and gem collection. It retains such features as long timber counters and a "flying fox", for transferring cash and receipts between the counter and a central office at mezzanine level.

Lark Quarry

At **Lark Quarry Dinosaur Trackways** ❻ (tours 10am, noon, 2pm; admission charge; tel: 4657 1812; www.dinosaurtrackways.com.au), 110 km (68 miles) southwest of Winton, fossilised footprints record the stampede of a herd of dinosaurs pursued by a larger dinosaur across a prehistoric mudflat 100 million years ago. As the inland sea receded,

the tracks turned to stone, creating an indelible record of pursuit and flight. Almost 4,000 dinosaur footprints are clearly visible in an area of just 210 sq. metres (2,260 sq. ft).

Despite exposure to the elements and visitors for many years, the footprints have remained intact. They are now shielded within a modern interpretative centre. The road from Winton is less than ideal, but the journey is worth it. Fuel up before you leave and carry food and water.

Kynuna and McKinlay

From Winton, it's 160 km (100 miles) northwest on the Landsborough Highway to **Kynuna** ❼, a small settlement best known for the **Blue Heeler Pub** (tel: 4746 8650), where station hands, truckies, shearers and bush characters rub shoulders with nomads and 4WD pilgrims. A former Cobb & Co. staging post, it has become an almost mandatory stop for travellers on the Matilda Highway.

Near by is the billabong mentioned in *Waltzing Matilda*, also known as the **Combo Waterhole**,

Map on page 220

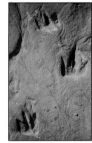

The Lark Quarry dinosaur tracks came to light in the 1960s, when a local station manager digging for opal discovered what he thought to be fossilised bird tracks.

BELOW: Winton's Waltzing Matilda Centre.

Map on page 220

TIP

To experience Outback life at first hand, spend a night or two at Carisbrooke Station, 85 km (53 miles) southwest of Winton, where graziers Charlie and Anne Philpott have converted their shearers' quarters to tourist accommodation (tel: 4657 3984).

BELOW: camel racing in Boulia.

accessed from a turn-off 13 km (8 miles) south of Kynuna. One of a string of semi-permanent coolibah-lined lagoons on the Diamantina River, the site is lent romance by the stone causeways built by Chinese labourers from 1883. From the car park, it's a 40-minute return walk to the waterhole. Camping is not permitted here.

McKinlay ❽, 76 km (47 miles) northwest of Kynuna, has never been quite the same since Australian actor Paul Hogan used the former McKinlay Federal Hotel as a set for his film *Crocodile Dundee*. Locals shook their heads as the film's set designers worked over the old place, replacing aluminium windows and doors with old-fashioned joinery. Renamed the **Walkabout Creek Hotel** (tel: 4746 8424), the building now represents McKinlay's one and only tourist attraction.

Boulia

Boulia ❾ is a small township in far western Queensland, 303 km (188 miles) south of Mount Isa and 366 km (227 miles) west of Winton. The population stands at about 300 – with another 300 or so people scattered over the shire's 61,000 sq. km (23,500 sq. miles), whose boundaries skirt the Northern Territory border and the edge of the Simpson Desert.

Boulia's main celebration is the annual Camel Races in mid-July. The "Ute Muster", held at the same time, is an opportunity for Outback petrol heads to see who has the fastest and fanciest "ute" (farm truck).

It would invite disillusionment to suggest that the district is nuggeted with attractions, but Boulia is not without mystique. The district is famous for an inexplicable and peculiarly Queensland phenomenon known as the Min Min Lights. Weird and luminous, these lights appear, hover, disappear and reappear with no apparent cause or pattern. The lights were first reported in 1912 following a fire in the Min Min Hotel, 105 km (65 miles) east of town.

Boulia has turned the phenomenon to account with **The Min Min Encounter** (Herbert Street; daily 8.30am–5pm, Sat–Sun 9am–2pm; admission charge; tel: 4746 3386). Supported by animatronics, fibre optics and high-tech wizardry, the 45-minute show features tales of close encounters with Min Min Lights told by those who experienced them.

Another attraction is the National Trust-listed **Stone House** (Pituri Street; daily 8am–5pm; admission charge; tel: 5437 6481). Built during the pastoral boom of the mid-1880s, and now Boulia's oldest surviving structure, it's the centrepiece of a museum complex housing a collection of Aboriginal artefacts and fossilised remains.

The town is also proud of its **Aquatic Centre** (Burke Street; daily; tel: 4746 3527). The centre's heated pool, air-conditioned gymnasium and indoor sports stadium are just what's needed after a hard day on the road. ❑

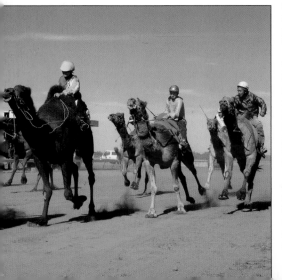

RESTAURANTS, CAFÉS & BARS

Boulia

The Australian Hotel
Herbert Street
Tel: 4746 3144
Open: L & D daily. **$**
Traditional pub menu of
steak, seafood and
chicken dishes in a typi-
cal Outback dining room.

Cloncurry

Gidgee Bar and Grill
Matilda Highway
Tel: 4742 1599
Open: D Mon–Sat. **$$**
Generous reef 'n' beef
offerings such as rib fillet
with grilled bugs, prawn
Bearnaise, pea purée
and soufflé potatoes.

Leichhardt Hotel-Motel
11 Scarr Street
Tel: 4742 1389
Open: L & D daily. **$$**
Well-prepared bistro
meals concentrating on
premium grain-fed steak
and fresh Gulf-sourced
seafood. Extensive wine
list with Grange vintages.

Wagon Wheel Motel
54 Ramsay Street
Tel: 4742 1866
Open: D daily. **$$**
A la carte menu runs to
four pages of primarily
steak and seafood
dishes, with a separate
menu for pizza and pasta.

Hughenden

Great Western Hotel
14 Brodie Street
Tel: 4741 1454
Open: L & D daily. **$**
Huge T-bone steaks are

the feature of this family-
oriented hotel-restaurant.

Mount Isa

Dom's Italian Restaurant
79 Camooweal Street
Tel: 4743 4444
Open: L & D Tues–Sat. **$**
Eclectic Italian menu
based on traditional
dishes. Well-presented,
affordable fare.

**Frog and Toad Bar
and Grill**
The Buffs Club, corner Grace
and Camooweal Streets
Tel: 4743 2365
Open: L & D daily. **$**
Hearty fare served in a
spacious room. Bistro for
lunch and dinner. Coffee
shop for light meals. Live
entertainment Wed–Sun.

The Grill Shop
Town Leagues Club, corner
Miles Street and Ryan Road
Tel: 4749 5455
Open: L & D daily. **$**
One of the Isa's better
club restaurants. A la
carte modern Australian
with fresh ingredients.

Keen's Bar and Grill
Mount Isa Irish Club,
1 Nineteenth Avenue
Tel: 4743 2577
Open: D daily. **$$**
The club also offers an
all-day breakfast in the
coffee shop and a lunch
buffet in the Members'
Bar noon–2pm.

Mount Isa RSL Club
89 Barkly Highway
Tel: 4743 2172
Open: L & D daily. **$**

Country-style meals in
the club bar. Few frills
but generous servings.

Overlander Hotel
119 Marian Street
Tel 4743 5011
Open: L & D daily. **$**
The hotel bistro delivers
generous helpings of
steak, seafood and
chicken dishes.

RE's
Red Earth Boutique Hotel,
corner West Street and
Rodeo Drive
Tel: 4749 8888
Open: L & D daily. **$$**
Classy and affordable
fare in a stylish hotel.
Popular with the corporate
sector. Book ahead.

Winton

**The Coolibah Country
Kitchen**
Waltzing Matilda Centre,

Elderslie Street
Tel: 4657 1466
Open: L daily. **$**
Coffee, cakes and pas-
tries baked in-house.
Salads and light meals
are also available. BYO.

Tattersalls Hotel
78 Elderslie Street
Tel: 4657 1309
Open: L & D daily. **$**
In Winton's oldest hotel
(1885), publicans Paul
and Sanya Nielsen serve
premium-quality steaks
from all over Australia.

PRICE CATEGORIES

Prices are for a three-
course meal per person
with house wine:
$ = A$60 and under
$$ = A$60–100
$$$ = A$100 and over

RIGHT: whistle-wetting in Winton.

SOUTHWEST QUEENSLAND

A region of vast distances, serene billabongs and diverse wildlife. Its isolation inspired both QANTAS and the Flying Doctor Service. Amid flood plains and red, sandy desert, the Outback spirit survives

Brisbane

Map on page 230

The best time to see Queensland's Southwest is after rain. Wild flowers burst into bloom, corellas wheel overhead and waterholes brim with yellowbelly. The transformation is little short of miraculous. The channels and gullies of Cooper Creek join to form a brown stream 30 km (19 miles) wide, and the red soil is cloaked in green.

Of course, the greening of the Outback is a comparatively rare phenomenon. For most visitors, the overriding impression is one of human fortitude amid a harsh, arid and unrelenting vastness. There's a curious appeal in this. In dry times – and times are mostly dry – the landscape expresses a kind of primeval power that is at once exhilarating and humbling. Perhaps that is what makes those who inhabit this unforgiving landscape such a flinty, independent breed – philosophical about setbacks, sanguine about prospects, laconic of wit.

The Southwest is studded with communities clinging to the ledge of existence. When Betoota's publican and last resident walked out a few years ago, the town became yet another vacant dot on the map. Other settlements have a more permanent air, Longreach among them. For visitors approaching Southwest Queensland by air, Longreach Air-

port is the first port of call before transferring to car or bus.

Self-drive allows independence, but a bus tour is by far the more informative experience, provided you don't mind amplified patter interspersed by repeated playings of *On the Road from Gundagai*. A competent driver/guide knows the name of every tree, flower, bird and critter that crosses your path. He'll impart astounding facts about the bush and introduce you to some of its colourful characters.

LEFT: cattle country, where every pub has character. **BELOW:** the Dog Fence on the border with New South Wales.

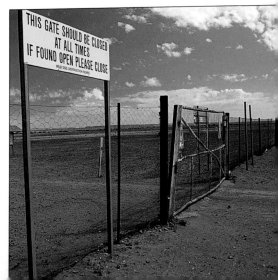

THIS GATE SHOULD BE CLOSED AT ALL TIMES
IF FOUND OPEN PLEASE CLOSE
WILD DOG DESTRUCTION BOARD

Longreach

Longreach ❶ is a city of about 4,000 people in the heart of the Outback, 1,200 km (746 miles) from Brisbane. The ennui that marks other Outback centres is less obvious here, possibly because Longreach retains its purpose as a service centre for the surrounding sheep and cattle runs.

Its most visible attractions are historical. Flying in, the first thing you see is the **QANTAS Founders' Outback Museum** (Landsborough Highway; daily 9am–5pm; admission charge; tel: 4658 3737; www.qfom. com.au), cementing Longreach's claim as birthplace of the airline. It's a sore point in the west. Winton and Longreach each claim the successful airline as their own – Winton, because the founders met in the Winton Club, Longreach because this was where they based their operation. An uneven compromise has been struck: Winton kept the

boardroom; Longreach has the A$9 million aviation museum.

The 747-200B jumbo jet is hard to miss, towering over everything (you can tour inside at extra cost); it's a big advance on the open cockpit Avro 504K used for the airline's inaugural flight from Longreach to Winton in 1921. There's a replica of an Avro 504K inside the museum, along with a slew of informative interactive displays. Near by, the original 1922 QANTAS hangar houses a replica of an Apollo biplane. The first QANTAS booking office in Eagle Street now serves as an information office for the museum.

Just beyond the museum is the **Australian Stockman's Hall of Fame and Outback Heritage Centre** (Landsborough Highway; daily 9am–5pm; admission charge; tel: 4658 2166; www.outbackheritage. com.au), an arresting building, designed as a tribute to the early explorers, stockmen and drovers of

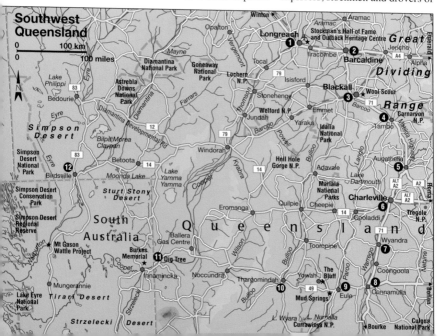

the Outback. Now, alongside the bush memorabilia, pioneering relics and dioramas of early Outback life, the centre has grown to incorporate new themes such as Aboriginal culture and European exploration.

One Longreach legend is 19th-century cattle duffer (thief) Harry Readford, alias Captain Starlight, who, in 1870, drove 1,000 cattle stolen from Bowen Downs Station through unexplored terrain into South Australia. When a distinctive white bull sold en route gave the game away, Readford was apprehended – only to be acquitted by a jury in Roma, an Outback town well known for incomprehensible "not guilty" verdicts. Readford is commemorated in Longreach by a hill known variously as **Cassidy's Knob** and **Starlight's Lookout**. The hill overlooks the surrounding plains where, so the story goes, Readford posted a lookout to keep watch while his henchmen gathered the stolen herd.

Barcaldine

Barcaldine ❷, 107 km (66 miles) east of Longreach, is a well-tended sheep-and-cattle town of 1,900 people, and the birthplace of the Australian Labor Party. It was here, during the strike of 1891, that shearers organised themselves into armed camps and were confronted by a military force equipped with guns. As a gesture of solidarity 1,000 striking shearers marched under torchlight to the Tree of Knowledge where they burned effigies of Premier Sir Samuel Griffith. The iconic ghost gum in Oak Street remained alive until 2006, when vandals poisoned it.

When 13 of the shearers' leaders were sentenced to three years' hard labour on St Helena Island in Moreton Bay, the shearers resolved to win political power to protect the interests of working people. They met under the Tree of Knowledge to endorse shearer Tommy Ryan, who became the first Labor Party candidate to win office in the parliament, inspiring the formation of the Australian Labor Party.

Barcaldine was also the first town to obtain artesian bore water, hence the oases of thriving gardens, leafy streets and orchards of citrus fruits

Map on page 230

Longreach was where QANTAS (the Queensland and Northern Territory Aerial Service) set up its first operational base in 1922.

BELOW: the Australian Stockman's Hall of Fame.

In 1891, beneath the branches of the so-called Tree of Knowledge, the sheep shearers of Barcaldine held their historic protest meetings against pay and working conditions. The ancient gum tree still stands as a monument to workers and their rights.

BELOW: loading the road train.

amid desert country. Sadly, the presence of a steady water source did not prevent conflagrations sweeping through the town. Of the six hotels that once stood in Barcaldine, only two – the **Artesian Hotel** and **The Union** – have remained unburned.

Barcaldine's history is chronicled at the impressive **Workers' Heritage Centre** (Ash Street; Mon–Sat 9am–5pm, Sun 10am–5pm; admission charge; tel: 4651 2422; www.australianworkersheritagecentre.com.au). Opened during the centenary celebrations of the Labor Party in 1991, the centre commemorates the role played by workers in the social and political development of Australia. Displays include a schoolhouse, a hospital and a powerhouse, and it's set in pleasant landscaped grounds around a central billabong.

Also worth seeing is the **Masonic Temple** (corner Yew and Beech Street). Built in 1901, and restored in 1980, the façade of this Outback gem has been painted to resemble stone blocks, pilasters and friezes.

Drop in at the Barcaldine Tourist Information Centre for a copy of the heritage trail guide (Ash Street; Mar–Sept daily 8.15am–4.30pm, Oct–Feb Mon–Fri 8.15am–4.30pm; tel: 4651 1724).

Blackall

Signs on the outskirts of **Blackall** ❸, 100 km (62 miles) south of Barcaldine, announce the town as home of shearer Jackie Howe, whose record with hand blades – 321 sheep in 7hr 40min, set at Alice Downs Station in 1892 – has never been bettered. Howe died in 1920, but his bronze statue looms large outside a replica of the **Universal Hotel** that he once owned. He is depicted wearing his trademark singlet, while hefting a sheep to the board for shearing. Jackie Howe designed his singlet without sleeves to allow freedom of movement. Other shearers adopted the idea and, in time, these practical work shirts (known as "Jackie Howes") became a symbol of rugged masculinity.

Howe also influenced the future of Australian politics. In 1891, as a member of the shearers' union committee, he contributed to the events

that led to the formation of the Australian Labor Party. Barcaldine may claim the Tree of Knowledge as the ALP's most sacred site, but Blackall hosted the first meeting of the shearers' union in 1886, an event marked by a memorial in Shamrock Street.

Blackall also asserts ownership of the **Black Stump** (a lump of petrified wood) which gave rise to the expression "beyond the black stump" to describe impossibly remote locations. According to historians, the Black Stump was used by surveyors to steady their theodolites while taking observations of latitude and longtitude around the year 1887. The original Black Stump has long since vanished, but there's a display and a mural where the stump used to be on Thistle Street.

Northeast of Blackall is the **Wool Scour**, built in 1906, and the last steam-driven wool washing plant in Australia, which operated commercially until 1978. The scour runs on steam May–September, but is powered at other times by electric motor.

Blackall's most fascinating site – the **Black's Palace** – on privately owned Marston Station has been closed due to public liability issues. At the time of writing, moves were afoot to reopen it. Here, anthropologists have recorded around 1,000 Aboriginal drawings on sandstone cliffs – stencils of boomerangs and axes, and drawings of spears, shields, lizards and abstract shapes.

Tambo and Augathella

From Barcaldine, the Matilda Highway heads south through Tambo and Augathella to Charleville.

Tambo ❹, 208 km (129 miles) from Barcaldine, has a population of 500 served by two hotels, a general store and two post offices – one dating from 1876, the other from 1904. The 1876 building, now the **Old Telegraph Museum** (12 Arthur Street; Mon–Fri 10am–5pm, Sat 10am–2pm; tel: 4654 6133), is a rare example of late 19th-century public works architecture, built when Tambo was the main communications point north of Charleville. It stands with other heritage buildings on the main street – the courthouse, post office and shire hall.

 Map on page 230

TIP

For a relaxing break from your Outback road trip, take the waters at the Blackall Aquatic Centre (Salvia Street; tel: 4657 4975) – a 50-metre (164-ft) pool and spa fed by naturally heated water from the Great Artesian Basin.

BELOW: the Workers' Heritage Centre in Barcaldine.

TIP

Charleville community life centres around the RSL Club in Watkins Street and the Warrego Club in Galatea Street. Every second weekend there's a rodeo, a gymkhana, a race meeting, a ball or a shearing competition. Talk to a local. You could find yourself attending a rodeo or wetting a line in a fishing competition. It could add a whole new dimension to your trip.

BELOW: painting the town red in Augathella.

Provided you have a 4WD, Tambo is the departure point for a challenging 320-km (200-mile) trip that traces early bullock routes through gorges and along rivers to the Great Dividing Range. Tambo Shire Council (21 Arthur Street; tel: 4654 6133) can provide maps and trail guides for this journey, which takes in sites of early European settlement and examples of Aboriginal rock art.

The main point of interest at **Augathella** ❺, on the Matilda Highway 118 km (73 miles) south of Tambo, resides with the town's whimsically named junior rugby team, the Augathella Meat Ants. Slightly odd wrought-iron sculptures of meat ants dot the town in support of this team. The Augathella reach of the Warrego River offers excellent fishing for Murray cod, yellowbelly, golden perch and catfish. Otherwise, not a lot happens.

Charleville

Eighty-four kilometres (52 miles) to the south is **Charleville** ❻, a classic Outback town characterised by wide streets, bottle trees and a vulnerability to flooding (on the rare occasions rain falls). Sited on the Warrego River along a stock route from New South Wales to western Queensland, Charleville was surveyed in 1867, developing as a service centre for the surrounding pastoral industry. In 1888, it became the terminus for the western railway line, confirming its strategic position, and in 1893 Cobb & Co. set up a factory for the construction of mail coaches and buggies.

Charleville's heritage architecture reflects eras of prosperity in the late 19th century and the 1920s. At the centre of one of the richest districts, the town has several substantial buildings. The Queensland National Bank (1889), now the **Historic House Museum** (Alfred Street; Mon–Fri 9am–3pm, Sat 9am–noon; admission charge; tel: 4654 3349), is an excellent example of early Queensland architecture, and there is an impressive collection of machinery and vehicles in the grounds, including an early fire engine and a Cobb & Co. coach. Other noteworthy

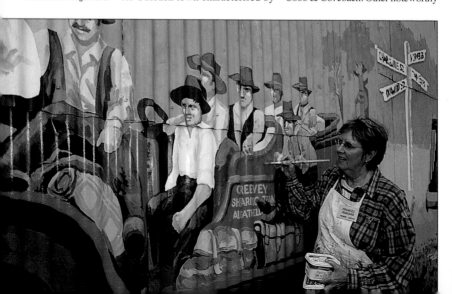

structures include the **Town Hall** (1926) and **Corones Hotel** (1929).

Charleville was at the forefront of the country's infant aviation industry; QANTAS commenced commercial services from here in 1922, taking up where Cobb & Co. had left off; Amy Johnson passed through here in the 1920s; and the US Air Force personnel commandeered Charleville Airport during the Japanese invasion scare of 1942. The Royal Flying Doctor Service (RFDS) established a base in Charleville the following year. You can visit the **RFDS Control Centre** in Old Cunnamulla Road (daily 8am–4pm; donation for entry; tel: 4654 1233).

One of Charleville's more innovative attractions is the **Cosmos Centre** in QANTAS Drive (Apr–Oct daily 10am–6pm, Nov–Mar 10am–5pm; admission charge; bookings essential for night-time; tel: 4654 7771; www.cosmoscentre.com), an observatory that makes use of clear night skies to view planets and star clusters through its sophisticated telescopes. In the galactic theatre you can see presentations describ-ing Aboriginal Dreamtime cosmology and the origins of the universe, while interactive displays explore the history of astronomy. The latest addition is a filter enabling visitors to look at the sun through a telescope.

The Charleville Visitor Information Centre (Enterprise Drive; Apr–Sept daily 9am–5pm, Oct–Mar Mon–Fri 9am–5pm; tel: 4654 3057) can give you details of all the attractions and activities on offer.

Wyandra and Cunnamulla

About 100 km (62 miles) south of Charleville and halfway to Cunnamulla, sits **Wyandra** ➐ – a hamlet of 60 souls blessed by a pub, some old buildings, a museum and, amazingly, a beach. Call into the **Gladstone Hotel** and rub elbows with locals who may, if you show interest, reminisce about Wyandra's heyday, when the town supported two pubs, two ice works, two stores and a garage. It's very quiet in Wyandra nowadays. The best thing is the sandy beach on a picturesque bend of the **Warrego River**, where it

Map on page 230

Every Outback town has its oddity, and Charleville's is the Steiger Gun, a rain-making cannon introduced in 1902 by meteorologist Clement Wragge in an attempt to break a drought by blasting hot air into the sky. A battery of these devices was fired into the atmosphere but, alas, not a drop of rain fell. One of these bizarre rain guns is displayed outside the scout hall, south of Charleville.

BELOW: bilby and baby.

Save the Bilbies

The Queensland Parks and Wildlife Service in Charleville (Park Street; Mon–Fri 8.30am–4.30pm; tel: 4654 1255) runs a breeding programme for endangered native species; you can see yellow-footed rock wallabies here. The centre is also behind the Save the Bilby Fund, a national appeal and breeding programme for bilbies, tiny marsupials whose numbers dropped to 100 at one stage. They are bred here and released into an area of Currawinya National Park surrounded by a predator-proof fence. The **Bilby Show** (Racecourse Complex, Partridge Street; Apr–Sep Mon, Wed, Fri, Sun 6–7pm) provides a fascinating insight into this rare nocturnal bandicoot.

*Cunnamulla's oddity
is the Cyprus Pine in
Stockyard Street, also
known as the Robber
Tree, where, in 1880,
station hand Joseph
Wells hid after a bank
heist. Dogs tracked
Wells to the tree,
where he was spotted
clinging to the
branches. When Wells
was sentenced to
death, opponents of
capital punishment
took to the streets, but
they could not save
him from the gallows.*

BELOW: café proprietor
in Wyandra.

would be easy to spend time fishing for yellowbelly or reading a book. Explorer Edmund Kennedy camped on this sandy expanse in 1847, noting "a two-mile stretch of water 60 yards wide". He named it Camp 18. Locals prefer to call it **Wyandra Beach**. Once a busy railhead, Wyandra lives happily with its ghosts. If you're looking for the railway station, it's been moved to the racecourse, where it serves as a catering hut on race days.

So to **Cunnamulla ⑧** – an Outback town at the intersection of two major stock routes, and the southernmost town in western Queensland. With its tree-lined streets and pleasant hotels it has old-fashioned country charm, and it lies on the Warrego River, a great place for boating, fishing or swimming.

The town was established to service the huge sheep farms which developed in the 1880s; the railway arrived in 1899, and since then Cunnamulla has been a major hub for the district. For details of what to see and do in town, visit the **Cunnamulla Information Centre** (Cente-

nary Park, Jane Street; Apr–Nov Mon–Fri 9am–4.30pm, Sat–Sun 10am–2pm, Dec–Mar Mon–Fri 9am–4.30pm; tel: 4655 2481).

Other points of note on Cunnamulla's heritage trail include the **Post Office** (1868), the **State School** (1885) and **St Catherine's Convent** (1914). As a respite from heat, dust and history, take time to visit the **Allan Tannock Weir**, 5 km (3 miles) south of Cunnamulla. Created with flood mitigation in mind, this placid expanse provides a haven for anglers and birdwatchers – and is a boon to all who come to the Outback in search of peace.

Eulo to Noccundra

Eulo ⑨, 66 km (41 miles) west of Cunnamulla, is a friendly town of about 50 people – virtually all engaged in a cottage industry of one sort or another, from opal cutters and beekeepers to artists and bush poets.

The main focus is the **Eulo Queen Hotel**, named after the original licensee, Isabel MacIntosh, whose clientele comprised opal miners slaking their thirst after a hard day's slog.

So the story goes, Isabel accumulated so many opals that she became known as the Opal Queen of Eulo. The present Eulo Queen offers clean rooms and decent food. It's a good place to meet the locals.

Nine kilometres (5 miles) west of Eulo, a sign announces the proximity of natural mud springs – fissures in the earth's surface that act as pressure valves for the Great Artesian Basin. These mounds have a hard crust but are spongy underneath. So many bores have been sunk that pressure from below has lessened markedly, but the mounds occasionally emit loud bangs.

Yowah, a small opal-mining town, is accessed via the Quilpie turn-off, about 20 km (12 miles) west of Eulo. Continue towards Quilpie for another 45 km (28 miles), then turn left. Depending on the season, Yowah's population fluctuates wildly from 50 to 400 – a number which includes many amateur fossickers combining an Outback experience with the chance of finding an opal.

The town is surprisingly cosmopolitan. Sand greens and earth fairways have been shaped to form a nine-hole golf course, and there is an annual Opal Festival on the third weekend of July. **The Bluff**, 2 km (1¼ miles) east of town, affords scenic views of the mine workings and a rare opportunity to take in the unrelenting and awe-inspiring vastness all around.

Getting to **Thargomindah** , 200 km (124 miles) west of Cunnamulla, is 90 percent of the fun. Aside from an old Fargo fire truck, the ruin of a disc plough and a historic house, there's not much to see or do here.

But Thargomindah does have one significant claim to fame; it is the first Australian settlement to harness bore water successfully to drive a hydroelectricity plant. In 1893, this was innovative stuff. The *Sydney Bulletin* hailed Thargomindah as a world centre for electricity, surpassed only by London and Paris. The hydroelectricity system lasted until 1951.

The first European to probe the district was grazier Vincent Dowling, who in 1859 rode from northern New South Wales to the Bulloo

Map on page 230

TIP

Former graziers Ian and Nan Pike have established a date and fig plantation on the Paroo River. Most popular of their many products is the refreshing date wine, which can be sampled at the cellar door just off Eulo's main street (Mar–Oct; tel: 4655 4890). For a truly memorable experience turn up at sunset, relax in a bath filled with hot Artesian mud, sip a glass of date wine and, as night falls, gaze at the stars.

BELOW: Cunnamulla.

TIP

The best times to visit Noccundra are during the second weekend of October, when local stockmen converge for the rodeo, or in the third weekend of May, when the population swells to 500 or 600 for the race meeting. Stockmen and truckies make up the core clientele of Noccundra's one pub; 4WD pilgrims, older travellers (also known as grey nomads) and recreational aviators take up the slack.

BELOW: there are oil fields in southwest Queensland.

River, returning three years later to establish Thargomindah Station. Gazetted in 1874, Thargomindah became a service centre for surrounding properties and, later, a stopover for teamsters taking wool to Bourke and the paddle steamers plying the Darling River.

Out here, it's the terrain – the mulga, gibber and flood plains and red sandy desert – that captures the eye… and there's plenty to observe on the 140-km (87-mile) run from Thargomindah to **Noccundra**. Close up, the colour and pattern of the landscape takes on a dreamlike quality. From a light plane *(see box opposite)*, you see geometrically precise seismic oil-exploration lines criss-crossing around the Jackson Oilfield.

The road to Noccundra, now sealed, invites conventional car access. Nonetheless, it remains a one-pub town of four residents. The pub, built of stone, dates from 1882, when it served as a watering hole for drovers and later as a mail hitch for Cobb & Co. Even now, it's sufficiently remote to allow light planes to taxi to the door.

The Dig Tree

The road is rough in parts but, having come so far, it makes sense to continue 230 km (143 miles) west to the **Dig Tree** ⓫ on Nappa Merrie Station, living symbol of one of Australia's great tragedies. Here, William Brahe and three others waited more than four months at a base camp near Cooper Creek while explorers Robert Burke and William Wills made their dash to the Gulf of Carpentaria. Brahe left just seven hours before Burke, Wills and King staggered back into the camp on 21 April. The explorers found the warm ashes of a fire and, carved into a tree, the words "Dig.3ft.N.W.April.21,1861". The starving Burke drove off Aborigines who had been giving him fish as he thought them "too cheeky". Both he and Wills died soon afterwards. Only King, who had been taken in by a local tribe, survived to tell the tale.

Australian history leaves fragile monuments. Yet the Dig Tree still grows beside the billabong on Cooper Creek. The carving has been grown over, but the message is partly decipherable.

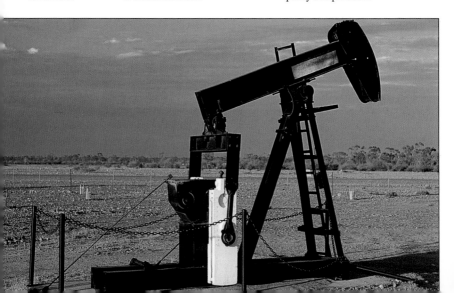

On this stretch of the Cooper, pelicans glide on waterholes that echo to the calls of corellas, galahs, plovers, dotterels, herons, egrets and parrots. Bream, catfish and tortoises swim beneath the surface.

Toompine and Quilpie

Visitors heading to Birdsville via Toompine, Quilpie and Windorah should retrace their route to the east, turning left at Thargomindah. About 75 km (47 miles) north of Thargomindah, **Toompine**'s one point of interest is its pub. When built in about 1893, it was the focal point for a bustling mining settlement. Today, all it has for company is a cemetery. The building has entered a state of decay. 'Roo shooters and opal miners frequent the bar, which is adorned with signs like "The Only True Wilderness Is between a Greenie's Ears". For all that, they're a friendly mob, ready with a beer and a tale.

Another 75 km (47 miles) north of Toompine is **Quilpie**, whose population stands at around 600, making it the big smoke in these parts. Tourism brochures depict Quilpie as the land of opals and oil. It is also the land of cattle and sheep, with 60,000 head passing through the railhead in a good season.

Quilpie's fascination with opal – the district is a major producer of boulder opal – finds expression at **St Finbarr's Roman Catholic Church** on Buln Buln Street, where opal lines the altar, font and lectern.

Windorah, 237 km (147 miles) northwest of Quilpie, is known for its landmark of huge red sandhills just 10 minutes' drive out of town. It's situated alongside Cooper Creek, and it doesn't get much more "Outback" than here, with its stunning vistas and picturesque ruins. There's an old wooden pub, a general store, a post office, a service station run by a blind mechanic – and not much else.

Try to time your visit to coincide with one of the events that take place here annually, when the population swells to 200 and the town comes to life: there's bronco branding, a rodeo and yabby racing (yabbies are small freshwater crayfish). The Windorah Visitor Information Centre (Maryborough Street; Apr–Oct daily

Map on page 230

TIP

Quilpie has become a hotbed of Outback art – largely thanks to local artist Lyn Barnes, whose gallery occupies premises in the former Brick Hotel in Brolga Street. For Barnes and fellow artists such as Char Speedy, Pat Hall and Leah Cameron it's a case of paint what you know; red dirt landscapes, shearing sheds, cattle yards, campfires and lonely homesteads.

BELOW: the Dig Tree.

Flying over the Outback

Winton-based **QOTS** (Queensland Outback Tourist Services; tel: 4657 1340; mob: 0427 571 340) will fly up to five passengers in a six-seater Piper Saratoga to almost anywhere in Outback Australia or the Great Barrier Reef. Pilot Peter Evert's most popular package is his Outback Pub Crawl, where passengers are taxied to the door of pubs in towns like Noccundra, Innamincka and Birdsville.

Air Central West (tel: 4658 9187; mob: 0427 622 329) offers go-anywhere charters in a six-seater from Longreach Airport, while **Outback Airtours** (tel: 4654 3033; www.outbackairtours.com), based in Charleville, offers charter packages for groups of four passengers or fewer.

Map
on page
230

8.30am–5pm, Nov–Mar Mon– Fri 8.30am–5pm; tel: 4656 3063) can help you.

Birdsville and the Simpson Desert

Located 1,600 km (1,000 miles) west of Brisbane, remote **Birdsville** ⑫ clings to the edge of the Simpson Desert, close to the route that Burke and Wills followed on their ill-fated expedition. On the first weekend in September its population expands from 120 to 6,000 as people converge on the town for the Birdsville Races, which celebrates 125 years of horse racing in 2006.

One of Australia's most famous pubs, the National Trust-listed **Birdsville Hotel**, is booked out at race time, and is busy from March through to November. Built from sandstone in 1884, the hotel has been tastefully renovated, and attracts Outback characters and tourists from far and wide.

The town's other hotel – the **Royal Hotel**, erected in 1883 – is a relic of Birdsville's pastoral past. In gracious ruins, it housed the Aus-tralian Inland Mission's Nursing Home from 1923 to 1937. The town's only other surviving masonry building (apart from the Birdsville Hotel) is the **Courthouse**, built between 1888 and 1890, and still in use by the police and judiciary.

Housed in the **Birdsville Working Museum** (Waddle Drive; April–Oct daily 8am– 6pm; admission charge; tel: 4656 3259) is a large and interesting collection of working machinery used by early settlers – including kerosene-powered fans and horse-driven water pumps. The museum, in a big tin shed, is the life-long project of former rodeo rider John Menzies, who demonstrates the ingenuity of early bush technology in three 50-minute shows daily (9am, 11am and 3pm).

Beyond Birdsville lies the **Simpson Desert National Park**, Queensland's largest national park. It's dominated by vast parallel dunes up to 20 metres (66 ft) high and interspersed by claypans, saltpans, sand drifts, plains and gibber-ironstone flats. This starkly beautiful environment provides the natural habitat for more than 180 bird species, ranging from tiny insect-eating wrens to large birds of prey, and is also home to the mulgara, a rare marsupial.

If you have a 4WD and want to cross the park, heed the advice on page 250 and only travel in two-vehicle parties between April and October. Contact the Ranger-in-Charge, Simpson Desert National Park (tel: 4658 1761) before you go.

Conventional cars can tackle the **Birdsville Track**, which stretches south of Birdsville to Maree in South Australia. taking a desolate course of 520 km (320 miles) between the Simpson Desert to the west and Sturt Stony Desert to the east. Take similar precautions as those for travelling through the national park, and ensure that you notify a responsible person of your plans prior to travelling. ❑

BELOW: bird's eye view of Birdsville.

RESTAURANTS, CAFÉS & BARS

Barcaldine

Lee Garden Chinese Restaurant
Corner Landsborough and Capricorn Highways
Tel: 4651 1451
Open: L Tues–Sun Apr–Oct, D Tues–Sun all year. **$**
Established in 1989, offering a mix of affordable Chinese and Western-style meals.

The Witches' Kitchen
Union Hotel, 61 Oak Street
Tel: 4651 2269
Open: L & D daily Apr–Oct. Hours vary rest of year. **$**
Head witch Neroli Pelizzari conjures up steaks, roasts and enchanted chicken dishes.

Birdsville

Big Red Café
Tel: 4656 3099
Open: L & D daily Apr–Oct. **$**
Owners Karsten John and Jackie Stallard's unique desert café offers espresso, cakes and world cuisine. Resident artist/musician Wolfgang John's paintings and CDs express the feeling of the landscape. Karsten, who is Wolfgang's son, does a line in campfire twirling.

Birdsville Hotel
Adelaide Street
Tel: 4656 3244.
Open: L & D daily. **$**
Bistro dining daily for lunch and dinner. Menu features locally raised grass-fed organic beef, as well as seafood and vegetarian dishes.

Birdsville Bakery
Tel: 4656 4697
Open: L daily Apr–Oct. **$**
Baker Dusty Miller rustles up fresh bread, pies and sausage rolls in his café/bakery. Evening meals include hamburgers, pizzas and fish and chips.

Blackall

Tatts Bar and Bistro
Acacia Motor Inn, 110 Shamrock Street
Tel: 4657 6022
Open: D Mon–Sat. **$**
Old-fashioned country food – and plenty of it.

Charleville

Charleville RSL Club
36 Watson Street
Tel: 4654 1449
Open: L & D daily. **$**
Bistro-style fare amid the clatter of poker and keno machines. A notch up from pub grub and a good place to observe locals at leisure.

Outback Restaurant
Mulga Country Motor Inn, Cunnamulla Road
Tel: 4654 3255
Open: D Mon–Sat. **$$**
Fare includes such unexpected exotica as Tahitian prawns and mushroom gratin.

Longreach

Jolly Jumbuck Restaurant
Sir Hudson Fysh Drive
Tel: 4658 1799
Open: L & D daily. **$$**
À la carte fare in an open restaurant set in gardens.

Longreach Club
31 Duck Street
Tel: 4658 1016
Open: L Mon–Sat, D daily. **$**
Chef Robin Grey dishes up generous helpings of steak and pork spare ribs – and also appears front of house to regale guests with Outback yarns.

McGinness's Restaurant
QANTAS Founders' Outback Museum, Sir Hudson Fysh Dr
Tel: 4658 3737
Open: L daily. **$**
Pleasant café fare.

PRICE CATEGORIES
Prices are for a three-course meal per person with house wine: **$** = A$60 and under **$$** = A$60–100 **$$$** = A$100 and over

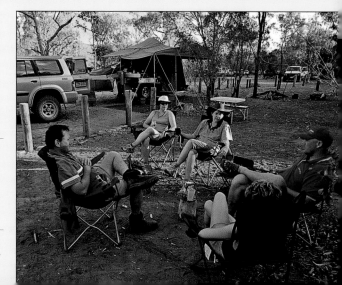

RIGHT: alfresco refreshments.

Outback Pubs

To enter an Outback pub in Queensland is to experience life slowed to near-standstill. Wags and bush characters linger over leisurely beers. Everyone has a tale to tell – and the walls resonate with a sense of place and community.

The state's most colourful pubs survive from the pioneering days, when hotels mushroomed wherever gold was discovered or a new railhead was established. Over the years, many historic hotels have succumbed to fire and neglect – but the thirsty traveller can still savour a coldie in quirky century-old establishments that have defied the broom of progress.

Probably the most famous is the **Birdsville Hotel**, 1,600 km (1,000 miles) west of Brisbane, just north of the Queens-land–South Australian border. Built in 1884, it began as a watering hole for local graziers and passing drovers. These days it enjoys the patronage of locals and 4WD adventurers. Due to a shortage of timber, the walls are constructed of solid sandstone, keeping the bar cool and tranquil even when desert winds howl. Battered hats, stubby-holders and photographs of locals decorate the main bar. Adjacent is the Green Lizard Lounge, so named because of a beer drought that forced locals to drink creme de menthe.

Despite this momentary shortage of amber fluid, Birdsville makes no claim to be the inspiration for the late country balladeer Slim Dusty's famous song, *The Pub with No Beer*. (That honour belongs to Lee's Hotel in Ingham, where US servicemen celebrating the Coral Sea victory literally drank the pub dry.)

Other notable scrub pubs in southwest Queensland include the 1882 **Noccundra Pub**, a stone-built former mail hitch for Cobb & Co. (21 km/13 miles down the turn-off at Nockatunga along the Adventure Way); the 1893 **Toompine Pub**, gracefully decaying between Quilpie and Thargomindah; and the **Eulo Queen**, named after original licensee Isabel MacIntosh, who earned her sobriquet after accumulating a fortune in opals from sozzled prospectors.

Corones Hotel is synonymous with Charleville – occupying nearly a block of the town's main street. Built during the eco-nomic boom of the 1920s, this famous hotel fell into disrepair during the 1960s but has since been restored (though not quite to its original grandeur). For several decades Corones Hotel was regarded as the epitome of hospitality in the west. It's worth visiting, if only to see the wood panelling and grand staircase in the foyer, not to mention the raised "pulpit" from which Harry "Poppa" Corones controlled goings-on in the bar.

Southwest of Blackall, in the foothills of the Yang Yang Ranges, the traveller comes upon the **Yaraka Hotel**, centrepiece of an idyl-lic Outback hamlet where, not so long ago, locals relied on a rusty hand-operated bowser for fuel and a manual telephone exchange for communication. Yaraka exists because this is where, in 1917, funding for the Great West-ern Railway petered out. Terminally disap-pointed, the rails point with abandoned hope towards their next destination, Windorah, 145 km (90 miles) to the southwest. Recently the once-a-week service to Yaraka ceased altogether, leaving Yaraka's 15 inhabitants even more isolated – but not lonesome. When Les Thomas, publican of the hotel, throws a barbecue the whole town turns up.

Another great bush pub is the **Wellshot Hotel**, 27 km (17 miles) east of Longreach, where Ilfracombe publican Jo Scott hosts a cast of characters that includes stockmen, Maori shearers and travellers. It's a pub with plenty of Outback atmosphere – little altered since its construction over a century ago.

Winton's **North Gregory Hotel** also enjoys popularity – partly because this is where Banjo Paterson delivered his debut performance of *Waltzing Matilda* in 1895, partly because it's a pleasant place to enjoy cold beer on a hot day. To be precise, the present North Gregory Hotel is not the one that Banjo Paterson patronised, although it does occupy the same site. In all, there have been four North Gregory Hotels. The other three burned down – which explains why the present hotel is built of brick.

Between Winton and Cloncurry are two more well-known bush pubs – the **Blue Heeler** at Kynuna and the **Walkabout Creek** at McKinlay (see *Mount Isa and the West*) and further north again, Normanton's luridly hued **Purple Pub**.

East from Normanton, and about 400 km (250 miles) inland from Cairns, is the National Trust-listed **Einasleigh Hotel**, built in 1909 during a moment of copper mining euphoria. The hotel gained notoriety in 1994 as the focus for community protest against the proposed closing of the Cairns to Forsayth railway. The town's 40 residents blockaded the railway for four days, holding the Last Great Train Ride hostage. Passengers and crew were accommodated and fed in the hotel until the blockade was lifted.

Another Far North Queensland icon is the **Lion's Den Hotel**, located at Helensvale on the coastal road from Cairns to Cooktown. Set in tropical rainforest, this 1875 pub bulges with memorabilia, beginning with a welcome sign that reads: "You keep your dog outta my bar and I'll keep my bullets outta your dog." Don't be afraid. The locals are friendly, especially after a beer or two – plus you can enjoy steak and pizza or cool off in the pub's reportedly crocodile-free swimming hole.

It's impossible to mention every Outback pub. For this writer, the pub at **El Arish**, north of Tully, remains a personal favourite. Named after the Middle Eastern village where Australia's Light Horse Infantry made its last cavalry charge in World War I, El Arish is a green, well-tended place with a happy-go-lucky pub.

Here I fell into conversation with a personable chap called Johnny Pawpaw (apparently he owned a pawpaw plantation). Mr Pawpaw explained that I was sitting on Big Bill's bar stool. Big Bill, sadly, had passed away but locals continued to reserve his seat as a mark of respect. I moved, only to learn that my new stool had been earmarked for Old McDonald, the pub philosopher. Old McDonald, said Mr Pawpaw, was alive and well – but could get upset if he found someone on his stool, a seat indicated by the portraits and poems pinned to the wall in his honour.

Rather than risk giving further offence, I stood – devoting my attention to a photo board showing pub regulars kicking up their heels at a cross-dressing party. Mr Pawpaw revealed that this was pretty mild stuff compared to what went on at some of the dos. At the El Arish pub, said Mr Pawpaw, you could leave your wallet on one part of the bar, your cigarettes somewhere else and your keys in yet another location – and they would still be there at the end of the night. That's the sort of pub it was. And we drank to that. ❏

LEFT: XXXX hits the spot. **RIGHT:** every pub's a hotel, but not every hotel's a pub. This is both.

TRANSPORT

GETTING THERE AND GETTING AROUND

GETTING THERE

By Air

About 30 international airlines fly directly to Queensland, with most bound for either Brisbane or Cairns. The QANTAS-owned Australian Airlines also flies directly to the Gold Coast International Airport from a range of Asian cities, including Japan, Hong Kong and Singapore.

Flights between Australia and Europe take about 22 hours, although with stopovers and delays the journey could take more like 30 hours. A stopover in an Asian capital (or on the Pacific Coast or Hawaii if travelling from Canada or the US) is worth considering.

The cost of flights to Australia can be high. The peak season for travel is around December, with prices tapering off from January to April. Apex fares will reduce the flat economy fare by about 30–40 percent during the less busy periods. If you are flexible and can fly at short notice, check with discount flight centres for fares on unsold tickets. Note that with many of the heavily discounted fares, refunds and changes in flight times are generally ruled out. A small departure tax, payable in Australian dollars, is levied on all travellers leaving Australia, but this is now included in the cost of an international ticket.

Travellers planning to cover several different parts of Australia in their trip will find it is probably cheaper for a travel agent to arrange flights from point to point before they leave home.

If you are planning to fly to Queensland from other parts of Australia you will most likely travel with one of the three major domestic carriers in Australia. Apart from QANTAS, there are two "no-frills" carriers, the QANTAS-owned Jetstar and Virgin Blue Airlines. They link the southern capitals with a number of points in Queensland, including Brisbane, the Gold Coast, Cairns, the Sunshine Coast, the Fraser Coast, Proserpine, Rockhampton, Mackay, Hamilton Island and Townsville. The regional airline, QANTASLink, also transports passengers from other states to some of Queensland's destinations. It links Townsville with Sydney and Alice Springs with Cairns, for instance.

AIRLINES

British Airways:
Tel: 1300 767 177
(Australia)
Tel: 08705 222 999 (UK)
Tel: 1 800 403 0882 (US)
www.ba.com
QANTAS:
Tel: 13 13 13 (Australia)
Tel: 0845 774 7767 (UK)
Tel: 1 800 227 4500 (US)
www.qantas.com.au
United Airlines:
Tel: 13 17 77 (Australia)
Tel: 0845 844 4777 (UK)
Tel: 1 800 538 2929 (US)
www.unitedairlines.com.au
Singapore Airlines:
Tel: 13 10 11 (Australia)
Tel: 08706 088 886 (UK)
Tel: 1 800 742 3333 (US)
www.singaporeair.com.au

By Sea

Sydney is generally the destination point for cruise liners travelling to Australia, but the following companies include Brisbane and Cairns and sometimes Port Douglas as a port of call on at least some of their itineraries.

Carnival Australia handles bookings for many of the cruise liners visiting Australia. Tel: 132-469 (in Australia); www.carnivalaustralia.com
Cunard Line, tel: 0845 071 0300 (UK); www.cunard.com
P&O, tel: 0845 355 5333 (UK); www.pocruises.com

Princess Cruises, tel: 1800-
PRINCESS (US); www.princess.com

By Train

Countrylink has a daily XPT service
between Sydney and Brisbane.
The train leaves Sydney in the
afternoon and travels overnight;
the return trip is during the day.
The trip takes about 14 hours.

There is another daily service
which involves travel by the XPT
to Casino in northern New South
Wales and then coach travel for
the remainder of the journey to
Brisbane, stopping at Surfers
Paradise along the way. Travel
from Sydney is during the day
while the return leg from Brisbane is overnight.

Book tickets online at
www.countrylink.info or tel: 132-232.

By Road

People arriving in Queensland by
road will generally be travelling
on one of the highways from New
South Wales. The Pacific Highway is the closest to the coast
and usually the fastest way to do
the 970-km (603-mile) trip from
Sydney.

Australia's major coach company, Greyhound Australia, travels both the Pacific Highway and
inland along the New England
Highway from Sydney to Brisbane.

Travellers can also take a
Greyhound coach from Tennant
Creek in the Northern Territory to
Townsville via Mount Isa. But be
prepared for a long haul.

Greyhound Australia, tel:
131-499 or 4690 9950;
www.greyhound.com.au

GETTING AROUND

By Air

Packed as it is with well-known
attractions, it is easy to under-
estimate the distances in
Queensland. To put it in

perspective, this is a state six
times the size of the United
Kingdom and twice the size of
Texas in the United States. The
distance from Brisbane to Cairns
is 1,807 km (1,120 miles).

To reduce the time spent on
the road, some travellers choose
to treat the state as a series of
short hops on a plane. Australia's three major domestic carriers are the best bet for people
wanting to travel between the
various destinations on the
Queensland coast or to Hamilton
Island. But to get any further
north than Cairns, to any other
islands or to inland and Outback
Queensland requires a ticket
with one of the regional carriers.

The largest regional airline in
Queensland is **MacAir**. It flies
from four major destinations –
Brisbane, Cairns, Townsville and
Mount Isa – to a total of 31 des-
tinations in regional and Outback
Queensland. **Sunshine Express
Airlines** flies passengers from
Brisbane to Hervey Bay, Marybor-
ough and Biloela. **Skytrans Air-
lines** has scheduled flights from
Cairns to a range of locations fur-
ther north, including Townsville,
Cooktown, Lockhardt River, Yorke
Island and Horn Island.

There are a variety of airlines
and charter operations servicing
the islands off Queensland's
coast. **Australian Helicopters**
makes daily flights on demand
from Gladstone, six hours north
of Brisbane, to Heron Island,
during daylight hours. It also
makes the short trip from
Mackay to Brampton Island daily
on demand. Tel: 4978 1177.

An air charter service run by
Midstate Airlines flies to Bramp-
ton Island from Mackay, Shute
Harbour and Hamilton Island.
Hinterland Aviation makes the
60-minute trip from Cairns to
Lizard, Bedarra and Dunk
Islands, or it is possible to book
a charter flight with Skytrans.
QANTAS/QANTASLink, tel: 131-
131; www.qantas.com.au
Jetstar, tel: 131-538 or 03-8341
4901; www.jetstar.com.au

Virgin Blue, tel: 136-789 or
3295 2296; www.virginblue.com.au
MacAir, tel: 4729 9444 or 1800-
622 247 (in Australia);
www.macair.com.au
Sunshine Express Airlines,
tel: 5450 6222;
www.sunshineexpress.com.au
Australian Helicopters,
tel: 4978 1177;
www.australianhelicopters.com.au
Midstate Airlines, tel: 1800-815
378 or 4194 1955
Hinterland Aviation, tel: 4035
9323; www.hinterlandaviation.com.au
Skytrans Airlines, tel: 1800-818
405 (in Australia);
www.skytrans.com.au

From the Airport

Brisbane International Airport is
about 16 km (9.6 miles) or a 20-
minute drive from the city centre.
The domestic airport is 2 km
(1.2 miles) further out. The **Airtrain** service leaves the international and domestic terminals
every 15 minutes in peak times
and can deliver new arrivals to
the city's Central Train Station,
Roma Street, or a number of
other destinations in about 20
minutes. Tel: 131-230 or 3216
3308; www.airtrain.com.au.

An alternative for travel to the
centre of Brisbane is the airport
bus service run by **Coachtrans**. It
meets all major flights seven
days a week and ferries arrivals
to the Brisbane Transit Centre at
Roma Street and all central business district (CBD) hotels. The
one-way fare to the Brisbane
Transit Centre is A$9 per person
and to any hotel door A$11 per
person. Tel: 3238 4700;
www.coachtrans.com.au.

Taxis can be found outside the
arrivals hall on Level 2 and will
cost about A$25 for a trip to the
centre of town plus an additional
A$2 for departing taxis.

People wanting to bypass Brisbane completely can travel easily
from the airport the 80 km (50
miles) south to the Gold Coast or
178 km (107 miles) north to
Noosa and the Sunshine Coast.

The Airtrain runs twice-hourly express services to the Gold Coast. The journey takes about 90 minutes, and trains arrive at Nerang Station in the Gold Coast hinterland. From there it is a 15–20 minute drive to the towers of tourist accommodation that line the Gold Coast's beaches. To smooth the trip it is possible to book a 24-hour "door-to-door" service where arrivals are met at Brisbane airport by porters who assist them with getting their luggage to the station. When the train arrives at the Gold Coast they are picked up in a chauffeur-driven vehicle and transferred to their accommodation. The cost of the service, which includes the train trip, is A\$39 for adults and A\$20 for children one-way or A\$75 for adults and A\$37 for children return. The cost is reduced if there is more than one person travelling.

Coachtrans runs from the airport to the Gold Coast via the Gateway Bridge. It drops off passengers at all hotels from Sanctuary Cove to Coolangatta. Tel: 3238 4700; www.coachtrans.com.au.

To get from Brisbane Airport to the Sunshine Coast there is an hourly bus service operated by Sun-air. Buses run 5.50am–8.50pm daily, and the cost is about A\$44 for adults and A\$28 for children one-way door-to-door or A\$28–32 for adults

and A\$17–20 for children to be dropped off at one of its transit stops on the Sunshine Coast, including Noosa, Noosa Heads and Coolum. Transfers can also be arranged for people arriving outside its scheduled hours. Tel: 5478 2811; www.sunair.com.au.

The Gold Coast Airport is on the Gold Coast Highway at Bilinga on the southern end of the Gold Coast. From there it is a five-minute drive to Coolangatta, 15 minutes to Broadbeach and 25 minutes to Surfers Paradise. If keeping costs low is important there is a free Airport Link shuttle bus out to the Gold Coast Highway, where travellers can pick up public transport.

The **Gold Coast Tourist Shuttle** provides a door-to-door service to accommodation on the Gold Coast, charging A\$15 for adults and A\$8 for children one-way or A\$27 and A\$14 respectively for return tickets. Tel: 5574 5111 or 1300-655 655 (in Australia); fax: 5574 5122; www.gcshuttle.com.au.

Taxis line up at a rank outside the terminal and a trip to Coolangatta will cost about A\$7 while Broadbeach will be about A\$28 and Surfers Paradise A\$35.

In Cairns there are two companies offering transfers from the airport. **Australia Coaches** runs a shuttle bus to hotels and the city centre. Tickets cost A\$8 per

person and children under three are free. Tel: 4048 8355.

Sun Palm Express Coaches drops off in the centre of town and goes further afield, taking passengers to the northern beaches, Palm Cove, Port Douglas and Cape Tribulation. Prices range from A\$16 for adults and A\$7.50 for children to the northern beaches up to A\$50 for adults and A\$30 for children for the twice-daily trip to Cape Tribulation. Tel: 4084 2626; www.sunpalmtransport.com.

Taxis and limousines are available at the airport. The average taxi fare into the centre of Cairns is about A\$16.

Public Transport in Brisbane

Public transport in southeast Queensland is divided into 23 zones, but the integrated Translink ticketing system makes it possible to travel on Brisbane's buses, trains and ferries from Noosa to Coolangatta on a single ticket.

There are various ways to explore Brisbane on the water. The inner-city ferry runs from Sydney Street Wharf to North Quay, stopping at places such as South Bank and Eagle Street Pier from 6am to midnight. There are two cross-river ferry services, one running between Tenerife and Bulimba, the other between Holman Street and Thornton Street. They run about every 10 minutes 5.30am–11.30pm.

The Citycat runs from Bretts Wharf at Hamilton to the University of Queensland and stops at places such as New Farm Park, South Bank Parklands and West End. The full trip takes about an hour, and Citycats run 6am–11.30pm daily.

Tickets for the ferries may be purchased on board, from the Ferry Information Centre at the Riverside Ferry Terminal or from about 300 sellers throughout Brisbane. All ferries operate in zones one and two of Brisbane,

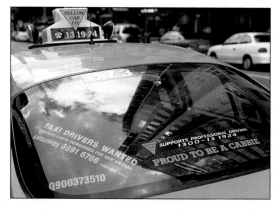

and the maximum ticket price is A$2.50 for adults, or an off-peak daily ticket is A$3.80.

Brisbane's buses operate from the city, ferry wharves and railway stations. The main bus termini are in Adelaide and Queen Streets. **The Loop** is a free red bus service which circles Brisbane's CBD, stopping at Central Station, Queen Street Mall, the Botanic Gardens, Riverside Centre and King George Square.

There is also a Brisbane City Council-operated **City Sights** tour. It takes in the CBD, South Bank, Chinatown, Spring Hill and Milton. Tickets can only be bought on the bus, and are A$22 for adults and A$16 for concessions.

Brisbane's **Citytrain** network extends from the centre of the capital city south to Beenleigh and Robina on the Gold Coast, and north to Caboolture and Gympie, east to Cleveland and west to Ipswich and Rosewood. To get to areas not serviced by the rail network there are integrated rail and bus options operating between Nerang and Surfers Paradise, linking Broadbeach and Noosa Heads. If travelling after dark, embark and alight at the areas marked with blue-and-white stripes on the platform. These areas have enhanced lighting, an emergency phone and video-camera surveillance. **Transinfo**, tel: 131-230.

Train

For those wanting to go further afield, the **Queensland Rail** network (www.traveltrain.com.au) fans out across the state to the dry interior and northward to Cairns, offering travellers an alternative to hours of driving or sitting on coaches. Several of the long-distance trains have a vehicle car, for people wanting to combine a driving holiday with train travel. The **Tilt Train** is the fastest way to travel the rails in Queensland. It does a 25-hour sprint from Brisbane to Cairns

twice a week, leaving town on Mondays and Fridays at 6.25pm and beginning the return leg on Sundays and Wednesdays at 8.15am.

All passengers travel business class, and if the scenery isn't enough to keep boredom at bay, there's always the personal entertainment system in the back of every seat.

The Tilt Train travels more frequently between Brisbane and Rockhampton, making the nine-hour journey six times a week. On this service passengers have a choice of travelling business or economy class. Fares vary depending on the time of year and whether the passenger is entitled to any concessions, but an economy ticket to Rockhampton will cost about A$100 (business class A$150), and to Cairns A$200 (business class A$300).

The Sunlander is a slower train travelling the coastal route from Brisbane. On Sundays and Thursdays it leaves Brisbane at 8.55am and arrives in Cairns at 4pm the following day. The return leg leaves Cairns on Tuesdays and Saturdays at 8.35am and arrives in Brisbane at 3.25pm on the following day.

On Tuesdays and Saturdays the train leaves Brisbane at 8.55am and terminates at Townsville at 8.20am the following day. The journey begins in Townsville on Mondays and Thursdays at 3.55pm and arrives in Brisbane about 24 hours later.

Passengers travelling on The Sunlander to Cairns have a choice of making the 31-hour journey in sitting class, an economy-class berth, a first-class berth and the de luxe class known as Queenslander class. The Queenslander class includes accommodation in a twin-berth sleeping cabin and all meals, which are prepared by a chef and served in the restaurant car. Tickets range in price from around A$200 for sitting class to A$725 for Queenslander class.

Queenslander class is not

available on the trips between Brisbane and Townsville.

Three trains make regular journeys into the Queensland Outback. The **Spirit of the Outback** travels the 1,300 km (808 miles) between Brisbane and Longreach, following the east coast from Brisbane to Rockhampton and then heading west through Blackwater, Emerald and Barcaldine to Longreach. Trains depart Brisbane twice a week, on Tuesdays and Saturdays, and Longreach on Mondays and Thursdays, and the journey takes about 24 hours. There are three options for travel; sitting class, economy and first class, with tickets ranging from around A$170 to A$360.

To see the southwest corner of the state take **The Westlander**. It leaves Brisbane, crosses the Great Dividing Range and travels to Charleville on Tuesdays and Thursday evenings, making the return leg on Wednesdays and Friday evenings. The trip takes about 17 hours and can be made in first-class or economy-class sleeping compartments or in seated accommodation. Full-fare adults pay about A$235 for a first-class berth, A$150 for an economy berth and A$100 for a seat.

The Inlander makes the 977-km (607-mile) trip from Townsville to the mining town of Mount Isa twice a week, leaving Townsville on Sundays and Wednesday afternoons and Mount Isa on Mondays and Friday afternoons. Passengers have a choice of first-class and economy berths as well as sitting class. Fares range from about A$120 to A$270.

There are several shorter train trips which can be a wonderful way to see some of the state's sights in a day trip. The **Kuranda Scenic Railway** travels from Cairns through rainforest and past waterfalls to the pretty village of Kuranda in under two hours. The train departs twice daily (except for Saturdays, when

it makes one trip), leaving Cairns at 8.30am and 9.30am and returning at 2pm and 3.30pm. Fares are A$35 for adults and A$17.50 for children.

The old "tin hare" is the nickname for **The Gulflander**, the train which runs from Normanton to Croydon in Gulf Country in the north of the state *(see also page 212)*. It runs once a week, leaving Normanton at 8.30am on Wednesdays to arrive in Croydon at 1pm. The return trip is made on Thursdays at 8.30am. The cost is A$48 for adults and A$24 for children.

The tongue-twisting **Savannahlander** is a 1960s train which travels at a maximum of 50 kph (30 mph) for its journey from Cairns up the Kuranda railway and through Savannah country to the Outback town of Forsayth. The journey leaves Cairns on Wednesdays at 6.30am and arrives in Forsayth on Thursdays at 5.45pm. The return trip is made on Fridays at 8.45am. **Citytrain**, tel: 131-230 or 3606 5555; www.citytrain.com.au **Queensland Rail**, tel: 1300-131 722; www.traveltrain.com.au

For tickets on the Savannahlander contact **QR Travel Centre Cairns** at the railway station in Bunda Street, tel: 4036 9249.

Boat

No visit to Queensland is complete without some time spent on at least one of its islands. In some cases it is possible to fly by seaplane or helicopter to the island, but for a more run-of-the-mill arrival, and for those with

vehicles, the alternative is using one of the many ferry services. In the south of the state **Moreton Island** and **North Stradbroke Island** are both pleasant day trips from Brisbane, and they are serviced by a number of daily vehicle- and passenger-ferry services. The Moreton Island ferries run from Lytton and Scarborough on the mainland while the North Stradbroke ferries run from Cleveland.

To get to the sand dunes of Fraser Island there are a several vehicle ferries, known as barges, operating from Rainbow Beach and Hervey Bay on the mainland to various points on the island.

With the start of the Great Barrier Reef, at Lady Elliot Island, 80 km (50 miles) northeast of Bundaberg, the transport arrangements become more complicated. Some resort islands, such as Heron Island, add the cost of a high-speed catamaran in the overall charge to guests, while others, such as the popular Great Keppel and Green Islands, are serviced by a multitude of ferry and tour operators based in Rosslyn Bay and Cairns respectively.

Most boats to the major islands in the Whitsundays group – such as Hook, Daydream, Lindeman, South Molle – leave from Shute Harbour, about 8 km (5 miles) east of Airline Beach, or from the Abel Point Marina, 1 km (⅔ mile) west. The alternative is to travel from one of the many boats leaving Hamilton Island, an option that will suit people who fly in from other parts of Australia or Queensland.

To get from Townsville to Magnetic Island, there are frequent high-speed catamarans that take about 25 minutes to make the journey. Access to Dunk and Bedarra Islands is via a catamaran from Mission Beach. For people who have a hankering to see the island at the tip of Cape York, Thursday Island, there is a regular ferry service provided by Peddells Thursday Island Tour.

Here are some of the operators providing access to Queensland's islands.

Moreton Island and North Stradbroke Island

Combie Trader, tel: 3203 6399; www.moreton-island.com
MI Cat, tel: 3909 3333; www.micat.com.au
Stradbroke Ferries, tel: 3286 2666; www.stradbrokeferries.com.au
Sea Stradbroke, tel: 3488 9777
Stradbroke Flyer, tel: 3286 1964

Fraser Island

Fraser Island Vehicle Barge, tel: 4120 3333 or 1800-227 437 (in Australia); www.kingfisherbay.com

Whitsunday Islands

Fantasea Cruises, tel: 4946 5111; www.fantasea.com.au

Magnetic Island

Sunferries Magnetic Island, tel: 4771 3855; www.sunferries.com.au

Dunk and Bedarra Islands

Mission Beach Dunk Island Connections, tel: 4059 2709; www.missionbeachdunkconnections.com.au

Thursday Island

Peddells Thursday Island Tours, tel: 4069 1551; www.peddellsferry.com.au
Horn Island Ferry Service, tel: 4069 1011; operates between Thursday Island and Horn Island.

Cruising

Cruising is a popular way to see the Whitsunday Islands. Operators provide plenty of options, including crewed sailing boats, tours and the chance to skipper a boat yourself. Bareboating (skippering yourself) does not require a special licence, and the operator will provide any introductory training needed. Vessels for hire include yachts, catamarans, motor cruisers and powerboats, with operators based at Airlie Beach, Hamilton Island and Shute Harbour.

Note that skippers with a boating licence must abide by the same drink-driving rules that apply to the road; their blood alcohol level must not exceed 0.05 percent. Weather forecasts should be obtained, even for a short trip, by contacting one of the following numbers: tel: 1300-360 426 (all of Queensland); 1300-360 427 (marine warnings); 1300-360 428 (southeast Queensland).

For more information on cruising see page 271.

Coach

People without their own wheels will have no trouble getting to the major tourist destinations in Queensland by coach. **Greyhound Australia** travels the coastal route from Surfers Paradise to Cairns. Inland it's possible to take one of their coaches west to Mount Isa and Camooweal near the Northern Territory border. Coaches leave Brisbane for Rockhampton, Toowoomba, Longreach, Mount Isa and Cairns.

For people planning to travel by coach to other parts of Australia, there is a range of money-saving passes to reduce travel costs. The Aussie Explorer Pass operates as a series of pre-set itineraries and is valid for travel for a fixed number of days. For instance, there's a pass which begins in Brisbane and allows travel up the coast to Cairns. It is valid for 183 days and is good for about 2,000 km (1,250 miles).

Backtracking is not allowed on concession passes.

A **Day Pass** is for travel on consecutive days and comes in three-, five-, seven- and 10-day options. Backtracking is allowed, but kilometres are limited.

For the greatest freedom of travel there is an **Aussie Kilometre Pass**, where a bank of km is purchased. A 10 percent discount is available on Greyhound passes for holders of various cards and memberships, including Youth Hostel Association or Hostelling International, Nomads and ISIC.

To travel beyond Cairns by coach, **Coral Reef Coaches** does a twice-daily run between Cairns and Cape Tribulation, dropping off and picking up at the Daintree, Mossman and Port Douglas.

There are plenty of coach companies running half- and one-day tours to various points of interest. **Greyhound Australia**, tel: 131-499 or 4690 9950; www.greyhound.com.au
Coral Reef Coaches, tel: 4098 2800; www.coralreefcoaches.com.au

Car

Visiting overseas drivers do not need a Queensland driver's licence or an International Driving Permit, provided they have an up-to-date driving licence from their home country. If the licence is not in English, it is a good idea to carry a translation.

Most of Queensland's road rules are based upon international rules, and it is simply a matter of following the signs, sticking to specified speed limits and so on. But there are a few points that drivers should be aware of:

● Australians drive on the left-hand side of the road.

● Drivers must give way to the right, unless otherwise indicated, to pedestrians (keep an eye out for zebra crossings), and to all emergency vehicles.

● The speed limit in most built-up city and suburban areas is **60 kph (37 mph)**, unless otherwise indicated.

● It is the responsibility of the driver to ensure restraints (including for children and babies under 12 months old) are used by passengers at all time.

● There is a 0.05 percent blood alcohol limit for drivers, which is widely enforced by the use of random breath tests carried out by the police.

● Use of hand-held mobile phones is not permitted while driving.

For safety issues, see page 250.

Vehicle Hire

Car-rental companies have offices located in Brisbane, including the airport, as well as major tourist centres, the Gold Coast, Noosa, Cairns and Townsville. It is also possible to hire campervans, 4WD vehicles and motorbikes. If you have not already organised car hire as part of a package, you should shop around for the best deal: the smaller, independent operators tend to be cheaper.

Don't forget insurance. Many companies have an excess charge of A$700–1,500, which means that you pay that amount in the case of an accident. It is wise to pay a little extra per day to reduce the figure. When you are getting a quote, ask for the full amount, including insurance and charges for items such as baby restraints. Many car-hire

RULES OF THE ROAD

Driving in Queensland can involve negotiating anything from roads that are under water during the wet season to kangaroos appearing out of nowhere. To have a problem-free holiday it is important to bear in mind the following suggestions:

● Seek local advice about road conditions, particularly in the wet season from October to April. Contact the RACQ (see below) for information prior to travelling.

● Distances between towns can be great in Queensland; always carry a spare tyre, other basic spare parts, tools, water (around 20 litres/40 pints per person) and fuel. Don't overload the vehicle and don't carry spare fuel inside the vehicle.

● Use a 4WD on unsealed roads and in remote areas,

and carry communication equipment other than a mobile phone, such as a radio, a satellite phone or an emergency positioning beacon.

● Before embarking on long journeys into the Outback, you should report to the police before you leave and again when you arrive at the other end.

● Where possible, travel with other vehicles to remote locations.

● If a road is covered in water, don't cross unless you know other vehicles have done so. Use ferry crossings instead if possible. If you have to cross, ensure the road surface is firm and stay in the middle of the road.

● Allow plenty of room before overtaking road trains, and be

prepared for the "windrush", which can pull smaller vehicles towards the road train.

● Animals and livestock can present a serious danger, particularly at sunrise, sunset and at night. Try to avoid driving at these times.

● Drive with your headlights on low beam during the day, as dusty conditions can make it difficult to see other vehicles on the road.

● If you run into trouble in the Outback, do not leave your vehicle. It will provide protection from the heat, and is easier to spot than an individual.

● Some areas of Outback Queensland may require permits to access Aboriginal land, and there may be restrictions about carrying alcohol into these areas.

companies do not insure normal vehicles for off-road travel, which means that the driver is liable.

For disabled drivers, all the major hire companies have a small number of cars with hand controls. Contact them well in advance to book.

Major car-hire companies

Avis, tel: 136-333; www.avis.com.au
Budget, tel: 5536 5377 or 1300-362 848 (toll-free); www.budget.com.au
Thrifty, tel: 5570 9999 or 1300-139 009 (toll-free); www.rentthrifty.com

Campervan hire companies

Apollo, tel: 3265 9200 or 1800-777 779 (toll-free); www.apollocamper.com
Britz, tel: 03-8379 8800 or 1800-331 454 (toll-free); www.britz.com
KEA Campers, tel: 4051 1989; www.keacampers.com

For information on travel by campervan or caravan contact

Caravan Parks Association of Queensland, tel: 3357 4399; www.caravanqld.com.au
Campervan and Motorhome Club of Australia, tel: 02-4978 8788; www.cmca.net.au

Four-wheel-drive-hire companies

Britz, tel: 4032 2611; www.britz.com
Four Wheel Drive Hire Service, tel: 4032 3094; www.4wdhire.com.au
Meteor Car and Truck Rentals, tel: 4035 2505; 1300-306 809 (toll-free); www.meteorrentals.com.au

Breakdown Services

The **RACQ** (Royal Automobile Club of Queensland) provides roadside service to members, and has reciprocal arrangements with motoring organisations overseas. Most car hire outlets arrange their own roadside service, but the RACQ is a good point of contact for all sorts of motoring advice.

It provides up-to-date information on road conditions on its website www.racq.com.au. For membership, insurance and emergencies, call tel: 131-905; for road

travel conditions (24-hour), tel: 1300-130 595. For 24-hour roadside assistance contact, tel: 131-111.

The Queensland Department of Main Roads is another useful source of information, including the free map, Guide to Queensland Roads, tel: 3834 2011; www.mainroadsqld.gov.au

ACCOMMODATION

SOME THINGS TO CONSIDER BEFORE YOU BOOK THE ROOM

OVERVIEW

Queensland has a whole range of options when it comes to finding somewhere to stay. For years there have been award-winning super-luxury five-star establishments, often on secluded tropical islands, luring the wealthy. Celebrity magazines are always being fed, oh so discreetly, stories of the latest movie star, rock singer or world leader, who has booked a clutch of rooms in resort X in order to avoid attention. Unsuccessfully, it seems. But even these places need to look to their laurels, because the state now has its first six-star hotel, Palazzo Versace on the Gold Coast. Presumably on the princess-and-the-pea principle, guests sensitive enough to be able to discern the difference can choose between multiple variants of pillow.

For everyone else there's an enormous choice of conventionally starred hotels and – mainly in the beach resorts – holiday apartment blocks. Many of the latter are only let out in week-long chunks. Boutique hotels are making inroads; motels are plentiful and are often the only option in the Outback; plenty of pubs

provide rooms of varying standards or have motel units, usually in a separate adjunct.

Bed-and-breakfast establishments are often found in old heritage buildings. Many of these reflect the British model where there will be a few bedrooms within a largish house and breakfast is provided in a communal dining room. However, the term "bed and breakfast" is also applied when a few provisions are left in a guest room along with a kettle and a toaster, and the guest does the work. Tea- and coffee-making equipment and supplies are usually provided in accommodation of all levels. Usually it's in the bedroom; if not, try the communal room(s).

Budget travellers will find a thriving backpacker scene. Queensland has always been popular with students, who often combine surfing and sightseeing with a bit of work. In the fruit-picking season many hostels double as employment exchanges. Farmers know that's where they will find cheap, hard workers. At these times hostels can get very busy, and it becomes even more advisable than usual to book ahead.

Campsites are generally well maintained and spacious and, almost without exception, will have cabins to rent. One interest-

ing phenomenon, particularly in the bush, is the donga. It's a prefab hut with spartan furnishing – usually a bed, table and chair. These only cost a few dollars and, although primitive, often include basic air conditioning.

Visitor Information Centres can offer advice on accommodation, and some of them will book on your behalf. Many hotels offer lower rates outside peak seasons (which vary and relate to disparate factors like school holidays). Watch out for "schoolies' week" in November, when kids who've finished their exams take over whole towns and discover that if you drink a lot, you fall over (see www.schoolies.org.au).

The increase in internet use means that most accommodation providers are at least looking at getting their own websites. Listings here include those who had sites at press time, but it's worth doing a search to see if others have joined up. It is an easy way of checking availability and tariffs.

There are also a number of clearing houses selling unsold rooms at hefty discounts, especially in the cities and main tourist centres. Check out:
www.wotif.com
www.flightcentre.com.au
www.okjack.com.au

TRANSPORT

ACCOMMODATION

ACTIVITIES

A – Z

BRISBANE

The City

Banana Benders
118 Petrie Terrace
Tel: 3367 1157
www.bananabenders.com.au
Right in the middle of town, with a range of accommodation styles. Airport shuttle, internet access and backpacker party nights. **$**

Brisbane Hilton
190 Elizabeth Street
Tel: 3234 2000
www.hilton.com
The levels of luxury you would expect from a five-star hotel and a plum city centre location as well. **$$$$**

Carlton Crest Hotel
Corner Ann and Roma Streets
Tel: 3229 9111
www.carltonhotels.com.au
Right opposite King George Square, close to the river and central shopping district, this hotel is good value. **$$$**

The Chifley on George Hotel
103 George Street
Tel: 3221 6044
www.constellationhotels.com.au
Five minutes' walk to city, casino or government district. Heated outdoor pool and gymnasium. The popular spa rooms overlook the river and South Bank. **$$$**

The Chifley at Lennons
66 Queen Street
Tel: 3222 3222
www.constellationhotels.com.au
A 20-storey tower in the city's heart, opposite Myers on the Mall. 152 units plus suites, non-smoking floors. Good value. **$$$**

The City

Astor Metropole
193 Wickham Terrace
Tel: 3144 4000
www.astorhotel.com.au
Right by the windmill, this is a friendly mid-scale starting point for a look around the city. **$$**

Conrad Treasury
130 William Street
Tel: 3306 8888
www.conrad.com.au
Makes the most of the features of the old treasury building and has a handy on-site casino. **$$$$**

Dockside Central Hotel
44 Ferry Street, Kangaroo Point
Tel: 3891 6644
Each spacious apartment has a fully equipped kitchen and a balcony with a sweeping view. It's across the river from the city centre, but there's a ferry at the bottom of the garden. Can be very economical for a group or family. **$$$**

Goodearth Hotel
345 Wickham Terrace
Tel: 3831 6177
www.goodearth.com.au
Prices include breakfast. There are 167 units in this hotel, which is situated close to Queen Street Mall and Central Station. It features excellent views of the city. **$$**

Palace Backpackers
Corner Ann and Edward Streets
Tel: 3211 2433
www.palacebackpackers.com.au
Opposite Central Railway Station. Basic lodgings close to cheap

eateries. Plenty of noisy entertainment in the bar, which stays open late. Good-value meals and rooftop sundeck. **$**

Royal on the Park
Corner Alice and Albert Streets
Tel: 3221 3411
www.royalonthepark.com.au
Pleasant luxury city-centre hotel in a quiet setting opposite the Botanical Gardens. **$$$$**

Rydges South Bank
9 Glenelg Street
Tel: 1300 857 922
www.rydges.com
Really handy for all the attractions of the South Bank. Throw in some great views of the city to make this a sound choice if you have the budget. **$$$$**

Stamford Plaza
Corner Margaret and Edward Streets
Tel: 3221 1999
www.stamford.com.au
The Stamford Plaza is a classy heritage hotel with good restaurants; all of its rooms have river views, and it is close to the city's main attractions. **$$$$**

The Suburbs

City Backpackers
380 Upper Roma Street
Tel: 3211 3221
www.citybackpackers.com
Bright and breezy operation that even runs its own pub and promises the best nightlife in the city. This doesn't necessarily make it the most restful retreat. **$**

Comfort Inn & Suites Northgate Airport
186 Toombul Road, Northgate
Tel: 3256 7222
www.choicehotels.com
The closest motel to the airport has good facilities. Recommended if you're hiring a car because you're far from city traffic and parking problems. **$$**

Kingsford Riverside Inn
114 Kingford Smith Drive, Hamilton
Tel: 1800 777590
budgetaccommodation.com.au
Bed and breakfast close to the popular "Brekkie Creek" pub. Convenient for the airport. **$$**

Thornbury House Bed & Breakfast
1 Thornbury Street, Spring Hill
Tel: 3839 5334
Breathe in a bit of history in this discerningly decorated 1886 Queenslander in characterful Spring Hill. **$$$**

PRICE CATEGORIES

Price categories are for a double room without breakfast:
$ = under A$70
$$ = A$70–120
$$$ = A$120–200
$$$$ = over A$200

GOLD COAST

Main Beach

Palazzo Versace
Sea World Drive
Tel: 5509 8000
www.palazzoversace.com.au
Supposedly a six-star hotel, the Versace has the style and extravagance associated with the brand. If that's to your taste, immaculate service and standards add up to the ultimate luxury hotel. **$$$$**

Sheraton Mirage
Sea World Drive
Tel: 5591 1488
www.starwoodhotels.com
Across the road from the Versace and on the seaward side, the Mirage claims a mere five stars. All the space, pools and facilities you could want, but slightly uninspiring. **$$$$**

Surfers Paradise

BreakFree Savannah Resort
46 Surf Parade,
Broadbeach
Tel: 5504 4444
www.savannahresort.com.au
Chic apartments in the heart of cosmopolitan Broadbeach. **$$$$**

Chateau Beachside
Corner Esplanade and Elkhorn Avenue.
Tel: 5538 1022
www.chateaubeachside.com.au
Right on the beach and as good a base as any. Cheap buffet breakfasts in the café. **$$$**

Courtyard by Marriott
Corner Surfers Paradise Boulevard and Hanlan Street
Tel: 5579 3499
www.marriott.com
High-rise pampering just a block back from the beach, with balcony

views down the coast. Ask for a room from the 20th floor upwards. **$$$**

Gold Coast International Backpackers Resort
28 Hamilton Avenue
Tel: 5592 5888
goldcoastbackpackers.com.au
One of the new breed of backpackers that is more like a resort. **$**

Islander Resort Hotel
Corner Beach Road and Gold Coast Highway.
Tel: 5538 8000
www.islanderresort.com.au
One of many hotels which are just back from the beach and therefore cheaper than their high-profile neighbours. **$$**

Pelican Cove
Corner Back and Burrows Streets.
Tel: 1800 354025
www.pelicancove.com.au
Two- and three-bedroom self-contained units right on the waterfront, 10 minutes from Wet 'n' Wild and Dreamworld. **$$**

Quality Hotel Mermaid Waters
Corner Markeri and Sunshine Boulevard, Mermaid Waters
Tel: 5572 2500
www.asiahotels.com
More than 100 rooms, some in a quiet area near casino and Pacific Fair shopping centre. A 20-minute scenic walk to the beach. Courtesy bus to Surfers Paradise Mon–Fri. **$$$**

Burleigh Heads

Aussie Resort
1917 Gold Coast Highway
Tel: 5576 2877
Simple apartment accommodation for the keen surfer. **$$$**

Best Western Outrigger Burleigh Heads Resort
2007 Gold Coast Highway
Tel: 5535 1111
www.outrigger.bestwestern.com.au
Balconies to all rooms and a recent refurbishment make this resort worth considering. **$$$**

Hill Haven Holiday Apartments
2 Goodwin Terrace
Tel: 5535 1055
www.hillhaven.com.au
Self-contained two- and three-bedroom, beautifully furnished holiday apartments, adjoining Burleigh Head National Park. All have ocean views from balconies. **$$$**

Coolangatta

Beachcomber International Resort
122 Griffith Street
Tel: 5599 0909
High-rise block of apartments with every mod con you could want. **$$$**

Oaks Calypso Plaza Resort
87-105 Griffith Street
Tel: 5599 0000
www.theoaksrhm.com.au
This attractive, low-rise hotel is far from the high-rise strip, near the surf beach, with a tropi-

cal swimming lagoon and water slide. Special deals offered. **$$$**

Ocean View Motel
Corner Clark Street and Marine Parade.
Tel: 5536 3722
coolangatta.net/oceanviewmotel
Looks like an old-fashioned traditional 1960s motel next to all the glossy high-rises but service is impeccable and it's great value. **$**

South Stradbroke Island

Couran Cove Island Resort
Tel: 5597 9000
www.couran-cove.com.au
Sleek, well-designed apartments over the water or cabins in the woods at this lovely island site. Cycle from one beach to another, watch the wildlife and spoil yourself. **$$$$**

PALAZZO VERSACE

DARLING DOWNS

Goondiwindi

Best Western MacIntyre Motor Inn
15 McLean Street
Tel: 4671 3051
www.bestwestern.com.au
Tidy modern motel that does all that could be asked of it. **$$**

O'Shea's Royal Hotel/Motel
48 Marshall Street
Tel: 4671 1877
Reasonable pub accommodation right on the main drag. **$$**

Ipswich

Ipswich City Motel
86 Warwick Road
tel: 3281 2633
www.ipswichcitymotel.com.au
A swimming pool, play area and barbecue facilities make this a popular place for families. **$$**

Ipswich Heritage Motor Inn
51 Warwick Road
Tel: 3202 3111
Excellent motel where the proprietor, a former professional musician, will cook your dinner and then play requests at the piano. **$$**

Kingaroy

Burke and Wills Motor Inn
95 Kingaroy Street
Tel: 4162 5131
www.burkeandwills.com.au
A good motel made better by the presence of a notable restaurant. **$$**

Taabinga Homestead
7 Old Taabing Road, Haly Creek. Tel: 4164 5531
www.taabingahomestead.com
This lovingly maintained 1840s homestead, not far from Kingaroy, functions both as a working farm and bed and breakfast facility.

Miles

Miles Outback Motel
11 Murilla Street
Tel: 4627 2100
www.goldenchainmotels.com.au
New motel with all the usual facilities as well as lock-up garages. **$$**

Possum Park
36865 Leichardt Highway
Tel: 4627 1651
www.possumpark.com.au
Remarkable old military camp, 20km north of Miles, where old bunkers, Nissen huts and railway carriages

have been converted into mid-range accommodation. **$**

Roma

Overlander Homestead Motel
Warrego Highway
Tel: 4622 2805
www.maranoa.org.au
An ersatz colonial inn, it scores well for facilities and service. **$$**

Villa Holiday Park
Northern Road
Tel: 4622 1309
www.big4.com.au
Just out of town, it has the standard mix of tent and van sites as well as cabins with AC. **$**

Stanthorpe

Stannum Lodge Motor Inn
1 High Street
Tel: 4681 2000
www.stannumlodge.com.au
A swimming pool is among the many facilities at this sound selection. **$$**

The Vines
2 Wallangarra Road
Tel: 4681 3844
www.thevinesmotel.com.au
There are the standard

motel rooms but also a couple of self-contained cottages. **$$**

Toowoomba

Country Gardens Motor Inn
94 James Street
Tel: 4632 3099
countrygardensmotorinn.com.au
This winner of architectural awards combines form with a high level of comfort. **$$**

Warwick

Abbey of the Roses
8 Locke Street
Tel: 4661 9777
www.abbeyoftheroses.com
One of those places to seek out. It's an old abbey with National Trust listing and a peaceful location to set it off. **$$**

SUNSHINE COAST

Bribie Island

Avon Lodge
132 Avon Avenue, Banksia Beach. Tel: 3410 7318
Comfortable B&B. **$$**

Caloundra

Dicky Beach Family Holiday Park

4 Beerburrum Street
Tel: 5491 3342
www.dicky.com.au
Well-run large site which combines camping and caravan sites with on-site accommodation. **$**

Rydges Oasis Resort
Corner North and Landsborough Parade.
Tel: 5491 0333

www.rydges.com
Close to the ocean and packed with facilities. **$$$**

Suncourt Motel
135 Bulcock Street
tel: 5491 9118
caloundrasuncourtmotel.com.au
Colourful modern motel covers all the bases with some style. **$$**

Coolum

**Coolum Beach
Caravan Park**
David Low Way
Tel: 5446 1474
www.maroochypark.qld.gov.au
Right on the beach, with
185 powered van sites
and 118 unpowered
camping sites. **$**
Coolum Seaside
23 Beach Road
Tel: 5455 7200
www.coolumseaside.com
Self-contained apart-
ments with a pool and
the standard holiday
accoutrements. **$$$$**
Surf Dance Coolum
29 Coolum Terrace
Tel: 5446 1039
www.surfdance.com
Another family-friendly
apartment block which
ticks all the boxes. **$$$**
Villa Coolum
102 Coolum Terrace
Tel: 5446 1286
www.villacoolum.com
Ground-floor units make
this a good holiday base
for those with young
children. **$$$$**

Eumundi

Eumundi Caravan Park
141 Memorial Drive
Tel: 5442 8411
Attractive setting and
relaxed atmosphere. **$**

Fraser Island

**Fraser Island
Wilderness Retreat**
Happy Valley
Tel: 4127 9144
www.fraserislandco.com.au/retreat
Individual timber lodges
sit amid landscaped gar-
dens on the coast. **$$**
**Frasers at
Cathedral Beach**
Happy Valley
Tel: 4127 9177
www.fraserislandco.com.au/frasers
The more economic

option is to camp on this
spacious site or rent one
of the cabins. **$$**
**Kingfisher Bay Resort
and Village**
North White Cliffs
Tel: 4120 3333
www.kingfisherbay.com
Well-appointed eco-
resort with wooden villas
surrounded by rainfor-
est. Gorgeous. **$$$**

Gympie

Gympie Muster Inn
21 Wickham Street
Tel: 5482 8666
Central, well-managed
motel. **$$**
Hilltop Motel
Bruce Highway
Tel: 5482 3577
www.hilltopmotel.com.au
Just north of Gympie,
this is a simple, good-
value establishment. **$**

Hervey Bay

Beachside Motor Inn
298 The Esplanade, Pialba
Tel: 4124 1999
www.beachsidemotorinn.com.au
Nicely turned-out beach-
side motel. **$$**
Boat Harbour Resort
650 The Esplanade, Urangan
Tel: 4125 5079
www.boatharbourresort.com
Appealing beachfront
resort with wooden
cabins and houses sur-
rounding a pool. **$$**
Grange Resort
33 Elizabeth Street, Urangan
Tel: 4125 2002
www.thegrange-herveybay.com.au
Luxurious town house.
$$$

Maleny

**Maleny Country
Cottages**
347 Cork's Pocket Road
Tel: 5429 6195
www.malenycottages.com.au
Curl up in comfort in the

woods and get back to
nature, helped by the
abundant wildlife in the
grounds. **$$$$**
Maleny Hills Motel
932 Montville Road
Tel: 5494 2551
www.malenyhills.com.au
Clean, if uninspiring,
units provide a good
base for exploring. **$**

Maroochydore

Reflections
3 Picnic Point Esplanade
Tel: 5443 9707
www.reflections-apartments.com
Right on the Maroochy
River and handy for the
ocean, these apart-
ments are popular for
family holidays. **$$$**
The Sebel
20 Aerodrome Road
Tel: 5479 8000
www.mirvahotels.com.au
104 two-bedroom apart-
ments in this glittering
new block. **$$$$**

Maryborough

**McNevins Parkway
Motel**
188 John Street
Tel: 4122 2888
www.mcnevins.com.au
Two restaurants in this
comfortable modern
motel give it the feel of
a small resort. **$$**
**Royal Centre Point
Motel**
326 Kent Street
Tel: 4121 2241
Award-winning accom-
modation in this splen-
did old pub makes it a
favourite. **$$**

Noosa

**Breakfree French
Quarter Resort**
62 Hastings Street
Tel: 5474 8122
www.frenchquarter.com.au
High-quality option on

the river side of
Hastings. **$$$$**
Halse Lodge
2 Halse Lane
Tel: 5447 3377
www.halselodge.com.au
Backpackers retreat
in a rambling old
Queenslander. **$**
Noosa Blue Resort
16 Noosa Drive
Tel: 5447 5699
www.noosablue.com.au
Sleek modern resort on
the hill overlooking the
water. **$$$$**
Noosa Village Motel
10 Hastings Street
Tel: 5447 5800
www.noosavillage.com.au
Surprisingly affordable
for its location. **$$**
**Seahaven Beachfront
Resort**
13 Hastings Street
Tel: 5447 3422
www.seahavennoosa.com.au
Overlooks the beach but
has plenty of pools and
facilities if you can't be
bothered to walk far. **$$$**
**Sheraton Noosa Resort
and Spa**
Hastings Street
Tel: 5449 4888
www.sheraton.com
One of two five-star
hotels in Noosa, with
superlative service.
$$$$
Tingirana
25 Hastings Street
Tel: 5474 7400
www.tingirana.com.au
The other five-star
resort, near the beach.
Breathtaking style. Home
to the renowned Sea-
sons restaurant. **$$$**

PRICE CATEGORIES

Price categories are for
a double room without
breakfast:
$ = under A$70
$$ = A$70–120
$$$ = A$120–200
$$$$ = over A$200

CAPRICORN COAST

Agnes Water/ Town of 1770

1770 Getaway
303 Bicentennial Drive
Tel: 4974 9323
www.1770getaway.com.au
Villas, set in manicured
gardens, all designed on
a hexagonal matrix. **$$$**

Beach Shacks
578 Captain Cook Drive
Tel: 4974 9463
www.1770beachshacks.com
Well-stocked bungalows
by the beach. **$$$**

Bundaberg

**Alexandra Park
Motor Inn**
66 Quay Street
Tel: 4152 7255
A nod to colonial archi-
tecture in this roomy and
comfortable motel. **$$**

Inglebrae
17 Branyan Street
Tel: 4154 4003
www.inglebrae.com
Sumptuous rooms in an
old Queenslander. **$$**

Carnarvon Gorge

**Carnarvon Gorge
Takarakka Bush Resort**
Carnarvon Gorge Road
Tel: 4984 4535

www.takarakka.com.au
Canvas cabins sleep up
to five. Campsites too.
$$

**Carnarvon Gorge
Wilderness Lodge**
O'Briens Road
Tel: 4935 9177
www.carnarvon-gorge.com
Reasonable facilities in
these woodland cabins,
but expensive. **$$$$**

Clermont

Peppercorn Motel
51 Capricorn Street
Tel: 4983 1033
www.peppercornmotel.com.au
Sixteen units in standard
format with a pool. **$$**

Emerald

**The Emerald Meteor
Motel**
Corner Opal and
Egerton Streets
Tel: 4982 1166
www.emeraldmeteormotel.com.au
Spotless, well-
maintained motel. **$$**

Explorers Inn
Springsure Road
Tel: 4982 2822
www.emeraldexplorersinn.com.au
Unremarkable but com-
fortable motel on the
edge of town. **$$**

Gladstone

Harbour Sails Motor Inn
23 Goondoon Street
Tel: 4972 3456
Modern development in
the centre of town that's
hard to fault. **$$$**

Great Keppel Island

**Great Keppel Island
Holiday Village**
Tel: 4939 8655
www.gkiholidayvillage.com.au
Budget resort where the
fact of being on the
island is the attraction
rather than facilities. **$$**

Mercure Resort
Tel: 4939 5044
www.greatkeppelresort.com.au
"Fun-loving resort"
where the kids will
never run out of things
to do. **$$$**

Heron Island

Heron Island Resort
Tel: 4972 9055
www.heronisland.com
Accommodation from
comfortable to over-the-
top, priced accordingly.
Spectacular diving a
real bonus. **$$$$**

Mount Morgan

Ferns' Miners Rest
Corner Burnett Highway and
Showground Road
Tel: 4938 2350
Modern cottage units
set back off the road
with everything you
might need. **$$**

Rockhampton

Criterion Hotel
150 Quay Street
Tel: 4922 1225
www.thecriterion.com.au
One of the iconic build-
ings of Rockhampton,
and a fine example of a
Victorian Hotel. Some of
the rooms are faithful to
the style of the period. **$**

Riverview Lodge
48 Victoria Parade
Tel: 4922 2077
Well-placed, basic bud-
get rooms. **$**

SOUTHERN REEF AND WHITSUNDAYS

Airlie Beach

Airlie Beach Hotel
Corner The Esplanade and
Coconut Grove
Tel: 4964 1999
www.airliebeachhotel.com.au
Absolutely prime
seafront location with
four-star facilities
makes this one of the

busier hotels in town,
but justifiably so. **$$$**

**Best Western Colonial
Palms Motor Inn**
Corner Shute Harbour Road
and Hermitage Drive
Tel: 4946 7166
colonialpalms.bestwestern.com.au
Large, comfortable
rooms looking across
the main road to the

sea come with friendly
service. **$$**

Coral Point Lodge
54 Harbour Avenue,
Shute Harbour
Tel: 4946 9500
www.coralpointlodge.com.au
Gorgeous views over to
the Whitsundays from
this homely guest
house/hotel. **$$**

Coral Sea Resort
25 Oceanview Avenue
Tel: 4946 6458
www.coralsearesort.com
The only absolute water-front resort in Airlie Beach offers a range of apartment-style suites, most with spa baths, just three minutes' walk from the action. **$$$**

Magnums Backpackers
366 Shute Harbour Road
Tel: 4946 6266
www.magnums.com.au
The most central hostel at Airlie has also won awards for being the friendliest. It offers dormitory, twin share and double accommodation, and the cheapest beer in town. **$**

Brampton Island

Brampton Island Resort
Tel: 4951 4499
www.brampton-island.com

Beautiful isolated resort that doesn't have the day trippers of some of the other islands. **$$$$**

Mackay

Larrikin Lodge YHA
32 Peel Street
Tel: 4951 3728
www.yha.com.au
Acclaimed hostel in an old Queenslander where the boast of homely comforts rings true. **$**

Whitsunday International Hotel
176 Victoria Street
Tel: 4957 2811
Simple, uncomplicated hotel close to the town centre which represents sound value. **$$**

Whitsundays

Daydream Island Resort and Spa
Tel: 4948 8488
www.daydreamisland.com

Popular resort on this tiny island offers everything for a fun family holiday, including outlandish novelty golf. **$$$$**

Hayman Island Resort
Tel: 4940 1234
www.hayman.com.au
One of the area's ultimate destinations. Offers a level of luxury that guarantees a regular throughput of world leaders and film stars. **$$$$**

Long Island Resort
Tel: 4946 9400
www.clubcroc.com.au
Relaxed resort on its own bay with the emphasis on water sports and fun but quiet woodland walks if you want to get away from it all. **$$$$**

Reef View Hotel
Hamilton Island
Tel: 4946 9999
If you like plenty of

other people around, this is the resort for you. There are 382 rooms and plenty of day trippers popping in to add to the numbers. **$$$$**

PRICE CATEGORIES

Price categories are for a double room without breakfast:
$ = under A$70
$$ = A$70–120
$$$ = A$120–200
$$$$ = over A$200

TOWNSVILLE AND SURROUNDINGS

Cardwell

Mudbrick Manor
Stoney Creek Road
Tel: 4066 2299
www.mudbrickmanor.com.au
The adobe building is a bit gimmicky, but the facilities and attention to detail are what count. **$$**

Charters Towers

Park Motel
1 Mosman Street
Tel: 4787 1022
Clean and efficient motel in a quiet street just a few strides from the centre. **$$**

York Street Bed & Breakfast
58 York Street

Tel: 4787 1028
Nip back to the 19th century in this Victorian house, where the decor recreates a bygone era. Twenty-first-century facilities though. **$$**

Hinchinbrook Island

Hinchinbrook Island Wilderness Lodge & Resort
Tel: 4066 8270
www.hinchinbrookresort.com.au
Accommodation is in architect-designed tree houses linked by an aerial boardwalk. If you're scared of heights take a beach cabin instead. **$$$$**

Ingham

Herbert Valley Motel
Bruce Highway
Tel: 4776 1777
Good functional place to overnight in. **$**

Palm Tree Caravan Park
Bruce Highway
Tel: 4776 2403
A few cabins, as well as the usual powered and unpowered sites. **$**

Magnetic Island

Base Backpackers
1 Nelly Bay Road, Nelly Bay
Tel: 4778 5777
www.basebackpackers.com
Well-run and right by the beach, with dorms or en

Brisbane ●

suites. Good bar and café too. **$**

Magnetic Island Tropical Resort
56 Yates Street, Nelly Bay
Tel: 4778 5955
www.magneticislandresort.com
Simple A-frame cottages in 3 hecta (8 acres) of forest that back-to-natu experience. **$$$**

Sails on Horseshoe
13 Pacific Drive
Tel: 4778 5117
Modern, comfortable units just back from this peaceful beach. **$$$**

Port Hinchinbrook

Port Hinchinbrook Resort and Marina
Bruce Highway
Tel: 4066 2000
www.porthinchinbrook.com.au

Huge marina and residential development has some high-spec cabins to rent. **$$$**

Ravenswood

Imperial Hotel
Macrossan Street
Tel: 4770 2131
Wonderfully atmospheric old hotel where the rooms have been carefully maintained with fans, mosquito nets and bathrooms along the landing, to take you back to its 19th-century heyday. **$**

Townsville

Beach House Motel
66 The Strand
Tel: 4721 1333
www.beachhousemotel.com.au
A pool overlooking the beach is the distinguishing feature of this standard motel. **$$**

Jupiters Hotel and Casino
Sir Leslie Thiess Drive
Tel: 6372 5255
www.jupiterstownsville.com.au
By the water and well placed to enjoy rejuvenated Strand. **$$$**

Strand Park Hotel
59-60 The Strand
Tel: 4750 7888
www.strandparkhotel.com.au
Sparkling all-suite hotel with views across to Magnetic Island. **$$$**

CAIRNS TO CAPE TRIBULATION

Cairns

Acacia Court Hotel
223-227 The Esplanade
Tel: 4051 5011
www.acaciacourt.com
Choice of rooms with balconies and ocean or mountain views, or cheaper, motel-style rooms. **$$–$$$**

Galvins Edge Hill B&B
61 Walsh Street
Tel: 4032 1308
www.cairns.aust.com/galvins
Peacefully located, genuine old Queenslander. The guest accommodation has two bedrooms, bathroom, lounge and breakfast room that opens onto the natural rock swimming pool. **$$**

⸺ Hotel
⸺ Abbott and
⸺ Streets
⸺ 188
⸺pointed
⸺el and
⸺ **$$**
⸺ns

landscaped gardens. A short walk from the Esplanade area. **$$$**

Outrigger Cairns Resort
53-57 The Esplanade
Tel: 4046 4141
www.outrigger.com
Penthouses and luxury one- and two-bedroom serviced apartments, close to the central district and attractions. Pool, fitness room, sauna and spa. **$$$$**

Shangri-La Marina
Pierpoint Road
Tel: 4031 1411
www.shangri-la.com
Fronting Marlin Marina and the inlet, this hotel set in lush tropical gardens has great views and a great location. Luxury accommodation with private balconies or patio. Facilities include a large pool. **$$$$**

Sofitel Reef Casino
35 Wharf Street
Tel: 4030 8888
www.reefcasino.com.au
Central five-star operation with a casino downstairs, an animal sanctuary on the roof but little discernible atmosphere. **$$$$**

Cape Tribulation

The Beach House
Cape Tribulation Road
Tel: 4098 0030
www.capetribbeach.com.au
Dormitory and family cabins, as close to the beach as the National Parks Authority will allow. Swimming pool and bistro/bar, as well as kitchen and laundry facilities. **$$$**

Coconut Beach Rainforest Lodge
Cape Tribulation Road
Tel: 4098 0033
www.voyages.com.au
Set in 100 hectares (250 acres) of rainforest with accommodation in timber villas. Attractions include excursions led by rainforest guides, 4WD tours and Great Barrier Reef cruises. **$$$$**

Daintree

Daintree Eco Lodge and Spa
20 Daintree Road
Tel: 4098 6100
www.daintree-ecolodge.com.au
Luxurious tree houses and award-winning spa.

The place to come to be spoiled. **$$$$**

Kenadon Homestead Cabins
Tel: 4098 6142
www.daintreecabins.com
Comfortable cabins with great views from the back deck. **$$**

Green Island

Green Island Resort
Tel: 4051 0455
www.greenislandresort.com.au
If Cairns gets too much, take to the island for unmitigated luxury. **$$$$**

PRICE CATEGORIES

Price categories are for a double room without breakfast:
$ = under A$70
$$ = A$70–120
$$$ = A$120–200
$$$$ = over A$200

Lake Eacham

Crater Lakes Rainforest Cottages
Lot 1, Eacham Close
Tel: 4095 2322
www.craterlakes.com.au
Four individually themed cottages bordering a national park. Fully equipped, including double spa bath and wood-burning stove. **$$$**

Malanda

Fur 'n' Feathers Rainforest Tree Houses
247 Hogan Road
Tel: 4096 5364
www.rainforesttreehouses.com.au
Private wildlife sanctuary with half a dozen spectacular tree houses deep in the rainforest. **$$$**

Malanda Falls Caravan Park
38 Park Avenue
Tel: 4096 5314
www.malandafalls.com.au
Delightful woodland setting and fine cabins. **$**

Mareeba

Jackaroo Motel
340 Byrnes Street
Tel: 4092 2677
www.jackaroomotel.com
Top motel accommodation with lots of facilities and helpful staff. **$$**

Mission Beach/ Dunk Island

Castaways on the Beach Resort
Corner Pacific Parade and Seaview Street
Tel: 4068 7444
www.castaways.com.au
Set on a tropical beach, with large rooms, one- and two-bedroom units, and a split-level penthouse – all with wonderful views. **$$$**

Dunk Island Resort
Tel: 4068 8199
www.dunk-island.com
Unspoiled beaches with the usual activities and facilities. Upmarket. **$$$**

The Horizon at Mission Beach
Explorer Drive, South Mission Beach
Tel: 4068 8154
www.thehorizon.com.au
The views from this resort-style hotel, on a headland above Mission Beach, are magnificent. Set amidst rainforest, rich in wildlife. Huge range of facilities. **$$$**

Mission Beach Ecovillage
Clump Point Road
Tel: 4068 7534
www.ecovillage.com.au
Comfortable units nestle in the trees around a lagoon-style pool in this well-run resort. **$$$**

Sanctuary Retreat at Mission Beach
72 Holt Road, Bingil Bay
Tel: 4088 6064
www.sanctuaryatmission.com
Freshly refurbished after damage from Cyclone Larry. Accommodation is in simple wooden cabins dotted through the rainforest and an empty beach just down the road. Peaceful retreat. **$**

Scottys Beach House
167 Reid Road
Tel: 4068 8676
Popular family-run place opposite the beach, offering budget accommodation in dormitories or motel-style rooms. **$**

Mossman

Silky Oaks Lodge
Finlayvale Road, Mossman
Tel: 4098 1666
www.silkyoakslodge.com.au
Rainforest hideaway on the edge of Mossman

Gorge; 45 tree houses and five river houses with all creature comforts, plus a spa, restaurant, rainforest excursions and canoe trips. **$$$$**

Palm Cove

The Mango Lagoon Resort & Wellness Spa
81-85 Cedar Road
Tel: 4055 3400
www.mangolagoon.com.au
Stylish suite and apartment accommodation, set amid lush landscaped gardens, with pools and waterfalls. A vast menu of massages and therapies. **$$$$**

Outrigger Beach Club & Spa
123 Williams Esplanade
Tel: 4059 9200
www.outrigger.com
Striking new resort. The top-floor suites have their own glass-encased pools and stunning views of the beach. **$$$$**

Palm Cove Camping Ground
149 Williams Esplanade
Tel: 4055 3824
Ideal spot for campers and campervans, just across from the beach. **$**

Paradise on the Beach Resort
119 Williams Esplanade
Tel: 4055 3300
www.paradiseonthebeach.com
High standards throughout this mid-range hotel. **$$$**

Sebel Reef House & Spa
99 Williams Esplanade
Tel: 4055 3633
www.reefhouse.com.au
Much-heralded boutique resort with elegant, over-sized rooms and suites. Lush gardens, a courtyard pool and a delightful restaurant complete the picture. **$$$$**

Port Douglas

Hibiscus Gardens Spa Resort
22 Owens Street
Tel: 4099 5315
www.hibiscusportdouglas.com.au
In exotic gardens with two pools, this hotel has a Balinese theme, with extensive use of natural wood and terracotta. Some apartments with private spas. **$$$–$$$$**

Martinique on Macrossan
66 Macrossan Street
Tel: 4099 6222
www.martinique.com.au
Nineteen comfortable apartments with kitchenettes, plus a saltwater swimming pool. **$$$**

Port Douglas Motel
9 Davidson Street
Tel: 4099 5248
www.portdouglasmotel.com
No views to speak of, but inexpensive by Port Douglas standards and perfectly serviceable. **$$**

Sheraton Mirage
Davidson Street
Tel: 4099 5888
www.sheraton-mirage.com
A luxury resort on the beach, with saltwater swimming lagoons, a freshwater pool, a world-class golf course, floodlit tennis courts, gym and health centre. Accommodation is in rooms, suites or villas with up to four bedrooms. **$$$$**

Ravenshoe

Kool Moon Motel
6 Moore Street
Tel: 4097 6047
A standard, unpreten-
tious place. **$**

Pond Cottage B&B
844 Tully Falls Road
Tel: 4097 7189
www.bnbnq.com.au/pondcottage
Platypus, wallabies and
possums are amongst
the inhabitants you're

likely to encounter at this
secluded resort, 10 km
(6 miles) from Raven-
shoe in the heart of the
Misty Mountains. **$$$**

Yungaburra

Curtain Fig Motel
16 Gillies Highway
Tel: 4095 3168
www.curtainfig.com
Far above the average
motel, with all the usual

features and extremely
helpful owners. **$$**

**Eden House Garden
Cottages**
20 Gillies Highway
Tel: 4095 3355
www.edenhouse.com.au
Sumptuous cottages in
the grounds of a historic
Queenslander. **$$$**

Kookaburra Lodge
Corner Oak Street and
Eacham Road
Tel: 1268940

www.kookaburra-lodge.com
Comfortable and homely
motel rooms. **$$**

**Mount Quincan Crater
Retreat**
Peeramon Road
Tel: 4095 2255
www.mtquincan.com.au
Luxury log cabins with
wood-burning fireplace
and a double spa bath
with a view. Isolated
location by a small
crater. **$$$$**

CAPE YORK

Bamaga

Resort Bamaga
Corner Lui and Adidi Streets
Tel: 4069 3050
www.resortbamaga.com.au
Good resort with four-
star facilities. **$$$**

Chillagoe

**Chillagoe Bush Camp
and Eco Lodge**
Hospital Avenue
Tel: 4094 7155
A high-quality set-up to
enhance that Outback
experience. **$**

Chillagoe Cabins
Queen Street
Tel: 4094 7206
www.chillagoe.com
Three cabins with
enough in them to war-
rant four stars, they are
set in lush gardens. **$$**

Cooktown

Pam's Place
Corner of Charlotte and
Boundary Streets
Tel: 4069 5166
www.scottysbeachhouse.com.au
Motel rooms and self-
contained cabins. **$$**

**Peninsula Caravan
Park**
Howard Street

Tel: 4069 5107
A well-equipped caravan
park popular both with
holidaymakers and the
local wallabies. It also
has some rather
luxurious cabins. **$**

Seaview Motel
Webber Esplanade
Tel: 4069 5377
Central motel offering a
wide range of accommo-
dation: townhouses,
motel rooms, self-con-
tained apartments. **$$**

Sovereign Resort
Corner Charlotte and
Green Streets
Tel: 4069 5400
The top of the range in
Cooktown, it can be
eerily quiet outside
peak season. **$$$**

Horn Island

**Gateway Torres Strait
Resort**
24 Outie Street
Tel: 4069 2222
Hard to get excited
about these units, but
it's the only option on
Horn Island. **$$$**

Laura

Quinkan Hotel
Tel: 4060 3255

The only pub, and very
much the social centre
of the settlement, can
provide a cheap room at
the back. **$**

Lizard Island

Lizard Island Resort
Anchor Bay
Tel: 4060 3999
www.lizardisland.com.au
Another Voyages resort
fulfilling the role of playground for the rich and
famous. Access is by
plane from Cairns
unless you spend sev-
eral hundred dollars on
chartering your own
boat from Cooktown.
$$$$

Mount Surprise

**Bedrock Village
Caravan Park**
Garnett Street
Tel: 4062 3193
www.bedrockvillage.com.au
One-stop shop with tent
and caravan sites plus
cabins. Mini-golf, pools
and barbecues. **$**

Mount Surprise Hotel
Garland Street
Tel: 4062 3118
The standard pub
option in town. **$**

Brisbane ●

**Mount Surprise Tourist
Caravan Park**
23 Garland Street
Tel: 4062 3193
Caravan park, motel,
café, gem shop and ser-
vice station. The owners
raise miniature horses
and native birds. **$**

Thursday Island

Federal Hotel
Corner Victoria Parade and
Jardine Street
Tel: 4069 1569
www.federalhotelti.com.au
Historic hotel with latest
facilities. **$$$**

PRICE CATEGORIES

Price categories are for
a double room without
breakfast:
$ = under A$70
$$ = A$70–120
$$$ = A$120–200
$$$$ = over A$200

Jardine Motel
Corner Normanby Street and
Victoria Parade
Tel: 4069 1555
www.jardinemotel.com.au
Pleasant beach resort
in tropical gardens. **$$$**

Weipa

Heritage Resort
Corner Commercial Avenue
and Kerr Point Drive
Tel: 4069 8000
www.heritageresort.com.au

Modern outfit with fine
rooms, it caters for a lot
of anglers. **$$$**
Weipa Camping Ground
Newbold Drive
Tel: 4069 7871
www.weipa.biz

Camp under the trees
on the shore of Alba-
tross Bay or take one of
the 17 cabins. **$$**

SAVANNAH WAY

Burketown

Burketown Pub
Corner Musgrave and Beames
Streets
Tel: 4745 5104
Focal point of the town
with some reasonable
motel units. **$**
Caravan Park
Sloman Street
Tel: 4745 5118
burketowncaravanpark.com.au
Cabins are perfectly
adequate, or there's
room to pitch a tent. **$**

Croydon

Club Hotel
Corner Brown and Sircom
Streets
Tel: 4745 6184
A terrific atmospheric
old pub with reasonable
modern units. **$**

Georgetown

Latara Motel
Gulf Developmental Road
Tel: 4062 1190

georgetownaccommodation.com
Not as bad as the pink
savannah-style façade
would suggest, there
are good rooms and
attractive grounds. **$$**

Gregory Downs

Gregory Downs Hotel
Tel: 4748 5566
Basic rooms are avail-
able at this friendly
Outback pub. **$**

Karumba

Gulf Country Van Park
69 Yappar Street
Tel: 4745 9148
The usual mixture of
tent and van sites along
with some old cabins. **$**
Pelicans Inn
2 Gilbert Street
Tel: 4745 9555
www.pelicanskarumba.com.au
New in 2005 and sitting
right on the river, there's
something to suit every-
one with six classes of
accommodation. **$$**

Lawn Hill Gorge

Adels Grove
Lawn Hill Creek
Tel: 4748 5502
www.adelsgrove.com.au
There's a choice of a
campsite, pre-erected
tents or very basic
rooms, which come as
part of a dinner, bed
and breakfast deal.
There is a campsite in
Lawn Hill Gorge (now
called Boodjamulla)
National Park. Book in
advance. **$**

Normanton

Gulfland Motel
11 Landsborough Street
Tel: 4745 1290
www.gulflandmotel.com.au
In the midst of tropical
greenery, this is a stan-
dard motel. **$$**
**The Purple Pub and
Brolga Palms Motel**
Corner Landsborough and
Brown Streets
Tel: 4745 1324

Some good-quality
motel rooms across the
yard behind this land-
mark pub. **$$**

Undara Volcanic National Park

Undara Experience
Savannah Way
Tel: 4097 1411
www.undara.com.au
There's a campground,
but the stylish choice is
to take a room in one of
a row of old railway car-
riages that have been
converted to provide
cosy bedrooms. Plenty
of Outback activities
laid on. **$$**

MOUNT ISA

Boulia

Desert Sands Motel
Herbert Street
Tel: 4746 3000
Unpretentious motel
with everything you
would expect in its 12
units. **$$**

Cloncurry

Gidgee Inn
Matilda Highway
Tel: 4742 1599
The most salubrious of
Cloncurry's places to
stay is built of rammed
red earth. The rooms

are of high quality but
the service can be off-
hand. **$$**
**Gilbert Park Tourist
Village**
McIlwraith Street
Tel: 4742 2300
www.toptouristparks.com.au
A well-organised camp-

site that also rents out some spotless cabins. **$**
Wagon Wheel Motel
54 Ramsay Street
Tel: 4742 1866
A strip of 1960s motel rooms behind this busy pub provide all the necessaries. **$**

Hughenden

Royal Hotel Resort
21 Moran Street
Tel: 4741 1183
Perfectly decent motel but not distinctive. **$**
Wrights Motel
16 Gray Street
Tel: 4741 1677
Unflashy, solid place that won't win any prizes but does the job. **$$**

Mount Isa

All Seasons Verona Hotel
Corner Marian and Camooweal Streets
Tel: 4743 3024
www.mercure.com.au
Sound choice for comfort and efficiency. Popular restaurant. **$$$**
Barkly Hotel
55 Barkly Highway
Tel: 4743 2988
Popular pub on main road into town with 42 sound rooms. **$$**
Inland Oasis Motel
195 Barkly Highway
Tel: 4743 3433
www.budgetmotelchain.com.au
A well-presented modern motel. Like all accommodation in Mount Isa, it

can fill up quickly on days when extra workers have been shipped in for shift at the mine. **$$**
Riverside Tourist Caravan Park
195 West Street
Tel: 4743 3904
Neat, well-maintained site with half a dozen decent cabins. **$$**

Richmond

Ammonite Inn
88 Goldring Street
Tel: 4741 3932
Plenty of good units as well as pub rooms. **$$**

Winton

Matilda Country Tourist Park

43 Chirnside Street
Tel: 4657 1607
www.toptouristparks.com.au
Sixty powered sites and some fine cabins make this a reasonable budget choice. Tours of Lake Quarry and bush-poetry evenings. **$**
North Gregory Hotel
67 Elderslie Street
Tel: 4657 1375
Standard pub rooms in a later incarnation of the hotel where Banjo Paterson first performed Waltzing Matilda. **$**
Winton Outback Motel
95 Elderslie Street
Tel: 4657 1422
www.wintonoutbackmotel.com
Clean, well maintained and handily placed for the centre of town. **$$**

THE SOUTHWEST

Barcaldine

Ironbark Inn
Landsborough Highway
Tel: 4651 1788
Reasonable motel rooms in this friendly establishment which features a large open-air dining room. **$$**
Shakespeare Hotel
95 Oak Street
Tel: 4651 1610
In a street full of old-style country pubs, this one offers good-value basic rooms. **$**

Birdsville

Birdsville Caravan Park
Florence Street
Tel: 4656 3214
Various levels of comfort in the cabins here, but all in a scenic setting. **$**
Birdsville Hotel
Adelaide Street
Tel: 4656 3244

Many actually go to Birdsville just to see this historic pub, so it makes sense to stay in one of its comfortable units. **$$**

Blackall

Acacia Motor Inn
Corner Shamrock and Short Streets
Tel: 4657 6077
High-class units and a restaurant in this central motel. **$$**
Blackall Caravan Park
53 Garden Street
Tel: 4657 4816
Friendly site where guests are encouraged to mingle round the campfire. There are a handful of units. **$**

Charleville

Corones Hotel
33 Wills Street
Tel: 4654 1022

www.hotelcorones.com
Terrific old wooden pub with first-floor verandas, lots of atmosphere and reasonable rooms. **$$**
Warrego Motel Charleville
73 Wills Street
Tel: 4654 1299
www.warregomotel.com
Standard units that do the job without fuss or flair. **$**

Cunnamulla

Country Way Motor Inn
17 Emma Street
Tel: 4655 0555
We're in standard motel territory, but done well. **$$**

Longreach

Albert Park Motor Inn
Sir Hudson Fysh Drive
Tel: 4658 3181
Lots of room, and

grounds teeming with wildlife. The most luxurious place in town. **$$**
Longreach Motor Inn
84 Galah Street
Tel: 4658 2322
Another fairly large enterprise that scores with attention to detail. **$$**

PRICE CATEGORIES

Price categories are for a double room without breakfast:
$ = under A$70
$$ = A$70–120
$$$ = A$120–200
$$$$ = over A$200

ACTIVITIES

THE ARTS, NIGHTLIFE, SHOPPING, SPORT, EVENTS AND CHILDREN'S ENTERTAINMENT

THE ARTS

Art Galleries

The best way to find out what's on in Queensland's art galleries is to buy a copy of *Art Almanac*, a monthly booklet that lists galleries and their current exhibitions. It costs A$2 and is available at good bookshops and galleries. Brunswick Street in Brisbane's Fortitude Valley is a good starting point for gallery-hopping, and includes Craft Queensland, an incubator for upcoming artists. There are also galleries aplenty in neighbouring suburbs such as Newstead and New Farm. Some of Queensland's public and commercial galleries are listed below.

Fire-Works Gallery
11 Stratton Street
Newstead, Brisbane
Tel: 3216 1250
A mixture of indigenous and other contemporary artworks. Open Tues–Fri 11am–5pm, Sat 11am–3pm.
Heiser Gallery
90B Arthur Street
Fortitude Valley, Brisbane
Open Tues–Sat 10.30am–6pm.
Institute of Modern Art
420 Brunswick Street
Fortitude Valley, Brisbane

Tel: 3252 5750; www.ima.org.au
Housed inside the Judith Wright Centre of Contemporary Arts. Open Tues–Fri 11am–5pm, Sat 11am–4pm.
Jan Murphy Gallery
486 Brunswick Street
Fortitude Valley, Brisbane
Tel: 07 3254 1855
Represents contemporary Australian artists such as Ben Quilty and Marina Strocchi. Open Tues–Sat 10am–5pm.
Libby Edwards Galleries
482 Brunswick Street
Fortitude Valley, Brisbane
Tel: 3358 3944
Open Tues–Sat 11am–5pm.
Philip Bacon Art Gallery
Brunswick Street
Fortitude Valley
Brisbane
Tel: 3358 3555;
www.philipbacon.com.au
One of Australia's best-known private galleries.
Queensland Art Gallery
Melbourne Street
South Brisbane
Tel: 3840 7303; www.qag.qld.gov.au
The state art gallery has an extensive collection of Australian art, including contemporary and indigenous artworks. A modern art gallery 200 metres/yards from the original Queensland Art Gallery is scheduled to open in late 2006. Open Mon–Fri 10am–5pm and weekends 9am–5pm.

Suzanne O'Connell Gallery
93 James Street
New Farm, Brisbane
Tel: 3358 5811
Australian indigenous art specialist including paintings, fibre and woodcarvings. Open Wed–Sat 11am–4pm.

Gold Coast
Gold Coast City Art Gallery
135 Bundall Road
Surfers Paradise
Tel: 5581 6567
An outdoor sculpture walk by Australian and international artists is part of the permanent display here. Open Mon–Fri 10am–5pm, Sat–Sun 11am–5pm.
Ipswich Art Gallery
D'Arcy Doyle Place
Nicholas Street
Ipswich
Tel: 3813 9222
Queensland's largest regional gallery. Open 10am–5pm.
Schubert Contemporary
Marina Mirage, Seaworld Drive
Main Beach, Gold Coast
Tel: 07 5571 0077
Open daily 10am–5.30pm.
Deals in some of the biggest names in Australian art.

Sunshine Coast
Keep an eye out for galleries in the Sunshine Coast hinterland villages of Montville, Maleny and Eumundi.

Noosa Regional Gallery
Pelican Street, Tewantin
Tel: 5449 5340; www.noosaregional
gallery.org
An annual exhibition of artists'
books is one of the innovative pro-
grammes at this regional gallery.
Open Tues–Sun 10am–4pm.

Cairns & Further North

Cairns Regional Gallery
97 Grafton Street
Tel: 4031 6865
**Daintree Timber Museum and
Gallery**
12 Stewart Street
Daintree
Tel: 4098 6166
Marina Gallery
Wharf Street
Port Douglas
Tel: 4099 4310
Reef Gallery
16 Macrossan Street
Port Douglas
Tel: 4051 0992

Theatre

The **Queensland Theatre Company** (QTC) is the state's most
prominent drama company.
Established in 1970, the company caters to a broad range of
theatrical tastes, staging a main-
stage season of nine plays a
year. Under the artistic direction
of award-winning playwright and
director, Michael Gow, it presents everything from classic
comedies to Christmas crowd-
pleasers for families. Part of its
vision is to assist in the development of new writing and actors'
and it does this by staging a
week of professional play read-
ings annually, which includes
new plays by local talent.

The banner for developing new
and emerging Queensland theatrical talent is also held by **La Boite
Theatre Company**, a company
that was founded in 1925. Known
for performing in the round, the
company continued its tradition of
providing intimate and accessible
performances when it moved to
its new home at the **Roundhouse
Theatre** in Kelvin Grove in 2004.

Blockbuster musicals, opera
and orchestral performances are
usually performed in the Lyric
Theatre or the Concert Hall at
the **Queensland Performing Arts
Centre** on the river at South
Bank. The Queensland Theatre
Company often performs in its
Playhouse Theatre with smaller,
less mainstream performances
held in the Cremorne Theatre in
the same complex.

The **Judith Wright Centre of
Contemporary Arts** and the
Brisbane Powerhouse are multi-
function arts venues, hosting
plays, dance and art exhibitions
at the edgy end of the scale.
Brisbane Powerhouse
119 Lamington Street
New Farm
Tel: 3358 8600
www.brisbanepowerhouse.org
**Judith Wright Centre of
Contemporary Arts**
420 Brunswick Street
Fortitude Valley, Brisbane
Tel: 3872 9000
www.jwcoca.qld.gov.au
**Queensland Performing
Arts Centre**
Corner of Grey and Melbourne
Streets, South Brisbane
Tel: 3840 7444 or 136 246
www.qpac.com.au
Includes the Lyric Theatre, the
Playhouse and the Cremorne
Theatre (which seats just 315).
Queensland Theatre Company
78 Montague Road
South Brisbane
Tel: 3010 7600
www.qldtheatreco.com.au
Roundhouse Theatre
6–8 Musk Avenue
Kelvin Grove, Brisbane
Tel: 3007 8600

Concerts and Opera

The **Queensland Orchestra** is
the state's only professional
symphony orchestra. It performs
about 70 concerts a year,
ranging from classics to new
commissions and baroque
music. The Concert Hall at the
Queensland Performing Arts
Centre in Brisbane is home base,
but the orchestra also tours to
other towns in the state as well
as regional areas.

For a special insight into specific members of the orchestra,
go along to one of the Sunday
afternoon performances by the
Ferry Road Chamber Players.
The chamber music series is a
collaboration between orchestra
members and local musicians
at the orchestra's Ferry Road
studio.

Opera Queensland is the
second-largest opera company in
Australia. It performs three major
operatic productions in Brisbane
each year at the Queensland Performing Arts Centre.
Opera Queensland
16 Russell Street
South Bank, Brisbane
Tel: 3735 3030
www.operaqld.org.au
Queensland Orchestra
53 Ferry Road
West End, Brisbane
Tel: 3377 5000 or 136 246
(bookings)
www.thequeenslandorchestra.com.au

Dance

The **Queensland Ballet** stages
more than 100 performances a
year, from a repertoire that
extends from classic ballets to
modern dance. The company
of 22 dancers makes its home
in the Thomas Dixon Centre
for Dance in Brisbane's West
End, a building that started
life in the 1900s as a shoe
factory.

The **Australian Ballet**, the
main classical dance company,
is based in Melbourne, but has
two seasons each year in Sydney

and brings some performances to the Lyric Theatre at Brisbane's Queensland Performing Arts Centre.

A trip to Brisbane can also offer the chance to catch the latest performance by some of Australia's best contemporary dance companies on tour.

Queensland Ballet
Thomas Dixon Centre
Corner of Drake Street and Montague Road
West End, Brisbane
Tel: 3013 6666
www.queenslandballet.com.au

NIGHTLIFE

Fashionable Bars

The Bowery
676 Ann Street
Fortitude Valley, Brisbane
Tel: 3252 0202
www.thebowery.com.au
Craggy brick walls and plush banquettes make this converted terrace a cosy place for a drink. Live jazz weeknights and live DJs at weekends.

Cru Bar and Cellar
22 James Street
Fortitude Valley, Brisbane
Tel: 3252 2400

www.crubar.com.au
Sweeping gold curtains, open-air seating and a stellar wine list draw Brisbane's beautiful. Open daily 11.30–1am.

Glass
420 Brunswick Street
Fortitude Valley, Brisbane
Tel: 3252 0533
www.glassjazz.com.au
Crowds cluster around the yellow light-box bars in this drinking hole in the Judith Wright Contemporary Art Centre.

Jade Buddha
1 Eagle Street Pier
Eagle Street, Brisbane
Tel: 3221 2888
Part-owned by Pat Rafter, this bar has river views, live jazz on Sundays and casual eating options. Open Fri and Sat 11.30am–3am; Mon–Thurs 11.30am–1am and Sun 11.30am–12am.

Old Favourites

Breakfast Creek Hotel
2 Kingsford Smith Drive
Breakfast Creek, Brisbane
Tel: 3262 5988
www.breakfastcreekhotel.com
Well known for its steaks, this historic pub has been given a new twist with Substation No. 41, its cocktail bar housed in a former substation on the hotel's site.

Empire Hotel
339 Brunswick Street
Fortitude Valley, Brisbane
Tel: 3852 1216
Watch the Valley's passing parade from the verandas of this local favourite. Live DJs.

Friday's
Riverside Centre
123 Eagle Street, Brisbane
Tel: 3832 2122
An institution.

Regatta Hotel
543 Coronation Drive
Toowong, Brisbane
Tel: 3870 7063
One of Queensland's oldest pubs, built in 1874.

Story Bridge Hotel
200 Main Street
Kangaroo Point, Brisbane
Tel: 3391 2266
This revamped former bikers' bar is a well-known place for a tipple.

Music Venues

Brisbane has a well-deserved reputation for its live-music scene. The cluster of venues in Fortitude Valley makes it easy to wander from one to another checking out the latest bands.

Arena Entertainment Complex
210 Brunswick Street
Fortitude Valley, Brisbane
Tel: 3252 5690

The Beat
677 Ann Street
Tel: 3852 2661

Brisbane Entertainment Centre
Melaleuca Drive, Boondall
Tel: 3265 8111

Brisbane Jazz Club
1 Annie Street
Kangaroo Point, Brisbane
Tel: 3391 2006

The Colombian Club
14–20 Constance Street
Fortitude Valley, Brisbane
Tel: 3257 3851

The Rev
25 Warner Street
Fortitude Valley, Brisbane
Tel: 3852 3373

RNA Showgrounds
Gregory Terrace, Brisbane
Tel: 3852 1831

GAMBLING

Queensland is home to four casinos. In Brisbane there are 80 gaming tables and 1,300 gaming machines at the **Conrad Treasury Casino**, housed within the sandstone walls of the former Treasury building at the top of the Queen Street Mall. Its glitzy sister, Conrad Jupiters Casino, is an unmissable landmark on Broadbeach Island on the Gold Coast. In Cairns the place to go is the Reef Casino, a boutique casino, with 44 gaming tables, and Townsville plays host to the Jupiters Townsville Hotel and Casino.

Conrad Treasury Casino
Queen Street Mall
Brisbane
Tel: 3306 8888

Conrad Jupiters Casino
Broadbeach Island
Gold Coast Highway
Broadbeach
Tel: 5592 8100

Reef Casino
35–41 Wharf Street
Cairns
Tel: 4030 8888

Jupiters Townsville Hotel and Casino
Sir Leslie Thiess Drive
Townsville
Tel: 4722 2373

The Tivoli
52 Costin Street
Fortitude Valley, Brisbane
Tel: 3852 1711
The Troubadour
1/322 Brunswick Street
Tel: 3252 2626
The Zoo
711 Ann Street
Tel: 3854 1381

Outside Brisbane

Troccadero Entertainment Centre
9 Trickett Street
Surfers Paradise
Tel: 5538 4200

Cinema

Check the daily newspaper for cinema listings, and the weekend papers for the best film reviews.

For mainstream films in Brisbane try the **Regent** at 167 Queen Street (tel: 3027 9999) or the cinemas in the Myer Centre. Art-house films are screened at the **Palace Centro Cinema** at 39 James Street, Fortitude Valley (tel: 3852 4488) and the **Dendy** Cinema at 346 George Street, Brisbane (tel: 3211 3244).

Look out for listings for outdoor cinemas in the summer. The following are locations of some of Queensland's cinemas.

Gold Coast

Coolangatta BCC
Showcase on the Beach
Tel: 5536 9300
Gold Coast Arts Centre
135 Bundall Road

Surfers Paradise
Tel: 5581 6515
Pacific Fair BCC
Pacific Fair Shopping Centre
Broadbeach
Tel: 5572 2666
Village Theatre Sanctuary Cove
Masthead Way
Sanctuary Cove
Tel: 5577 8999

Sunshine Coast

Noosa
29 Sunshine Beach Road
Noosa Heads
Tel: 5447 5130
Townsville
Townsville BCC Cinemas
Sturt Street (corner of Blackwood Street)
Tel: 4771 4101
Cairns
Cairns BCC
108 Grafton Street
Tel: 4051 1222
Cairns Central
Cairns Central Shopping Centre
Tel: 4052 1166
Mount Isa
Cinema Mount Isa
22 Marian Street
Tel: 4743 2043

Comedy

Sit Down Comedy Club
Paddington Tavern
186 Given Terrace
Paddington, Brisbane
Tel: 3369 4466
Dockside Comedy Bar
Ferry Street
Kangaroo Point, Brisbane
Tel: 3391 1110

SHOPPING

What to Buy

Aboriginal Art

Aboriginal artists sell their work in art centres, specialist galleries and craft retailers and through agents. Each traditional artist owns the rights to his or her particular stories, motifs and tokens. Indigenous fabric designs by artists such as Jimmy Pike are eagerly sought. Bark paintings are the most common form of Koori (Aboriginal) art, but look out for contemporary works on board, boomerangs and didgeridoos.

Clothing

A distinct style of clothing has evolved in rural Australia (an area collectively known as "the Bush"). Driza-Bone oilskin coats, Akubra hats (wide-brimmed and usually made of felt) and the R. M. Williams range of bushwear (including boots and moleskin trousers) are good examples. Blundstone boots, made in Tasmania and renowned for their durability, are another.

Food and Drink

Local delicacies include macadamia nuts, bush honey, royal jelly, chocolates and the inevitable Vegemite, a savoury spread. Australian wines can be bought at any pub or bottle shop, with fair-quality wines starting at A$10 a bottle.

Gemstones

Australia is the source of about 95 percent of the world's opals. "Boulder" opals – bright and vibrant – come from Quilpie.

Where to Buy

Australiana

Australian Geographic Shop
Shop 248, Myer Centre

Queen Street, Brisbane
Tel: 3220 0341
Many excellent Australian products for the great outdoors. Also throughout Queensland.

Done Art and Design
34 Orchid Avenue
Surfers Paradise
Tel: 5592 1282
This popular Australian artist puts colour and vibrancy into all his works.

Opals Down Under
Bruce Highway, Palmview
Sunshine Coast
Tel: 5494 5400
A wide range of opals including local boulder opals and the renowned black opal.

Quilpie Opals
Queen Street Mall
Brisbane
Tel: 3221 7369
One of Queensland's opal specialists.

R. M. Williams
Airport Drive
Eagle Farm, Brisbane
Tel: 3860 6600
Domestic Airport, Cairns
Tel: 4035 9702
Suppliers of bush gear including riding boots, Akubras *(see Clothing)* and oilskin bushman's coats. Also at Cairns Airport.

Tjapukai Aboriginal Cultural Park
Kamerunga Road, Smithfield, Cairns
Tel: 4042 9999
Aboriginal art and crafts from Queensland and elsewhere.

International Brands

Queensland's Gold Coast has a collection of big-name international designer stores, and a number of others have moved into the newest addition to the Queen Street Mall in Brisbane, Queens Plaza.

These are some of Queensland's most exclusive designer outlets:

Cartier
Shop 3, The Moroccan
9 Elkhorn Avenue
Surfers Paradise
Tel: 5529 3744

Furla
Shop 1B, 3170 Surfers Paradise Boulevard
Surfers Paradise
Tel: 5570 3799

Gucci
Shop 6, Elkhorn Avenue
Surfers Paradise
Tel: 5531 6966

Hermès
Shop 154, 74 Seaworld Drive
Main Beach
Tel: 5532 4959
9–11 Elkhorn Avenue
Surfers Paradise
Tel: 5538 4388

Louis Vuitton
Ground Level, Queens Plaza
Queen Street Mall
Brisbane
Tel: 3223 3666
74 Seaworld Drive
Main Beach
Tel: 5591 3852
26 Orchid Avenue
Surfers Paradise
Tel: 5539 0026
18 Abbott Street
Cairns
Tel: 4031 5600

Prada
Shop 1, The Moroccan
11 Elkhorn Avenue
Surfers Paradise
Tel: 5539 8858

Tiffany & Co.
Ground level, Queens Plaza
Queen Street Mall
Brisbane
Tel: 3003 1837

Books

Major bookstores **Angus and Robertson**, **Dymocks Booksellers** and the Queensland chain **QBD** (www.qbd.com.au) can be found in the main centres. The US giant **Borders** is on Albert Street in Brisbane (tel: 3210 1220). There are also smaller, independent bookshops.

Brisbane

American Book Store
197 Elizabeth Street
Brisbane
Tel: 3229 4677
Originally specialised in stocking US titles not generally distributed in Australia, this bookshop still

makes a business of selling the hard-to-get titles.

Avid Reader
193 Boundary Street
West End, Brisbane
Tel: 3846 3422

Bent Books
205 Boundary Street
West End, Brisbane
Tel: 3846 5004
A second-hand bookshop stocking a wide range of genres, including gay and lesbian history and fiction.

Coaldrake's Bookshop
Shop 8, 32 Park Road
Milton, Brisbane
Tel: 3367 0559. Also in Brisbane's Fortitude Valley.
Specialises in literature, history, travel and children's books.

Folio Books
80 Albert Street, Brisbane
Tel: 07 3221 1368
Architecture, design and graphic-arts book specialist.

Mary Ryan's Bookshop
40 Park Road
Milton, Brisbane
Tel: 3510 5000
Also in other southeast Queensland locations including Noosa, Toowoomba and the Gold Coast.

Noosa

Written Dimension Bookshop
Shop 2, Cinema Centre
Beach Road, Noosa Heads
Tel: 5447 4433

Port Douglas

Whileaway
43 Macrossan Street
Tel: 4099 4066

Townsville

Mary Who? Bookshop

414 Flinders Street Mall
Tel: 4771 3824

Shopping Centres

Brisbane

The main shopping action in Brisbane can be found on the Queen Street Mall. The half-kilometre retail precinct has five major shopping centres, two department stores and four shopping arcades. **Queens Plaza** is the newest addition, bringing some international brands to Queensland for the first time, while the **Myer Centre**'s six levels of speciality shops include many of Australia's fashion favourites. The 1920s **Brisbane Arcade** has fashion designers, antiques, jewellers and tea shops.

Nearby **Fortitude Valley** is home to edgy fashion designers (check out Ann and Brunswick Streets), stylish homeware shops and gourmet eateries (James Street). For an interesting wander around gift shops, antique stores and boutiques, try Latrobe Terrace in the suburb of Paddington.

Direct Factory Outlet
1 Airport Drive
Brisbane Airport
Tel: 3305 9250
The factory outlets for many of Australia's favourite fashion and homeware chains all under one roof. Open daily 10am–6pm.

Toowong Village Shopping Centre
9 Sherwood Road
Toowong
Tel: 3870 7177
David Jones and Kmart plus 80 speciality shops in Brisbane's west.

Westfield Shopping Centre
Corner Gympie and Hamilton Roads, Chermside
Tel: 3359 0755
One of six big Westfield Malls in southeast Queensland, this one is accessible by public transport and offers all the major stores.

Gold Coast

Centro Surfers Paradise
Cavill Mall
Surfers Paradise
Tel: 5592 0155

Pick up anything from food supplies to sunglasses at this centre in the heart of Surfers.

Marina Mirage
74 Seaworld Drive
Main Beach
Tel: 5577 0088
Australian and international fashion designers are among the 80 luxury speciality shops in this waterfront collection.

Pacific Fair Shopping Centre
Corner of Gold Coast Highway and Hooker Boulevard
Broadbeach
Tel: 5581 5117
The Gold Coast's largest shopping centre, with 270 speciality shops and Myer department store.

Cairns

Cairns Central
Corner of McLeod and Spence Streets
Tel: 4041 4111
More than 180 speciality shops and department stores.

Department Stores

Queensland's main department stores are Myer and David Jones. They offer an extensive range of goods from hardware to homeware. Target and Kmart are variety stores at the lower end of the price spectrum.

David Jones, Queens Plaza, 149 Adelaide Street, Brisbane; tel: 07 3243 9000 or 13 33 57 for general enquiries;
www.davidjones.com.au

Myer, 91 Queen Street, Brisbane; tel: 3232 0121; www.myer.com.au. Other locations include suburban Brisbane, Broadbeach, Cairns, Strathpine and Toowoomba.

Target, Brisbane Myer Centre, corner of Elizabeth and Albert Streets; tel: 3231 6700. www.target.com.au. Other locations include suburban Brisbane, Broadbeach, Cairns, Hervey Bay, Mackay, Maroochydore, Rockhampton and Townsville.

Kmart. Tel: 1800 634 251 (customer enquiries); www.kmart.com.au. There are no stores in Brisbane city, but several in suburban Brisbane and others in Broad-

beach, Bundaberg, Cairns, Gladstone, Innisfail, Mackay, Maroochydore, Mount Isa, Rockhampton and Toowoomba.

Markets

Queensland's markets offer a myriad of buying opportunities, from organic produce to wonderful creations by local artists.

While some markets are open weekly, other "community" and "farmers'" markets are only open a couple of days each month, and in the tropical north of the state some markets are only open at certain times of the year. Most stallholders handle cash only.

Brisbane

Brisbane Marketplace
250 Sherwood Road
Rocklea
On Saturdays this location, 11 km (7 miles) from the CBD, is a fresh-food market selling everything from seafood to deli products, and on Sundays a flea market. Open 6am–12pm both days.

Jan Power's Farmers' Market
Brisbane Powerhouse
119 Lamington Street, New Farm
One for the foodies, this organic market includes cooking demonstrations and visiting chefs. Open 7am–noon. 1st and 3rd Saturday of the month.

Riverside Markets
Riverside Centre and Eagle Street, Brisbane
Started by a handful of artists a couple of decades ago, there are now hundreds of stalls selling arts, crafts and gourmet goodies. Free, live performances add to the atmosphere. Open Sun 7am–4pm.

South Bank Markets
Stanley Street Plaza
South Bank Parklands
See these outdoor art-and-craft markets in full swing on a Friday evening. Open Fri 5pm–10pm; Sat 11am–5pm; Sun 9am–5pm.

Valley Markets
Brunswick Street
Fortitude Valley
Join locals in discovering the next upcoming jewellery designers or get a quick massage at this

Brisbane institution. Open Sat–Sun 8am–4pm.

Cairns

Cairns Night Market
71–75 The Esplanade
Cairns
Housed in a permanent building, these markets cater to the souvenir shopper. Open 5pm–11pm.

Kuranda Markets

Time a day trip to this rainforest village for a day when the two markets are open. The original markets are open Sun, Wed, Thur and Fri 9am–3pm and the Heritage Markets daily 9am–3pm.

Gold Coast

Carrara Markets
Nerang–Broadbeach Road
Carrara
The biggest markets on the Gold Coast offer everything from fruit and vegetables to clothing and plants. Open Sat–Sun 7am–4pm.

Surfers Paradise

Beachfront Markets
The Esplanade
Surfers Paradise
About 70 stalls selling locally made art, accessories and homewares at these night markets. Open Wed and Fri 5.30pm–10pm.

Noosa

Eumundi Markets
Memorial Drive
Eumundi
About 15 minutes from Noosa, this pretty village draws throngs of tourists and locals to its twice-weekly markets. Go there to enjoy the relaxed hinterland vibe. Open Sat 6.30–2pm; Wed 8am–1.30pm.

Noosa Farmers' Market
Weyba Road, Noosa
Popular with locals, all the produce sold at this thriving market is produced by the stallholders. Open 7am–noon, 2nd and 4th Saturdays of the month.

Townsville

Cotters Market
Flinders Street Mall
Stallholders sell pottery, jewellery and fresh produce from the Flinders Mall. Open Sun 8.30am–1pm.

BUYING TICKETS

Performance venues often sell tickets through ticket agencies such as Ticketek and Ticketmaster. Names and numbers of venues are published in all listings of what's on.

Ticketek
Brisbane Myer City Box Office
Shop 95, Elizabeth Street, Brisbane. Also in other locations, including Cairns, Surfers Paradise and Townsville.
Tel: 13 28 49
www.ticketek.com.au

Ticketmaster
Rebel Sport
Shop 1, Queen Adelaide Building, Queen Street Mall, Brisbane. Also at Broadbeach, Chermside and Toowoomba.
Tel: 13 61 00
www.ticketmaster.com.au

From May to December in Townsville there are night markets on Fridays at Strand Park 5.30–9.30pm.

SPORT

Spectator Sports

If you are keen to see one of the big football or cricket games, you'd be well advised to ask your travel agent to find out about tickets prior to arrival. The ticket agency, **Ticketek** (tel: 13 28 49; www.ticketek.com.au), handles ticketing for most of the big games in Queensland. The main spectator sports sites are as follows:

The Gabba
Vulture Street
Woolloongabba
Tel: 3008 6166;
www.thegabba.org.au
Hosts the major cricket matches and Australian Rules Football.

Suncorp Stadium
Tel: 3331 5000;
www.suncorpstadium.com.au
Hosts Queensland's rugby league, rugby union and soccer matches.

Dairy Farmers Stadium
Golf Links Drive
Kirwan (near Townsville)
Tel: 4760 7594;
www.dairyfarmersstadium.org.au
Home ground to the North Queensland Cowboys national rugby league team.

Horse-Racing

The principal thoroughbred racing clubs in Queensland are the **Queensland Turf Club** (tel: 3268 2171; www.qtc.org), which races at Brisbane's Eagle Farm Racecourse, and the **Brisbane Turf Club** (tel: 3268 6800; www.doomben.com), which races at Doomben Racecourse.

The winter carnival in June is the main event in the racing calendar, featuring the Queensland Oaks Day, Stradbroke Day and the Brisbane Cup, all held at Eagle Farm.

Doomben Racecourse
Hampden Street
Ascot
Tel: 3268 6800

Eagle Farm Racecourse
Lancaster Road
Ascot
Tel: 3268 2171

Outdoor Activities

Bushwalking

Visitors wanting to go bush while they are touring Queensland have plenty of choices. There are about 220 national parks and state forests. The subtropical rainforest of Lamington National Park near the NSW border, the Aboriginal rock art in the Carnarvon National Park in the Rockhampton area

and Eungella near Mackay are some of the most frequently visited areas. The Queensland government has been progressively establishing walking tracks through some of the most beautiful parts of the state as part of its "Great Walks" programme. The walks range from a couple of hours of walking to multi-day trips, and are located on Fraser Island, in the Conway Range near Airlie Beach and the Mackay Highlands.

More information about these walks is available from the Environmental Protection Agency or Queensland Parks and Wildlife Service (www.epa.qld.gov.au).

For advice on bushwalks, see the Queensland Walks website (www.queenslandwalks.com.au). It includes regional information, links to bushwalking clubs and advice on how to prepare for a bushwalk.

Environmental Protection Agency
Customer Service Centre
160 Ann Street
Brisbane
Tel: 3227 8185
Queensland Parks and Wildlife Service
Campsite bookings
Tel: 13 13 04;
www.qld.gov.au/camping

Cycling

As long as you avoid the humidity and downpours of the height of summer, cycling in Queensland is to be recommended. A first point of contact should be the state's advocacy organisation, **Bicycle Queensland** (58 Gladstone Road, Highgate Hill; tel: 3844 1144; www.bq.org.au). Its website contains information on cycle shops and bicycle-user groups, local groups which often have regular ride programmes. The **Transport Queensland** website (www.transport.qld.gov.au/cycling) carries information on cycle routes and maps published by local councils from the Gold Coast to Townsville.

To make a relatively easy start, pedal some of the 400 kilometres of cycling track in Brisbane.

Golf

The **Queensland Golf Union** (tel: 9264 8433; www.queensland gold.org.au) is a good starting point for golf players from abroad looking for information on public-access courses. Queensland has built a reputation for its golf-resort courses, with more than 10 on the Gold Coast and others on the Sunshine Coast and further north near the Whitsundays and Port Douglas.

The following list of some of Queensland's high-quality courses includes a number of resort courses.
Brisbane
Brookwater Golf Club
Tournament Drive
Springfield
Tel: 3814 5500
North Lakes Resort Course
Bridgeport Drive
North Lakes
Tel: 3480 9299
Royal Queensland
Curtin Avenue West
Eagle Farm
Tel: 3268 1127
Gold Coast
The Glades
Glades Drive
Robina
Tel: 5569 1900
Hope Island
Hope Island Resort
Hope Island Road
Hope Island
Tel: 5530 9000
The Pines
Sanctuary Cove Resort
Caseys Road
Sanctuary Cove
Tel: 5577 6175
Sunshine Coast
Hyatt Regency Coolum
1 Warran Road
Coolum Beach
Tel: 5446 1234
Noosa Springs
Links Drive
Noosa Heads
Tel: 5440 3333
North Queensland
The Links at Port Douglas
Off Old Port Road
Port Douglas
Tel: 4087 2222

Paradise Palms Golf Course
Captain Cook Highway
Near Cairns
Tel: 4059 9900
Turtle Point Golf Course
Laguna Whitsundays Resort
Kunapipi Springs Road
Whitsundays
Tel: 4947 7777

Snorkelling and Diving

Seeing the Great Barrier Reef up close and personal through either diving or snorkelling is a must for any Queensland holidaymaker. Apart from the 2,900 individual reefs and 70 coral cays that make up the Great Barrier Reef, there are also dive sites near shipwrecks and outcrops off the southern coastline that can be explored from the Fraser Coast, Sunshine Coast or the Gold Coast. Water temperatures stay warm all year round, and August through to January generally offer the best visibility for divers.

Snorkelling is a great introduction to the reef's fascinating underwater world and simply requires the ability to swim and a reasonable level of fitness. Most day trips from Cairns offer some instruction and in some cases a guided safari for snorkellers. While snorkelling may involve jumping out of a boat at some places, including the Low Isles, Green Island and Heron Island, it is possible to walk into the water. Less confident swimmers can also ask about using a "float coat" to provide extra buoyancy while snorkelling.

Operators in Cairns, Port Douglas, Townsville and the Whitsunday Islands offer a range of options to holidaymakers keen to do some diving. At the lowest level is the introductory dive. It doesn't require scuba-diving certification, and after some initial instruction the diver will be accompanied by a qualified instructor on a single dive. Any other diving trips require certification, and the dive courses offered by dive companies make it possible to acquire initial open-water certification while on holiday.

Day trips from Cairns to reefs like Hastings, Saxon and Norman are usually the domain of less experienced divers, while the experienced diver is likely to opt for live-aboard boats doing four- to seven-day trips. Cod Hole is the most famous dive site off Cairns and is often included in an extended trip to the Ribbon Reefs or the Coral Sea for experienced divers.

As a starting point for planning a trip have a look at the Dive Queensland website (www.dive-queensland.com.au). This is an association of dive-tourism operators and includes information on day trips, extended diving trips, diving insurance and training institutions.

Dive Queensland
PO Box 5120
Cairns, Queensland 4870
Tel: 4051 1510

Sailing & Sea Kayaking

Boating enthusiasts will find Queensland offers plenty of opportunities to indulge in their sport. Most are drawn to the 74 islands of the Whitsundays, where even novices are permitted to go "bareboating", cruising the calm waters without any crew.

There are dozens of operators hiring yachts, catamarans, tall ships and sea kayaks at Airlie Beach and Shute Harbour. To begin arranging boat charter before leaving home see the **Whitsunday Tourism** website (www.whitsundaytourism.com) or contact the **Whitsunday Central Reservation Centre** (tel: 4946 5299).

To get in touch with fellow sailors and participate in local events, contact the **Whitsunday Sailing Club** at Airlie Beach (tel: 4946 6138; www.whitsundaysailingclub.com.au).

Swimming and Surfing

Queensland's surf beaches are concentrated in the southern corner of the state. Surf schools have become something of a boom industry, with lots of newcomers entering the business.

Surfing Australia runs coaching accreditation courses, and also accredits surf schools. Some unaccredited schools may still be excellent, and some accredited ones may not be. Generally the ex-professional surfers offer very good services, and there is no denying the value of their years of experience. But beware – there are some surf coaches getting around who can barely surf themselves. It's worth doing a bit of research and asking around before deciding where to go. Some schools worth checking out:

Cheyne Horan's School of Surf
Surfers Paradise
Tel: 1800 227873
www.cheynehoran.com.au
With world champion Cheyne Horan

Godfathers of the Ocean
Surfers Paradise
Tel: 61 7 5593 5661
With ex-professional surfer Michael Munga Barry

Have a Go Surf Coaching
Coolangatta
Tel: 0417 191 629
With former pro surfer Dave Davidson

Surfing Queensland Coaching Academy
North Stradbroke Island
Tel: 0407 642 616
email: info@surfingqueensland.com

Walkin' On Water
Coolangatta
Tel: 0418 780 311
email: surf@walkinonwater.com

Wave Sense
Noosa Heads

Tel: 61 7 54749076
www.wavesense.com.au
Former world number two Serena Brooke takes some women-only sessions.

Intermediate to serious surfers should try Burleigh Heads, Surfers Paradise and Coolangatta, while surfers of all skill levels will find something to like about Noosa Heads, and Noosa Main Beach is ideal for beginners. Airlie Beach marks the beginning of the Great Barrier Reef, which means calm-water beaches only for the rest of the coastline. *For recommended surf schools, see left.*

Visitors looking to cool down in Brisbane could take advantage of **Streets Beach** at South Bank, a man-made beach complete with white sand, palm trees and its own year-round life-saving patrol. Major hotels and resorts have their own pools, but many serious lappers find that these are a bit short for a good workout. There are six public pools in Brisbane that are open year-round and heated, including the 50-metre Centenary Pool (400 Gregory Terrace, Spring Hill) and the 50-metre Fortitude Valley Pool (432 Wickham Street; tel: 3257 1240).

Tennis

Play in the early morning and/or late afternoon to avoid the sun. Ask about equipment hire when ringing to book a court. A good stop for information is **Tennis Queensland** (tel: 3871 8555). Its

website (www.tennisqueensland.com.au) will also let you search for a tennis club in the area.

EVENTS

Autumn (Mar–May)

Australian Surf Life-Saving Championships, Mar/Apr, the peak event for Australia's 34,000 surf life-savers comes to the Gold Coast.

Kilkivan Great Horse Ride, April, an annual event which draws more than 1,000 riders.

Dent to Dunk Race, May. For more than a century yachts have been competing in this 220-km (137-mile) annual race from Hamilton Island to Dunk Island in the Whitsundays. Tel: 4948 1493.

Australian-Italian Festival, May, one of northern Queensland's biggest events, held in Ingham near Townsville.

Winter (June–Aug)

Cooktown Discovery Festival, mid-June. An annual re-enactment of Captain Cook's emergency landing on the banks of the Endeavour River includes a gala ball and a ute and 4WD muster. Tel: 4069 6004.

Bedourie Camel Cup, early July. Camel-racing draws crowds from all over the Outback. Tel: 4746 1205.

Gold Coast Airport Marathon, early July. Tel: 5564 8733.

Mount Isa Rodeo, mid-Aug. Australia's biggest and richest rodeo.

The Ekka, mid-Aug. City meets country at the Royal Queensland Show in Brisbane.

Noosa Jazz Festival, late Aug/early Sept.

Spring (Sept–Nov)

Birdsville Races, first weekend in September. Annual racing event held to raise money for the Royal Flying Doctor Service. Tel: 4656 3300.

Big River Jazz, early Sept. An annual three-day jazz festival in Rockhampton.

Riverfestival, early Sept. A celebration of the Brisbane River, the city's culture and environment.

Brisbane Writers' Festival, mid-Sept. A four-day festival to celebrate reading and writing held at South Bank.

Cairns Festival, Sept. Arts, music, dance and theatre take centre stage at this annual festival. Tel: 4033 7454.

Australian Nationals, Sept. Australia's drag-racing championships hit Ipswich. Tel: 3849 6881.

Australian Camp Oven Festival, Oct 2006. A biannual event held at Millmerran in Queensland's Western Downs region. Events include the camp-oven cooking competition and damper throwing. Tel: 4695 1423.

Indy 300, Oct. See Champ cars and V8s race on the Gold Coast in this premier motor-racing event. Tel: 5588 6800.

Noosa Triathlon, late Oct. A week-long festival of multi-sport events, including the Noosa Triathlon. Tel: 5449 0711.

Schoolies, Nov–early Dec. A period when high-school graduates from Australia's eastern states converge on Surfers Paradise to celebrate the end of their exams. Best avoided if possible.

Summer (Dec–Feb)

Australian PGA Championship, mid-December. Australia's oldest professional golf championship is held at the Hyatt Regency Coolum. Tel: 1800 009 499 (in Australia).

Woodford Folk Festival, late-Dec–1 Jan. Hundreds of folk music-lovers gather to bring in the new year. Tel: 5496 1066.

Big Day Out, Jan. An annual rock, electronic and contemporary outdoor music event held on the Gold Coast.

Australia Day, 26 Jan. Celebrations held all over Queensland. www.australiaday.gov.au/qld/

CHILDREN

There are plenty of exciting attractions aimed at children in Queensland. Theme parks on the Gold Coast have everything from water slides at **Wet'n' Wild Water World** to movie sets at **Warner Brothers Movie World**. Dolphins and polar bears can keep smaller kids amused at **Sea World**, while the rides at **Dreamworld** cater to older children.

Australia Zoo (tel: 5436 2000) on the Sunshine Coast is the place to catch Steve Irwin, otherwise known as the Crocodile Hunter, in action with his charges. There are 14 shows daily, and, although crocodiles may be the main attraction, the zoo allows visitors to feed the Asian elephants and cuddle koalas. Cuddly koalas can also be found at the **Lone Pine Sanctuary** (3378 1366) near Brisbane, the first and largest koala sanctuary in the world.

The **Queensland Museum** (3840 7555) on Brisbane's South Bank is full of inspiring interactive exhibitions for kids. They can learn how to measure an earthquake, play a thongophone and piece together a human jigsaw. At the **Cobb & Co. Museum** at Toowoomba are examples of transport from the horse-drawn era. The excitement of huge cattle sales can be seen on Wednesdays at **Dalrymple Sales Yards** (tel: 4761 5300) on the Flinders Highway at Charters Towers. At **Tjapukai Aboriginal Cultural Park** in Cairns (tel: 4042 9999) the daily shows include an evening of corroboree around a fire.

A-Z

AN ALPHABETICAL SUMMARY OF PRACTICAL INFORMATION

Admission Charges

Entry to attractions in Queensland varies widely. The "worlds" – Dreamworld, Warner Bros Movie World and Sea World – have some of the highest admission charges: adults pay A$62 and children A$40. Wet 'n' Wild World is cheaper at A$40 for adults and A$26 for children.

If you're planning to go to Sea World, Wet 'n' Wild Water World and Warner Bros Movie World, there is a money-saving pass which entitles holders to entry to all three attractions and costs A$164 for adults (or A$159 if bought online) and A$106 for children (or A$103 online). They are valid for 14 days after entry to the first attraction.

While some attractions, such as Australia Zoo, Curumbin Bird Sanctuary and the Daintree Discovery Centre can also be relatively pricey, they all offer family tickets, which can help keep a lid on costs if travelling with children.

There are also plenty of museums and art galleries where entry is free or A$5–A$8 for adults and a couple of dollars for children. The Brisbane website, www.ourbrisbane.com, has an excellent section pointing out attractions and activities that are free.

Budgeting for Your Trip

Australia has low inflation, and the basics – food, accommodation, admission charges – are still comparatively inexpensive. A plate of noodles or pasta in an average restaurant costs about A$10. A bottle of Australian wine from a liquor store starts at about A$8, a 260ml glass of beer (about half a pint) costs from A$2.50, and a cup of coffee or tea about the same.

Hiring (renting) a small car costs from A$45 per day. Petrol (gasoline) costs around A$1.10 per litre, more expensive than in the US but cheaper than in most European countries. A half-day coach sightseeing tour is A$36–150 per person.

A room at a backpacker hostel can be as little as A$20 a night, and a room in a five-star hotel A$250 and upwards. Queensland has a full range of accommodation in between.

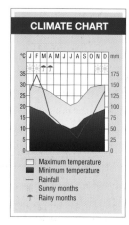

CLIMATE CHART

☐ Maximum temperature
■ Minimum temperature
— Rainfall
  Sunny months
🌧 Rainy months

Business Hours

Banks generally open 9.30am–4pm Monday to Thursday, and 9.30am–5pm on Friday. Most shops are open 9am–5.30pm Monday to Friday and to 5pm Saturday. Many of the larger shops in southeast Queensland and in the major tourist centres to the north now open all day Sunday as well. Thursday night is late-night shopping, when some shops stay open until 8 or 9pm. In Surfers Paradise there is late-night shopping seven days a week, and Brisbane's Queen Street Mall stays open until 9pm on Friday nights. Major supermarkets and convenience stores also often have extended trading hours.

C limate

Queensland has just two seasons: summer (from October to March) and winter. The difference is more pronounced in the south, and the inland regions of the state have the greatest range in temperature. There, temperatures can drop below 0°C (32°F).

In the north of the state there is a wet season from mid-December through to April, when rainfall and thunderstorms are common and there are occasional tropical cyclones.

April to September during the Australian autumn and winter is often the best time to visit Queensland, particularly the north of the state. It is a time when rainfall and temperatures are lower. In Cairns the temperature range in winter is 16–26°C (55–90°F) and in summer it can exceed 36°C (125°F), when the humidity is high.

Brisbane has summer temperatures that range from 20°C to the high 30s (86°F plus) and winter temperatures of 10–20°C (35–68°F).

Crime and Safety

Common-sense rules apply when visiting Queensland. Because of its high tourist profile, petty theft can be an issue in popular visitor locations. Keep wallets out of sight; do not leave valuables visible in the car or luggage unattended. Take care when using ATMs to withdraw cash, particularly at night or in dimly lit areas, and keep an eye out when using public telephones to make sure someone doesn't sneak up behind you.

Drink spiking is far from commonplace, but to ensure your safety police suggest travellers go with someone to the bar if they offer to buy you a drink, never accept a drink from a container or already opened drink that is being passed around, and avoid leaving a drink unattended. The emergency number for police, ambulance and the fire brigade is 000, or 112 from a mobile phone.

Report any theft to the police straight away, as you will need a police report if you wish to make a claim on travel insurance. The details of the closest police station will be listed in the White Pages under "Police". Non-urgent enquiries can generally be made at police stations from 8am to 4pm, but it is worth phoning first, as stations in the country may have more limited opening hours.

Customs

Australia has extremely strict regulations about what can and cannot be brought into the country. Before disembarking from the plane, visitors are asked to fill in an Incoming Passenger Card. Australian Customs officers check the information on the cards when passengers disembark, and may initiate a baggage search. There are heavy fines for false or inaccurate claims. It is always best to declare an item if in doubt.

Strict quarantine laws apply in Australia to protect the agricultural industries and native Australian flora and fauna from introduced diseases. Animals, plants and their derivatives must be declared on arrival. This may include items made from materials such as untreated wood, feathers or furs. The import or export of protected species, or products made from protected species, is a criminal offence. It is also illegal to export any species of native flora or fauna without a permit.

All food products, no matter how well processed and packaged, must be declared on arrival.

All weapons are prohibited, unless accompanied by an international permit. This includes guns, ammunition, knives and replica items.

Medicinal products must be declared. These include: drugs that are illegal in Australia (narcotics, performance enhancers, amphetamines); legally prescribed drugs (carry your doctor's prescription with you); non-prescription drugs (painkillers and so on); and vitamins, diet supplements and traditional preparations.

Customs Information Centre, tel: 1 300 363 263 (in Australia); 61 2 6275 6666 (outside Australia); www.customs.gov.au

Duty-Free Allowances

Anyone over the age of 18 is allowed to bring into Australia A$400-worth of goods not including alcohol or tobacco;

2,250 ml (about 4 pints) of alcohol (wine, beer or spirits); 250 cigarettes, or 250 grams of cigars or tobacco products other than cigarettes. Members of the same family who are travelling together may combine their individual duty/tax-free allowances.

D isabled Travellers

Queensland caters reasonably well for people with disabilities, but you would be wise to start making enquiries and arrangements before leaving home. A good place to begin is with the **National Information Communication Awareness Network (NICAN)**, a national organisation that keeps a database of facilities and services with disabled access, including accommodation and tourist sights. It also keeps track of the range of publications on the subject.

Accessible Queensland is a comprehensive website (www.accessiblequeensland.com) linking people with disabilities to maps, transport and other information. Information is separated into regions, making it easy to locate a service in your area of interest.

The **Paraplegic and Quadriplegic Association of Queensland** (PQAQ) provides an information phone line to help link people with disabilities with service providers.

PQAQ, PO Box 5651 West End, Queensland 4101; tel: 07 3391 2044 or 1800-810 513 (in Australia)
NICAN, PO Box 407 Curtain, ACT 2605; tel: 1 800 806 769.

The **Queensland Holidays** website (www.queenslandholidays.com.au) is also an excellent resource. Listings for attractions include clear information about disabled access.

E lectricity

The current is 240/250v, 50Hz. Most good hotels have universal outlets for 110v shavers and small appliances. For larger appliances such as hairdryers, you will need a converter and a flat three-pin adaptor.

Embassies and Consulates

The following are the closest contacts for travellers needing assistance when in Queensland.
British Consular Agency, Level 26 Waterfront Place, 1 Eagle Street, Brisbane; tel: 07 3830 5748 or 07 3830 5748 (after-hours emergencies); www.britaus.net
Canadian Consulate General, Level 5, 111 Harrington Street, Sydney; tel: 02 9364 3000; recorded information: 02 9364 3050; www.canada.org.au
Consulate General of Ireland, Level 30, 400 George Street, Sydney; tel: 02 9231 6999
US Consulate General, MLC Centre, Level 10, 19–29 Martin Place, Sydney; tel: 02 9373 9200; after-hours emergencies, tel: 02 4422 2201

Overseas Missions

Canada, Australian High Commission, Suite 710, 50 O'Connor Street, Ottawa, Ontario K1P 6L2; tel: (613) 236 0841 (plus consulates in Toronto and Vancouver)
   Ireland, Australian Embassy, Fitzwilton House, Wilton Terrace, Dublin 2; tel: (01) 664 5300; email: austremb.dublin@dfat.gov.au
   United Kingdom, Australian High Commission, Australia House, The Strand, London WC2B 4LA; tel: (020) 7379 4334; www.australia.org.uk
   United States, Australian Embassy, 1601 Massachusetts Avenue, Washington DC NW 20036-2273; tel: (202) 797 3000; email: library.washington@dfat.gov.au (plus consulates in New York, Los Angeles, San Francisco, Miami, Detroit, Atlanta etc)

Emergency Numbers

The emergency number for police, ambulance and the fire brigade is 000, or 112 from a mobile phone.

Entry Requirements

Visitors to Australia must have a passport valid for the entire period of their stay. Anyone who is not an Australian citizen also needs a visa, which must be obtained before leaving home – except for New Zealand citizens, who are issued with a visa on arrival in Australia.

ETA visas The Electronic Transfer Authority (ETA) enables visitors to obtain a visa on the spot from their travel agent or airline office. The system is in place in over 30 countries, including the US and the UK. ETA visas are generally valid over a 12-month period; single stays must not exceed three months, but return visits within the 12-month period are allowed. ETAs are issued free, or you can purchase one online for A\$20 from www.eta.immi.gov.au.

Tourist visas These are available for continuous stays longer than three months, but must be obtained from an Australian visa office, such as an embassy or consulate. A A\$20 fee applies. Those travelling on tourist visas and ETAs are not permitted to work while in Australia. Travellers are asked on their applications to prove they have an adequate source of funding while in Australia (around A\$1,000 a month).

Temporary residence Those seeking temporary residence must apply to an Australian visa office, and in many cases must be sponsored by an appropriate organisation or employer. Study visas are available for people who want to undertake registered courses on a full-time basis. Working holiday visas are available to young people from the UK, Ireland, Japan, the Netherlands, Canada, Malta and Korea who want to work as they travel.

Department of Immigration and Multicultural Affairs, tel: 13 18 81, or the nearest mission outside Australia; www.immi.gov.au.

TRANSPORT

ACCOMMODATION

ACTIVITIES

N
I
A

G ay and Lesbian

Queensland may not be the gay Mecca that you would find in Sydney, but there is a thriving gay community in the state's capital and Noosa, is a favoured spot to wind down after the Sydney Gay Mardi Gras in March.

Further north there are several exclusively gay and lesbian hotels and resorts, including **Turtle Cove Resort** near Cairns (tel: 07 4059 1800) and **Pink Flamingo** in Port Douglas (Tel: 07 4099 6622).

To find the rainbow edge to Brisbane's nightlife try **The Wickham Hotel** in Fortitude Valley. There's also the **Sportsman Hotel**, which is the oldest gay bar in town. The annual Brisbane Pride Festival (www.brisbanepride.org.au) is held in June. The highlight of the month-long festival is generally a parade and fair day.

In Cairns there is Nu-trix Nightclub (53 Spence Street; tel: 07 4051 8223, open Wed–Sun from 9pm) and Montage Bar at Skinny Dips Resort (18–24 James Street; tel: 07 4099 6622).

Check out the gay press for more details about places to go and meeting spots. *Queensland Pride* is a free monthly newspaper, and *Q News* is a free fortnightly newspaper; both are based in Brisbane.

The International Gay and Lesbian Travel Association is a professional body for people involved with gay tourism. Visitors can find providers of different travel services on its consumer website. Gay and Lesbian Tourism Australia fulfils a similar function within Australia. **International Gay and Lesbian Travel Association**, tel: 02-9818 6669; www.traveliglta.com **Gay and Lesbian Tourism Australia**, tel: 0414 446 401; www.galta.com.au

H ealth and Medical Care

Australia has excellent medical services. For medical attention out of working hours go to the casualty department in one of the large hospitals or, if the matter is less urgent, visit one of the seven-day medical clinics in the major towns and tourist centres. Look under "Medical Centres" or "Medical Practitioners" in the Yellow Pages, or ask at your hotel.

No vaccinations are required for entry to Australia. As in most countries, HIV and AIDS are a continuing problem despite efforts to control its spread. Heterosexual and homosexual visitors alike should wear condoms if engaging in sexual activity.

Emergency medical assistance, tel: 000, or 112 from a mobile phone.

Pharmacies

"Chemist shops" are a great place to go for advice on minor ailments such as bites, scratches and stomach trouble. They also stock a wide range of useful products such as sunblock, nappies (diapers) and non-prescription drugs.

If you have a prescription from your doctor, and you want to take it to a pharmacist in Australia, you will need to have it endorsed by a local medical practitioner.

Local Health Hazards

The biggest danger for travellers in Australia is the sun. Even on mild, cloudy days it has the potential to burn. Wear a broad-

brimmed hat and, if you are planning on being out for a while, a long-sleeved shirt made from a light fabric. Wear SPF 15+ sunblock at all times, even under a hat. Avoid sunbathing between 11am and 3pm.

Care should be taken while swimming at Queensland's surfing beaches, which stretch from Rainbow Bay in the south to Agnes Water south of Gladstone. The best advice is to swim only at beaches that are patrolled, and to swim between the yellow and red flags. Never swim at night after a few drinks or immediately after a heavy meal.

Dangerous Animals

Take care to swim inside stinger-resistant swimming enclosures when holidaying in the north of the state between November and April. It is during those months that the deadly box jellyfish in the area a couple of kilometres off the mainland beaches. A "stinger suit" or a full wetsuit can also provide the necessary protection. These may be available for hire. For more information on marine stingers see www.marinestingers.com.au.

Freshwater and saltwater crocodiles live in Queensland's waterways north of Rockhampton. They may be found close to the shore in the sea, or in rivers and creeks. Warning signs usually alert people to the areas where it is dangerous to swim. Also avoid camping, preparing food or cleaning fish within 50 metres (55 yards) of the water's edge.

Mosquitoes can also be more than an occasional annoyance on a summer evening, carrying viruses such as Dengue Fever and Ross River Fever. The best way to avoid contracting these viruses – which lead to high fevers, headaches and joint- and muscle-pains – is to cover up, use insect repellents and mosquito nets.

Dangerous snakes are part of Australia's landscape. In Queensland there are 120 species of snake and about 20 of them are considered dangerous. Most snakes will not attack unless directly provoked. Avoid trouble by wearing covered shoes when walking in the bush, and checking areas such as rock platforms and rock crevices before making yourself comfortable. Seek medical advice for any bite.

Other animals to be wary of include dingoes, as they have been known to attack humans, and the deadly redback spider.

Holidays

Banks, post offices, offices and most shops close on public holidays (see box on page 278).

Different cities in Queensland have an additional Exhibition holiday. Brisbane celebrates its Exhibition holiday in mid-August. School holidays run from early December to the third week in January, and there are two weeks at Easter, late June and early July and late September to early October. It can be difficult to get discounted air fares and at these times.

Internet Cafés

Internet cafés have proliferated in recent years, and travellers to Australia should have no trouble finding internet access in major cities and tourist locations. Many hotels and hostels now have facilities for people travelling with their own laptops, and local libraries fill the gap in communities where there is no commercial internet facility. Often access in libraries is free, or there may be a nominal charge.

Left Luggage

There are no left-luggage facilities at Brisbane Airport for security reasons. However, Cairns Airport has a baggage-storage facility run by Smart Carte Australia (tel: 0407 359 678). There are lockers for luggage on all three levels of Brisbane's Transit Centre at Roma Street. To check the facilities available at other Queensland train stations see www.traveltrain.com.au.

Lost Property

You should report loss or theft of valuables to the police immediately, as most insurance policies insist on a police report.

At Brisbane Airport direct any enquiries about property lost in the terminal to the Visitors Information Desk on level two in the arrivals hall, tel: 07 3406 3190. Enquiries about lost baggage should be directed to the airline involved.

Lost property found at a City-train station in Brisbane is held for three days at that particular station before being forwarded to Roma Street Station, tel: 07 3235 1859 between 10.15am and 2.25pm Mon–Fri. For anything left on Brisbane's ferries, tel: 07 3229 7778, 9am–5.30pm daily.

To locate property left on a Brisbane bus, contact the Brisbane City Council call centre, tel: 07 3403 8888. The lost-property office is located at 69 Ann Street, Brisbane.

For items missing on Greyhound Australia coaches, contact its lost-property department, tel: 07 3868 0901, or visit the nearest coach terminal.

Maps

The accredited Visitor Information Centres, indicated by the yellow "i" against a blue background, give away useful maps of their areas. The Queensland Holidays website carries a map of Queensland showing the locations of the Visitor Centres. Visit the RACQ Travel Centres (www.racq.com.au) for touring maps. They can also be mailed overseas to international visitors. For a detailed street map, look for either UBD or Gregory's Street Directory.

Media

Publications

Brisbane's daily newspaper is the Courier-Mail, an energetic tabloid which appears on Monday to Saturday. On Sunday the major Brisbane newspaper is the Sunday Mail. Both are part of the News Corporation stable.

Australia has two national papers, the Australian and the Financial Review, both excellent publications at the serious end of the scale. The weekly Bulletin is a long-running magazine with good news analysis, and there is also a weekly Australian edition of Time magazine.

Foreign newspapers and magazines are available at newsagents in Brisbane, the airport and other major tourist districts, usually within a couple of days of publication.

Radio and Television

The Australian Broadcasting Commission (ABC) runs a national television channel as well as an extensive network of radio stations. ABC Television is broadcast on Channel 2 and offers excellent news and current affairs, as well as local and imported drama, comedy, sports and cultural programmes. The commercial TV stations, Channels 7, 9 and 10, offer news, drama, soaps, infotainment, travel shows and, between them, coverage of all the major international sporting events. Many hotels provide access to a large number of cable-television stations.

The radio stations include Triple J (107.7 FM in Brisbane and 107.5 in Cairns), rock and comment for the twentysomethings; Classic FM (106.1 FM in Brisbane and 105.9 FM), continuous classical music; and Radio National (792 FM and 105.1 FM in Cairns), excellent national news and events coverage. Commercial radio stations include Triple M FM (104.7 in Brisbane), for popular local and international rock, and Nova 1069 for contemporary music (106.9 FM). For frequencies in other parts of Queensland, check with locals.

Of particular interest to overseas travellers is Australia's ethnic/multicultural broadcaster,

SBS. The organisation's television channel offers many foreign-language films and documentaries, and Australia's best coverage of world news. SBS Radio (93.3 FM in Brisbane) offers programmes in a variety of languages.

Money

Currency

The local currency is the Australian dollar (abbreviated as A$ or simply $), made up of 100 cents. Coins come in 5, 10, 20, and 50 cent units and 1 and 2 dollar units. Notes come in 5, 10, 20, 50 and 100 dollar units. Single cents still apply to many prices, and in these cases the amount will be rounded down or up to the nearest 5c amount. Carry smaller notes for tipping, taxis and payment in small shops and cafés.

There is no limit to the amount of foreign or Australian currency that you can bring into or out of the country, but cash amounts of more than A$10,000 (or its equivalent) must be declared to Customs on arrival and departure.

Banks

The four big banks in Australia are the National, the Commonwealth, Westpac and ANZ. Trading hours are generally 9.30am–4pm Monday to Thursday and 9.30am–5pm on Friday. A few of the smaller banks and credit unions open on Saturday mornings. Most banks will have an internal board or a window display advertising exchange rates; if not, ask a teller.

Credit Cards and ATMs

Carrying a recognised credit or debit card such as Visa, MasterCard, American Express or Diners Club is always a good idea when travelling. A credit card should provide access to EFTPOS (electronic funds transfer at point of sale), which is the easiest and often the cheapest way to exchange money – amounts are automatically debited from the selected account. Many Australian businesses are connected to EFTPOS.

There are literally hundreds of ATMs around Queensland, allowing for easy withdrawal of cash, and again a linked credit card will provide access to both credit and other bank accounts. Some of the islands do have limited banking facilities, so it is worth checking before going there for an extended period.

Exchange

Most foreign currencies can be cashed at the airport, with major exchange outlets operating to fit in with flight arrival times. Queensland has many bureaux de change, which generally open 9.30am–5pm, but you'll usually get a better rate at one of the big banks.

Lost Cheques and Cards

If you lose your travellers' cheques or want replacement cheques, contact the following:
American Express, tel: 1 800 688 022
Thomas Cook and MasterCard Travellers' Cheques, tel: 1 800 127 495
Visa Travellers' Cheques, tel: 1800 127 477
If you lose your credit card, call:
American Express, tel: 1 300 132 639
Diners Club, tel: 1 300 360 060
MasterCard, tel: 1 800 120 113 (world service puts you in contact with local authority)
Visa, tel: 1 800 450 346 (Australian cardholders)

Travellers' cheques

All well-known travellers' cheques can be cashed at airports, banks, hotels and similar establishments, and are as good as cash with many of the larger retail outlets and the shops in major tourist areas. Smaller restaurants and shops may be reluctant to cash cheques, so you should also carry cards or cash.

Banks offer the best exchange rates on cheques in foreign currencies; most banks charge a fee for cashing cheques. Travellers' cheques can also be purchased in larger towns at one of the major banks.

Postal Services

Post offices are open 9am–5pm Mon–Fri, with some branches opening Sat morning. The General Post Office (GPO) is located at 261 Queen Street in Brisbane and opens 7am–6pm weekdays.

Domestic Post

Posting a standard letter to anywhere in Australia costs 50c. The letter will reach a same-city destination overnight, but may take up to a week if it is being sent to a remote part of the country.

Yellow Express Post bags can be used to send parcels and letters overnight to Australian capital cities and between major towns in Queensland. The cost ranges from A$4 to A$9.70, and represents very good value for money when compared to courier costs.
Postal enquiries: tel: 13 13 18.

Overseas Post

The cost of overseas mail depends on the weight and size of the item. Postcards cost A$1.20 by airmail to the UK and the US. Standard overseas mail takes about a week to most destinations.

PUBLIC HOLIDAYS

1 January New Year's Day
26 January Australia Day
March/April Good Friday, Holy Saturday, Easter Monday
25 April Anzac Day
May (1st Mon) May Day
June (2nd Mon) Queen's Birthday
25 December Christmas Day
26 December Boxing Day

TRANSPORT

There are two types of express international mail. Express Mailing Service International Courier (EMS) will reach the UK in three to four working days. The minimum cost for a package is A$35. Express Post International (EPI) will arrive in the UK within four working days, and is priced according to weight and size. The cost of a prepaid envelope for documents or a letter starts at A$11.

EMS and EPI, tel: 13 13 18.

Faxes

There are many places from which you can fax documents, including hotels, video stores, newsagents, a variety of small businesses, and post offices, where the rates are reasonable.

 axis

The cost of a taxi ride in Queensland depends on a number of factors: the flagfall, the per-kilometre rate, the per-minute rate and the booking fee. The per-kilometre rate in southeast Queensland for metered cabs is A$1.50, and for exempted cabs A$2.50; for cabs outside of southeast Queensland it is A$1.58. The waiting time or per-minute fee is 60 cents per minute for all metered taxis and 56 cents for exempted taxis. The booking fee is A$1.10.

Flagfalls vary according to the time of day, with the lowest, A$2.50, applying 7am–7pm Monday to Friday except for public holidays, and the highest, A$5.70, applying from midnight to 5am on Sunday.

There are nine secure taxi ranks in the Brisbane CBD, Fortitude Valley and Petrie Terrace, which are staffed by taxi marshals and security guards and monitored by Queensland Police, and in some cases closed-circuit television cameras.

Telephones

Local calls in Australia are untimed, and cost about 25c from private phones and 40c from public phones. Instead of making calls from hotel rooms, which can be double or triple the price, you should aim to use public phones. Phonecards are widely available from newsagents and other outlets displaying the Telstra logo. There are four cards, ranging from A$5 to A$50.

Most interstate (STD) and international (ISD) calls can be made using phonecards. These calls are timed, and can be expensive, but cheaper rates are available after 6pm and at weekends.

Queensland has two types of telephone directory. The White Pages is an alphabetical listing of residential and business phone numbers. The Yellow Pages lists commercial operations under subject headings.

Calls made from Brisbane to other parts of Queensland are charged at STD rates, although it is no longer necessary to dial an area code first. However, you do have to dial an area code to call interstate in Australia. All regular numbers in Australia (other than toll-free or special numbers) are eight digits long. The area code for Queensland is 07.

Numbers beginning with 1 800 are toll-free. Numbers beginning with 13 are charged at a local rate, even if the call is made STD. Numbers beginning with 018,

041, 015 and 019 are mobile phone numbers.
Directory enquiries: 1223
Overseas assistance: 1225
Information on costs: 12552
International calls: 0011, followed by the national code of the country you are calling.

Mobile Phones

Most of the large urban areas and major rural centres are covered by a telecoms "net". Smaller towns and remote regions are not covered, which means that mobiles have virtually no use as a safety communications device when travelling in the Outback.

Many visitors will find that they can bring their own phones with them and use them without too much trouble. Contact your provider before leaving home to find out what is involved. To hire a phone during your stay, look under "Mobile Telephones" in the Yellow Pages, and shop around for the best deal – this is a very competitive market. There are also outlets offering mobiles for hire in some of the airport terminals.

Time Zone

Queensland is on Eastern Australian Standard Time (EST), which is 10 hours ahead of Greenwich Mean Time, 15 hours ahead of New York and 18 hours ahead of California. Unlike other states on Australia's east coast, Queensland does not observe daylight saving.

Tipping

Tipping is not obligatory, but a small gratuity for good service is appreciated. It is not customary to tip taxi drivers, hairdressers or porters at airports. Porters have set charges at railway terminals, but not at hotels. Restaurants do not automatically include service charges, but it is customary to tip waiters up to 10 percent of the bill for good service.

ACCOMMODATION

ACTIVITIES

A – Z

Tourist Information

For tourist information before you leave home, see the Tourism Australia website, www.australia.com
United Kingdom: Gemini House, 10–18 Putney Hill, London SW15 6AA; tel: 020 8780 2229.
USA: 2049 Century Park East, Suite 1920, Los Angeles CA 90067; tel: (310) 229 4870.

Within Queensland each of the major regions has its own tourist information centre.

V isitor Info Centres

Here are the main tourist information centres in Queensland:
Atherton Tableland
Corner of Silo Road and Main Street, Atherton.
Tel: 07 4091 4222;
www.athertontableland.com
Brisbane
Corner Albert and Queen Streets, Brisbane.
Tel: 07 3006 6290;
www.ourbrisbane.com
Bundaberg City
186 Bourbong Street, Bundaberg.
Tel: 1800 308 888;
www.bundabergregion.info
Cairns – The Gateway Discovery Centre
51 The Esplanade, Cairns.
Tel: 07 4051 3588;
www.tropicalaustralia.com.au
Capricorn Coast
Ross Creek Roundabout, Scenic Highway, Yeppoon.
Tel: 07 4939 4888 or 1800 675 785;
www.capricorncoast.com.au
Capricorn Information Centre
Tropic of Capricorn Spire, Gladstone Road, Rockhampton.
Tel: 07 4927 2055 or 1800 676 701;
www.capricorntourism.com.au
Charleville
Enterprise Drive, Charleville.
Tel: 07 4654 3057;
www.murweh.qld.gov.au
Coolangatta
Shop 14B, corner Griffith and Warner Streets, Coolangatta.
Tel: 1300 309 440;
www.veryGC.com

Gladstone
Marina Ferry Terminal, Bryan Jordan Drive, Gladstone.
Tel: 07 4972 9000;
www.gladstoneregion.org.au
Hervey Bay
Corner Urraween and Maryborough Hervey Roads, Hervey Bay.
Tel: 07 4125 9855;
www.herveybaytourism.com.au
Kuranda
Centenary Park, Kuranda.
Tel: 07 4093 9311;
www.kuranda.org
Mackay
320 Nebo Road, Mackay.
Tel: 07 4944 5888;
www.mackayregion.com
Mission Beach
Porters Promenade, Mission Beach.
Tel: 07 4068 7099;
www.missionbeachtourism.com
Mount Isa
19 Marian Street, Mount Isa.
Tel: 07 4749 1555;
www.outbackatisa.com.au
Noosa
Hastings Street, Noosa Heads.
Tel: 07 5447 4988;
www.tourismnoosa.com.au
Rockhampton Tourist and Business Information Centre
Customs House, 208 Quay Street, Rockhampton.
Tel: 07 4922 5339;
www.rockhamptoninfo.com
Southern Queensland Visitors Information Centre

Level 2, Brisbane International Airport and Ground Floor, Virgin Blue Domestic Terminal, Brisbane.
Tel: 07 3406 3190 and 07 3114 7260;
www.southernqueensland.com.au
Stradbroke Island Tourism
Junner Street, Dunwich.
Tel: 07 3409 9555;
www.stradbroketourism.com
Surfers Paradise
Cavill Avenue, Surfers Paradise.
Tel: 1300 309 440;
www.veryGC.com
Toowoomba
86 James Street, Warrego Highway, Toowoomba.
Tel: 07 4639 3797
www.toowoomba.qld.gov.au
Townsville – Flinders Mall Information Centre
Flinders Mall, Townsville.
Tel: 07 4721 3660;
www.townsvilleonline.com.au
Whitsunday Information Centre
Bruce Highway, Prosperpine.
Tel: 07 4945 3711.

W ebsites

Enter "Queensland tourism" into any search engine, and you will access a vast number of sites. Here is a selection of the more comprehensive and reliable:
www.atn.com.au
www.queenslandholidays.com.au
www.discoveraustralia.com.au
www.oztravel.com.au
www.tourismqueensland.com.au
www.outbackholidays.info
www.visitqueensland.com.au
www.ourbrisbane.com

What to Wear

Whatever the season, you can forget your overcoat. Even a sweater may not be necessary unless you are travelling in the Outback in winter, where temperatures will be cold at night. Generally the most you will need are long-sleeved T-shirts to protect against sunburn and mosquitoes. A light raincoat will serve in any season. Comfortable walking shoes and good-quality sunglasses are essential.

FURTHER READING

General

Australia. The Greatest Island, R Raymond.
Australia's Living Heritage: Arts of the Dreaming, J Isaacs.
Aboriginal Myths, Legends and Fables, AW Reed.
Archaeology of the Dreamtime, J Flood.
Down Under, B Bryson.
Tucker Track – A curious history of food in Australia, W Fahey.
Wilderness Australia, D McGonigal.

History

Crackpots, Ratbags and Rebels, R Holden.
The Explorers, ed. T Flannery.
The Fatal Shore, R Hughes.
A Shorter History of Australia G Blainey.

Natural History

Australia's Natural Wonders, M Richardson.
Australia, the Wild Continent, M Morcombe.
Australian Wildlife, J Kavanagh.
Green Guide: Mammals of Australia, T Lindsey.
Green Guide: Snakes and Other Reptiles of Australia, by G Swan.
The Slater Field Guide to Australian Birds, P, P & R Slater.

Australian language

The Dinkum Dictionary, S Butler.
Let's Talk Strine, A Lauder.

Fiction/poetry

The Bodysurfers, R Drewe.
Dirt Music, T Winton.

For the Term of His Natural Life, M Clarke.
A Fortunate Life, A Facey.
Fly Away Peter, D Malouf.
A Fringe of Leaves, P White.
An Item from the Late News, T Astley..
Journey to the Stone Country,

FEEDBACK

We do our best to ensure the information in our books is as accurate and up-to-date as possible. The books are updated on a regular basis, using local contacts, who painstakingly add, amend and correct as required. However, some mistakes and omissions are inevitable and we are ultimately reliant on our readers to put us in the picture.

We would welcome your feedback on any details related to your experiences using the book "on the road". Maybe we recommended a hotel that you liked (or another that you didn't), or you'd like to tell us about a new attraction or any other details about the country itself. The more details you can give us (particularly with regard to addresses, e-mails and telephone numbers), the better.

We will acknowledge all contributions, and we'll offer an Insight Guide to the best letters received.

Please write to us at:
Insight Guides
PO Box 7910
London SE1 1WE
United Kingdom
Or send an e-mail to:
insight@apaguide.co.uk

A Miller.
Last Drinks, A McGahan.
Matthew Flinder's Cat, B Courtenay.
Morgan's Run, C McCullough.
Over the Top with Jim, H Lunn.
Short Stories, H Lawson.
Territory, J Nunn.
The True History of the Kelly Gang, Bliss, Illywhacker, Oscar and Lucinda, all P Carey.
The Vivisector, P White.

Other Insight Guides

Titles which highlight destinations in this part of the world include:

Insight Guide: Australia, a superbly illustrated guide to all the best that Down Under has to offer.

Insight Guide: New South Wales, a detailed look at Sydney and its state, from the beaches to the remote outback.

Insight Guide: Tasmania, a comprehensive guide to Australia's smallest state.

Insight Pocket Guide: Sydney, a series of itineraries written by a local author guides you to the best of one of the world's most beautiful cities.

282

ART & PHOTO CREDITS

AFP/Getty Images 42,
aeropix/Alamy 117, 240
Apa 1
ASP Tostee/Getty Images 60/61
Australian Picture Library/J P &
E S Baker 107
Australian War Memorial 38
Bill Bachman/Alamy 152
Ian Beattie/Auscape 139
David Bragg/Newspix 35L
Brisbane City Council archives
26
Brian Cassey/Rex Features 185
Anthony Cassidy/Getty Images
110
Cephas Picture Library 102, 129,
144, 158, 172, 207, 217
Coo-ee Picture Library 23
Courtesy of Hamilton Island 4B,
257
Michael Coyne/Axiom 30
Danita Delimont/Alamy 104,
119R
Jerry Dennis/Apa 3B, 4C, 5B, 6T,
6C, 6B, 7T, 7C, 7BL, 7BR, 8CL,
8CR, 8B, 9T, 14, 31, 32, 33, 34L,
34R, 41, 47, 50, 51, 58/59, 62,
68, 69, 70, 70T, 71, 72, 72T, 73,
74, 75, 76T, 77, 78, 78T, 78C,
79, 79T, 81, 81T, 82, 85, 88, 89,
91, 91T, 93, 93T, 94L, 94R, 95,
96T, 96C, 97, 98T, 99L, 99R,
100, 100T, 101, 103, 106T, 108,
110T, 111, 112T, 117T, 118,
119L, 119T, 139T, 141T, 142T,
147, 148T, 149, 151, 151T,
152T, 153, 154, 154T, 155,
155T, 156, 156T, 157, 160, 161,
162, 163B, 163C, 163T, 164,
164C, 165, 166, 166T, 167, 168,
168T, 169, 170, 170T, 171,
171T, 173, 179, 180C, 183, 184,
185T, 186, 186T, 187, 189,
190, 196, 197, 201, 202T, 203,
208, 209, 211, 212, 213, 214,
215, 216, 216T, 218, 219, 220T,
221, 222T, 223, 223T, 224,
224T, 225, 225T, 227, 228, 229,
231, 231T, 232, 232T, 233, 234,
236, 237, 238, 241, 242, 243,

246, 248T, 253, 254, 258, 264,
266, 267, 269, 270, 271, 272,
279, 280
Georgette Douwma/Nature
Picture Library 53, 54
Jean-Paul Ferrero/Auscape 135
Bob Finlayson/Newspix 35R
Jürgen Freund/Auscape 83
Jürgen Freund /Nature Picture
Library 10/11, 55, 188
Michael Gebicki 204, 205
General Photographic
Agency/Getty Images 43
David Gregs/Alamy 138
Kevin Hamdorf/Apa 9CL, 177,
178, 179T, 180, 180T, 181, 199,
210T, 249, 250, 260, 276
Patrick Hamilton/Newspix 49
Heeb/Prisma/Superstock 109
Steve Holland/AP/EMPICS 92
Chris Howes/Wild Places
Photography/Alamy 182
Mark A. Johnson/Alamy 150,
200
Tom Keating/Wildlight 146
Kobal Collection 39
Ludo Kuipers/Australian Picture
Library 206, 206T
Nick Laham/Getty Images 222
National Library of Australia 19,
22,
National Library of Australia/The
Bridgeman Art Library 18
Newspix 24, 40
Mary Evans Picture Library 17,
21, 29, 37,
Laurie McGuiness/Surfpix 44,
Tony Perrottet 191
petpics/Alamy 239
Photolibrary.com 4T, 115, 120,
122, 123, 124, 125, 127, 128,
132, 136/137, 140, 141, 143,
Picpics/Alamy 12/13
Steven Pohlner/APA 9CR, 83T,
98, 105, 126, 126T,
Jamie Robertson/Nature Picture
Library 52
G. Salter/Lebrecht 48
State Library of Victoria 20
Doug Steley/Alamy 36

Topham Picturepoint 27, 124T
Tourism Queensland 133, 134T,
137, 142
David Wall/Alamy 114, 120T,
121,
Dave Watts/Alamy 235
Wildlight/Philip Quirk 112
Wildlight/Andrew Rankin 176
Simon Williams/Surfpix 45, 46
Mari Witkiewicz/Alamy 226
Jonathan Wood/Getty Images 2/3

PICTURE SPREADS

Pages 56/57: Georgette Douwma/
Nature Picture Library 56TL;
Jurgen Freund/Nature Picture
Library 56CR, 56BR, 57CL, 57BR;
Doug Perrine/Nature Picture
Library 56/57, 56BL; Dave
Watts/Nature Picture Library 57TR
Pages 86/87: AP/Steve Holland/
EMPICS 86BL; Farjana K. Godhuly/
AFP/Getty Images 87BL; Steven
Pohlner/APA 86BR; Cameron
Spencer/Getty Images 86/87;
AP/Mark J Terrill/EMPICS 87BR;
Jonathan Wood/Getty Images
87CR
Pages 130/131: All pictures Jerry
Dennis/Apa except: Darroch
Donald/Alamy 130/131TC
Pages 174/175: All pictures Jerry
Dennis/Apa
Pages 194/195: Brent Hedges
195BL; Jerry Dennis/Apa 194CR,
195TR, 195CR, 195BR; Dave
Watts/Nature Picture Library
194/195, 194BL, 194BR, 195CL

Cartographic Editor: Zoë Goodwin

Map Production: Phoenix Mapping
Ltd.
Map section reproduced with kind
permission of UBD, ©Universal
Publishers Ltd DG 02/06

©2006 Apa Publications GmbH & Co.
Verlag KG, Singapore Branch

Production: Linton Donaldson

GENERAL INDEX

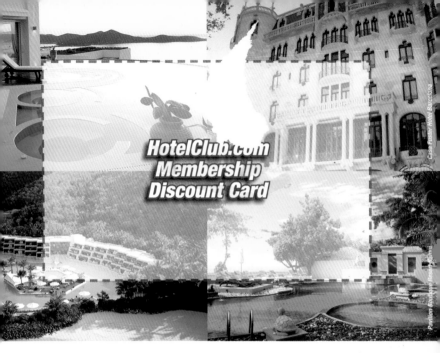

Casa Foster Hotel Barcelona

Pavilion Bodrque Resort Rahmi

Register with
HotelClub.com
and get US$20!

At *HotelClub.com*, we reward our Members with discounts and free stays in their favourite hotels. As a Member, every booking made by you through *HotelClub.com* will earn you Member Dollars.

When you register, we will credit your account with *US$20 FREE Member Dollars*. All you need to do is log on to *www.HotelClub.com/city*. Complete your details, including the Membership Number and Password located on the back of the *HotelClub.com* card.

Over 2.2 million Members already use Member Dollars to pay for all or part of their hotel bookings. Join now and start spending Member Dollars whenever and wherever you want – you are not restricted to specific hotels or dates!

With great savings of up to 60% on over 20,000 hotels across 97 countries, you are sure to find the perfect location for business or pleasure. Happy travels from *HotelClub.com!*

INSIGHT GUIDES
www.insightguides.com

HotelClub.com

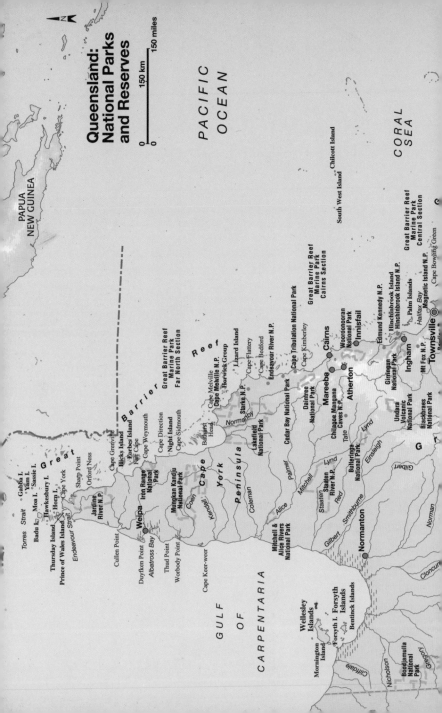